Get the eBooks FREE!

(PDF, ePub, Kindle, and liveBook all included)

We believe that once you buy a book from us, you should be able to read it in any format we have available. To get electronic versions of this book at no additional cost to you, purchase and then register this book at the Manning website.

Go to https://www.manning.com/freebook and follow the instructions to complete your pBook registration.

That's it!
Thanks from Manning!

Aurelia in Action

Aurelia in Action

SEAN HUNTER

MANNING
SHELTER ISLAND

For online information and ordering of this and other Manning books, please visit
www.manning.com. The publisher offers discounts on this book when ordered in quantity.
For more information, please contact

> Special Sales Department
> Manning Publications Co.
> 20 Baldwin Road
> PO Box 761
> Shelter Island, NY 11964
> Email: orders@manning.com

Manning Publications Co.
20 Baldwin Road
PO Box 761
Shelter Island, NY 11964

Development editor:	Toni Arritola
Technical development editor:	Andrew Siemer
Review editor:	Ivan Martinović
Project manager:	Tiffany Taylor
Copy editor:	Safis Editing
Proofreader:	Katie Tennant
Technical proofreader:	Troi Eisler
Typesetter:	Dennis Dalinnik
Cover designer:	Marija Tudor

ISBN: 9781617294785
Printed in the United States of America
1 2 3 4 5 6 7 8 9 10 – DP – 23 22 21 20 19 18

To the welcoming and always enthusiastic Aurelia community

brief contents

contents

preface

I first came across Aurelia in a *.NET Rocks!* podcast interview with the framework's creator, Rob Eisenberg. I particularly remember that evening because I had more than my usual podcast-listening time commuting from work, due to a flat tire (the third that month—but that's a different story). At this stage, Rob had just started working on a new single-page application (SPA) framework, which differentiated itself from most other popular frameworks by its focus on clean code and use of convention over configuration to eliminate boilerplate code. Having used other frameworks like Caliburn Micro—which Rob had created for the WPF/Silverlight space for desktop applications—the idea of a framework that followed a similar approach in the world of JavaScript immediately struck a chord with me. As is often the case with information gleaned from podcasts during a daily commute, I stashed away the knowledge and didn't think about it for some time.

Later that year, we were starting a new frontend project and had to choose an SPA framework. With the plethora of options available, the process was daunting. After trawling the web for information that would allow us to make the best decision for the team moving forward, I realized that all the available options provided the same benefits, and much of the choice came down to how much the team would enjoy working with the framework, how quickly we could get something up and running, and how easy it would be to maintain the project going forward. The nugget of information gleaned from the podcast earlier that year came back to me, and I started comparing code samples from Aurelia to other frameworks. The beauty and simplicity of the

Aurelia MV* model for building SPAs by using components contrasted starkly with the other approaches I came across. This was enough for us to give Aurelia a shot.

Throughout the course of the next year, we built three projects with Aurelia, the first of which went from proof of concept to functioning production application in only a few weeks. This led to an unofficial tour of UK Aurelia user groups, where I had the privilege of meeting some super-smart people working in the .NET and web-development space. At this stage, Aurelia was still in alpha and early beta, and many people hadn't come across it yet. Although initially sceptical of yet another SPA framework, many developers (particularly in the .NET space) were impressed by Aurelia's intuitive, component-based development style.

The content of these talks (getting started with Aurelia, and component-based development with Aurelia) turned out to be the seeds that grew into this book. Because I (and most other developers I come across) tend to learn far better by example than by theory alone, I've built the content around a fictional virtual-bookshelf application (like Goodreads.com) called my-books. You'll start by creating a bare-bones application via the Aurelia CLI and then progressively layer on various features that users would want in a virtual bookshelf.

Fortunately, you can fit more into a book than you can a one-hour talk. In this book, I aim to teach you everything you need to know to build compelling, real-world applications in Aurelia from the ground up.

acknowledgments

Some people would say I'm crazy to even thinking about attempting to write a book while at the same time welcoming a newborn into my family earlier this year, and they'd be right! Writing a book was, to put it mildly, more work than expected. I'd like to thank my wife Matilda for supporting me throughout the process and taking on more than her fair share of our family responsibilities. I couldn't have gotten through it without her.

Next, I thank my editor at Manning, Toni Arritola. As I'm writing this, I'm remembering back to when I received my first round of feedback for chapter 1. There was more red than white on the page after all the review comments! I've learned a great deal from working with Toni over the past year. This book and my writing technique have benefited beyond measure from her involvement. I'd also like to thank my Manning technical development editor, Nick Watts, and tech proofer Troi Eisler. Their input made an enormous difference in the quality and clarity of my technical explanations and code samples.

Next, I thank everyone who submitted feedback on the Manning forum and the *Aurelia in Action* GitHub repository throughout the MEAP process. It's been a great motivation to see people reading the chapters and working through them as they've been released. Much of the feedback has been factored into the book throughout the MEAP. I also thank the book's technical peer reviewers, led by Ivan Martinović: Alain Couniot, Alessandro Campeis, Álvaro Falquina, Ashley Grant, Aurelien Gounot, Binh Vo, Geoff Barto, Jeff Smith, Joseph Tingsanchali, Luca Campobasso, Matt Harting, Peter Perlepes, Phil Taffet, Philippe Charrière, and Wayne Mather.

Finally, I thank the Aurelia core team, both for their wonderful contributions to the Aurelia open source community by creating and maintaining the project, and for their assistance with the book. Special thanks go to Ashley Grant for reviewing some of the early chapters and providing feedback that I was able to use throughout the rest of the book, and of course to Rob Eisenberg, who was fundamental in helping to get the book out to the Aurelia community.

about this book

When I first began web development with .NET 2.0 and ASP.NET Web Forms, there was only one paradigm for web applications: the server-side paradigm. This pattern involves making a request for the full page content, including scripts, images, and ads, every time the user performs an action on the page. For the kinds of web applications we were building when I started, this paradigm worked for the most part. If users wanted a richer and more interactive experience, it was typically implemented as a desktop application.

With the introduction of jQuery, we saw the possibility of pushing more of the logic that was previously done on the server side of our websites to the client side, communicating back and forth with the server using AJAX. The problem with this approach was that jQuery doesn't provide guidance for how to structure a client-side application, so many projects implemented during this era devolved into spaghetti code as the size and complexity of the client-side application grew. Smart developers recognized this problem and took the opportunity to create frameworks to simplify building rich user interfaces on the client side. Popular examples include Angular1, Backbone.js, and Knockout.js. With these frameworks, it became easy to write full applications as SPAs that would traditionally have been built as desktop apps.

A lot has changed since these frameworks were introduced. Over the past eight years, we've seen an almost exponential improvement in both web browser platform development and the JavaScript language itself. With these improvements, opportunity came knocking with a chance to build something better. Aurelia has answered.

It takes full advantage of this new environment, allowing you to build sophisticated SPAs with less framework-specific code than was possible in the past.

Aurelia in Action was written to give you a kick-start in building SPAs with Aurelia. To begin, we'll walk through a mental model that describes how the framework works and how the main building blocks fit together. From there, we'll begin developing the my-books virtual bookshelf sample application. This application starts as a simple shell, which you'll enhance as you learn the various tools and techniques in the Aurelia framework. By the end of the book, you'll have built my-books into a full-featured SPA with reusable components, form validation, routing, HTTP interaction, and more. This approach will get you up to speed with Aurelia best practices, while at the same time providing a solid reference project that you can return to for inspiration when building your own Aurelia applications.

Who should read this book

Aurelia in Action is intended to be read by intermediate developers with at least a basic level of web-development experience. If you've built web applications with a server-side technology like ASP.NET MVC or Ruby on Rails with a smattering of jQuery, or have dabbled in the path with another client-side technology like Backbone.js or Angular, you'll have all the prerequisite knowledge you need to grok the concepts and exercises presented here. Like most web-development technologies today, you can learn most of what you need about Aurelia by reading the online documentation and blogs. But what I aim to do is save you time and effort by weaving all the information you need to know about Aurelia into a consistent narrative that takes you all the way from creating a basic Hello World application to a fully functional SPA, ready for deployment to production.

Roadmap

The book has 3 parts and 16 chapters. Part 1 introduces Aurelia, covering the key framework building blocks and giving you a bird's-eye view of the kinds of problems Aurelia can help you solve:

- Chapter 1 outlines what Aurelia is, what kinds of applications you can build with it, and why you'd want to do that in the first place.
- Chapter 2 introduces the my-books sample application and steps through the process of creating the first iteration of this application using the Aurelia CLI. We'll pause at key points in the process to give you glimpses of key framework concepts like components, routing, and event handling.

Part 2 explores each of the key tools and techniques available in the Aurelia framework. These chapters go beyond the basics, covering everything you'll need to build real-world applications:

- Chapter 3 takes a more in-depth look at two of the major component types you'll use in Aurelia: custom elements and attributes. You'll style the my-books application, refactor to components, and get your first look at how to integrate third-party JavaScript dependencies.

- Chapter 4 looks at the Aurelia templating system. You'll learn the ins and outs of rendering data to an Aurelia view and handling user interaction with DOM events.

- Chapter 5 introduces two of the more advanced component types in your Aurelia tool belt: value converters and binding behaviors. You'll use these component types to create an autocomplete-style filterable table, and optimize some of the my-books user interactions.

- Chapter 6 outlines the Aurelia component lifecycle. You'll enhance the my-books application, refactoring to more fine-grained components and wiring them together using intercomponent communication techniques like the Event Aggregator and custom events.

- Chapter 7 is all about forms. You'll add an edit-book form to my-books, learning how to use check boxes, radio controls, form validation, and more.

- Chapter 8 covers HTTP interaction. You'll connect your burgeoning SPA to a Node.js REST API using Aurelia's HTTP client libraries.

- Chapter 9 introduces the concept of SPA routing, why it's important, and how you can use Aurelia's router to add sophisticated URL-based navigation to your applications.

- Chapter 10 covers authentication, answering questions like, "How can I secure an application without cookies?" You'll combine techniques from previous chapters, like value converters, routing, and HTTP interceptors, to secure the my-books application.

- Chapter 11 gets fancy with dynamic component composition. You'll learn how to build your views at runtime, adding a new dimension of flexibility to your applications.

- Chapter 12 introduces the web-component standards and shows you how to use features like the shadow DOM to create templated components.

- Chapter 13 goes deep into extending Aurelia, showing you how to override Aurelia's default conventions, inspect what the binding system is doing under the hood, and create custom attributes that can take a dynamic set of options.

- Chapter 14 describes the basics of Aurelia's animation system and framework hooks, teaching you how to animate components using CSS or JavaScript animations.

Part 3 covers what you'll need to know to prepare a production-ready Aurelia application package:

- Chapter 15 shows how you can use a combination of unit testing and end-to-end testing to iterate quickly on your projects with the confidence that they're working as designed.

- Chapter 16 gives you the tools you'll need to build a deployment package and release to production. You'll package and deploy the my-books application to the Firebase cloud host.

The first two chapters will help you understand the high-level concepts in the Aurelia framework, so I recommend reading them first to build a mental model of how everything fits together. These chapters will also help you set up your development environment and create the initial version of the my-books project.

Chapters 3–6 also cover key concepts fundamental to the remainder of the book, so unless you've already got a basic knowledge of the Aurelia framework, it would be a good idea to read these before moving on. Each chapter builds on the same sample application, so the remainder of the book is designed to be read sequentially. But if you do want to jump ahead to a specific topic, you can do so by cloning the project's GitHub repository and changing your working directory to the prior chapter. For example, if you wanted to jump to chapter 10, you could move to the Chapter-9-Complete directory to begin right where chapter 9 left off.

About the code

This book contains many examples of source code both in numbered listings and inline with normal text. In both cases, source code is formatted in a `fixed-width font like this` to separate it from ordinary text.

In many cases, the original source code has been reformatted; we've added line breaks and reworked indentation to accommodate the available page space in the book. Additionally, comments in the source code have often been removed from the listings when the code is described in the text. Code annotations accompany many of the listings, highlighting important concepts.

Source code is provided for chapters 2–16. Code listings are available on the publisher's website at www.manning.com/books/aurelia-in-action and on GitHub at https://github.com/freshcutdevelopment/Aurelia-in-Action. Some of the code listings and exercises are also provided as gists that can be run interactively with GistRun: https://gist.run. Such examples are clearly marked.

Because the book follows the iterative development of one sample application, there's a folder per chapter in the GitHub repository. They follow the convention *Chapter-[Number]-Complete*. If you run into problems with any of the code samples, you can use the completed versions to cross-reference and troubleshoot problems with your project, or skip to the completed version. The GitHub repository is an active, open source project, so any feedback is welcomed in the form of a GitHub issue or pull request.

Online resources

Need additional help? The Aurelia project website (http://aurelia.io) is the best place to go to review the online documentation and ask for help. The site includes a discourse forum (https://discourse.aurelia.io) frequented by many community members and Aurelia core framework contributors. Asking a question here will get you the help you need from developers working in the trenches with Aurelia.

Book forum

Purchase of *Aurelia in Action* includes free access to a private web forum run by Manning Publications where you can make comments about the book, ask technical questions, and receive help from the author and from other users. To access the forum, go to https://forums.manning.com/forums/aurelia-in-action. You can also learn more about Manning's forums and the rules of conduct at https://forums.manning.com/forums/about.

Manning's commitment to our readers is to provide a venue where a meaningful dialogue between individual readers and between readers and the author can take place. It is not a commitment to any specific amount of participation on the part of the author, whose contribution to the forum remains voluntary (and unpaid). We suggest you try asking him some challenging questions lest his interest stray! The forum and the archives of previous discussions will be accessible from the publisher's website as long as the book is in print.

about the author

Sean Hunter is a web developer with nearly 10 years of experience. He's extremely passionate about all things Aurelia and has been working with the framework in production since the early beta days. Sean got a taste for teaching developers how to get started with Aurelia while visiting user groups across the UK, and he's been excited to expand on this teaching effort with this book. These days, Sean is working in a variety of web-development technologies with companies across Australia, and he blogs at https://sean-hunter.io.

about the cover illustration

The figure on the cover of *Aurelia in Action* is captioned "Habit of One of the Guards to the King of Morocco." The illustration is taken from Thomas Jefferys' *A Collection of the Dresses of Different Nations, Ancient and Modern* (four volumes), London, published between 1757 and 1772. The title page states that these are hand-colored copperplate engravings, heightened with gum arabic.

Thomas Jefferys (1719–1771) was called "Geographer to King George III." He was an English cartographer who was the leading map supplier of his day. He engraved and printed maps for government and other official bodies and produced a wide range of commercial maps and atlases, especially of North America. His work as a map maker sparked an interest in local dress customs of the lands he surveyed and mapped, which are brilliantly displayed in this collection. Fascination with faraway lands and travel for pleasure were relatively new phenomena in the late eighteenth century, and collections such as this one were popular, introducing both the tourist as well as the armchair traveler to the inhabitants of other countries.

The diversity of the drawings in Jefferys' volumes speaks vividly of the uniqueness and individuality of the world's nations some 200 years ago. Dress codes have changed since then, and the diversity by region and country, so rich at the time, has faded away. It's now often hard to tell the inhabitants of one continent from another. Perhaps, trying to view it optimistically, we've traded a cultural and visual diversity for a more varied personal life—or a more varied and interesting intellectual and technical life.

At a time when it's difficult to tell one computer book from another, Manning celebrates the inventiveness and initiative of the computer business with book covers based on the rich diversity of regional life of two centuries ago, brought back to life by Jefferys' pictures.

Part 1

Introduction to Aurelia

Chapters 1 and 2 provide an overview of the Aurelia framework and the kinds of problems it's designed to solve. You'll learn how to create a new Aurelia project and set up the fundamentals that every SPA needs, including rendering and templating, routing, and HTTP communication. You'll also get a taste of some patterns and practices—such as convention over configuration, component-based development, and dependency injection—that you can use with Aurelia to create high-quality code that's fast to implement while at the same time being easy for you and your team to understand and maintain.

Introducing Aurelia

This chapter covers

- Examining what Aurelia is and is not, and why you should care
- Identifying applications suited to development using the Aurelia framework
- Looking at what you'll learn in this book
- Touring the Aurelia framework

Aurelia is a frontend JavaScript framework focused on building rich web applications. Like other frameworks, such as Angular and Ember.js, Aurelia is a single-page application (SPA) development framework. This means that Aurelia applications deliver the entire user experience (UX) on one page without requiring the page to be reloaded during use. At its core, writing an Aurelia application means writing a JavaScript application. But Aurelia applications are written with the latest versions of JavaScript (ES2015 and beyond, which we'll dig into as we go along, or TypeScript). The Aurelia framework has all the tools you need to build the rich and responsive web applications that users expect today, using coding conventions closely aligned to web standards.

1.1   Why should you care?

Imagine you're having a Facebook chat session with your friend Bob, and every time you send a message, you need to wait because there's a three-second delay while the page reloads to show you whether you've successfully sent the message, whether Bob has received it, and whether you've received any other messages from Bob in the meantime. In this scenario, it would be difficult to have a fluid conversation because of the jarring pause between entering your message and receiving feedback from the application. You may ask Bob a question, only to find that by the time the page reloads, he's already answered it. Today, however, the experience is much different. As soon as you start typing a message, Bob can see that you're composing a message for him, and when you click Send you receive visual feedback in the form of a checkmark to indicate that the message was delivered successfully. It's easy to gloss over functionality like this today because it's a part of so many applications we use all the time, such as Slack, Skype, and Facebook Messenger.

Now imagine that you've been tasked with building a line-of-business application for your department. The HR department has implemented an employee-of-the-month system where staff nominate and vote on who most deserves a monthly prize. This app would be expected to provide things like the following:

- A responsive voting system
- Live updating charts showing an overview of who has the most votes
- Validation to prevent employees from voting more than once

> **DEFINITION** *Responsive web applications* can be used across a variety of devices, from smartphones to desktop PCs. Typically, this is achieved using CSS media queries to resize various sections of the page or even hide them entirely so that the UX is optimal for the device at hand.

The features listed for your HR application are common examples of the kinds of things that users—like your fictional HR department—expect in rich web applications. Applications like Facebook and Slack have raised the bar in terms of what users expect from all web applications. I've noticed a trend over the past few years where clients have begun to expect the same kind of richness out of a line-of-business application that they're used to seeing in applications they use outside of the office. Using an SPA framework like Aurelia makes it vastly simpler to build these kinds of applications, compared with the traditional request/response style of architecture used with frameworks such as ASP.NET MVC, JSP, or Ruby on Rails, to name a few.

Given that you want to create rich, responsive web applications, the next logical question is, which technology should you use to do this? A useful technique for answering this kind of question is to analyze the kinds of attributes that are important to you and your team with a set of questions like this:

- *How complicated are the applications you're trying to build?* You don't want to use a jackhammer to crush a walnut when a nutcracker will do the job. Conversely, you want to make sure that you have a sufficient foundation in place that will support the kind of application you're trying to build.

- *How important is web-standards compliance to the team?* A framework that adheres more closely to web standards is more likely to look familiar to anybody with web-development experience, regardless of whether they've used a given framework in the past. Such a framework is also more likely to play nicely with other web technologies such as third-party libraries and frameworks.

- *What past development experience does the team have?* Frameworks and libraries can have a steeper or shallower learning curve, depending on the experience of the team.

- *How is the team organized?* Do you need designers and developers to be able to work together on the same project? Do you have a team of 1 to 5 or 100 to 500?

- *What kind of commercial and community support do you need?* How important is it to be able to pick up the phone or send an email to the team or company responsible for the framework? What kind of community are you looking to join?

Let's look at where Aurelia sits in terms of each of these questions; in doing so, you'll get a feel for the kinds of problems Aurelia helps you solve, and some of the features available in Aurelia's toolbox.

1.1.1 How complicated are the applications you're building?

With most SPAs, it's helpful to have a minimal set of tools to build the kind of experience that users expect. If these tools aren't present in the framework, then you may need to either bring them in as a third-party project dependency or build a bespoke implementation. Aurelia provides a core set of functionalities that most SPAs need out of the box, as a set of base modules. Most of these modules are available as optional plugins, so if you don't need a part, you can leave it out. The following subsection presents a basic list of the features that Aurelia offers. I'll include only a brief definition at this point to give you a taste of what's available. We'll dive into each of these topics in more detail later.

THE BASICS: SPA BREAD AND BUTTER

The following functionality is bread and butter to almost every SPA, regardless of the complexity level:

- *Routing*—SPA users expect your application to behave like a standard website. This means that they should be able to bookmark a URL to get back to it later and navigate between the different states of your application using the browser's Forward and Back buttons. The Aurelia router solves this problem by allowing you to build URL-based routing into the core of your application. Routing also allows you to take advantage of a technique called *deep linking*, which allows users to bookmark a URL from deep inside the application (for example, a specific product on an e-commerce site) and return to it later.

- *Data binding and templating*—Virtually every SPA needs a way to take input from the page (either via DOM events or input fields) and push it through to the JavaScript application. Conversely, you'll also need to push state changes back to the DOM to provide feedback to the user. Take a contact form as an example. You need a way of knowing when the email field is modified so that you can validate it in your JavaScript application. You also need to know what the value of the input field is so you can determine the validation result. Once you validate the input field, you need to return the result to the user. Data binding and templating are Aurelia's way of achieving this.
- *HTTP services*—Most SPAs aren't standalone; they need to communicate with or get their data from external services. Aurelia provides several options out of the box to make this easy, without the need to pull in any third-party JavaScript libraries like jQuery AJAX.

GETTING MORE ADVANCED—BEYOND BREAD AND BUTTER

As an SPA increases in size and complexity, you'll often run into a new set of problems. When you run into these problems, it's useful to have the tools to solve them:

- *Components*—One set of tools Aurelia provides for dealing with complexity is components. Components are a way of taking a user-interface (UI) layout and breaking it into small chunks to be composed into an entire view of your SPA. In a way, you can think of the components of your page like objects in a back-end system built using object-oriented programming (OOP), such as Ruby, Java, or C#.
- *Intercomponent communication*—Following the OOP analogy, wherein OOP objects can notify each other of application-state changes, your components also need a way of talking to each other. Aurelia has several options for how you can implement this kind of behavior. The appropriate option again depends on the complexity of your application in terms of the number of components and how interrelated they are. We'll dive into intercomponent communication in depth in chapter 6.

Most SPAs start basic and become more complicated over time. Aurelia allows you to reach for tools to deal with a given level of complexity when you need to but avoids overloading you with that complexity unnecessarily. By the end of this book, you'll be equipped to handle SPAs with varying complexity levels, and you'll know the suitable tool to retrieve from your Aurelia toolbox to solve the problem at hand.

1.1.2 *How important is web-standards compliance to the team?*

Imagine you're tasked with building an international website that needs to be accessible by users across the globe, some of whom may be vision impaired or have poor-quality internet connections. Enter *web standards*. Web standards provide a common base for the web. Devices and browsers are built to web-standards specifications, and as such, sticking to these specifications when building websites gives you the best chance of supporting a plethora of devices. These standards are also focused on accessibility; a working group called the Web Content Accessibility Guidelines (WCAG) is devoted to it. Following web standards also gives you a set of tools to enable support for users with a diverse set of accessibility requirements. A simple example of this is alt text (alternative text) on images, which allows screen readers to give vision-impaired users a description of the images on your site.

At the same time, you can reduce your future development costs by building on a stable and well-understood technology set. This makes it easier to bring new team members onto a project who don't necessarily know Aurelia, and allows you to make use of the vast array of third-party JavaScript and CSS libraries that weren't built with Aurelia in mind, which in turn improves maintainability and reduces development costs.

Wherever possible, Aurelia uses existing browser technology rather than reinventing the wheel. A simple example of this is HTML markup. Aurelia uses standards-compliant HTML, which allows both humans and screen readers to read the page source without needing to understand how Aurelia works. As we explore the framework, I'll highlight various points where the core team have leaned on an existing standard web technology to implement a given feature.

1.1.3 What past development experience does the team have?

In the world of web development, the number of new technologies to learn can often seem overwhelming. Given this reality, any boost your team can get in terms of building on past development experience can save you a lot of time. Some of the concepts in Aurelia will feel familiar to those with OOP experience, such as patterns like dependency injection, Model-View-ViewModel, or Event Aggregator. Don't worry if these concepts aren't familiar to you at this point, because we'll delve into each of these throughout the course of the book. On the other hand, Aurelia should also be easy to pick up for people with a good amount of experience with vanilla JavaScript, HTML, and CSS due to Aurelia's close adherence to web standards.

1.1.4 How is the team organized?

The concept of *separation of concerns* between your HTML file (which provides the structure of the page), your CSS file (which determines how the page looks), and your JavaScript (which determines how the page behaves) has existed in web development for some time. The idea is that by splitting these concerns and managing them separately, you should be able to work on any of them independently of the others. It also means that team members with the relevant skill set should be able to work on one piece of the picture without needing to know the in-depth details of the other pieces. For example, a developer should be able to put together the basic HTML structure and JavaScript behavior to then be styled by a team member with more of a focus on UX or design.

Aurelia's opinion on this is that that this concept of separation of concerns is no less important in the world of SPA development than it is in a more traditional server-centric web-development approach.

This approach gives you maximum flexibility. You still have the option of having one person manage an entire vertical slice of the application—JavaScript, HTML, and CSS—but you also have the option of splitting these out if that's the way you'd prefer to work within your team or company, as depicted in figure 1.1.

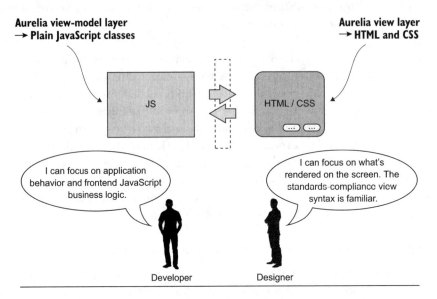

Figure 1.1   Aurelia maintains a separation of concerns between the structure, style, and behavior of pages. This allows for these pieces to be worked on independently, and by the person best suited for the job.

1.1.5   *What kind of commercial and community support do you need?*

Besides the technical details of any technology choice, an important aspect to consider is how well the product is supported. The level of support available for a given technology can have an enormous impact on how successful it is within your company. Following are some metrics to consider.

LEARNING/TRAINING

How easy is it to take somebody with no experience in the technology and up-skill them to the stage that they're productive with it? Several factors play into this:

- *Documentation*—Aurelia has a detailed set of documentation on the project website (http://aurelia.io/docs). This is actively maintained by the project core team. Often, issues that are raised on GitHub result in a documentation update that clarifies how a feature should be used.
- *Training*—Aurelia has a training program that makes it possible to receive in-person or online training from an Aurelia expert. This training is official and endorsed by the Aurelia core team. Often, it's even provided by core team

members, giving you direct access to people with the most experience working with Aurelia.

- *Community*—If you haven't come across it before, Gitter is a chat client like Slack but focused on allowing threaded conversations on open source projects. The Aurelia community has an active Gitter chat room, and often you'll get a detailed answer to any questions you might have. You can also ask questions and learn about best practices on the Aurelia Discourse forum (https://discourse .aurelia.io/).

SUPPORT

Like most popular JavaScript frameworks today, Aurelia is open source. But unlike most alternatives, Aurelia is one of two SPA frameworks that has commercial support available. Where frameworks such as Angular or React are developed and maintained by Google and Facebook respectively, it's not possible to pay for somebody from these companies to assist you if you get into trouble or want a little extra guidance on a project. Conversely, Blue Spire—the company behind Aurelia—offers commercial support contracts that can be tailored to the needs of your company.

Support is also available in the standard forms that you'd expect from an open source project. Aurelia core team members are quick to respond to GitHub issues or questions on Gitter.

For somebody from a technical background, it can be easy to overlook the fluffier aspects of choosing a technology like support and training. But these aspects make a difference when you look at how a technology will be picked up and used by the company long term.

1.2 *What kind of projects make Aurelia shine?*

To understand what kind of projects Aurelia works best with, let's look at the web-development models that are available, and how they might consider the context of a sample application. Imagine that you're tasked with building an ecommerce system. This system consists of a set of the following distinct groups of functionalities:

- *Blog*—News and updates about new products or events. This needs to be searchable and is mainly a read-only system.
- *Product list*—A listing of all the products that your company has on offer.
- *Administration*—Administrators need to be able to add new products and view statistics of what users are doing on the site.

You can structure an SPA several ways, but for our purposes, you can split these into the following four main categories:

- Server-side application with a sprinkling of JavaScript
- Client-side-rendered SPA
- Hybrid SPA
- Server-side rendered SPA with client-side continuation

1.2.1   *Server-side application with a sprinkling of JavaScript*

Figure 1.2 represents a traditional PHP/JSP/ASP.NET/Ruby on Rails–style website. In this model, the user requests the product list. The server is then responsible for rendering it to HTML and returning it to the user. Once the page has reached the client side, you may have a few simple JavaScript widgets such as a product-image lightbox jQuery plugin.

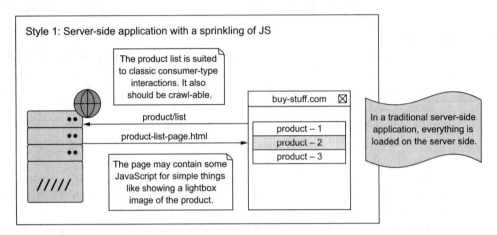

Figure 1.2   Server-side applications retrieve the entire page load as one rendered resource from the server (in addition to any CSS and JavaScript that is typically loaded separately).

The benefits of this approach are as follows:

- *The entire page is rendered on the server*—By scaling the server, you can improve page-load times without worrying about a device's native client-side render performance.
- *The crawler issue*—Page crawlers can effectively crawl a site for products and blog entries because JavaScript (which has patchy support by these technologies at best) isn't required to render the page.
- *Initial page load is generally fast*—The user isn't returned to the page by the server until the page is ready to go.

But there are drawbacks, such as slower subsequent page loads. Although the initial page-load time is relatively quick, subsequent interactions to the page also go through the same lifecycle of a full HTTP request to the server and rerender the entirely new page in the browser. This is OK for features such as the blog and product list but isn't ideal when the user needs to perform a set of interactions on the site and receive rapid feedback (such as commenting on a blog or creating a new product).

1.2.2   SPA rendered on the client side

In contrast to the server-side application, in this scenario the entire payload is loaded up front and returned to the browser in a single batch in a client-side SPA. This payload contains the application scripts and templates along with (optionally) some seed data required on the initial page load (see figure 1.3). In this case, the page is rendered on the client side rather than the server side. Traditionally, in this model, you have the entire e-commerce website returned when the user visits the initial page. Following this, as the user browses through various pages such as products and blog entries, you rerender the page on the client side based on data you received from the server via AJAX.

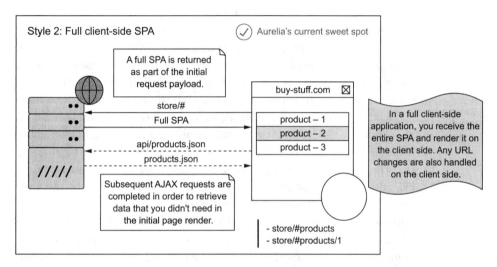

Figure 1.3   Full client-side SPA. An entire application is bundled and returned in one or two responses from the server and rendered in the browser. Subsequent AJAX requests completed to populate data that isn't required in the initial page load.

The benefits of this approach are as follows:

- *Your app feels lightning fast*—As the user clicks around, viewing products and comments on blog threads, the response times are fantastic, with minimal friction. The only time the client needs to talk to the server is when it needs data that the user hasn't seen before. This is often optional data that may not need to be loaded at all. In these cases, it's generally easy to show a spinner or a similar indicator to give the user instant feedback that the data they want is being fetched, and then proceed to show them the rerendered UI once the data has been received.
- *Selectively load and render UI fragments with AJAX*—After initial page load, you can also make the page feel more responsive by executing multiple concurrent asynchronous calls to the backend API. When these asynchronous calls com-

plete, you can provide the results to the user by rerendering only the impacted DOM fragment. An example is retrieving the list of products as JSON from an HTTP response and rerendering only the product list, leaving the rest of the page intact.

The drawbacks are as follows:

- *Large response payload*—Because the entire page loads in one request, users are forced to wait while this happens. Typically, you'd show a spinner or a similar visual device to smooth this interaction. But with large applications, this can be time consuming. Because 47% of users expect a website to load in 2 seconds or less, there's a risk that you may lose some of the visitors to your site if the initial application load exceeds this boundary.
- *Unpredictable page-load times*—Because you're delivering a substantial chunk of JavaScript and state to the application, page-render times can also be unpredictable. If you visit the page from a modern device with a fast processor and high internet bandwidth, there's a good chance you'll have the lightning-fast experience you've come to expect from SPAs. But what if you're in the outback in Australia attempting to load the application on a 5-year-old smartphone over a flaky 3G connection? The experience will be altogether different. Conversely, a traditional server-rendered web application is more predictable (at least in terms of the time required to render the application before it's returned to the user). HTTP servers can be more easily updated and scaled to improve these render times, bringing the issue back into something that you can control, rather than being subject to whatever device the user happens to be visiting the page from.
- *The crawler issue*—Some technologies, such as web crawlers, aren't built with the ability to process JavaScript. This can be a significant issue when building a public-facing SPA that needs to appear in search engine results.

BEST OF BOTH WORLDS

A good option would be to split the application into several separate sites. The blog might still be done in the traditional server-side rendered style (mainly for SEO purposes). But you could potentially develop the administrative site and shopping cart as separate microsites, providing the user with that rich interaction needed for this style of UI.

1.2.3 *The hybrid approach: server side with SPA islands*

Imagine a new set of requirements have come down from management. After great initial success, the company is looking to expand the use of the site and sell directly from the site. As such, the site needs some interactive pieces like a shopping cart and order screen. Taking the hybrid approach, you'd create the following three new routes in the website (see figure 1.4):

- site/store/cart
- site/store/order
- site/admin

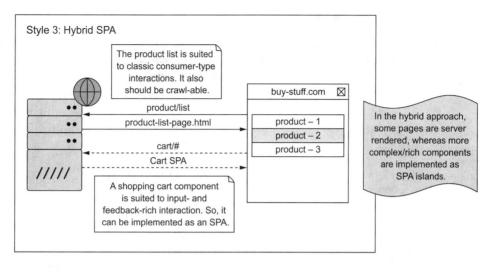

Figure 1.4 Hybrid SPA approach. In this model, the main *content* parts of the site are done with the traditional server-side approach. The *product list* and *blog* endpoints return the relevant HTML rendered from the server. But you then create multiple smaller SPAs to add rich interaction to the parts of the site that need it, such as the store.

Each of these new routes hosts an individual SPA. This approach avoids the need to immediately rewrite the entire site as an SPA, but still gives you the benefit of building the rich interactive parts of the site in a technology designed for that purpose. It also avoids the large payload size to some extent by splitting the SPA into smaller chunks that can be more quickly retrieved from the server and rendered.

The benefits of this approach are as follows:

- *The crawler issue has been solved*—This resolves the SEO and unpredictable page-load issues while still providing an interactive experience.
- *Faster on-ramp*—If you've already got a server-side application, you don't need to rewrite it as an SPA from the ground up, but instead can break out components of the application that are good candidates for SPA-style interaction over time.

The drawbacks are as follows:

- *Added complexity*—Managing application state and page navigation can get tricky when these concerns are dealt with both at the client-side and server-side level. With each new feature, there's a cognitive burden of deciding where everything fits best.
- *Tightly coupled frontend and backend*—In this style of architecture, your backend API is vulnerable to changes on the frontend, and vice versa. Without a clean boundary between the UI and the backend, API changes on either side are likely to trigger changes on the other. This increases the maintenance burden and makes it less likely you'll be able to use your backend API for other client types (such as mobile) in the future.

1.2.4　*Server-side-rendered SPA*

The Aurelia team has released a technology called *Server Render*. As the name implies, using this approach, the application is rendered on the server side before it's returned to the browser. This technology resolves both the *unpredictable page-load times* and *crawler* issues. This goes a long way toward expanding the set of applications that fall into Aurelia's sweet spot. You can find out more about server-side rendering on the Aurelia documentation site (https://aurelia.io/docs/ssr/introduction/). Take a look at figure 1.5.

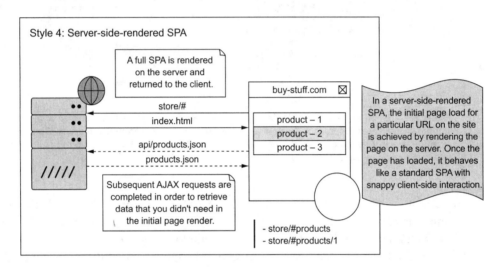

Figure 1.5　In this server-side-rendered SPA model, the initial page render is done on the server side, but once the application has been loaded into the browser, the SPA framework takes over, and subsequent interactions are done on the client side.

The benefit of this approach is that, in a way, this model gives you the best of both worlds. The initial render can be done on the server side, which resolves the issues of unpredictable page-load times and crawler accessibility, but still provides the rich interactive experience that users expect when the page is loaded. This approach may add more complexity to the system architecture by requiring the setup of additional components on the server side.

1.2.5　*Where does Aurelia sit?*

At its heart, Aurelia is designed to manage your entire web application in the style of a client-side-rendered SPA. Any web application where you need a significant level of interaction from the user that goes beyond simple content consumption is a good fit for Aurelia. Example applications that would be a great fit for Aurelia include the following:

- A messaging client
- A reporting/analytics portal for a website

- A CRUD (create, read, update, delete) application (like a typical forms-over-data example)
- An office-style application (such as Google Docs)
- An admin portal for a website (like the WordPress admin panel)

What these have in common is a user-interaction model more like a traditional desktop application than what you'd historically think of as a website. In the e-commerce example in figures 1.2–1.5 (buy-stuff.com), a great candidate would be a separate sidekick site to the main website that would be used to handle the administrative operations. You might also use Aurelia to build the shopping-cart or blog-comment website components as modules of the larger site.

1.2.6 What makes Aurelia different?

With the substantial number of SPA frameworks available today from the heavy hitters like Angular, React, and Vue, to up-and-comers like Mithril, it's important to consider what makes Aurelia different. What unique value does Aurelia provide that makes it a standout choice for building your web applications? I present you with the Aurelia cheat sheet, four reasons that you can give to your teammates when they ask you this question:

- *It gets out of your way.* Aurelia applications are developed by combining components built with plain JavaScript and HTML. In contrast, many other MV* frameworks today require a comparatively large amount of framework-specific code in both the view layer and the model/controller layer. This increases the concept count, making them more difficult to master and maintain.
- *Aurelia is developed following the convention-over-configuration pattern.* Convention over configuration means having reasonable defaults rather than requiring developers to manually specify every option. But what if the convention doesn't suit you? Aurelia makes it easy to override the default conventions when necessary, and we'll go into this in more detail as we proceed through the chapter.
- *When it comes to web standards, Aurelia's a pro.* Although other frameworks may pay lip service to web standards, Aurelia has them at its core, in its bones. Wherever possible, Aurelia adopts the standard browser implementation of a feature, rather than creating a framework-specific abstraction. A simple example of this is Aurelia's HTML templates, which come directly out of the Web Components Specifications (covered in depth in chapter 12).
- *When it comes to open source, community is king.* Aurelia has a thriving open source community. With core team members, and other Aurelia aficionados available on Slack (https://aurelia-js.slack.com/), Gitter, Stack Overflow, and GitHub help, you can always get the help you need to keep up the momentum while building your Aurelia applications.

1.3   *A tour of Aurelia*

Often, when you arrive at your hotel in a new city, one of the first things the concierge provides is a tourist map. Perhaps it's not a street-level map with the detail of the individual winding roads you need to take, but it's enough to give you an idea of where the major attractions and suburbs are. With a high-level map in hand, if you get lost, you can generally find your way by aiming for the attraction you want to visit and heading in the right direction. If you need a bit more detail, you might pull out a smartphone to navigate your way through some tricky areas. Similarly, you can think of figure 1.6 as your high-level map of the Aurelia framework.

Aurelia applications are built by combining view/view-model pairs called *components*. A view is a standards-compliant HTML template, and a view-model is a simple JavaScript class. Binding is used to connect fragments of the view (such as an <input value>) with properties on a view-model. Events raised on the view (such as an input-value change) trigger a corresponding method call in the view-model. Aurelia uses dependency injection to construct instances of view-models, providing them with their dependencies at runtime. These dependencies can be service classes (as seen in figure 1.6) or framework dependencies, such as the @inject decorator.

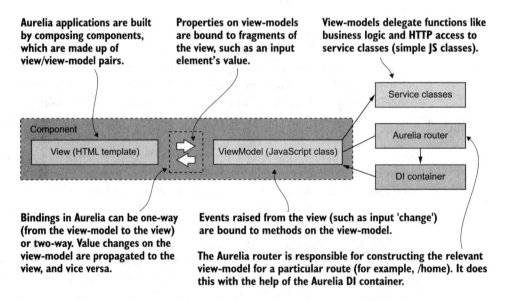

Figure 1.6   A high-level map of the Aurelia framework. At its core, Aurelia is an MV* framework.

> **DEFINITION**   Decorators are a new ECMAScript feature that at the time of writing are in stage 2 of the TC-39's proposal process for ECMAScript. Fortunately, the Babel transpiler allows us to use them today, even though they need to make it to stage 4 of this proposal process before they're officially adopted as a part of the language. Decorators allow you to easily and transparently

augment the behavior of an object, wrapping it with additional functionality (for example, logging). Decorators are used throughout the Aurelia framework to change the way that objects behave and can be recognized by their @ prefix. One example of this is the `@bindable` decorator from the Aurelia framework package. Properties can then be declared as `@bindable` using the imported decorator.

The Aurelia router is used to pick the correct component to load for a given application URL.

The map is highly detailed, but don't worry if you see blocks that you're not familiar with. We'll delve into each area of this diagram to give you a well-rounded understanding of how Aurelia does its thing. Like the concierge, I'm going to draw a line through some of the paths that you'll follow through the framework. These are the code paths that users interacting with the system will trigger every time they load a page or click a button. Like pulling out a smartphone to see a given location in greater detail, we'll zoom in on specific parts of the map that represent important aspects of the framework that we'll expand on throughout this book. Like any good tour, there will be a few interesting detours along the way, but by the time I'm finished guiding you through, you'll have a much clearer idea of where you're going. Let's get started.

1.3.1 Binding

Aurelia's core building blocks, components, are view/view-model pairs, where the view is an HTML template and the view-model is a simple JavaScript class.

> **NOTE** Some components, such as custom attributes and value converters, don't have a corresponding HTML file, but we'll come back to these later.

A technique called *binding* is used to connect DOM fragments on the view (such as `<input value>` or `<h1>` content) to corresponding properties on the view-model. Changes to properties on the view-model are automatically propagated to the view, causing the relevant fragment of the DOM to be rerendered with the updated value. Several options are available to control the behavior of how and when the view or view-model is notified of changes in the pair. This binding workflow is illustrated in figure 1.7.

1.3.2 Handling DOM events

Aurelia's binding system also handles DOM events. Events raised on the view, such as `input value change`, `checkbox checked`, and `button clicked`, are connected to corresponding view-model methods via *binding commands*. Binding commands in Aurelia are declared in the view template and are used to connect a view event with a view-model method, such as `delegate` and `trigger`—we'll delve into these in detail in chapter 4. As in the case of binding, Aurelia provides tools (such as binding behaviors, which you'll encounter in chapter 3) to control when and why the view-model is notified of events raised from the view. Aurelia's event-handling workflow is illustrated in figure 1.8.

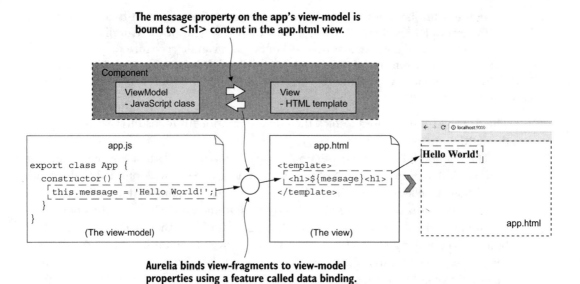

Figure 1.7   The app view-model (from the app.js file) is bound to its pair (the app view from the app.html file). When the app view-model is constructed, the 'message' property is set to the 'Hello World!' value. This value is bound to the view using data binding. When this view is rendered, the bound value of the message property is rendered to the view, and you can see the "Hello World!" text rendered in the Chrome browser.

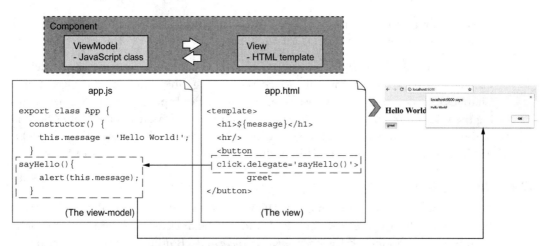

Figure 1.8   The Aurelia delegate binding command is used to delegate the click event to the sayHello method on the app.js view-model. When the button is clicked, the event is raised, and the sayHello method is called. This results in a greeting alert being presented to the user.

1.3.3 Routing

One of the tools required in most SPAs today is routing. Routing provides a way of mapping URLs to application routes. The benefit is that you can build an SPA in a way that makes it feel like a real website, so conventions such as the Back button returning to the previous page work like the user expects. As mentioned, taking advantage of a routing tool in your SPA allows you to implement deep linking, which allows users to visit a path deep within your application (for example, /products?id=1) and have the page rendered with the state that they expect (in that case, the product with the given ID). Aurelia lets you configure an array of URLs called *routes*. When you navigate to a route, it looks up the URL entry in the dictionary and finds the view-model that corresponds to this route. It then constructs that view-model on your behalf. But how do you get from that constructed JavaScript class to something that's rendered on the page? Figure 1.9 gives you a vital clue, outlining how a typical routing setup in Aurelia works.

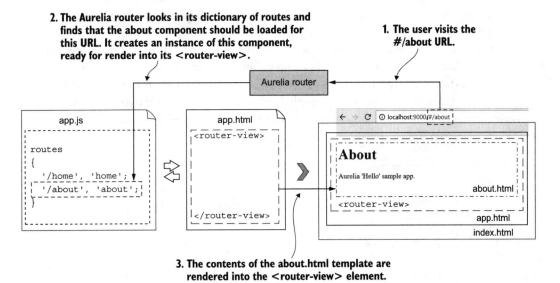

Figure 1.9 Zooming in on the routing component of your Aurelia map, the router works by looking up a URL (in the case of the example, the /about URL) and matching it to a route found in the route dictionary. The route dictionary determines which view-model to load. In this case, you've specified that you want the about view-model to load whenever a user visits the #/about URL.

In this example, you've added routing to your app.js view-model by configuring a set of URLs (home and about) that corresponds to components in your application. Figure 1.9 consists of two components: about and index. The router takes care of constructing the view-model for a component. The component is then rendered inside the <router-view> element in the app.html view.

To get a better understanding of how this process works, bear with me as I take you on a brief diversion that will give you some insights into Aurelia's personality.

Understanding Aurelia's personality provides some clues as to why the framework behaves the way it does. Aurelia is a framework with many strong opinions, held weakly. This means that for any scenario you might face in your application—in this case, picking the view to show in relation to a view-model—Aurelia thinks it should be handled a certain way. But like an open-minded person, Aurelia's opinions are flexible. If you have a different opinion about the framework, you can tell Aurelia, "No, in this case I want you to pick the view to render based on the Fibonacci sequence," and it will do that instead.

These opinions are often called *conventions*. Typically, the default conventions will get you where you need to be about 80% of the time; for the other 20%, you'll need to override them with your own. Your mileage may vary based on how opinionated you are, and how much your opinions diverge from the default.

One of Aurelia's opinions is that naming is important. Programmers typically put a lot of thought into how we name things. First, it appeals to our sense of organization (sometimes to the annoyance of those around us). But beyond that, it allows us to remember where everything is in a project and what it does. Naming conventions also allow our team members, when they first start a project, to make educated guesses about a file's content and have a fighting chance of being correct. Aurelia has the convention that each view-model file should be named the same as the view file but with a different file extension. For example, a view-model class named App should live in a file called app.js. The view corresponding to this view-model should then be named app.html (see figure 1.10).

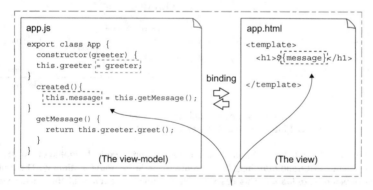

Example of how view/view-model pairs should
be named the same (apart from the filename)
so that they are bound together by convention

Figure 1.10   Naming the view-model and view files in this way allows
Aurelia to bind the view-model and view together by convention.

Aurelia has many other opinions, and we'll look at those later, but for now let's return to the dilemma of how you get from the view-model that the router loaded to the view rendered on the page. One option is to define a property in your view-model to hold the path of the view that you want to load. Then, when the view-model is loaded, the framework will look up this property, fetch the page, and render it into the DOM. This is a fine approach that's taken by many frameworks, but Aurelia instead uses conventions to create smart defaults regarding which view should be loaded given a specific view-model.

1.3.4 Inside the view-model, and what's this about components?

Now you know that users interact with the Aurelia framework either by navigating to a URL or by interacting with the view, which raises DOM events. In the first case, the appropriate view-model will be loaded and instantiated. In the second case, you're already on the page, so the view-model has been instantiated as a part of the application startup.

In the example application shown in figure 1.8, you've only got one view-model view pair (the app.js and app.html files). This pair is called a *component*. A component in Aurelia can represent a section of the UI (for example, it could be a nav bar or a product list). Components can also be used to encapsulate functionality within your application (for example, formatting a date field for display in the view with a value converter). Examples of these kinds of components include value converters, binding behaviors, and view-engine hooks. We'll cover these kinds of components in chapter 5. Using custom-element components is a way of reducing complexity as your application grows by splitting the application into a set of small, well-defined pieces that do one thing well. Those of you from an OOP background can think of this as another use case of the single-responsibility principle.

The first thing that Aurelia does after the view-model has been initialized is call the view-model constructor. This is the first step in something called the *component lifecycle*.

1.3.5 The Aurelia component lifecycle

As you interact with the components in the Aurelia application, these components go through a lifecycle. The lifecycle includes from when a component is constructed (for example, when you first visit a route that causes a component to be created) and rendered into the DOM to when you navigate away from this route, causing the component to be cleaned up and removed from the DOM.

Aurelia provides hooks into this lifecycle, allowing you to execute behavior relevant at that point in the life of the component. An example of this is the *activate* lifecycle hook. To hook into when a component is attached to the DOM, you can create an attached method on your component's view-model. You can think of this lifecycle like a tour bus, where you let the driver know in advance which attractions you're interested in seeing. The driver will then let you know at certain points in the tour that "We've reached the picnic spot," or "We've reached the scenic lookout destination." Then, when you arrive at a destination, you can decide on the action you want to take. We'll cover the Aurelia component lifecycle and look at each of the lifecycle hooks available in chapter 6 when we cover intercomponent communication with Aurelia.

1.3.6   *Loading data from an API*

Suppose that when your page loads, you want to retrieve a greeting from a REST API and render it in the app view. To load this data, you can hook into the `created` call-back method from the component lifecycle (as shown in figure 1.11), or the `activate` callback method from the router lifecycle in the case of a routed component (covered in chapter 9). Zooming in on the data-retrieval area of your map shows the `app.js` view-model using an external service called app-service to retrieve data from a back-end API using `aurelia-fetch-client`. Figure 1.11 illustrates a typical workflow used to retrieve data from an HTTP API and render it in the DOM.

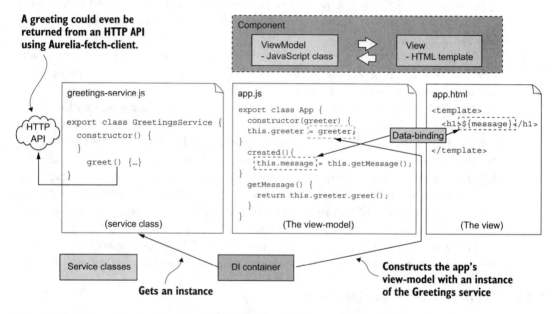

Figure 1.11   **The architecture of a sample Hello World application modified to show how a service class could be used to encapsulate functionality such as HTTP API access**

The Aurelia DI container is used to get an instance of the `GreetingsService` class and inject this into the app view-model when it constructs it. This service is then used to retrieve a greeting from an HTTP API. The greeting message is data-bound from the app view-model to the app view, so when your response returns from the HTTP API, it's immediately rendered to the DOM.

Having determined where you're going to implement this logic, how do you go about doing it? One of the most popular choices in Aurelia is via the use of a service class (figure 1.11). There's nothing special about a service class. In fact, it's a plain old JavaScript object (or POJO). Service classes allow you to separate the concern of retrieving data from an API from the view-model concerns of getting data rendered to the screen. In this case, you'd fill out the logic for retrieving the data via AJAX (most likely via `aurelia-fetch-client`, an HTTP client that makes your life much simpler than the jQuery AJAX `$.get` method, but we'll get into that in more detail later). An instance of this service class can be automatically injected into the view-model using dependency injection.

> **DEFINITION** Traditionally, objects in a system are responsible for managing their own dependencies. This can become challenging as the application grows in scale, increasing the complexity of the relationships between these objects. *Dependency injection* (DI) simplifies this problem by moving the responsibility of creating objects away from the objects themselves and placing it in the hands of the DI framework. This transition of responsibility is known as *inversion of control (IoC)*. Typically, in an application using DI, an object declares which dependencies it requires (often as constructor parameters), and the DI framework provides the relevant implementation of these dependencies at runtime.

1.3.7 Dependency injection with Aurelia

In your simple example view-model, there's only one basic screen (the app view), so it will be easy to create a new instance of the class directly in the constructor and do what you need to do. In the real world, however, applications are never that simple. Take Facebook as an example. It has a chat box, a notification widget that tells you how many unread messages you've got, an area that shows you all the ongoing conversations with your friends—and this is only on the chat side of things. If you were to build this in Aurelia, each area would be made up of a set of components. Dependency injection becomes useful when you have multiple components and need to manage dependences (such as service classes) between these components. We'll look at how DI simplifies this process in more detail when we explore intercomponent communication in chapter 6.

1.3.8 Rendering the view

After you've retrieved the data via the service class, you need some way of rendering it back to the screen. One approach that you may be familiar with is to use jQuery. In the world of jQuery, you start by pulling your JSON blob into an array of JavaScript objects. You then have to query the DOM to retrieve the `Table` element object. After that, you cycle through each of the values in the array and add these as rows to the table, but there are two downsides to this approach:

- *Performance*—It's possible to update the DOM efficiently by carefully replacing only the affected DOM branches that correspond to a change in your JavaScript model even with plain JavaScript or jQuery. But because this optimization step is tedious and time-consuming, many developers skip it and instead replace a larger fragment of the DOM than is necessary. Data binding performs this optimization for you, which makes skipping this step a non-issue.

- *Difference of abstraction level*—In an ideal world, when writing application code, you only need to concern yourself with the business problem you're solving. If you're in the flow of solving this problem, and then need to change gears and think instead about the mechanics of getting the relevant state changes reflected in the DOM, it can break you out of this flow. Any break in flow causes a slowdown in development pace and introduces an opportunity for errors to creep in. Imagine if every time you wanted to accelerate your car you needed to think about the process of how the internal combustion engine worked to produce forward motion. Focusing on these details might increase the likelihood of accidents. The accelerator pedal is an abstraction that obviates you needing to think about all of this. All you need to do is push the pedal, and off you go. Aurelia's binding system brings you to a higher level of abstraction, much like the accelerator pedal does when you're driving.

To render the results from your service-class call, save those results into a property bound to an element in the view. Aurelia then takes care of it, first notifying itself that a change has taken place, and then applying the relevant changes to the DOM. This keeps you at the same level of abstraction throughout the process and allows you to focus on the task at hand. It also allows Aurelia to optimize the changes to the DOM. Aurelia has a high-level picture of the changes that need to be made to the DOM. Given this perspective, it's able to find an optimal way to perform these changes to minimize browser rerendering, and so on. (We'll look at Aurelia's DOM optimizations in more depth later in this book.)

We started our virtual tour with user interaction on the page (either a URL navigation event or a DOM event). In the case of the navigation event, you've loaded the appropriate view-model and initiated it via the constructor, which is the first step in its component lifecycle. In the case of the DOM event, you've responded to an event triggered in the UI that was bound to a method in the view-model via data binding. In both cases, you responded to the event by retrieving data from a web API via a service class that was injected into your view-model via dependency injection. Once you received the data back from the service class, you saved it into a property value on the view-model that was data-bound to a property on the view. This caused that part of the view to rerender and display the list of values to the user.

You now have an idea of the kinds of problems that Aurelia solves and, at a high level, how it solves them. But if you're anything like me, you're eager to learn how to put this into practice. In the next chapter, you'll get your hands dirty creating an Aurelia application from the ground up. We'll build a virtual bookshelf SPA and begin by creating the ability to add and list books. By the end of this book, we'll have built a full-fledged SPA with multiple interrelated components, third-party libraries (such as Bootstrap and Font Awesome), and the ability to send and receive data from an HTTP REST API built with Node.js, MongoDB, and Express.js. This will give you an understanding of the variety of tools that Aurelia offers, and by the time you're finished, you'll have everything you need to build your own component-oriented SPA with Aurelia.

Summary

- Certain styles of web applications are difficult to develop using the traditional request/response style of web-application architecture.
- Many of these applications (such as admin portals or messaging applications) would've been built as desktop applications.
- The SPA architecture makes it easier to build this style of application, by providing a set of tools such as data binding and routing.
- Aurelia is an MV* SPA application framework that provides a similar set of tools to other frameworks, such as AngularJS or Ember.js, and is more similar to these frameworks than the SPA libraries, such as React, which are more of a rendering layer.
- Aurelia is the standout choice in today's web-development world due to its focus on clean code, simplicity, and convention over configuration.
- Aurelia applications are built by composing components of view/view-model pairs, where the view is an HTML template and the view-model is a JavaScript class.
- Data binding is used to handle events from the view in the view-model, propagate changes in view-model properties to the view, and propagate changes from the view back to view-models.
- Dependency injection is used to simplify the management of dependencies in Aurelia applications by moving the dependency-management responsibility out of the components themselves and into the DI container.
- Aurelia provides routing to allow developers to build SPAs that feel like real websites, supporting the standard web-interaction patterns that users are familiar with.

Building your first
Aurelia application

2

This chapter covers

- Introducing my-books, the virtual bookshelf built with Aurelia
- Bootstrapping an Aurelia application with the Aurelia CLI
- Creating components in Aurelia by building view/view-model pairs
- Responding to view events using binding commands
- Keeping track of UI state with the Aurelia router

"In theory, there is no difference between theory and practice. But in practice, there is."

—Yogi Berra

When I first started surfing, I took a lesson to get a jump-start on the basics. At the beginning of the lesson, the instructor explained the concept of catching a wave, that idea of springing up from the board at just the right moment to glide down the face. I got it, conceptually. When I attempted to catch the first wave, I face-planted and ended up with a nose full of saltwater. My understanding moved from concept to reality.

2.1   *Introducing my-books*

If you've ever used an application like Goodreads (www.goodreads.com), you'll be familiar with the concept of a virtual bookshelf. Throughout this book, you'll implement a virtual bookshelf called my-books that gives users the ability to record and share books that they've read. This application allows me to show you some of the shiny tools in Aurelia's tool belt that make it great for building data-centric SPAs. When you've finished this book, you'll be able to apply what you learned to create solutions beyond my-books. In this chapter, you'll start by creating a simple form to add and list books. In future chapters, you'll take this further with animations, communication with third-party REST APIs, automated testing, and more.

Even the grandest of applications has humble beginnings. The first version of my-books is no different. You'll start by creating a single page that allows you to view a list of books and add books to that list. The layout of the application will look something like figure 2.1. The entire application is hosted inside the index.html page. The main application component, app.js, includes a book-list component to render a list of books to the view.

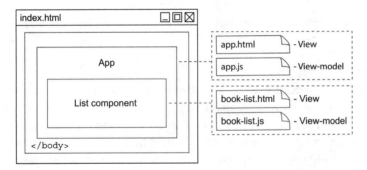

Figure 2.1   my-books application wireframe. You'll build up the my-books application via a set of iterations throughout the book. The first iteration consists of two main components: app and book-list.

The first step on your journey to creating my-books is to set up the project structure and the build pipeline—the process of taking your beautiful ES2015+ modules and getting them running in the browser. For this project, you'll use the Aurelia CLI to jump-start your new application. Before you do this, however, let's take a brief look at the various options available for creating new Aurelia applications.

2.2   *Building with Aurelia*

With Aurelia, one of the themes that may begin to stand out to you is freedom of choice. The web-development community is varied, both in terms of the kinds of applications we build and the opinions and approaches we have in mind when building them. Because of this, the Aurelia core team always makes sure to include alternative options where possible. As such, there are three main options available for developers creating a new Aurelia project. The appropriate approach depends on the goal you have in mind for your current project. I'll start by outlining each of the popular choices for creating new projects with Aurelia and mention some pros and cons for each. This should assist you in picking the most appropriate option for later projects. We'll then dive into creating a new project via the third option listed—the Aurelia CLI.

2.2.1   *Option 1: Download the quick start*

The quick start option is a ZIP package that you can download from the Aurelia website. This is useful if you want to download the project and get started without performing any kind of setup work installing framework dependencies. Typically, this isn't used for real-world applications because it performs transpilation from ES Next to ES5 on the fly in the browser (a slow process). Also, this project is missing some common dependencies out of the box, which you'd often need to add anyway. If you'd like to explore this option, you can download the ZIP file from http://aurelia .io/downloads/basic-aurelia-project.zip.

> **NOTE**   Aurelia is platform-agnostic, but at the moment there's only a ZIP file available, and no .tar.gz.

2.2.2   *Option 2: Skeleton application*

The second option is to download one of the sample skeleton applications from GitHub. These are basic shell projects with many of the things that you'll need in a standard SPA such as routing, a navigation menu, and framework dependencies, already created or referenced. The benefit of this option is that there are skeletons out there for many of the standard setups you might choose. For example, one of the skeleton-navigation applications uses TypeScript instead of ECMAScript, and one uses webpack as an alternative to SystemJS (these are different module-loading and application-bundling options). Don't worry if some of these terms aren't familiar to you; we'll unpack them as we proceed through the chapter. This option provides a great amount of flexibility, allowing you to tailor the project's build system specifically to your needs.

2.2.3   *Option 3: Aurelia CLI*

This option is your choice for today. Aurelia applications are built using ES Next or TypeScript. Because of this, a collection of Node.js tools are required to create Aurelia applications and perform tasks such as transpilation from ES Next/TypeScript to ES5, module loading, and build automation. Each of these tasks has many alternative tooling options, and the tools of choice within the JavaScript community change rapidly. The Aurelia CLI streamlines the process of creating and building Aurelia applications by setting up reasonable defaults for each of these tools, and in some cases allowing you to swap out a given default for your tool of choice (for example, TypeScript rather than Babel.js). The Aurelia CLI is also updated to incorporate new tooling options as they emerge, allowing you to easily integrate them into your development process. These tools make up a frontend build pipeline. When you get to section 2.2.4, you'll see how the Aurelia CLI can be used to make the process of building modern Java-Script applications easier to manage.

> **DEFINITION** You can think of a *build pipeline* as the standard build process you might be familiar with from the backend development world. It takes the source code that you write and translates it into something that the browser knows how to run.

It's time to get your hands dirty creating your first Aurelia application. In the next section, you'll create the first iteration of my-books using the Aurelia CLI.

2.2.4 Creating the my-books project

Before continuing with this section, please ensure that you have the prerequisites, Node.js and the Aurelia CLI npm package, installed. Installation instructions can be found in the appendix. Let's begin by generating a new my-books application with the Aurelia CLI.

> **TIP** If you bear with me, I'll get you to run a set of commands at the Aurelia CLI terminal to generate a basic Hello World application. That way, you'll have a concrete running example to refer to when I describe how this project fits together.

All Aurelia CLI projects start with the `new` command, which generates the application project structure and configures the build pipeline. Start by running the following command at the terminal/command prompt:

```
au new
```

After running this command, you'll be asked to enter the name of your project, as shown in figure 2.2.

```
Please enter a name for your new project below.

[aurelia-app]> my-books
```

Figure 2.2 The `au-new` command initiates a wizard that will ask you a series of questions required for Aurelia to set up your build pipeline and project structure. The answers to these questions determine which utilities are used at each step of the pipeline.

At the prompt, enter the name of your project: my-books. A new folder with this name will be created to host your Aurelia application as a subdirectory of your current directory.

After entering the project name, select the project setup option you want to use. To provide maximum flexibility in configuring the build pipeline, select 3 (Custom); see figure 2.3. This allows you to select your preferred transpiler, CSS processor, and more. Don't worry if you're unfamiliar with these terms; we'll briefly cover each concept as you go along.

```
[aurelia-app]> my-books

Would you like to use the default setup or customize your choices?

1. Default ESNext (Default)
   A basic web-oriented setup with Babel and Webpack for
   modern JavaScript development.
2. Default TypeScript
   A basic web-oriented setup with TypeScript and Webpack for
   modern JavaScript development.
3. Custom
   Select loaders (requirejs/systemjs), bundlers
   (cli/webpack), transpilers, CSS pre-processors and more.
```

Figure 2.3   The wizard advances you to the next setup options after you enter the project name.

After entering the custom project workflow, the first choice you're presented with is to select the *module loader/bundler*.

> ### Bundlers and module loaders
>
> Modules allow developers to write small, well-defined chunks of JavaScript functionality that don't blend into the rest of the application code. Consumers and maintainers of the module should be able to more easily understand what a module does. Various module loaders are available, each with its own advantages. You can find out more about module loaders, and RequireJS specifically, in my blog post at https://sean-hunter.io/aia-modules.
>
> Only the most recent browser implementations provide support for native JavaScript modules. *Bundlers* bring modular JS techniques to older browsers while at the same time allowing you to roll up all of your disparate JS files into one or more *bundle* files for improved page-load time. We'll look at bundling in more depth as we go along.

In the context of Aurelia, each view-model or service class is encapsulated within a module, providing a convenient way to organize your project. Additionally, the Aurelia framework is itself modular. As you'll see throughout this chapter, you can bring various framework features into your project by importing the relevant module. Select option 1 to use the RequireJS module loader (see figure 2.4). By selecting this option, you're also selecting the Aurelia CLI as your bundler.

```
[Default ESNext]> 3

Which module loader / bundler would you like to use?

1. RequireJS (Default)
   A file and module loader for JavaScript.
2. SystemJS
   Dynamic ES module loader
3. Webpack
   A powerful bundler

[RequireJS]>
```

Figure 2.4   Select which module loader you wish to use.

The next option to select is the transpiler. Enter 1 to select the BabelJS transpiler and use JavaScript rather than Typescript (see figure 2.5).

```
What transpiler would you like to use?

1. Babel (Default)
   An open source, standards-compliant ES2015 and ESNext
   transpiler.
2. TypeScript
   An open source, ESNext superset that adds optional strong
   typing.

[Babel]>
```

Figure 2.5   Select the transpilation option.

DEFINITION   *Transpilation* in the context of Aurelia is the process of taking your source files (ES Next or TypeScript) and translating them to the ES5 format supported by today's browsers.

Next, you're presented with a range of minification options for your project (see figure 2.6). These options allow you to tune how Aurelia minimizes your template files to be bundled and delivered to the browser. You may want to keep options 2 and 3 in

```
How would you like to setup your template?

1. Default (Default)
   No markup processing.
2. Minimum Minification
   Removes comments and whitespace between block level
   elements such as div, blockquote, p, header, footer ...etc
3. Maximum Minification
   Removes comments, script & link element [type] attributes
   and all whitespace between all elements. Also remove attribute
   quotes where possible. Collapses boolean attributes.

[Default]>
```

Figure 2.6   Select option 1 (Default) to skip markup minification.

your back pocket in case you want to remove additional whitespace and so on in production, minimizing your bundle file size and hence reducing initial page-load time. Let's go with option 1, because this demo project isn't constrained by performance requirements.

You're now presented with a set of *CSS processors* (see figure 2.7). CSS processors extend CSS to add variables, mixins, interpolations, and more. They can be extremely useful in creating more-maintainable styles for your SPA projects but would add unneeded complexity to the demo application. Select option 1 to skip importing a CSS processor.

```
What css processor would you like to use?

1. None (Default)
   Use standard CSS with no pre-processor.
2. Less
   Extends the CSS language, adding features that allow
   variables, mixins, functions and many other techniques.
3. Sass
   A mature, stable, and powerful professional grade CSS
   extension.
4. Stylus
   Expressive, dynamic and robust CSS.
5. PostCSS
   A tool for transforming CSS with JavaScript.
```

Figure 2.7   Select the CSS processor to use for your Aurelia project.

After this, you're asked to select a project testing option. Although you won't need to add tests right away, let's generate the default testing configuration anyway so it's in place once you get to chapter 15 (see figure 2.8).

```
Would you like to configure unit testing?

1. Yes (Default)
   Configure your app with Jasmine and Karma.
2. No
   Skip testing. My code is always perfect anyway.

[Yes]> 1
```

Figure 2.8   Select your testing option.

Now you're asked to select a code editor (see figure 2.9). Several popular options are available, and there's nothing to stop you from using a different editor later. You may be wondering why the editor choice is included in the CLI: the answer is that the CLI generates configuration files specific to each editor to improve your coding experience. For example, by selecting the Visual Studio Code (option 1), you indicate to the CLI that it should generate a jsconfig.js file that the editor can use to give you hints about the ESNext syntax.

```
What is your default code editor?

1. Visual Studio Code (Default)
   Code editing. Redefined. Free. Open source. Runs
   everywhere.
2. Atom
   A hackable text editor for the 21st Century.
3. Sublime
   A sophisticated text editor for code, markup and
   prose.
4. WebStorm
   A lightweight yet powerful IDE, perfectly equipped for
   complex client-side development.
5. None of the Above
   Do not configure any editor-specific options.
```

Figure 2.9   Select your default code editor.

As figure 2.10 shows, you now have the choice of whether you want to proceed with the project setup, given the displayed set of pipeline-configuration options, or abort and start again. This is useful if you realize that you need to tweak any of the configuration settings before the project is created. If you select option 3 (Abort), the wizard will exit, and you'll need to start again. Press Enter to proceed with the default option and create the project.

```
Project Configuration

    Name: my-books
    Platform: Web
    Bundler: Aurelia-CLI
    Loader: RequireJS
    Transpiler: Babel
    Markup Processor: None
    CSS Processor: None
    Unit Test Runner: Karma
    Integration Test Runner: None
    Editor: Visual Studio Code


Would you like to create this project?

1. Yes (Default)
   Creates the project structure based on your
   selections.
2. Restart
   Restarts the wizard, allowing you to make different
   selections.
3. Abort
   Aborts the new project wizard.

[Yes]> 1
```

Figure 2.10   You can see the list of selections you made, with default setup options configured as Babel for your transpiler, the Karma test runner, and Visual Studio Code for your editor.

The next step in the project-setup wizard (figure 2.11) determines whether project dependencies (such as RequireJS) should be installed as a part of the project-creation process. Installing the dependences should take only a few minutes, depending on your internet connection speed. Press Enter to go ahead with the default option.

```
Would you like to install the project dependencies?

1. Yes (Default)
   Installs all server, client and tooling dependencies
   needed to build the project.
2. No
   Completes the new project wizard without installing
   dependencies.

[Yes]> 1|
```

Figure 2.11   You can select Aurelia project dependencies in the wizard, for example, the npm package required to build and run your project. At this step, you can decide whether it should go ahead and install the dependencies or whether you'd like to install later.

After the project setup has completed, you should see the output shown in figure 2.12. If you run into any errors at this point, the best option is to start from scratch with a new project directory. It's also wise to verify that your version of npm and the Aurelia CLI are up to date to avoid any version-mismatch-related issues. The appendix provides further troubleshooting options if you get stuck here.

Updating npm and Aurelia
You can upgrade to the latest version of NPM using the `npm install npm@latest -g` command. You can get the latest version of the Aurelia CLI via npm using the `npm update aurelia-cli -g` command.

When you complete the last step in the project-setup wizard (figure 2.12) there are several other Aurelia CLI commands available, now that you have the default project structure in place. You can see a full list of the Aurelia commands by changing to your project directory (`cd my-books`) and running the `au help` command.

Your new Aurelia application includes the project structure and dependencies. We'll delve into this project structure in detail momentarily, but first, to verify that everything has been set up correctly, run the default project to see the obligatory Hello World page in the browser.

In addition to generating the project structure, Aurelia CLI commands can be used to execute the build-pipeline steps necessary to transpile and package your code, and then get your project running on a simple HTTP server.

```
Congratulations! Your Project "my-books" Has Been Created!

Getting started

Now it's time for you to get started. It's easy. First,
change directory into your new project's folder. You can use cd my-books to get there.
Once in your project folder, simply run your new app with au run. Your app will run fully
bundled. If you would like to have it auto-refresh whenever you make changes to your HTML, JavaScript or
CSS, simply use the --watch flag If you want to build your app for production, run au
build --env prod. That's just about all there is to it. If you need help, simply run au
help.


Happy Coding!
```

Figure 2.12 After completing the final step of the wizard, you're shown some of the other commands that the Aurelia CLI provides, such as au build, which you may want to run, now that you have the default project structure in place.

To launch the my-books application, change the directory to the my-books subdirectory and run the au run command:

```
cd my-books
au run
```

Running the au run command hosts the application in a simple HTTP server on port 9000. Open a browser and navigate to http://localhost:9000 to view the default Hello World page. Figure 2.13 demonstrates the page that you should see in the browser.

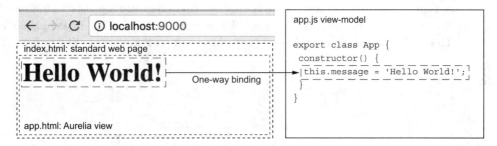

Figure 2.13 Default page shown when setting up a project via the au-new command. This is useful as a smoke test to ensure that everything has been shown correctly. The default application consists of an app.html view and an app.js view-model. One-way binding is used to render a message from the view-model to the view.

NOTE For the best results, use the current version of Google Chrome, Mozilla Firefox, Microsoft Edge, or Apple Safari. Older browsers such as IE9 are also supported but require polyfills. You can learn more about running Aurelia in older browsers on the Aurelia Hub website at http://mng.bz/3DPz.

> **Troubleshooting**
>
> If you experience this error when using the `au run` command—`SyntaxError: Block-scoped declarations (let, const, function, class) not yet supported outside strict mode`—there's a chance that you're running an unsupported version of Node.js. At the time of writing, this error can be resolved by upgrading to Node.js LTS. It's also worth checking the Aurelia documentation for details on the current prerequisites: http://aurelia.io/docs/build-systems/aurelia-cli.

Even though you'll remove this default page as you continue creating your virtual bookshelf, it's useful as a smoke test to ensure that everything has been configured correctly.

> **NOTE**   It can be difficult to keep track of all the moving parts in the frontend build pipeline. The project-creation wizard provides an effective shortcut, allowing you to set up all the required build-pipeline plumbing in minutes rather than hours. Additionally, because you're now using a pipeline configured by the Aurelia core team, you can lean on their experience. You can read through the source code of some of the gulp build tasks to familiarize yourself with the latest techniques and practices.

2.3 One-way and two-way data binding and event delegation

In the preceding section, you generated the my-books project structure and ran the default application using the `au run` command. But now you have a problem; your website is—to put it mildly—bare-bones. It's not much use having a virtual bookshelf that's only capable of greeting users. Users want to be able to manage their books. The initial layout of the my-books application will look something like figure 2.14.

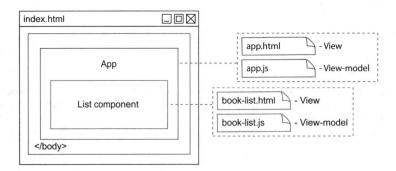

Figure 2.14   This is the my-books layout that you're aiming for in the first version of your application. It has one subcomponent (`book-list`) inside the main app shell, which shows a list of all the books that the user has added. This component consists of a view/view-model pair.

Knowing what granularity to break your application down into can be hard. To approach this problem, I often start with the high-level application inlined on one page, and then break this page down into different components when they have enough functionality to justify it. This is the approach we'll take now.

2.3.1 Adding the functionality inline

Start by modifying the app.js file to include the desired behavior, as shown in code listing 2.1. First, create the addBook method, which adds a new book to the list of books with the name stored in the bookTitle view-model property. It then clears the current value of bookTitle so that the next value can be added and logs the list of books to the console so that you can view the results. You can get started by opening the newly generated my-books project in your text editor of choice.

> **TIP** My text editor preference is Visual Studio Code (https://code.visualstudio.com). It has great support for JavaScript, and you can even get plugins for autocompletion of Aurelia classes and HTML snippets, like this fantastic one by Aurelia core team member Erik Lieben, at https://github.com/aurelia/vscode-extension.

Now that you've got a simple version running, you can start breaking it down into components to make the code cleaner and easier to reason through. As you saw in chapter 1, because the app view and view-model have the same name, Aurelia automatically binds them together. As result of this, the submit event on the form is delegated to the addBook method on the app view-model using the submit.trigger binding command. This wires up Aurelia to capture the submit event and call the addBook method whenever the event is fired.

The value attribute of the input field is configured for two-way binding with the bookTitle property's value using the value.bind syntax. When the value is changed in the book-title input field, the corresponding value is updated in the view-model, and vice versa. At the beginning of the form, the form-submit event is wired up to trigger the addBook view-model method using the submit.trigger binding command.

Start by modifying the app view-model created by the CLI at src/app.js, and then modify the file as shown in the following listing.

Listing 2.1 Initial implementation of the app view-model (app.js)

```
export class App {

  constructor(){
    this.books = [];
    this.bookTitle = "";
  }

  addBook () {
    this.books.push({title : this.bookTitle});
    this.bookTitle = "";
```

Array of books to be bound from app view

Book title to be bound from app view

Method to be called from view to add a book

Adds a new book to the array with the bound title

Resets the title

```
      console.log("Book List ", this.books);        ◁──┐  Logs the updated
    }                                                   │  book array

}
```

TIP   One thing that caught me out a few times when I started using this syntax
was that the brackets need to be included in the method name that you're binding to: addBook() rather than addBook. If you do the latter, you'll be scratching
your head wondering why the method isn't being called, so it's good to remember that from the start. This syntax is required because you're calling a function
on the view-model rather than reading the value of a property.

The second step is to modify the view at src/app.html to include an input form and
make use of the extra functionality exposed by the view-model. The following listing
shows the source code for the modified version of the app.html file, including a rudi-
mentary implementation of adding and listing books.

Listing 2.2   Initial implementation of app view (app.html)

```
<template>
  <h1>Add Book</h1>

  <form submit.trigger="addBook()">      ◁──┐  Triggers the addBook
                                             │  method on form submit
    <label for="book-title"></label>

    <input value.bind="bookTitle"       ◁──┐  Binds the bookTitle
        id="book-title"                    │  view-model property
        type="text"                        │  to the input value
        placeholder="book title...">

    <input type="submit" value="add" >

  </form>
</template>
```

This gives you a taste of some of the user interactions that you can set up using the
related concepts of event delegation and data binding. In this case, you set up the event
delegation on the submit DOM event, but it could also be used to bind to any event
raised by the DOM, allowing you to handle a plethora of different scenarios.

Likewise, you set up two-way binding to an input element as a starting point, but
this concept can be applied to any DOM element that takes input. A key point is that
even though you haven't specified the input binding as two-way, Aurelia has automatically created a two-way binding by convention because the binding command is
applied to an input element. The logic behind this convention is that you likely want
to send input back to the view-model. We'll elaborate on the various scenarios supported by data binding and event delegation in chapter 3 when we take a deep dive
into the Aurelia binding and templating engine.

You can view the first iteration of the add-book form by running the au run --watch
command and navigating to http://localhost:9000 in the browser.

TIP   Running the au run command with the --watch parameter will spin up the simple web server as before and watch for any file changes, which is useful as you modify the component to add form elements.

Type a value into the input box and click the Add button or press Enter. The value of the bookList array updates via two-way data binding and is logged to the console. This allows you to verify that your first event-delegation trigger and two-way data binding are working as expected. You should now see the add-book form rendered on the page: when you add a book to the list, it should be logged to the console, as shown in figure 2.15.

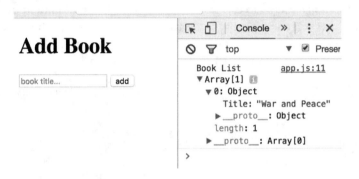

Figure 2.15   This is what the first iteration of your add-book form looks like in the browser.

Now that you can add books to the list, you need a way to view them on the page. Do this by rendering the list of books to an unordered list in the app view using the repeat.for="item of array" repeater. You can think of repeaters like an ES2015 for...of loop because they have the same semantics. They allow you to loop through the values of an array and inject content for each item into the DOM. This is often used in combination with the one-way data-binding string-interpolation syntax that you saw in chapter 1 (<h1>${message}</h1>) to render the value of the item in the current iteration. We'll cover repeaters in more depth in chapter 3.

   The following code listing shows the source-code changes required to render an unordered list of books to the app view. Modify the src/app.html view to display a list of the books that have been added to the list.

> **Listing 2.3   Modified app view to include books repeater (app.html)**

```
<template>

  <h1>Add Book</h1>

  ...
  <hr/>
```

```
  <ul>
    <li repeat.for="book of books"> ${book.title} </li>
  </ul>

</template>
```

The repeat.for="book of books" syntax can be
used to iterate over each of the items in an array.

Within the context of the `<li>` element (including attributes on the element as well as inside the element itself) you have access to the book in the current iteration of the loop. You then use a one-way binding expression, `${book.title}`, to render the Title property of the book in the current iteration to the page. Conceptually, Aurelia converts `<li repeat.for="book of books">` to `<template repeat.for="book of books">...</template>`, but this is abstracted to create a cleaner syntax for development time.

Run the `au run --watch` command at the terminal and navigate in the browser to http://localhost:9000. You should now see the unordered list of all the books rendered to the page, as shown in figure 2.16.

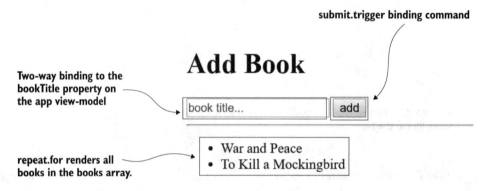

Figure 2.16   Adding books triggers the one-way binding expression from the view-model to the view for the `books` array to be updated, which causes the updated list to be rendered to the page.

Let's recap what you've learned so far. You've now used a combination of one-way data binding, two-way data binding, iterator expressions, and event delegation to take input from a form, add that input to a list, and render the updated values to the page. A key point here is that you didn't need to do anything special to refresh the list of books after the value was added. The `repeat.for` binding expression allows you to render a collection of items (such as an array, range, or map) from the view-model to the view. Changes on the collection are observed, meaning that additions or deletions from the collection are propagated to the view. This binding system allows you to implement an interaction model where users receive instant feedback based on actions they take on the page, without needing to individually wire up at which points the page needs to be refreshed.

Now that you've completed the first iteration of this page with all functionality developed inline as a part of the `app` component, it's time to look at breaking down the page to extract the first logical subcomponent. In the next section, you'll break out the `book-list` component, and in doing so you'll take your first look at Aurelia's custom-element feature.

> **Exercise: Binding**
>
> You've started the implementation of a simple Aurelia greeter application on GistRun at https://sean-hunter.io/aia-exercise-2-1. As an exercise, try modifying the application to change the greeting message to the contents of the input box on form submit. You can find the solution here: https://sean-hunter.io/aia-exercise-2-1-solution.

2.4 Creating components using Aurelia custom elements

At the beginning of section 2.3, I outlined a high-level blueprint of how the my-books page should be composed. The first step in implementing this view was introducing functionality for users to add and list books inline.

Now that you have the basic functionality in place, it's time to break out the first logical subcomponent to match the original blueprint, shown earlier in figure 2.14. The app component, which serves as the application shell, is at the root level of the application. The `book-list` app component has a subcomponent that renders the list of books to the page.

The new `book-list` component will be created as an Aurelia custom element. Custom elements are a way of extending the DOM by creating new HTML elements that can behave like regular DOM elements. To create custom elements, do the following:

- Create a new JavaScript class (the view-model).
- Create a corresponding HTML template (the view).
- Name the view and the view-model the same, apart from the extension, so that Aurelia can automatically bind them together.

Beginning at the top, start by creating the `book-list` custom element by defining two new files (src/book-list.js and src/book-list.html) as shown in listings 2.4 and 2.5. Technically, this isn't the cleanest place to put these (imagine what it would look like with thousands of files in this root directory), but it keeps things simpler for now. This view-model will be bare-bones to start with, exposing only a single `@bindable` property book to be bound from the parent element.

Listing 2.4   Initial implementation of the `book-list` view-model (book-list.js)

```
import {bindable} from 'aurelia-framework';        ◁──┐  Imports the bindable
                                                        attribute from the
export class BookList {          ┌── Defines a new bindable property,    aurelia-framework
  @bindable books;        ◁──────┤    books, on the view-model           package
}                                └──
```

In listing 2.4, you begin by importing the `@bindable` decorator. This is then used to set up a one-way data binding between the app parent component and `book-list` child component.

TIP   Decorators allow you to easily and transparently augment the behavior of an object, wrapping it with additional functionality (for example, logging). Decorators are used throughout the Aurelia framework to change the way that objects behave and can be recognized by their @ prefix. One example of this is the @bindable decorator that you imported from the Aurelia framework package. You then declare the book's property as @bindable using the imported decorator.

Next up, some housekeeping. To clean up the project structure, move the book-list repeater from the app.html view file into the book-list.html view file. This encapsulates the book-list functionality into its own view. Create the view that corresponds to this view-model in the src/book-list.html file to complete the new component. Create a new file called src/book-list.html and add the code shown in the following listing.

Listing 2.5   Initial implementation of the `book-list` view (book-list.html)

```
<template>
    <ul>
        <li repeat.for="book of books"> ${book.title} </li>    ◁─┐ Refactors the
    </ul>                                                        │ repeater into a
</template>                                                       │ new book-list
                                                                 │ view
```

Next, you'll need to remove this behavior from the app view. You can think of it like changing the level of abstraction. You've delegated the book-addition behavior to the child component (book-list) so that it no longer belongs in the app view. This lifts the level of abstraction in the app component by delegating the details of how books should be added down the component hierarchy.

Modify the app view at /src/app.html to use the newly created custom element, as shown in listing 2.6. This example contains some elements you've not seen yet. The <require> element is a custom element provided by the Aurelia framework that behaves similarly to a require statement used to import a module in JavaScript, or an import statement in ES6. This imports the references you want to use in your view.

The <book-list> custom element represents your new BookList component. Wherever you include a reference to this, you'll get a copy of it injected into the DOM. If you reference an element without first importing it with <require>, nothing will be rendered on the page, as Aurelia doesn't know how to interpret it.

Listing 2.6   Modified `app` view refactored to use custom elements (app.html)

```
<template>
    <require from="./book-list"></require>    ◁─┐ Imports the book-
    <h1>Books</h1>                              │ list custom element
    <form submit.trigger="addBook()">
        <label for="book-title"></label>

        <input value.bind="bookTitle"
            id="book-title"
            type="text"
            placeholder="book title...">
```

```
            <input type="submit" value="add">
        </form>
        <hr/>
        <book-list books.bind="books"></book-list>
</template>
```

Adds a book-list element to the view

By using the `<require from="">` custom element, you declare that the app.html file depends on the `book-list` module. This indicates to the framework that the module loader that you've got configured (in your case, RequireJS) should import that resource at runtime.

The `books.bind="books"` expression is a one-way data binding. It binds the `books` property of the parent view-model app to the same property on the child view model. That way, any books added to the list in the app view-model are automatically propagated to the `book-list` view-model. Figure 2.17 shows the data flow between these components.

The @bindable decorator can be used to share state between parent and child components. In this case, you set up a one-way binding between the books property on the app view-model and the books property on the book-list view-model.

This means changes to the books in the app view-model are propagated down to the book-list view-model.

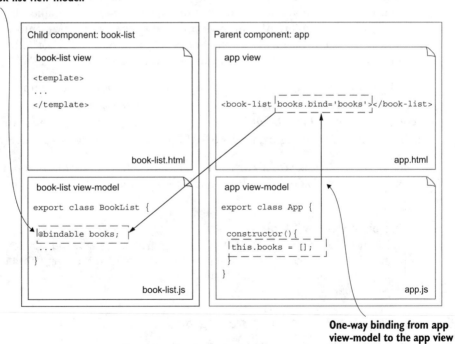

One-way binding from app view-model to the app view

Figure 2.17   As books are added to the `books` array in the `app` view-model, the changes are propagated down the component hierarchy using one-way data binding.

This pattern that you've followed for breaking down the UI into a set of custom elements is one of the key patterns you'll follow when creating Aurelia applications. As UIs grow in complexity, it's key to modularize the layout by breaking it down into small, well-defined pieces. The benefit is that you can then take these custom elements and either move them to different areas of your application to adjust as layout requirements change, or even reuse the components in different contexts. For example, imagine that you want to add the ability for users to upload a book-cover image to be stored with the book and displayed in the book list. Further, you also want to allow users to upload an Excel spreadsheet listing all their books to bulk load their entire library. If you build this upload functionality as a custom-element component, you can reuse this same element as-is to implement both of those requirements. The book-list component modularization you completed would also be useful in this case; to add the ability to render the book-cover image for each item in the list, the only component you need to modify is the book-list component. This keeps the change encapsulated, making it easier to reason about and test.

In this first iteration of the my-books application, you used custom elements to break down the Aurelia application layout into a set of modular components and linked these components together with data binding.

> **WARNING** You have a fine line to walk when componentizing your application. You want to make sure that creating a given component makes the application design simpler. Although decomposing the application into smaller units can make it easier to reason about each unit, it also adds complexity, as you need to think about how these units communicate.

You'll get a better feel of how to decide when to split out a new component through the course of the book as you expand on the my-books application. Currently, you're rendering a set of hardcoded books into the book-list. Next, you'll make this list more dynamic by loading from a REST API using aurelia-http-client.

> **NOTE** In chapter 6, you'll work with a more detailed view composition, and in the process you'll add the ability to mark books as read and provide a star rating.

> **Exercise: Custom elements**
> Try modifying the greeter in this gist (https://sean-hunter.io/aia-exercise-2-2) to encapsulate the greeting component in a new custom element. You can find the solution here: https://sean-hunter.io/aia-exercise-2-2-solution.

2.5 *Building services and retrieving data from a REST API*

I have a feeling that when you saw the view-model source code, you got the gist of what it was doing before you read the explanations. One reason for this is that in keeping with The Aurelia Way, the framework introduces minimal extraneous code. For example, there's nothing telling the book-list view-model where to find the view template. All you need to do is name it book-list.html, and the framework figures it out for you. This allows you to keep your classes as close to vanilla JavaScript as possible. The only item that may have caused a blip in your brain while you were reading through the view-model implementations is the @bindable attribute that you used to enlist a property for two-way data binding on the book-list view-model. Apart from that, they're just ES Next classes. Wouldn't it be nice if it were possible to implement data access in the same way?

In Aurelia, there's no specific concept for service/data-access logic. All you need to do is create a class that provides the data or functionality required by your view-model. This class is then injected by the Aurelia DI system.

Next, you'll add a backend to my-books to allow your saved books to be loaded on startup. You'll do this by adding a new class responsible for retrieving a list of books from the backend API. But first, the setup. The following steps are required to retrieve data from your API:

1　Create the books.json my-book JSON seed file to stand in as your REST API endpoint.
2　Install the aurelia-fetch-client using the au install CLI command.
3　Create the BookApi service class to implement the HTTP logic.
4　Update the book-list component to retrieve the seed data from books.json via the BookApi service.

To keep things simple and avoid creating a backend REST API for now, the current implementation of the my-books API is a JSON file. The REST API will return the contents of a flat JSON file that will be read from the file by the HTTP server. Create a new file named books.json at the root of your application at the same level as the index.html file called books.json, as shown in figure 2.18. Having the file at the root level ensures that the file is served by the HTTP server.

Copy and paste the code from listing 2.7 into the /books.json file.

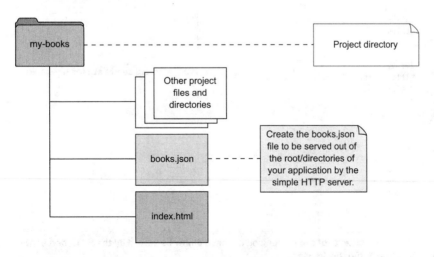

Figure 2.18　Add the books.json file to the root of the my-books project.

Listing 2.7   JSON file containing initial my-books seed data (books.json)

```json
[
    {
        "Id" : 1,
        "title" : "War and Peace",
        "description" : "Really enjoyed this one.",
        "rating" : 3,
        "status": "good"
    },
    {
        "Id" : 2,
        "title" : "Oliver Twist",
        "description" : "",
        "rating" : 2,
        "status" : "ok"
    },
    {
        "Id" : 3,
        "title" : "Charlie and the Chocolate Factory",
        "description" : "",
        "rating" : 5,
        "status" : "bad"
    }
]
```

If it's not still running, run the `au run --watch` command to initialize the Aurelia application. If you navigate to http://localhost:9000/books.json, you should see the JSON results, as shown in figure 2.19.

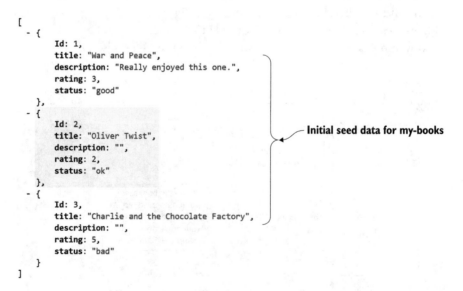

Figure 2.19   The contents of the books.json file should now be served by the HTTP server at http://localhost:9000/books.json.

The next step is to install `aurelia-fetch-client`. This library provides the `Http-Client` module, which is an HTTP client based on the fetch standard. This is a new way of using AJAX (a native alternative to `XmlHttpRequest`), which you'll delve into in more detail in chapter 8. Run the `au install` command to install the library:

```
au install aurelia-fetch-client
```

You may be given the option of installing optional CSS files. In this case, the CSS files are only related to unit testing the `aurelia-fetch-client`, so select `[no - option 2]` to skip additional CSS file installation. You can think of this command as being a two-step process:

1 Download and install the package from the npm repository.
2 Autoconfigure the aurelia.json file to add the script to the vendor bundle.

> ### Installing packages with the Aurelia CLI using the Aurelia Importer
> The Aurelia CLI has two commands for installing packages. These packages use either npm or Yarn (https://yarnpkg.com/en/) to download packages from the npm repository and install them into your Aurelia project. The two commands are as follows:
>
> - `au install {package}` (for example, `au install jQuery`) installs the package with npm or Yarn and attempts to configure it by making the necessary changes to the aurelia.json file.
> - `au import {package}` (for example, `au import jQuery`) configures a package that has already been installed by npm or Yarn by making the necessary changes to the aurelia.json file.

As part of the import step (step 2 of the `au-install` command), the new dependency needs to be added to the vendor bundle. When you generated the my-books project using the `au new` CLI command, the project's build configuration was automatically created for you at /aurelia_project/aurelia.json. The aurelia.json file has several jobs related to how the Aurelia application is run. One of these is bundle configuration.

When the `aurelia-run` command runs, one of the things it does is transpile the ES6/7 code into ES5 so that it will run in older browsers and concatenate these converted files into clumped files called bundles. The maximum concurrent requests on browsers today range from two to eight. With an application composed of many small files, you can imagine the effect that this has on page-load time. Reducing the number of HTTP requests to these bundles helps to avoid this. The au new CLI command generates a configuration containing two bundles by default: app-bundle.js, which contains your application code, and vendor-bundle.js, which contains the libraries that you depend on.

TIP   If the aurelia.json file isn't updated automatically, add the four lines related to this dependency from the following listing.

After running the `au install aurelia-fetch-client` command, the /aurelia_project/ aurelia.json file for your project will be updated.

Listing 2.8   Modified project file to include `aurelia-fetch-client` (aurelia.json)

```
...
  {
    "name": "vendor-bundle.js",
    "prepend": [
     "node_modules/bluebird/js/browser/bluebird.core.js",
     "node_modules/requirejs/require.js"
    ],

    "dependencies": [
        "aurelia-binding",
        "aurelia-bootstrapper",
        "aurelia-dependency-injection",
        "aurelia-event-aggregator",
        "aurelia-framework",
        "aurelia-history",
        "aurelia-history-browser",
        "aurelia-loader",
        "aurelia-loader-default",
        "aurelia-logging",
        "aurelia-logging-console",
        "aurelia-metadata",
        "aurelia-pal",
        "aurelia-pal-browser",
        "aurelia-path",
        "aurelia-polyfills",
        "aurelia-route-recognizer",
        "aurelia-router",
        "aurelia-task-queue",
        "aurelia-templating",
        "aurelia-templating-binding",
        "text",
        ...
        {
          "name": "aurelia-testing",
          "path": "../node_modules/aurelia-testing/dist/amd",
          "main": "aurelia-testing",
          "env": "dev"
        },
        {
          "name": "aurelia-fetch-client",
          "main": "aurelia-fetch-client",
          "path": "../node_modules/aurelia-fetch-client/dist/amd",
          "resources": []
        }
    ]
    ...
```

Adds aurelia-fetch-client package as a dependency

NOTE Bluebird is a third-party promise library with fantastic performance characteristics. According to tests done by the Aurelia core team, introducing the Bluebird library into an Aurelia project improved application load times by approximately 25% in Google Chrome and approximately 98.5% in Edge, compared with the native promise implementations.

Now that you can retrieve data from the books API, create a new JavaScript file, /src/book-api.js, as shown in the following listing. The `BookApi` client will fetch data from the backend REST API and return it asynchronously via `aurelia-fetch-client`.

Listing 2.9 Initial implementation of `BookAPI` (book-api.js)

```
import {HttpClient} from 'aurelia-fetch-client';
import {inject} from 'aurelia-framework';

@inject(HttpClient)
export class BookApi{

  constructor(http){
    this.http = http;
  }

  getBooks(){

    return this.http.fetch('books.json')
        .then(response => response.json())
        .then(books => {
          return books;
        });

  }

}
```

Imports the HttpClient class from the aurelia-fetch-client package

Imports the inject decorator from the aurelia-framework (used for DI)

Injects the HttpClient class into the book-api class using DI

Makes an HTTP GET call to the books.json endpoint using the fetch method

The fetch call returns a promise. Unwrap the promise using the .json method on the response object and extract the JSON result from the promise.

Takes the JavaScript object representation of the object returned from the API call stored in the books object and returns it to the caller

`BookApi` is a standard ES2015 class apart from the use of the `@inject` decorator. The first two lines import the required modules. Aurelia uses the concept of dependency injection to supply objects with the modules they depend on at runtime. The `inject` module provides an Aurelia decorator, which indicates that the framework should supply an object.

After importing the requisite modules, the `@inject` decorator is used to supply a singleton instance of the `HttpClient` module as a parameter of the constructor.

NOTE All injected instances in Aurelia are singletons by default within a given container where each component (such as a custom element or attribute) has its own container. It's possible to override this convention if needed.

When the Aurelia framework constructs the `BookApi` class, this instance will be injected. Within the constructor, the injected `HttpClient` instance is saved into the `http` class property. The `getBooks` method returns a promise. This promise consists of performing an HTTP fetch out to the books.json endpoint, extracting the JSON from the response object, and returning the resulting array of books.

> **NOTE** This is one simple example of how the fetch client can be used. We'll dive into much more detail around the functionality provided by this package in chapter 8 when you hook up the REST API for the my-books project.

Now that you have the functionality required for fetching the books array from the API endpoint, all you need to do is wire this up in the app view-model so that the stored list of books is retrieved and rendered to the user on startup. To include the logic to fetch a list of books from the REST API using the BookApi service class, modify the view-model at /src/app.js as shown in the following listing.

In listing 2.10, you begin by importing the BookApi service and the inject decorator. Then, you inject an instance of the BookApi service into the book-list view-model. Finally, in the constructor call, the getBooks method is applied on the injected BookApi service, the response of the promise returned from the getBooks method is unwrapped, and the resulting books are pushed into the @bindable books property.

Listing 2.10 Modified app view-model to retrieve books from the API (app.js)

```
import {bindable, inject} from 'aurelia-framework';      ⟵  Imports the inject
import {BookApi} from 'book-api';   ⟵                        decorator so that you
                                                             can inject an instance
                                    Imports the new          of the BookApi class
@inject(BookApi)            ⟵       BookApi class from
export class App {                  the book-api module

  constructor(bookApi) {            Injects a singleton instance
    this.bookTitle = "";            of the BookApi class into
    this.books = [];                the constructor
    this.bookApi = bookApi;
  }

  addBook () {                           Hooks into the bind
    this.books.push({title : this.bookTitle});    component-lifecycle
    this.bookTitle = "";                 method
  }
                                              Wires up a method to be
                                              fired on completion of the
  bind(){                                     getBooks request promise
    this.bookApi.getBooks().then(savedBooks =>   ⟵
                  this.books = savedBooks);   ⟵
  }                                               Refreshes the books array
}                                                 with values returned from
                                                  the HTTP API
```

Calling an asynchronous method on a service class that returns a promise with the results of a backend web API call is a popular Aurelia framework pattern. This pattern can be used to perform any kind of interaction you might need with an HTTP endpoint. For example, in the context of my-books, you could also use this to delete books using the HTTP delete verb or modify books with the put verb. We'll delve into a variety of use cases for this combination of service class and HTTP API in chapter 8, when we look in depth at using HTTP in Aurelia.

If you're still following along, kill the au run --watch process and relaunch it to restart your HTTP server. Your browser should then pick up the new dependency on aurelia-fetch-client and refresh with a new list of books loaded from your API, as shown in figure 2.20.

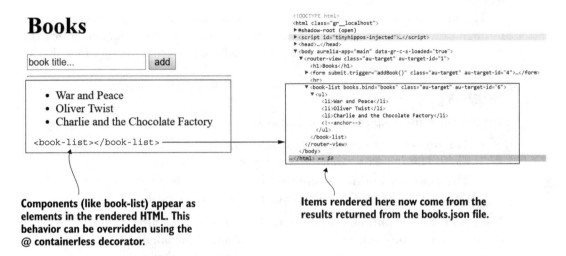

Components (like book-list) appear as elements in the rendered HTML. This behavior can be overridden using the @ containerless decorator.

Items rendered here now come from the results returned from the books.json file.

Figure 2.20 The book list rendered inside the book-list component is now made up of the books returned from the books.json HTTP endpoint.

TROUBLESHOOTING STEPS

If you encounter any errors at this point, it's worth checking the following:

- Ensure that aurelia.json contains the aurelia-fetch-client dependency.
- Ensure that you've imported the book-api service into your book-list view-model and that the import path is correct (you'll receive an HTTP 404 error if the path to this import is incorrect).
- If you're still running into problems, you can cross-check the status of your package.json and aurelia.json files against this gist: https://sean-hunter.io/chapter-2-dependencies.

The book-list component is now dynamic, loaded from an HTTP API rather than being hardcoded in the view-model. But looking at the results in figure 2.20, the layout still doesn't feel quite right. The my-books application is now only about adding and listing books, but you'll want to add more pages in the future to expand the functionality of the application. In the next step, you'll shift the responsibilities for adding and listing books into separate application routes using Aurelia's router. This gives you a more flexible application layout that you can expand on throughout the book.

2.6   *Maintaining page state with the Aurelia router*

Have you ever had an experience where you follow all the steps in a web application, get close to finishing the form, and then need to click the Back button to double-check something on a previous page? All too often, when you do this, your entire workflow loses its state and resets back to the beginning. This tends to frustrate users immensely. To remedy this, a modern SPA framework needs a powerful routing system that's easy to implement.

The next thing that my-books needs is a way of maintaining state as you transition through different logical pages of the application. You'll begin by implementing the Aurelia router. When it's in place, you'll set up a home view that the user initially sees when they load the page.

2.6.1   *Configuring the router*

The Aurelia router implementation consists of two parts:

- The routable area consists of anything inside the `<router-view>` custom element. This should be added to the component you want to route inside.
- The view-model of this component needs to include a `configureRouter` function that defines the routes that your application supports.

The layout of the application needs to be changed slightly to support the new routing system. To do this, you'll extract the book-retrieval functionality into a new `books` component, and strip the `app` component down to a basic shell.

Because there are a few steps that you need to get right for this refactoring to work correctly, I've outlined the process here, including which files need to be created or modified and when:

1　Modify the view-model ./src/app.js file to include the routing configuration.
2　Remove application logic from the view ./src/app.html file to create a basic application shell.
3　Define a new home page for the application by creating a new view-model ./src/index.js file and view ./src/index.html file.
4　Define a `books` page for the application by creating a new view-model ./src/books.js file and view ./src/books.html file. The logic for both the view and view-model should be moved out of the `app` component.
5　Stop and start the `au run --watch` process to make sure that all file changes are factored in correctly, and that the app and vendor bundles have been successfully recompiled.

TIP　For brevity, we sometimes need to shorten code listings so they only show the modified sections. If you have trouble following exactly which parts to modify, you can always find the full code listings (which you can copy and paste) in the *Aurelia in Action* GitHub repository, https://github.com/freshcutdevelopment/Aurelia-in-Action.

To begin with, replace the contents of the /src/app.js file to include the router.

Listing 2.11 app view-model modified to include the route configuration (app.js)

```
export class App {
  configureRouter(config, router) {
    this.router = router;
    config.title = 'my-books';
    config.map([
      { route: ['', 'home'], name: 'home', moduleId: 'index' },
      { route: 'books', name: 'books', moduleId: 'books' },
    ]);
  }
}
```

- **Defines the route configuration function**
- **The router on the view-model**
- **Sets the view title**
- **Adds the routes to the router**
- **Defines the home route**
- **Defines the books route**

The `configureRouter` function defines which routes the application supports. First, the router of the current view-model is set to the injected router instance. Following this, the title of the application is configured. The `map` function is then provided with the current list of available routes. In this example, you're only configuring some basics. Each route listed defines the following:

- `route`—The URLs that this route listens for.
- `name`—The name of the route is defined so that it can be referenced when setting up links in views.
- `moduleId`—The name of the component that this route should initialize.

Now that you've configured the initial set of routes, you need to use them in the application layout. Modify the application layout to change the app component into a shell that hosts several views. You can do this by including a reference to the `<router-view>` custom element. This element serves as a slot in the page where the Aurelia router can swap in content at runtime based on the active route. This is what gives the appearance that you're navigating to a different page, as you would in a traditional server-based web application, without the overhead of needing to perform a full page refresh.

Modify the view /src/app.html file so that it only includes `router-view`.

Listing 2.12 app view simplified to a router-view shell (app.html)

```
<template>
  <router-view></router-view>
</template>
```

- **Adds the router-view shell to the app view**

Include the `<router-view>` custom element. This is the shell that hosts the views that correspond to the routes defined in your array of routes. The shell is now configured, but the new home page that you configured in the router setup isn't available yet. Create a new /src/index.js view-model file, as shown in the following listing. This is relatively empty for now.

Listing 2.13   Initial implementation of `index` view-model (index.js)

```
export class Index{          ◁─┐  Empties the index.js
}                               │  view-model class
```

The index.js file is the view-model for the homepage of your application. At this stage, it's bare-bones, as you don't need any functionality here yet. By now you should be starting to become familiar with the steps for creating custom elements in Aurelia. Now that you've got the view-model created, add the corresponding view, as shown in the following listing, to complete /src/index.html. This view will serve as the my-books homepage.

Listing 2.14   Initial implementation of `index` view (index.html)

```
<template>
  <h1>my-books</h1>

    <p>
  my-books allows you to keep track of the books
  you've read by adding and rating them as you read.
  </p>

  <a route-href="route: books;">books</a>     ◁─┤  Reference to
</template>                                        stored route
```

The `route-href` expression creates an HREF to the route stored against the books key in the `route` array using the Aurelia custom attribute called `route-href`, referencing the books named route that you defined in the router configuration.

Next, create a view/view-model pair to serve as the books parent component, which now provides the functionality that was previously provided by the app component.

Create the view-model /src/books.js file using the code in the following listing. This becomes the new host of the book-management logic that previously sat in the view-model app.js file as part of encapsulating all the book management functionality into a new page.

Listing 2.15   Initial implementation of `books` view-model (books.js)

```
import {bindable, inject} from 'aurelia-framework';
import {BookApi} from 'book-api';

@inject(BookApi)
export class Books {                 ◁─┐  Refactors book management
                                        │  functionality from app view-
  constructor(bookApi){                 │  model into books view-model
    this.bookTitle = "";
    this.books = [];
    this.bookApi = bookApi;
  }

  addBook () {
    this.books.push({title : this.bookTitle});
    this.bookTitle = "";
  }
```

```
bind(){
    this.bookApi.getBooks().then(savedBooks => this.books = savedBooks);
  }
}
```

Create the corresponding view /src/books.html file. This contains the functionality moved across from the app.html page. All the book-management component references have been moved across to this new, encapsulated, book-management page.

Listing 2.16   Initial implementation of books view (books.html)

```
<template>
    <require from="./book-list"></require>        ◁⌐  Imports the book-list
    <h1>Books</h1>                                      custom element
    <form submit.trigger="addBook()">
        <label for="book-title"></label>

        <input value.bind="bookTitle"
            id="book-title"
            type="text"
            placeholder="book title...">

        <input type="submit" value="add">
    </form>
    <hr/>                                               Uses the book-list
    <book-list books.bind="books"></book-list>    ◁⌐  custom element
</template>
```

Next, include a reference to the book-list component that you created in the previous section, and move the custom-element reference into the books page, which now hosts all book-management-related functionality.

You've now completed all the layout refactoring required to move the book-management functionality into its own page. If you're following along, the application should now look like the image in figure 2.21 when it's initially loaded in the browser.

The my-books application layout has now been refactored to make use of the Aurelia router. The main index page serves as a starting point for the user and gives you an area to add more functionality as the application progresses. The book-management functionality has been refactored into a separate books page that's available via a link on the index page.

You can click the new Books link to navigate the browser to the books route at http://localhost/#/books, as shown in figure 2.22.

Troubleshooting

If you receive an error after creating a new route like the books route from listing 2.14, ensure that your routes are defined correctly in the configureRoute function that you defined in the view-model that backs the view containing <router-view></router-view>.

Aurelia renders the contents of the current route into
<router-view>: in this case, the / route index.html.

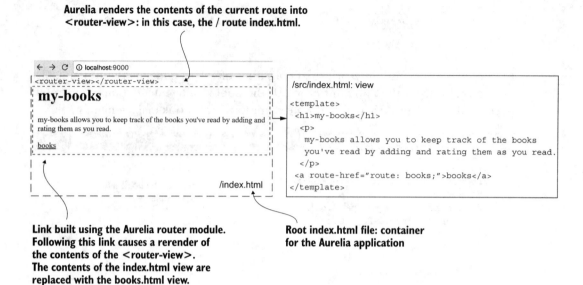

Link built using the Aurelia router module.
Following this link causes a rerender of
the contents of the <router-view>.
The contents of the index.html view are
replaced with the books.html view.

Root index.html file: container
for the Aurelia application

Figure 2.21   The my-books home route can be reached at http://localhost:9000 or http://localhost:9000/#/home.
When you navigate to this route, the contents of the <router-view> custom element are rerendered with the
contents of the index.html view template.

Navigating to the #/books route now re-renders the contents
of the router-view CustomElement with the books.html view.

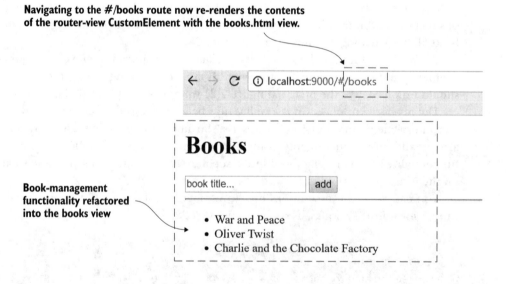

Book-management
functionality refactored
into the books view

Figure 2.22   The book-management functionality has been encapsulated into a new books page.
This page includes a book.js view-model that's indexed under the books route in the array of routes
configured in the app.js file. When the user navigates to /books, the content of <router-view> in
the app.html page is rerendered with the contents of the Books view.

With a few additional lines of code, my-books is starting to behave like a fully fledged SPA. Users can use the Back and Forward buttons to transition between the two logical states of the application. This only scratches the surface of what the Aurelia router can do. I'll cover it in a lot more depth in chapter 10.

2.7 Moving forward

So far, we've structured the my-books project in the simplest way possible, with all views and view-models stored in the src directory. Although this was fine to begin with, you can imagine how out of hand things could become as the application grows. Before we launch into chapter 3, let's reorganize the project structure to be more in line with Aurelia convention. The Aurelia project structure under src currently looks like figure 2.23.

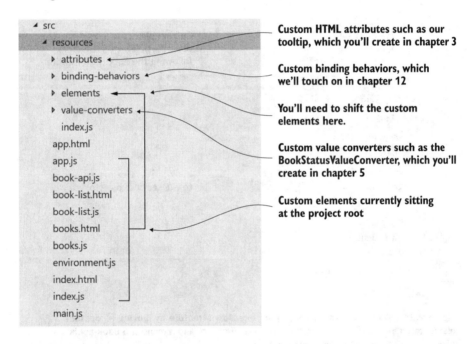

Figure 2.23   Current my-books directory structure with all views, view-models, and services sitting under the src directory.

Eager to get to chapter 3?

If you want to skip this reorganization exercise and jump directly into chapter 3, you can check out the *Aurelia in Action* GitHub repository (https://github.com/freshcut-development/Aurelia-in-Action.git) using the `git clone` command. From there, you can get the completed chapter 2 my-books project under \Chapter-2-Complete.

The resources folder holds several directories. Each of these directories should be used for the relevant kind of view resource (an external resource such as a custom element that you `require` into a view). We'll go into each of these view resource types in detail in chapters 3–5, but for now you only need to concern yourself with the custom-element resources that you've created so far. Start by moving the custom elements created in this chapter under the resources/elements directory. Next, create a new directory, src/services, and move the book-api.js service into it. Once you're finished, the directory structure should look like figure 2.24.

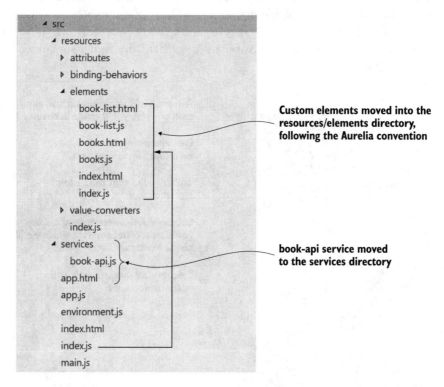

Figure 2.24   Reorganize the my-books src directory structure by moving all custom elements under the /src/resources/elements directory and moving the book-api.js service under a new directory, /src/services.

Now that the files are where they should be, you need to modify some of the paths in your app.js and book-list.js view-models to use the new locations. Modify the /src/app.js file as shown in the following listing to correct the `books` module path.

Listing 2.17   app view-model modified to fit the new directory structure (app.js)

```
export class App {
  configureRouter(config, router) {
  this.router = router;
  config.title = 'my-books';
```

```
config.map([
  { route: ['', 'home'], name: 'home', moduleId: 'index' },
  {
    route: 'books',
    name: 'books',
    moduleId: './resources/elements/books'       ◁─┐  Modifies moduleId to
  }                                                  │  point to new location
]);                                                  │  of books module
  }
}
```

Finally, you need to modify the /src/resources/elements/books.js file to import the book-api service from the services directory.

> **Listing 2.18 Importing the `book-api` from the services directory (books.js)**

```
import {bindable, inject} from 'aurelia-framework';          ┐  book-api service
import {BookApi} from '../../services/book-api';       ◁─────┤  changed to import from
...                                                          ┘  the services directory
```

2.8 my-books project status

In this chapter, you've created the initial implementation of the my-books virtual bookshelf. You've used routing to split the application into two pages, with the Aurelia router loading the correct view for a given URL. You've used Aurelia's binding commands and template repeaters to give users the ability to add books to a list and view the updated shelf contents as books are added. The final state of the project at the end of this chapter is depicted in figure 2.25.

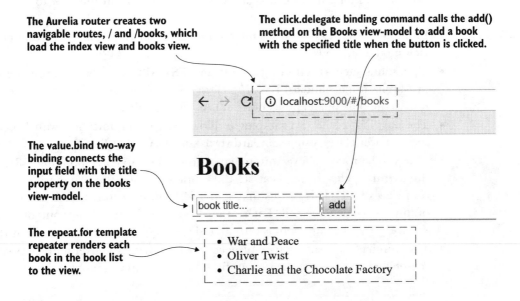

The Aurelia router creates two navigable routes, / and /books, which load the index view and books view.

The click.delegate binding command calls the add() method on the Books view-model to add a book with the specified title when the button is clicked.

The value.bind two-way binding connects the input field with the title property on the books view-model.

The repeat.for template repeater renders each book in the book list to the view.

Figure 2.25   The my-books book-management page state at the end of chapter 2

You can download the completed project from GitHub at https://github.com/fresh-cutdevelopment/Aurelia-in-Action.git using the `git clone` command. I recommend that you begin chapter 2 from the version checked out from GitHub, as the Aurelia package versions may change after this book has been published. Running the version from GitHub ensures that the code listings in the book are compatible with the dependent Aurelia framework libraries.

Like a tourist visiting Rome for the first time, you've been on a whirlwind tour of the Aurelia framework. You've seen all the major attractions but have a feeling that you're only scratching the surface of what it has to offer. In the next chapter, we'll expand on the book-management functionality added in chapter 2, enhancing the book-management form by adding constraints around when books can be added, and the ability to remove books from the library. In doing so, we'll dive into some of the more powerful features of Aurelia's templating and binding system.

Summary

- You've got three main options for creating Aurelia applications: the quick-start download, skeleton projects, and the Aurelia CLI.
- The Aurelia CLI is a Node.js application that allows you to easily create, run, and deploy Aurelia projects.
- Aurelia applications are made up of components, such as custom elements.
- Custom-element components generally consist of a view/view-model pair where the view is an HTML template and the view-model is an ES Next (or TypeScript) class, except in the case of HTML-only custom elements.
- Aurelia uses binding to propagate changes in data from the view to the view-model and vice versa.
- Binding is also used to transmit events raised on the view to corresponding view-model methods.
- Operations such as retrieving data from REST APIs are typically implemented in Aurelia using standard ES2015+ classes. This keeps Aurelia's concept count low, as the bulk of an application isn't Aurelia-specific.
- The `aurelia-fetch-client` plugin allows easy communication with backend services over HTTP using standard verbs such as GET or POST.
- The Aurelia router allows you to map Aurelia views to corresponding URLs. As the user navigates the application, the window location is updated with the current view's URL. This means that standard browser features, such as the Back button, work as expected. Each time the route changes, the content of the `<router-view>` component is rerendered with the contents of the current view.
- The Aurelia CLI creates a base project structure that, by convention, gives you a reasonable place to put the various files that make up your application.

Part 2

Exploring Aurelia

Part 1 of this book took you on a whirlwind tour of the Aurelia framework, covering the features and techniques you need to know at a high level. You created a basic my-books application through the Aurelia CLI; the application is OK by Hello World standards, but it's pretty bare bones. In the upcoming chapters, we'll expand on the techniques covered in part 1, and you'll build my-books into a full-fledged SPA with routing, authentication, form validation, and more.

Chapter 3 will teach you the ins and outs of Aurelia's two key component types: custom elements and attributes. Chapter 4 looks at how you can render data to your components using a combination of templating conditionals, binding, and repeaters. You'll also learn how to handle DOM events efficiently using the trigger and delegate binding commands. Chapter 5 rounds out our exploration of Aurelia's component types.

In chapter 6, you'll learn the tools and techniques you'll need to communicate between Aurelia components. Chapter 7 is all about forms: you'll learn how to create user-friendly forms with check boxes, selects, and radios. Chapter 8 shows how you can use the aurelia-fetch-client library to make HTTP calls to a backend REST API, and chapter 9 explores the challenges of implementing authentication in a client-side world where the old client-server cookie approach is no longer an option.

Shifting to the SPA development brings with it several advantages, not least of which is the improvement in speed and responsiveness due to the reduced frequency of full page reloads. But if you're not careful, you run the risk of confusing users because changes in application state aren't recorded in your browser history. In chapter 10, you'll learn how to avoid this pitfall using Aurelia's client-side router.

In chapter 11, you'll learn how to create truly flexible views using dynamic composition; this is a niche feature, but one that you'll be glad to have in your toolbelt when building applications in the wild. Then, chapter 12 delves into web component standards.

One of Aurelia's superpowers is the extensive number of simple extensibility points, and chapter 13 provides an overview of two: custom attributes with dynamic options, and custom binding behaviors. Finally, in chapter 14, you'll learn about Aurelia's CSS animation framework and see how to use CSS to weave animations throughout your project.

View resources, custom elements, and custom attributes

This chapter covers

- Exploring view resources
- Examining custom elements
- Using custom attributes

The core of the Lego toy ecosystem is the 8 x 8 x 10 mm Automatic Binding Brick, originally called the Mursten, which almost all other Lego construction toys are derived from. These standard Lego bricks have been combined to produce a multitude of different creations by millions of people around the globe.[1] What makes this toy different—and makes Lego one of the most successful toy companies in the world today—is that kids aren't limited to what the toy designers have imagined for them, but only by their own imagination. The same bricks can be used to build a car, a house, or a castle, by combining them in different ways. In the world of programming, we'd call the Mursten a *primitive*, a core building block that can be used to create a more complex system.

Historically, most of the more successful technologies have been built by defining these core primitives and building on top of them. A famous example of this is

---

[1] There are up to 915,103,765 different combinations, according to Wikipedia (https://en.wikipedia.org/wiki/Lego#Design).

HTML. HTML provides us with a set of simple components like <h1>, <body>, and <span>, which, when combined with CSS and JavaScript, can be used in many ways to produce any site on the web.

3.1 Understanding Aurelia's templating primitives

Aurelia follows the tactic of building from a set of core primitives. In this chapter, we'll look at some of the Aurelia templating-system primitives, how the framework builds on these primitives to provide higher-level features, and how you can use these features to build Aurelia components. The primitives explored in this chapter include the CSS resource, custom elements, and custom attributes, all of which inherit from ViewResource.

3.1.1 Aurelia's templating primitives

One of the core primitives of Aurelia's templating system is ViewResource. View resources are resources that you <require> into an Aurelia view to extend it with additional functionality.

Figure 3.1 provides an overview of the anatomy of the core primitives that make up Aurelia's templating engine. This serves as a mental model for how each of the

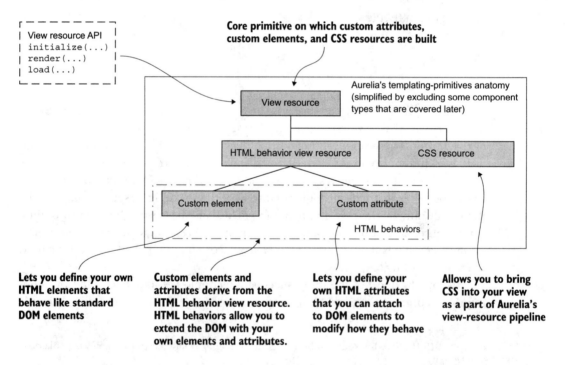

Figure 3.1   Pages in Aurelia are built by composing various kinds of resources—external items that are loaded into the view to extend it with additional functionality. These resources all derive from an Aurelia framework primitive called a view resource.

primitives in Aurelia's templating and binding system fit together. Don't be concerned if it looks complicated at first glance. There's a method to my madness. As we explore the various easy-to-use components of the Aurelia framework, I'll use this architecture to show you where each component fits in the bigger picture.

You'll start by adding some much-needed style to my-books, and in doing so, you'll get an overview of a subset of core view-resource types in the Aurelia framework: `Html-BehaviorResource` and `CSSResource`. Under the hood, all resources implement the basic view-resource API with methods to tell the framework how they should be initialized, rendered into the DOM, and dynamically reloaded. `CSSResource` allows you to `<require>` a CSS file into your view. The `CustomElement` and `CustomAttribute` view resources both inherit from a primitive called `HtmlBehaviorResource`. This isn't the complete picture. Other view resources, such as values converters, have been left out for simplicity.

3.2 CSS resources

Let's begin our tour of the Aurelia templating-primitive system by looking at the CSS resource. In this section, you'll use the CSS resource to add a nice coat of paint and polish to your virtual bookshelf.

3.2.1 Setting up the project dependencies

Before you begin adding custom styles using Aurelia CSS resources, you need to do some setup work. The style changes you're going to make in this section depend on two external dependencies:

- *Font Awesome*—This is an open source collection of scalable vector icons. Use this to add icons to buttons, and so on. You can find out more about Font Awesome and browse the catalogue on the project website at http://fontawesome.io/.
- *Bootstrap 4*—Because we like staying on the cutting edge, we'll also be using the latest version of the Bootstrap HTML, CSS, and JavaScript framework. You'll style your application by using some of the layout and style classes provided by the Bootstrap CSS library and use Bootstrap jQuery plugins to enhance parts of the UI without needing to write everything from scratch. Styling an application with Bootstrap isn't within the scope of this book, but you can find out more information on the project website at http://getbootstrap.com/docs/4.0/getting-started/introduction/.

For simplicity, include the Font Awesome dependency by adding a reference to the Font Awesome CDN (the Content Delivery Network–hosted version of these files) into the index.html file. Modify the ./index.html file as shown in the following listing to include the new dependency.

Listing 3.1   Including Bootstrap and Font Awesome (index.html)

```
<!DOCTYPE html>
<html>
  <head>
    <meta charset="utf-8">
    <title>Aurelia</title>
    <link href="https://maxcdn.bootstrapcdn.com
                    /font-awesome/4.7.0/css/font-awesome.min.css"
          rel="stylesheet" >            ⟵┐  Includes Font
  </head>                                   │  Awesome CSS
                                           │  via CDN
  <body aurelia-app="main">
    <script src="scripts/vendor-bundle.js"
            data-main="aurelia-bootstrapper">
    </script>
  </body>
</html>
```

To install Bootstrap 4, please follow the steps shown in section A.4 of the appendix. With the dependencies set up, you're ready to add a custom stylesheet to the app component. After completing the setup steps in the appendix, you'll have modified your app.js, app.html, aurelia.json, and package.json files, as shown in this gist: https://seanhunter.io/aurelia-bootstrap4.

3.2.2   Adding the CSS resources

First, download the my-books CSS file from GitHub at http://mng.bz/N674. Copy this file to the src directory of the my-books project. Before you begin using the ./src/styles.css file, look at an Aurelia view resource that makes it easy to add styles to components as part of Aurelia's view-resource pipeline.

An Aurelia CSSResource allows you to load stylesheets related to a component. You need to take two steps to add styles to your application:

1. Create the stylesheet.
2. Use the <require> custom element to load the stylesheet into your component.

Because these styles apply to your entire application, you'll include them in the app component. Modify your app.html file as shown in the following listing to require the style resources for your custom styles and reference the Bootstrap styles added using the steps described in the appendix.

Listing 3.2   Modifying the app view to include the stylesheet (app.html)

```
<template>
    <require from="bootstrap/css/bootstrap.css"></require>   ⟵┐ Imports
    <require from="styles.css"></require>   ⟵┐                  │ Bootstrap
    <router-view></router-view>             │ Imports the       │ styles
</template>                                  │ custom CSS
```

By including a `CSSResource` in your application, you tell Aurelia to inject a new `<style>` element in the location of your `<require>` custom element. Then, when the app.html file is loaded, Aurelia will go through the following steps to load the child view resources:

1 Load the `style.css` CSSResource.
2 Load the `<router-view></router-view>` custom element and, based on the current route, load the appropriate component. For example, if you visit http://localhost:9000#/books, the `<books></books>` custom element is loaded.

Figure 3.2 depicts the steps that Aurelia goes through to load each of the view resources on the `app.html` page, recursively traversing through the child components.

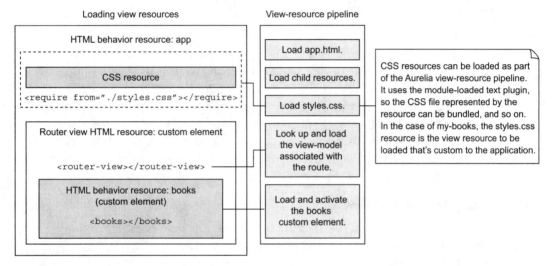

Figure 3.2 Aurelia views are loaded by recursively traversing through the DOM tree and loading all child resources found in each nested view. This is a simplified view because there are also child components underneath the `<books></books>` element.

This process of recursively loading view resources is the view-resource pipeline. Examples of view resources loaded in this way include custom elements and CSS resources. Loading this resource causes a new `<style>` element containing the style.css contents to be injected into `<head>` DOM element. You can inspect this behavior using the browser dev tools (F12 in Chrome), as shown in figure 3.3.

The CLI-configured module-loader plugin loads the CSS file contents. In your case, for example, this is done by RequireJS. This also means that they can be bundled as part of the app-bundle.js file as an alternative to including them inline.

Including the styles in this way works well if you don't mind your styles being applied to the entire Aurelia application (the default behavior for referenced CSS files). But what if you wanted to create a component (such as an email sign-up widget)

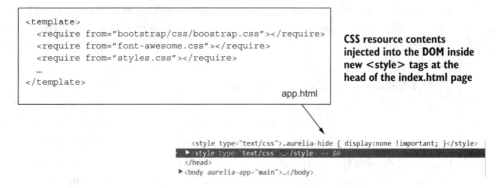

Figure 3.3   A CSS resource is processed and a new style tag with contents read from the referenced resource is injected into the DOM.

that would be styled in its own way, with the styles outside of the component not leaking into it and vice versa? In Aurelia, you can achieve this using an exciting feature called *scoped CSS resources*. Scoped CSS resources inject your CSS into the *Shadow DOM* (a new feature available as a part of the Web Components Specification). CSS injected into the Shadow DOM is only applied to the contents of the *shadow root* element (the root node of a Shadow DOM tree) for the component. We'll delve into scoped CSS resources in chapter 12. Now that you've included these CSS resources, modify each of the views to make use of these styles.

3.2.3   Styling the my-books views

In this section, we'll modify each of the views to use the new styles. The following views need to be updated to take advantage of the new theme:

- app.html
- book-list.html
- books.html
- index.html

If you'll bear with me and replace each of these views with the contents of the following four listings, you should end up with an application that behaves the same but follows the my-book theme.

Listing 3.3   Modifying the app view to include new styles and a nav bar (app.html)

```
<template>
    <require from="bootstrap/css/bootstrap.css"></require>
    <require from="styles.css"></require>
     <div class="container">
        <div class="header clearfix">
        <h3 class="text-muted">
          <span class="brand-highlight">my</span>-books
        </h3>
```

```
      </div>
      <router-view></router-view>
      <footer class="footer">
        <p>&copy; Aurelia Demo 2017</p>
      </footer>

    </div>

</template>
```

Listing 3.4 Modifying the `book-list` view to use the new styles (book-list.html)

```
<template>
    <ul class="books list-group list-group-flush">
      <li class="list-group-item" repeat.for="book of books">
        <div class="book row"
           <div class="col-10">${book.title}</div>
        </div>
      </li>
    </ul>
</template>
```

Listing 3.5 Modifying the `books.html` view to use the new styles (books.html)

```
<template>
 <require from="./book-list"></require>

 <h1 class='page-heading'>books</h1>
       <div class="card">
         <div class="card-block">
           <form class="form-inline" submit.trigger="addBook()">

             <label for="book-title"></label>

             <input class="form-control" value.bind="bookTitle"
                 id="book-title"
                 type="text"
                 placeholder="book title...">

               <input class="btn btn-success tap-right"
                       type="submit"
                       value="add">
         </form>
       </div>
     </div>
 <hr/>
 <book-list books.bind="books"></book-list>
</template>
```

Listing 3.6 Modifying the `index` view to use the new styles (index.html)

```
<template>
      <div class="jumbotron">
        <h1 class="display-3">
```

```
        <span class="brand-highlight">my</span>-books
      </h1>
      <p class="lead">
        my-books allows you to keep track of
        the books you've read by adding and rating them as you read.
      </p>
      <a route-href="route: books;">books</a>
    </div>

    <div class="row">
      <div class="col-lg-12">
          <p></p>
      </div>
    </div>
  </div>
</template>
```

Now that you've styled my-books and it's starting to look more like a real application, it's time to start enriching the `books` and `book-list` components that you created in chapter 2. You'll supplement these elements with a suite of additional elements to allow you to encapsulate the new behavior as you introduce it into your application. We'll also look at a new kind of view resource that you haven't come across yet called the *custom attribute*, and you'll use it to add tooltips across the buttons in your application.

At this point, it's worth stopping the `au run --watch` command and rerunning it to ensure that the application is recompiled with the latest dependencies.

> **Troubleshooting**
>
> If you encounter problems compiling the vendor bundle, it's likely an issue with the way the Bootstrap dependencies are configured. You can cross-check the impacted files against this gist to make sure each of the files has been updated correctly: https://sean-hunter.io/aurelia-bootstrap4.

3.3   *Custom elements*

HTML behavior resources include the custom element (mentioned in chapter 2 when you defined the `books` and `list-books` components) and the custom attribute. HTML behavior resources allow you to extend your HTML by providing your own HTML elements and attributes.

> **NOTE** Custom-element and custom-attribute classes are named using the standard JavaScript class-naming convention of InitCase. InitCasing is where the first letter in each word of the class name is capitalized, for example, `BookList`. The HTML view and JavaScript files are named using kebab-case, for example, book-list.html, where the name is made up of lower-case words separated by a hyphen.

3.3.1 Custom elements

Custom elements—as the name suggests—allow you to define your own HTML elements and use them within an Aurelia view. Custom elements are the default type of HTML behavior resource. This means that you can optionally provide the `Custom-Element` suffix. For example, you could've named the `BookList` custom element `BookListCustomElement`, and the result would've been identical. Alternatively, if you leave this suffix out, the Aurelia framework assumes that this is a custom element by default and hence will treat it like a custom element in terms of how it's registered and rendered into the view. Similarly, custom-element-view and view-model filenames should use kebab-case, for example book-list.html and book-list.js.

3.3.2 *my-books custom elements*

So far, you've encountered two major custom elements while developing the my-books application: `<books>` and `<book-list>`, as shown in listing 3.7. This listing provides a convenient high-level overview of the major building blocks of the my-books page:

- The `books` custom element is an orchestrator. It loads books, passes them to the `book-list` component, and allows books to be added to the array.
- The `book-list` custom element renders the list of books to the screen.

To start, use the `<require>` custom element to load the `book-list` custom-element resource into the view. In doing this, you'll instruct the Aurelia framework to search the view for any elements called `<book-list>`. When it finds them, it will follow the default convention, looking for a corresponding JavaScript class called `BookList` or `BookListCustomElement` by taking the name of the module and InitCasing it.

> **Listing 3.7** `books` **custom-element view (books.html)**

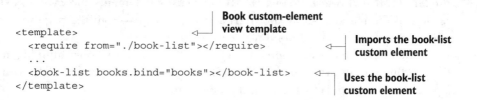

```
                              ┌─── Book custom-element
                              │    view template
<template>              ◁─────┘
  <require from="./book-list"></require>   ◁───┐  Imports the book-list
  ...                                          │  custom element
  <book-list books.bind="books"></book-list>  ◁──┐
</template>                                       │  Uses the book-list
                                                  │  custom element
```

Views in Aurelia can be built up by iteratively creating custom elements using the following pattern:

1. Create a new JavaScript file (for example, book-list.js) that exports the view-model class (for example, `BookList`) following the InitCase naming convention.
2. Create the corresponding HTML view file—for example, book-list.html—following the kebab-case naming convention.
3. Import the custom element into the page using the `<require>` custom element.
4. Use the custom element in the page.

NOTE The `from` attribute on the `<require>` element can either take a relative path from the current view, as shown in listing 3.7, or it can take a relative path from the root of the application. For example, you could instead reference the component from the root of your application using the full path, ./resources/ elements/book-list.

3.3.3 *HTML-only custom elements*

In the example custom elements you've seen so far in my-books, you've always created both a JavaScript class and a corresponding HTML view file. This is useful when you have behavior that needs to be implemented in the class. For example, in the `Books` class, you needed to implement the behavior that was fired because of the `addBook` button being clicked, as shown in the following listing.

Listing 3.8   View-model for the `books` component (books.js)

```
import {bindable, inject} from 'aurelia-framework';
import {BookApi} from '../../services/book-api';

@inject(BookApi)
export class Books{              ◁── View-model required
   ..                                 to handle the add-
   addBook () {                       button-click behavior
       this.books.push({title : this.bookTitle});
       this.bookTitle = "";
   }
   ..
}
```

But what about the case where you want to extract a fragment of the view markup that doesn't necessarily have any corresponding non-view behavior? In this case, you can use an *HTML-only custom element*. HTML-only custom elements allow you to extract a section of the markup—also known as a *DOM fragment*—from the page without the need to implement a corresponding view-model class.

To demonstrate this functionality, refactor the view in the books.html file, moving the heading into its own element. The following steps are required to refactor part of a parent view into an HTML-only custom element:

1 Create a new HTML file to hold the extracted markup.
2 Move the relevant markup from the parent view into the newly created HTML file.
3 Require the newly created HTML file into the parent view.
4 Reference the custom-element tag in the view.
5 Set up any bindings required to pass data from the parent view to the child view.
6 Use the new element.

STEP 1: CREATING A HEADING.HTML FILE

Create a new file, heading.html, under the src/resources/elements/heading.html path. This HTML file is the new home of your refactored markup. When completing this step, start by including an empty set of `<template>` tags in the new file upon creation. Otherwise, it's easy to forget to add them later and wonder why the view isn't being rendered correctly into the DOM. The newly created file should look like the following listing.

Listing 3.9 heading view, empty apart from `<template>` tags (heading.html)

```
<template>
</template>
```

STEP 2: MOVING THE MARKUP

Move the heading from the `books.html` file into the new `heading.html` file inside the template tags.

Listing 3.10 Modifying `heading` to include a hardcoded heading (heading.html)

```
<template>
    <h1 class='page-heading'>books</h1>
</template>
```

`<template>` tags indicate that this should be handled as an Aurelia view.

Extracted heading moved from books.html view

STEP 3: IMPORTING THE VIEW

To indicate to the Aurelia framework that this new child-view resource should be loaded as part of the Aurelia templating pipeline, import the new view into the parent view (books.html) by adding a new `require` statement to the top section of the view.

Listing 3.11 Importing HTML-only heading.html into the `books` view (books.html)

```
<template>
    <require from="./book-list"></require>
    <require from="./heading.html"></require>
...
</template>
```

New require statement to import the heading.html HTML-only view

One important thing to note here is that you've included the .html extension in the `from` attribute on the `<require>` element.

> **NOTE** When using the `<require>` element on HTML-only custom elements, you need to include the file extension of the view to indicate that it's an HTML-only custom element and Aurelia should not follow the default convention of searching for a corresponding JavaScript file.

STEP 4: REFERENCING THE `<HEADING>` ELEMENT

Now that you've created a new `<heading>` custom element, you need to include a reference to it. Replace the hardcoded heading text with the `<heading>` custom-element tag.

Listing 3.12   Modifying `books` to reference the `heading` component (books.html)

```
<template>
...
<require from="./heading.html"></require>
<heading></heading>                          ◁─┐  References the newly created
...                                                <heading> element
</template>
```

Rerun the application now to view the latest version. The heading displays the same as it did before you refactored. Check Chrome Developer Tools (F12) and you'll see that `<h1>` now sits under the custom-element tag in the DOM—highlighted in figure 3.4.

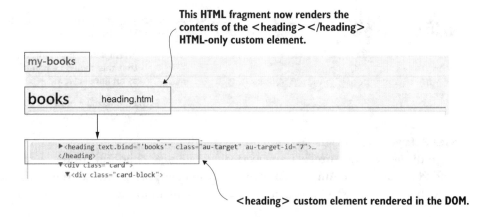

Figure 3.4   The page header should render as it did previously, even though it's now being loaded from an external view resource rather than being an inline element within the view. Chrome Developer view tools show that the `<h1>` tag now lives under the custom element.

Although this functionality is working now, and you've replaced the same heading functionality that you had before, it hasn't added any value yet. The value comes in the next step, when you add data bindings between the parent view and the child view, creating a flexible heading component that can be used anywhere in the application.

STEP 5: ADDING THE BINDINGS

Make your `<heading>` custom element flexible enough to handle heading text defined in the parent component. To do this, add a `bindable` attribute to the `<template>` element and specify the properties that you want to be able to bind between the parent and child views. In listing 3.13, you set up a two-way data binding between the parent and child views on the text property. You then render it out to the DOM using the string-interpolation binding expression, `${text}`. Modify the /src/resources/elements/heading.html template as shown in the following listing.

Listing 3.13 `heading` view modified to include data binding (heading.html)

```
<template bindable="text">
  <h1 class='page-heading'>${text}</h1>
</template>
```

◁── Sets up a two-way data binding on the text property

◁── Renders the heading text to the DOM

STEP 6: USING THE NEW ELEMENT

You need to consume this binding from the parent view. You can do so by using the `propertyName.bind=` binding convention on the heading custom element in the books.html view.

This refactoring will allow you to encapsulate the UI fragment related to rendering the `heading` into its own element. This element can then be standardized and referenced in any component throughout the application. It's probably overkill for our example, but it can be useful when you need to extract a part of the view without taking along any associated behavior.

Modify the `books` view to include this data binding, as shown in the following listing. In this case, you bind the `'books'` literal value to the bindable `text` property on the `<heading>` element, but there's nothing stopping you from binding to a property on the `books` view-model instead.

Listing 3.14 Modifying `books` to bind text into the heading (books.html)

```
<template>
...
<require from="./heading.html"></require>
<heading text.bind="'books'"></heading>
...
</template>
```

◁── Adds the text.bind binding expression to the `<heading>` element

3.4 *Custom attributes*

Custom elements are useful when you want to create an entirely new element in the DOM, but what if you want to change the way an existing element behaves? Custom attributes—the function is also in the name—provide a way of implementing new HTML attributes. These attributes can be appended to an HTML element's behavior. You can apply them to either a built-in element (such as `<input>` or `<div>`) or your own custom element (such as `<book-list>`). These are commonly used to bring third-party libraries into an Aurelia application. For example, you could implement a custom attribute for the Bootstrap tooltip JavaScript library to easily add a tooltip to any element in your application by adding the attribute like so: `<input tooltip> </input>`. Custom attributes are defined by creating a view-model class that operates on the element.

The default naming convention for custom attributes is to include a `Custom-Attribute` suffix, so the `tooltip` attribute would typically be called something like `TooltipCustomAttribute`. By using that naming convention, you instruct the Aurelia framework to treat this view resource as a custom attribute, meaning that Aurelia should search for any elements in the view that reference that custom-attribute name (the name of the class minus the `CustomAttribute` suffix), and construct a new instance of this class, injecting the DOM element that the attribute is attached to. Let's implement a tooltip custom attribute and look at what's required to consume it in the my-books application.

3.4.1   Creating a tooltip custom attribute

The following steps are required to create an attribute:

1 Create a new JavaScript file for the view-model named `attribute-name.js` (for example, `tooltip.js`).
2 Export a class from this file named `AttributeNameCustomAttribute` (for example, `TooltipCustomAttribute`).
3 Implement the behavior that you want (for example, initializing the Bootstrap tooltip).
4 Require the newly created `CustomAttribute` view resource into the view that needs it.
5 Add the new attribute to the target element.

Begin by creating a new JavaScript file, /src/resources/attributes/tooltip.js, and exporting the view-model class.

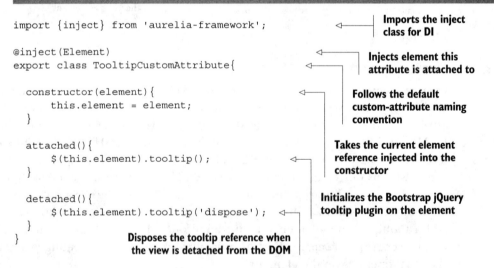

Listing 3.15   Creating the Bootstrap `tooltip` custom attribute (tooltip.js)

```
import {inject} from 'aurelia-framework';          Imports the inject
                                                   class for DI

@inject(Element)                                   Injects element this
export class TooltipCustomAttribute{               attribute is attached to

  constructor(element){                            Follows the default
      this.element = element;                      custom-attribute naming
  }                                                convention

  attached(){                                      Takes the current element
      $(this.element).tooltip();                   reference injected into the
  }                                                constructor

  detached(){                                      Initializes the Bootstrap jQuery
      $(this.element).tooltip('dispose');          tooltip plugin on the element
  }
}              Disposes the tooltip reference when
               the view is detached from the DOM
```

Custom-attribute and custom-element view-models can ask which HTML element they're attached to. They do this by asking for a reference to this element in the constructor via a dependency injection. This is key, particularly in custom attributes, where you'll often want to perform an operation on the element that the attribute is attached to. After you've accessed the element in the constructor, you can then perform the action needed. In this case, hook into the `attached` Aurelia lifecycle hook, which is called when the element is attached to the DOM. The reason that you do it here rather than in a different hook (for example, the constructor) is that you need to ensure that the element is available before you try to reference it.

Within the `attached` method, wrap the element in a jQuery object and initialize a tooltip on the element. From there, the Bootstrap JavaScript takes over and performs the steps necessary to attach the tooltip to the element. Hook into the `detached` lifecycle hook to dispose of the plugin object and clean up the DOM. This ensures that you don't leak resources by accidentally creating an ever-increasing number of these plugin references each time you navigate between Aurelia views.

Now that you've got the new custom attribute defined, it's a matter of requiring that element into the view, which you can do using the `<require from='attribute-name'>` syntax. Start by adding a `removeBook` button to your view (which is in fact a span styled as a button). Then use a *contextual property* repeater (`$index`) to pass the current book to remove. Contextual properties are properties made available to the view in certain binding scenarios (in this case, a repeater). We'll cover repeater contextual properties in depth in chapter 4. You then add the `tooltip` attribute to your view and attach it to the `<span>` element. The `title` for the tooltip is taken from the `title` attribute on the element (though this is built in the Bootstrap functionality rather than your attribute behavior).

Require the custom attribute into the view in the /src/resources/elements/book-list.html file.

> **Listing 3.16 Using the `tooltip` custom attribute in `book-list` (book-list.html)**

```
<template>
  <require from="../attributes/tooltip"></require>      ⟵  Requires the new
  ..                                                          tooltip attribute
                                                              into the view
          <div class="col-10">${book.title}</div>
          <div class="col-1">
            <span class="remove-button
                  click.delegate="removeBook($index)"  ⟵  Passes the index of the
                  tooltip                                     book in the current
                   title='Remove book from list'>             iteration to the
                                                              removeBook method
              <i class="fa fa-trash" aria-hidden="true"></i>
            </span>
          </div>
  ..
</template>
```

Adds the tooltip and title attributes to the button ⟼ (pointing to `tooltip` line)

Next, add a new `removeBook` method to the `BookList` view-model to remove a book from the `books` array with the index parameter passed from the view: `removeBook(index)`. Modify the ./src/resources/book-list.js file to incorporate this method.

Listing 3.17   Incorporating book removal into `book-list` (book-list.js)

```
import {bindable} from 'aurelia-framework';

export class BookList {
  @bindable books;

  removeBook(index) {                          ⟵─┐ Removes a book from
      this.books.splice(index, 1);                │ the list by index
  }
}
```

If you refresh the page at http://localhost:9000/#/books, you should see the tooltip displayed above the button, as shown in figure 3.5.

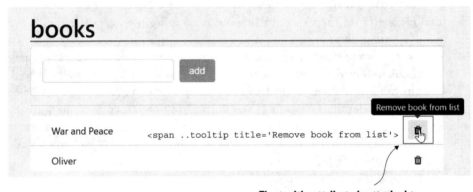

Figure 3.5   The book-list.html view updated to use the new tooltip custom attribute that adds a tooltip hover effect on the delete-book button

This tooltip isn't limited to this one element, however. You can attach it to any element in the application to easily provide a tooltip.

Currently, there are two major areas for improvement with your new attribute. First, you can display a tooltip only on top of the element; second, you currently apply the tooltip via a `title` attribute rather than doing things the Aurelia way using binding. Let's improve the attribute by resolving both issues.

3.4.2   Single-value binding

When building custom attributes, you'll often want to bind only a single value. For example, imagine that you have an `uploadable` attribute that transforms any element into a drag/drop upload area. In such a case, you may need to supply only the API path that the file should be uploaded to. Aurelia has a feature for this called *single-value binding.*

To see single-value binding in practice, enhance the `tooltip` custom attribute, allowing it to take its `title` as an option rather than having this value coming from a `data` attribute on the element. Because you've applied a single-value binding, Aurelia assigns the option value to a new `value` property on the tooltip object. This means you can access this value directly using `this.value`.

> **NOTE** This `value` isn't set until data binding is completed on the component, so the value is available in the component lifecycle hooks from `bind` onward. It's OK in this case, because you're accessing the value in the attached hook, which is fired after the binding has been completed.

First, modify the `tooltip` attribute in the tooltip.js file to take a single value for the title.

Listing 3.18   Modifying `tooltip` to use a single-value binding (tooltip.js)

```
...
export class TooltipCustomAttribute{
  ...
  attached(){
      $(this.element).tooltip({title: this.value});      ◁─┐ Modifies the tooltip
  }                                                          method to take the
  ...                                                        title option
}
```

Next, modify the corresponding view to pass this value along in the custom-attribute binding expression. Modify the /src/resources/elements/book-list.html view file.

Listing 3.19   Modifying `book-list` to use single-value binding (book-list.html)

```
<template>
  ...
          <span class="remove-button"                         Passes the literal title
            click.delegate="removeBook($index)"               value to the tooltip
              tooltip='Remove book from list'>      ◁─┐       attribute
            <i class="fa fa-trash" aria-hidden="true"></i>
          </span>
  ...
</template>
```

In this case, you're specifying a literal value for the title of the tooltip, but this could also be a binding expression, such as ${tooltipTitle}, if you wanted to bind this from the BookList view-model.

3.4.3   Options binding

Single-value bindings work well when you've only got one value to bind, but with the `tooltip` you already have two that you know of, and you may want to add more later. To achieve this, you can instead use an *options binding*. Options bindings allow you to supply a set of values to a custom attribute from the view. Modify the `tooltip` custom attribute in the tooltip.js file, as shown in listing 3.20, to allow for configuration of both the `title` and the `position` using an options binding.

With options bindings, you need to create a `@bindable` property on the custom attribute view-model for each value that you want to bind. In this case, expose both the `title` and `placement` attributes as `bindable` properties, making them available from the view. Again, you're able to use the values for both properties within the context of the `attached` hook because binding has already completed at this point, passing the values along from the view.

Listing 3.20   Modifying `tooltip` to use an options binding (tooltip.js)

```
...
export class TooltipCustomAttribute{                    Adds a bindable
                                                        property title
  @bindable title;
  @bindable placement;
                                       Adds a bindable
                                       property placement
  constructor(element){
      this.element = element;
  }

  attached(){
      $(this.element).tooltip({title: this.title,
  placement : this.placement});
  }                                         Initializes the tooltip with option
  ...                                       values from the bindable properties
}
```

Following this, you need to modify the view to pass both options. Multiple options can be passed to a custom-attribute binding expression using the `customAttribute-Name='propertyName1: value1; propertyName2: value2'` syntax, where the values are either a literal value or a JavaScript expression. Modify the /src/resources/elements/book-list.html file to pass the title and placement along in the binding expression.

Listing 3.21   Modifying `book-list` to use an options binding (book-list.html)

```
<template>                              Passes the index of the current iteration
...                                              into the removeBook method
            <span class="remove-button"
              click.delegate="removeBook($index)"
              tooltip="title: remove book from list;
                       placement: right">
                <i class="fa fa-trash" aria-hidden="true"></i>
            </span>
...                                      Passes the literal tooltip options
</template>                              values to the view-model in the
                                        binding expression
```

In this case, you've passed the literal values for both the `title` and the `placement` to the attribute-binding expression. If you refresh the browser now and place the pointer over one of the `remove-book` buttons, you should see the same title, but the tooltip should now float to the right, as shown in figure 3.6.

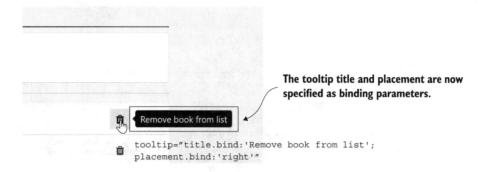

The tooltip title and placement are now specified as binding parameters.

```
tooltip="title.bind:'Remove book from list';
placement.bind:'right'"
```

Figure 3.6 Remove buttons now use the configurable tooltip to allow a placement and title to be specified as a part of the custom-attribute binding expression.

Because you leaned on an existing JavaScript library to do the bulk of the DOM manipulation work, you didn't need to go too much further with your custom attribute. We'll explore custom attributes in more detail in chapter 13 with an overview of dynamic options bindings, which will enable us to get a lot more sophisticated.

You should now have a reasonable understanding of two kinds of HTML behavior view resources: custom elements and custom attributes. Next, we'll look at several tools provided by Aurelia's templating engine that allow you to bring your custom elements and attributes to life.

3.5   *my-books project status*

You began this chapter by adding a hint of style to my-books using a CSS resource to load custom styles into the app view, combined with the Font Awesome and Bootstrap third-party libraries. Then you used an HTML-only custom element to encapsulate the header of the my-books page into a component without any non-view behavior. You also decomposed the application into a series of easy-to-reason-about components using custom elements and attributes.

The current project state is shown in figure 3.7. You can download the completed chapter 3 my-books project from GitHub at https://github.com/freshcutdevelopment/Aurelia-in-Action.git using the `git clone` command.

Chapter 2 gave you grounding in the basics of what the Aurelia templating and data-binding system has to offer. In chapter 4, we'll build on this foundation, delving into the details of how Aurelia's templating and binding system works under the hood. You'll also learn how and when to use the variety of binding tools available in Aurelia's toolbox, from one-way and two-way binding to the binding commands available for handling DOM events.

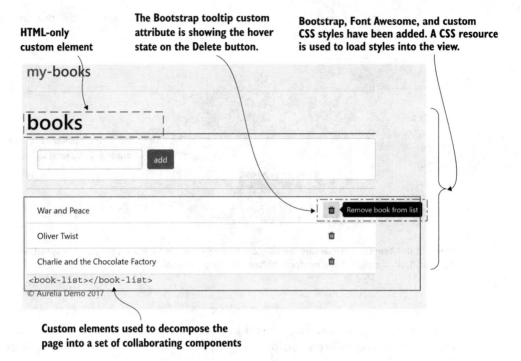

HTML-only custom element

The Bootstrap tooltip custom attribute is showing the hover state on the Delete button.

Bootstrap, Font Awesome, and custom CSS styles have been added. A CSS resource is used to load styles into the view.

Custom elements used to decompose the page into a set of collaborating components

Figure 3.7   Current my-books application book-management-page status. Styles have been added, and the page decomposed using custom elements and attributes.

Summary

- Aurelia's templating and binding system is built on a set of core primitives.
- One of these core primitives is the CSS resource, which allows you to load CSS into your Aurelia views.
- HTML behaviors are another kind of view resource that allows you to extend the DOM by adding custom HTML elements and attributes.
- Aurelia applications are built by composing custom elements, attributes, and other types of components.

Aurelia templating and data binding

This chapter covers

- Exploring Aurelia templating
- Understanding the Aurelia data-binding system
- Handling DOM events

The best UIs are intuitive; they make it obvious what the user can and can't do at any given point. One example of this is the clipboard feature in Microsoft Word: it's not possible to click the Cut or Copy buttons until you've selected the target text. This is made obvious by adding a grey hue to these buttons until the option is available.

User interface tweaks like these simplify the UX by guiding users through processes and minimizing decision making. An alternative approach would be to show an error or warning message when the user clicks the Copy button without having any text selected, which I'd argue is a much more invasive way of achieving the same result. One of the beautiful things about SPAs is how easy they make it to add these kinds of UI interactions. In this chapter, you'll learn how to use a combination of template conditionals, repeaters, and binding commands to build these kinds of interactions into your Aurelia applications.

4.1 Template conditionals

Template conditionals allow you to conditionally show or hide a fragment of the DOM based on an expression or view-model property. This allows you to design UIs that only show the user what they need at a given point in time. In this section, we'll look at Aurelia's template conditionals: `show.bind` and `if.bind`.

The template-conditional options in Aurelia are as follows:

- `show.bind`—Attach this to an element to have Aurelia show or hide the element using CSS.
- `if.bind`—Attach this to an element to have the element added or removed from the DOM based on the result of the binding expression.

You'll use both template-conditional options as you implement a new component of the application called `book-stats`. Begin by adding a simple counter to display the number of books that you've added after loading the page. What you should see after you've added this new component is a running total of the number of books added, which is shown only after at least one book has been added to the list. First, you need to create a new view/view-model pair for this component. After you've done that, introduce the template conditionals to control what's shown on the page.

The `BookStats` view-model (listing 4.1) is straightforward for the most part; however, it has one feature that you haven't come across yet: *computed properties*. This decorator allows you to create a property that will be notified for update when either the `originalNumberOfBooks` or the `books.length` values change. This is useful because it prevents Aurelia from needing to have a loop running in the background, constantly checking whether either of these values has been updated to determine if this component needs to be rerendered. As a rule of thumb, you should use this decorator whenever you need to do something in the view that depends on multiple properties in the view-model, or when you're binding to the result of a calculated expression, such as `bookTitle.length > 0`.

Create a new src/resources/elements/book-stats.js JavaScript file that contains your `BookStats` view-model class.

Listing 4.1 `book-stats` view-model first iteration (book-stats.js)

```
import {computedFrom, bindable} from 'aurelia-framework';      ◁──┐ Imports the
                                                                    @bindable and
export class BookStats{              Books is bound from           @computedFrom
                                     the parent view.              decorators
    @bindable books;         ◁──┘
    @bindable originalNumberOfBooks;
                                                                   ┌
    @computedFrom('originalNumberOfBooks', 'books.length')   ◁─────┘
```

The original number of books is bound from the parent view.

Adds a computed property that depends on both originalNumber-OfBooks and books.length

```
get addedBooks(){
    return this.books.length-this.originalNumberOfBooks;    ◁───┐
}                                                                │
}                                            Calculates the number
                                                 of added books  │
```

After you've created the view-model, the next step is to create the corresponding book-stats view. Create a new src/resources/elements/book-stats.html file, and include the template markup shown in the following listing.

Listing 4.2   book-stats view first iteration (book-stats.html)

```
<template>
    <div class="card text-center">
        <div class="card-block">
            <p class="card-text">
                <span show.bind="addedBooks"            ◁─┐  Adds a show.bind
                    class="badge badge-primary">           │  binding to the
                    new books ${addedBooks}                │  addedBooks property
                </span>                                    │  and renders the value
            </p>
        </div>
        <div class="card-footer text-muted">
            Book Stats
        </div>
    </div>
</template>
```

The show.bind expression is used to hide the addedBooks badge until books have been added to the list. You're also using the string-interpolation syntax again here to render the number of added books into the <span> content. The way the show.bind expression works is that it adds the aurelia-hide class to the element that it's been applied to, which has a style of display:none, as shown in figure 4.1. This class is removed when the binding expression evaluates to true.

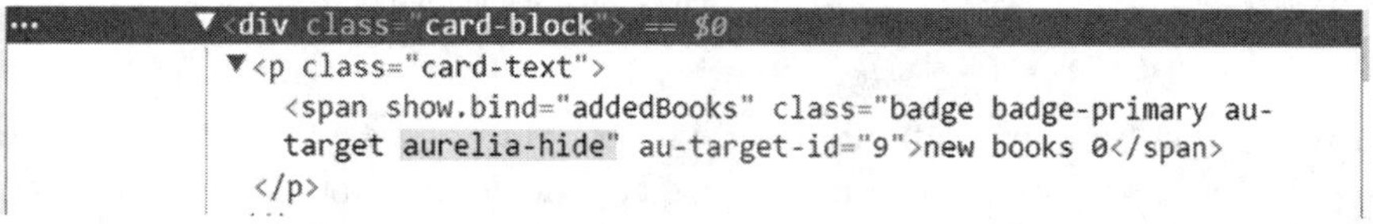

```
...      ▼<div class="card-block"> == $0
            ▼<p class="card-text">
                <span show.bind="addedBooks" class="badge badge-primary au-
                target aurelia-hide" au-target-id="9">new books 0</span>
            </p>
            ...
```

Figure 4.1   Chrome Developer Tools shows that the aurelia-hide class is added to an element.

A good rule of thumb is to use the show.bind conditional unless there's a good reason you need the element to be removed from the DOM entirely. This optimizes templating performance by avoiding unnecessary DOM manipulation.

Now that you've created your `book-stats` component, you need to use it in the `books` component. Do this by following the usual pattern of requiring the new view resource into the parent element and adding a new custom-element reference.

To begin with, add another conditional binding to the `book-stats` element—the `if.bind` conditional. This binding ensures that this resource isn't initialized and added to the DOM until the books list has been populated.

A convenient side effect of using this binding here is that the value of the `original-NumberOfBooks` view-model property is set to 3 once the book list has been loaded, so you have the correct value to send through in the data binding to the `book-stats` view-model.

Following this, bind the `books` array between the parent and child view-model (so that it can be used in the calculation) and set up a one-time binding on `original-NumberOfBooks`, setting it to the length of the `books` array. A one-time binding is an example of something called a *binding behavior*. As the name suggests, binding behaviors give you a way of tailoring how a binding behaves to the requirements in each scenario. In this case, you're indicating that the binding should be set only once, which will happen when the component is initialized, and any changes in the value of `books.length` won't be picked up by this binding expression. One-time binding is only one example of binding behavior offered by the Aurelia framework.

Modify the src/resources/elements/books.html as shown in the following listing.

> **Listing 4.3   Modifying `books` view to include the `book-stats` component (books.html)**

```
<template>
..
<require from="./book-stats"></require>          ◁──  Requires the new view
...                                                    resource into the view
<hr/>
<book-stats if.bind="books.length > 0"           ◁──  References the element and adds
     books.bind="books"                                an if.bind conditional binding
 original-number-of-books.one-time="books.length"> ◁─┐
</book-stats>                                         │  Binds the value of
</template>                          Binds the original number of │  the books from the
                                    books with a one-time binding │  parent to the child
                                                                     view-model
```

If you launch the application and add a new book, *Lord of the Rings*, you should now see the `book-stats` component rendered as shown in figure 4.2.

You've enhanced the my-books application by adding a statistics component using a combination of the `if.bind` and `show.bind` template conditionals. The next enhancement you'll make to the my-books application is to add some interesting styling to the book list while learning more about Aurelia repeaters, which you first glimpsed in chapter 2.

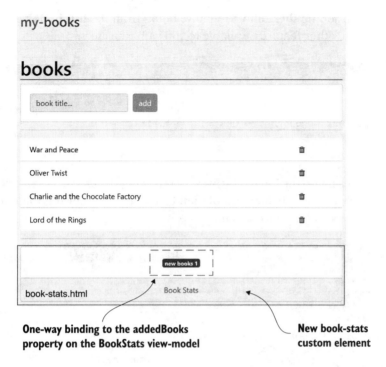

One-way binding to the addedBooks property on the BookStats view-model

New book-stats custom element

Figure 4.2 After including the new `book-stats` component, the my-books book-management view should display the number of books added in each session.

4.2 Repeaters

Repeaters are a kind of template expression that allows you to loop through a view-model collection and render it to the DOM. They're particularly useful for scenarios where you have a list of items (like your book list) or a table of data you want to render to your view. Repeaters allow you to iterate over almost any kind of JavaScript collection you can imagine, including the following:

- *Arrays*—(`repeat.for="book of books"`)
- *Ranges*—(`repeat.for="i of numberOfBooks"`)
- *Sets*—(`let books = new Set(); books.add({title: 'War and Peace'}; repeat.for="book of books"`)
- *Maps*—(`repeat.for="[bookRating, book] of books"`)
- *Maps*—(`"bookProperty of books | bookProperties"`)

Let's take another look at the `book-list` repeater that you created in chapter 2, which is reproduced in listing 4.4. Repeaters can be used on any element, but in the example, you used it to render each of the books in the list. In this section, we'll expand on the book elements, adding the ability to remove books from the list. In doing so, we'll explore some of the other features available to you with repeaters.

Listing 4.4   `book-list` view with repeater from chapter 2 (book-list.html)

```
<template>
    <ul>
        <li repeat.for="book of books"> ${book.title} </li>      ◁─┐ repeat.for
    </ul>                                                          │ renders
</template>                                                        │ each book.
```

Before you begin, clean up the `book-list` view by removing the `<book-stats>` element. Update the /src/resources/elements/books.html view, as shown in the following listing, to remove the `<book-stats>` element.

Listing 4.5   Removing the `book-stats` element from `books` view (books.html)

```
<template>
 <require from="./book-list"></require>
 <require from="./heading.html"></require>

 <heading text.bind="'books'"></heading>
    ...                                              First book-stats
 <hr/>                                               component
 <book-list books.bind="books"></book-list>    ◁─┘  implementation
                                                     removed

</template>
```

Within the repeater, you get access to several variables that give an insight into the context of the iteration. Let's look at what options you've got available.

4.2.1   *Aurelia repeater contextual properties*

Aurelia's binding system makes several properties available to the view within the context of binding scenarios. These are called *contextual properties*. The following properties are available within the context of an Aurelia repeater:

- `$index`—The index within the collection that you're repeating over
- `$first`—Boolean contextual property that returns `true` for the first item in the array
- `$last`—Boolean contextual property that returns `true` for the last item in the array
- `$even`—Boolean contextual property that returns `true` for the items in the array with even indexes
- `$odd`—Boolean contextual property that returns `true` for the items in the array with odd indexes

I use the $index property most often because it's useful whenever you need to perform an action on a specific item in the array. In your case, use this to implement the remove-book feature, removing an item with the specified index. Extend the behavior of the <book-list> element to make use of these contextual properties.

In this example, you first use the $even contextual property to style the even list items differently. This is a somewhat contrived example because you could achieve the same result through simple CSS. Following this, use the $first and $last properties to render details regarding which are the first and last items in the array.

Finally, pass the $index property through to the removeBook view-model method to indicate which book should be removed from the array. Although this is a somewhat contrived example (you wouldn't generally need to use this many contextual properties in one view), it provides you with an insight into the kinds of contextual information available within iterators.

It's worth mentioning that even though the binding between the books and book-list components is one-way, you can propagate the changes back up to the books view because you have a reference to the books array object. When you remove an item by index from the array, you're removing it directly from the array of books in the parent component. This communication is achieved by object reference rather than binding. In a real-world application, you'd use a technique such as an Event Aggregator or custom events (covered in chapter 6) to notify the parent component of the change in the child component. This avoids direct object manipulation on the parent and makes the intercomponent interaction more explicit and easier to reason about.

Replace the markup in the src/resources/elements/book-list.html view.

Listing 4.6 Including contextual properties in the book-list repeater (book-list.html)

```
<template>
  <require from="../attributes/tooltip"></require>
  <ul class="books list-group list-group-flush">
      <li class="list-group-item ${$even ? 'book-even' : ''}"
          repeat.for="book of books">
          <div class="book row">
            <div class="col-10">
                ${book.title} ${bookLocation($first, $last)}</div>
                  <div class="col-1">
                    <span class="remove-button"
                          click.delegate="removeBook($index)"
                          tooltip="title.bind:
                              'Remove book from list';
                              placement.bind:'right'" >
                <i class="fa fa-trash" aria-hidden="true"></i>
            </span>
          </div>
        </div>
      </li>
    </ul>
</template>
```

Annotations:
- Uses the $even context property to give the even rows a different style
- Your standard repeat.for iterator
- Uses $first and $last contextual properties to give insight into what element you're on
- The click event of the remove-button is delegated to the removeBook method passing the current $index within the array.

Next, finish up this implementation by modifying the /src/resources/elements/book-list.js view-model to add the `bookLocation` method referenced from the view. Modify this file as shown in the following listing.

Listing 4.7   Using contextual properties in the `book-list` view-model (book-list.js)

```
...
export class BookList {
...

    bookLocation(isFirst, isLast){           ◁──┐  The $first and $last
                                                    contextual properties that
        if(isFirst) return '- first book';          were passed as parameter
        if(isLast)  return '- last book';           values from the view

        return '';
    }

    ...
}
```

The view, which can be found at http://localhost:9000/#/books, should now look like figure 4.3.

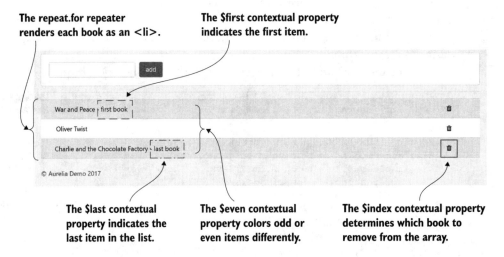

The repeat.for repeater renders each book as an `<li>`.

The $first contextual property indicates the first item.

The $last contextual property indicates the last item in the list.

The $even contextual property colors odd or even items differently.

The $index contextual property determines which book to remove from the array.

Figure 4.3   The my-books book-management page restyled using the contextual properties available within the list repeater, such as `$first`, `$last`, and `$index`.

NOTE   We've only scratched the surface of the features that repeaters offer. Aurelia repeaters allow you to repeat over other kinds of collections as well, such as ES6 sets or even object properties. The Aurelia Hub documentation has a fantastic page that goes into this in more detail: http://aurelia.io/docs/templating/basics#repeaters.

4.3 Data binding with Aurelia

Data binding is Aurelia's way of communicating between the view (HTML) and the view-model (JavaScript). So far, you've used several of the basic binding options available in the Aurelia framework, but in this section, we'll take things up a notch. We'll look first at the three key ingredients that make up an Aurelia binding expression. We'll then look at the several types of bindings available, called *binding behaviors*. By the end of this section, you'll know which data binding to reach for in any scenario during your Aurelia development workflow.

4.3.1 The three key ingredients of Aurelia's binding expressions

Aurelia's data-binding system is built using the *observable technique*. Conceptually, what this means is that when Aurelia parses an HTML file, it scans for HTML elements that have three key ingredients: attributes with attached binding commands, with an assigned JavaScript expression. Attributes and binding commands tell the framework what to bind to, and how the binding should be configured. Several binding commands are included in the framework, `bind`, `one-way`, `two-way`, and `one-time`, to name a few. A common example of a JavaScript expression is a simple view-model property name.

If Aurelia finds a property on the view's view-model with the name defined in the JavaScript expression, it will then attempt to rewrite it to make it *observable*. By this I mean that the property will have the ability to let Aurelia's binding system know when a change occurs. For example, imagine you have a form with a text box allowing a user to enter a greeting. As the user types a greeting into the text box, the updated value should be rendered to an `<h1>` element in the view. In Aurelia, this could be implemented with a couple of simple binding expressions, as shown in listings 4.8 and 4.9. In this case, Aurelia configures the `greeting` property for notification. Any time it changes (like when the `timeOut` completes and updates the greeting value), Aurelia queues the change for rendering to the browser. After a property is rewritten in this way, the framework can observe it for changes.

You can see this sample application in action and play with the binding expressions on this gist: https://sean-hunter.io/aia-binding-greeter.

> **Listing 4.8 The greeter app view (app.html)**

```
<template>
  <h1>${greeting}</h1>                    ◁─── Renders the
  <form class="form-inline">                    greeting to the view
    <input class="form-control"
           placeholder="greeting..."
           value.bind="greeting">         ◁─── Adds a bind command
    </input>                                    to the value attribute
  </form>
</template>
```

Listing 4.9   The greeter app view-model (app.js)

```
export class App {
  constructor(){
    this.greeting = 'Hello';            Initializes the
                                        greeting message

    setTimeout(x => {                   Updates the greeting
      this.greeting = 'hello from the future!';   at a two-second delay
    },2000);
  }
}
```

In most cases, all you need to do to observe a view-model property in Aurelia is mention it in a binding expression in the view. The only exception is if you need to observe a property that needs to reflect a change to the view when one of several view-model properties changes. The textbook example of this is a user.fullName property that needs to trigger a view update when a user's first or last name changes. In these cases, you'd need a computed property (which we touched on in section 4.1).

On the flip side, Aurelia can also observe changes on input fields—this is where the term *two-way data binding* comes into play. As Aurelia compiles the view, it will look for elements that have attributes with binding commands attached. It will also look for elements that conventionally require two-way binding and observe them.

For example, in the input binding from listing 4.8, Aurelia assumes (correctly) that you want to notify the view-model when the input value changes. But how does Aurelia know when the value changes? The answer is that it depends on the situation. Aurelia uses several strategies to observe various kinds of attributes. In the case of a value attribute, Aurelia subscribes to valueChanged events and notifies any subscribers (in the example, the only subscriber is the app view-model).

This should give you an indication that Aurelia has been optimized for observing changes to input elements in a way that's most suited to each element type. You may also be wondering what kinds of attributes you can bind to. That's the exciting part. You can bind to any DOM attribute. Some useful attributes to bind to include disabled, checked, and value. You can even bind to Aurelia's custom attributes such as show, hide, or style. Figure 4.4 depicts the three key ingredients of Aurelia's binding expressions in the context of the simple greeter-app example.

So far, you know you can instruct Aurelia to observe changes to attributes by applying binding commands. Binding commands have different modes that determine how and when you get notified of changes. The next piece of the puzzle is the expression. Binding commands take a JavaScript expression, which the framework parses and executes. This could be a literal string (boring), a view-model property, or even an inline JavaScript function (like meaningOfLife == 42). One thing to watch out for is this: if your expression includes a function that depends on multiple property values, Aurelia will be forced to constantly check to see if these values have been updated. This is a performance problem you can avoid, again with the aid of the computedProperty decorator.

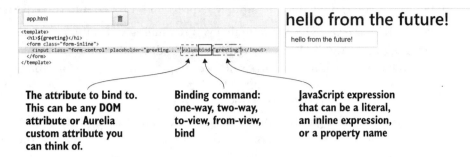

The attribute to bind to. This can be any DOM attribute or Aurelia custom attribute you can think of.

Binding command: one-way, two-way, to-view, from-view, bind

JavaScript expression that can be a literal, an inline expression, or a property name

Figure 4.4 The three key ingredients of an Aurelia binding expression: attributes, binding commands, and JavaScript expressions

To make things even more interesting, Aurelia gives us various tools to manipulate the value of the expression (for example, to change a UTC date to a local date—called *value converters*), and even change the behavior of the binding itself (for example, to only get notified of changes when the clock strikes 12) with binding behaviors. To give you something to look forward to, I'll hold you in suspense and cover binding behaviors and value converters in chapter 5.

With this basic understanding of the three key ingredients of Aurelia binding expressions, let's look at the different types of binding commands that the framework offers. We'll do this by tweaking the way that the <books> component behaves and adding some simple validation.

4.4 Binding commands

Binding expressions in Aurelia are a way of connecting HTML or SVG attributes to JavaScript expressions. The syntax for a binding expression is depicted in figure 4.5.

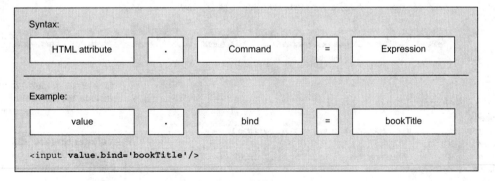

Figure 4.5 The Aurelia binding expression syntax follows the convention of an HTML attribute name followed by a period character, followed by a command name such as bind, followed by the equals character, and ending in a JavaScript expression, for example, <input value.bind ='bookTitle'/>.

In figure 4.5, you can see that the binding expression is broken into three parts:

- *HTML attribute*—The attribute that you're binding to (in this case, value).
- *Command*—Aurelia has several different binding commands available, each of which serves a different purpose (for example, .one-way sets up a binding from the view-model to the view only). We'll go through each of the available binding commands in this section; in this case, .bind.
- *Expression*—The JavaScript expression that should be evaluated to determine the value; in this case, this is a reference to the bookTitle property on the view-model.

The type of binding command you'll want to use depends on the data-flow requirements between your view and view-model for a given element. Let's go through each of the binding commands in the context of the <books> component to see when a given command would be useful.

4.4.1 One-way bindings

One-way bindings should be used when you want data to come only from the view-model to the view and not the other way around. For example, in line with what I mentioned earlier about making the UX as straightforward as possible, modify the Add button to include a one-way binding on the disabled attribute.

Modify the books.js file as shown in listing 4.9 to add a new canAdd property on the class. This property will return whether the book can be added based on the length of the bookTitle property. In this case, you used the computedFrom decorator again to indicate that the binding expression should be reexecuted any time the value of the bookTitle.length changes. If you left this out, the framework would need to constantly reevaluate this expression to determine whether the value had changed.

I've structured the code in this way to demonstrate how to use the computedFrom decorator. A simpler way to do this is to include the binding expression directly in the view: (input disabled.bind='bookTitle.length === 0').

> **Listing 4.10   Adding read-only property canAdd for one-way binding (books.js)**

```
import {bindable, inject, computedFrom} from 'aurelia-framework';      ◁──┐
import {BookApi} from '../../services/book-api';
                                                        Modifies the imports to also
                                                        include the computedFrom
export class Books {                                    decorator
    ...
    @computedFrom('bookTitle.length')           ◁──┐
    get canAdd(){                                   Indicates that you want
        return this.bookTitle.length === 0;  ◁──    to be notified when the
    }                                               bookTitle.length value
}                                                   changes
```

This needs to be a get property because it's calculated.

Calculates whether this is allowed based on title length

Next, modify the view in the /src/resources/elements/books.html file to take advantage of this new property.

Listing 4.11 Adding `disabled` one-way binding to the `canAdd` property (books.html)

```
<template>
  ..
  <div class="card">
     <div class="card-block">
   ..
              <input class="form-control" value.bind="bookTitle"
                   id="book-title"
                   placeholder="book title..."
                   type="text">

              <input class="btn btn-success tap-right"
                   type="submit"
                   value="add"
                   disabled.one-way="canAdd">          ◁─┐  Sets up a one-way
        ..                                               │  binding on the
      </div>                                             │  canAdd expression
   </div>
</template>
```

You've now added a binding expression that will send data from the view-model to the view (in this case, the disabled status on the button). If you reload the browser (see figure 4.6), you should see that the button is now disabled until a title value has been specified.

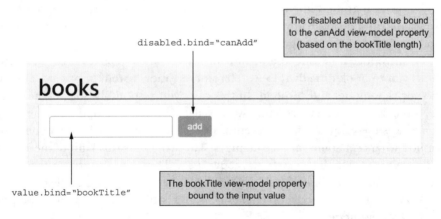

Figure 4.6 The books.html view has been modified to include a one-way binding on the disabled attribute of the Add button. This prevents books from being added unless a length has been specified.

In fact, you could've gotten away with using the `disabled.bind` expression due to the reasonable defaults coded into the Aurelia framework. In this case, you don't want to send the `disabled` value back to the view-model; based on its default conventions, Aurelia automatically sets up a one-way binding for you instead.

4.4.2 String-interpolation binding

You've already used string-interpolation-type binding quite extensively throughout the my-books application, so I won't include a specific example here, but it's worth noting that, like the `disabled` binding we just discussed, the string-interpolation binding is automatically one-way only and sends data from the view-model to the view to be rendered. Here are some scenarios in which string interpolation binding can be useful:

- Styling elements with the `class` or `style` attributes
- Rendering text from a view-model directly or by pushing it through a value converter

4.4.3 Two-way bindings

In contrast to one-way bindings, two-way binding expressions send data from the view-model to the view and back. The type of binding that Aurelia infers by default depends on the observer type. For example, the following observer types automatically set up two-way bindings:

- `AttributeValueObserver`—Used to bind to the `value` attribute on elements
- `CheckedObserver`—Used to bind to the `checked` attribute on checkbox elements

What this means is that you can write the `value.bind="bookTitle"` expression as `value.two-way="bookTitle"` instead, and it would have the same effect.

To prove that the value of the `bookTitle` is changed when the input and change events are fired on your input element, you can add a property observer in the view-model to watch these changes.

I'll introduce a new decorator in listing 4.12 called `@observable`. This decorator allows you to hook directly into Aurelia's observation system to observe any variables on your view-model and respond. In this case, you respond by logging `newValue` and `oldValue` so that you can see the two-way data binding live-updating the `bookTitle` property as the `<input>` change event is fired. This can be useful if you need to run a method whenever some variable changes. The syntax for this kind of method hook is `propertyName'Changed'(newValue,oldValue)`. These hooks are available on view-model properties decorated with the `@observable` and `@bindable` decorators.

Modify the /src/resources/elements/books.js file to add a property observer to the Books view-model.

> #### Listing 4.12 Adding an observer on the `bookTitle` property (books.js)

```
import {inject, computedFrom, observable} from 'aurelia-framework';    ⟵┐
import {BookApi} from '../../services/book-api';                           │
                                                                   Imports the
                                                                    observable
export class Books {                                                 decorator to
                                            Extracts bookTitle to be mark bookTitle
  @observable bookTitle = "";          ⟵┤ defined outside of the   as observable
  ...                                     constructor and marks
                                          it as @observable
```

```
bookTitleChanged(newValue, oldValue){
    console.log(`Book title changed,
                Old Value : ${oldValue}, New Value: ${newValue}`);
}
...
}
```

**Defines a hook to be called whenever
the value of bookTitle changes**

If you reload the browser and type in the `<input>` box, you should see the values logged to the console in Chrome Developer Tools, like in figure 4.7.

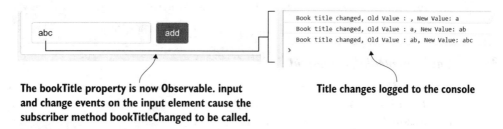

**The bookTitle property is now Observable. input
and change events on the input element cause the
subscriber method bookTitleChanged to be called.**

Title changes logged to the console

Figure 4.7 Typing values into the input box should now result in these values being logged to the console. Each time the `change` event is fired, the new value of the `bookTitle` property is logged to the console.

TIP You may have noticed the use of the backtick syntax in the console log statement from listing 4.12. This is an addition in ES2015 to allow you to easily create templated strings. These strings have placeholder syntax (defined using $\{\}$) into which you can inject variables. As you can see, this allows you to write code that's far more readable than string concatenation. If you're interested in learning more, I recommend checking out this article on MDN: https://sean-hunter.io/aia-template-literals.

At this point, you can also check whether the default two-way convention on input elements holds true. If you switch the binding mode on the input value to one-way in the view at /src/resources/elements/books.html, as shown in listing 4.12, then even when you type a value in the input box, the Add button should remain disabled because the view-model has never been notified that the bookTitle value should be changed.

Listing 4.13 Changing books to use two-way binding on bookTitle (books.html)

```
<input class="form-control"
value.one-way="bookTitle"
            id="book-title"
            type="text"
            >
```

**Switches default two-way data
binding out for one-way temporarily
to see the behavior**

This binding-mode output is highlighted in figure 4.8.

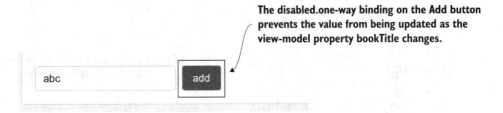

The disabled.one-way binding on the Add button prevents the value from being updated as the view-model property bookTitle changes.

Figure 4.8   With the binding changed to one-way, the disabled value is never updated because you don't receive a change notification when the value in the input field is changed. Hence, this value is never sent back to the view.

4.4.4   One-time binding command

The one-time binding command is a binding from the view-model to the view that unsubscribes from the property-change subscription after the first time the notification is called. This can be useful in the following cases:

- Executing the binding has a performance cost (such as retrieving data from an HTTP endpoint).
- You want to calculate the value only once (when the component is initialized and binding is executed). You may recall that you ran into that case when implementing the <book-stats> component.

To refresh your memory, take another look at this binding expression in listing 4.14. In the case of the `originalNumberOfBooks` property on the `BookStats` view-model, it makes sense to look at the value the first time the binding is fired (which is when the view-model is instantiated). After that, you don't want to receive any more notifications of changes in the `book.length` property, because they would give you an incorrect `original-number-of-books` value.

Listing 4.14   The books view demonstrating one-time binding (books.html)

```
...
<book-stats if.bind="books.length > 0"
            books.bind="books"
            original-number-of-books.one-time="books.length">    ◁─┐
</book-stats>
...                          Sets up a one-time binding command on
                             the original-number-of-books property
```

4.5   Handling DOM events

Handling DOM events in Aurelia is a piece of cake and follows the same conventions that you're now familiar with. In Aurelia, you can handle DOM events by adding `.delegate` or `.trigger` after specifying an event name on an element (either standard HTML or a custom element), and then specifying an Aurelia function to be called when that event is fired. For example, `click.delegate='addBook()'` reads thus: "On click, delegate the clicked event to the `addBook()` view-model method." Figure 4.9 depicts the syntax for handling DOM events in Aurelia.

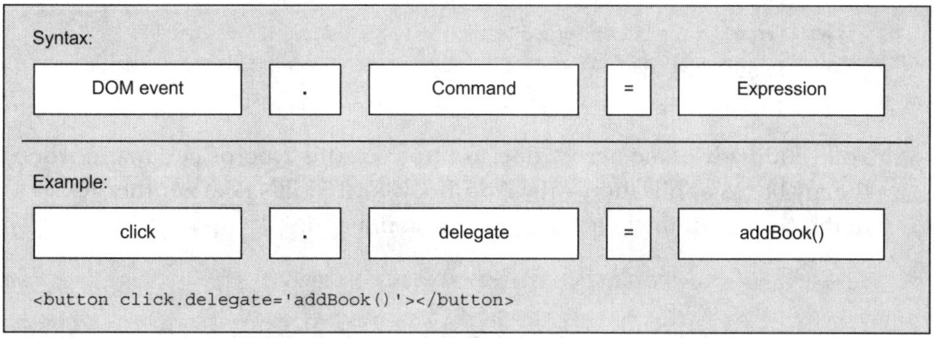

Figure 4.9 The Aurelia event-binding syntax follows the convention of a DOM event name followed by a period character, followed by a command name such as `delegate`, followed by the equals character, and ending in a JavaScript expression; for example, `<button click.delegate= 'addBook()'/>`.

Two binding commands can be used to handle events in Aurelia: `delegate` and `trigger`. Let's look at each of these in a bit more detail.

4.5.1 *Trigger*

The `trigger` command attaches an event handler directly to an element. The expression is invoked whenever the event occurs on that element. Because the `trigger` command attaches the handler directly to the element that it's applied to rather than bubbling it up from a nested element, you use it in cases where you need to listen to an event that doesn't bubble (we'll cover why this is the case in section 4.5.2).

Event bubbling

The browser has two models for how to handle events: capturing/trickling and bubbling. These models were originated by Netscape and Microsoft, who had different opinions on how this should work. It's easiest to understand these differences in the context of an example: if you have an inner element and an outer element, and the user clicks the inner element, this click applies to both the inner and the outer element.

The question that arose when this functionality was originally being implemented was, which event should fire first? Netscape's opinion was that the event should be fired on the outer element first, trickle down, and then fire on the inner element. Microsoft's opinion was that the event should be fired on the inner element first, and then bubbled up to the outer element. IE versions pre-9 support only the bubbling model, but IE9+ support both the bubbling and capturing/trickling model.

Here are some common examples of the kinds of cases where you'd want to use the `trigger` command:

- `<input focus.trigger  = "test()"> </input>`
- `<form  submit.trigger = "test()"> </input>`
- `<input change.trigger = "test()"> </input>`
- `<input reset.trigger  = "test()"> </input>`

You've already come across one example of this type of command when building the my-books application—the Add Book form. Let's take another look at this form in the context of the following `trigger` command:

```
form class="form-inline" submit.trigger="addBook()"
```

In the view, you bind the `addBook` method to the form `submit` event. Because of this, whenever the form is submitted, the `addBook()` method on the `Books` view-model is called. The semantics of the `trigger` binding command are depicted in figure 4.10.

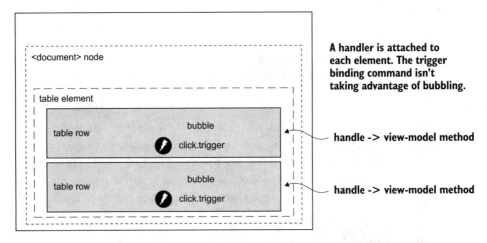

Figure 4.10   The `trigger` binding command is designed to be applied to events that don't bubble, and hence attaches an event handler to each element the command is applied to. Notice that a click-event handler is attached to each table row to trigger individually rather than simply handling a bubbled event higher in the DOM.

4.5.2   Delegate

The `delegate` command, in contrast, is attached to a top-level node such as the document node or the nearest Shadow DOM boundary.

The main benefit of using the `delegate` command is performance. Under the hood, Aurelia can optimize the `delegate` command by aggregating all the delegated event handlers under one handler abstraction, which then forwards the event to the appropriate target. You can think of this abstraction like a router for your events. It automatically sets up a map between your event target and the handler method, and

The Shadow DOM

Have you ever run into a situation where you had a section of your web page (perhaps even a reusable component) that you wanted to style differently from the rest of the page? Traditionally, this has been difficult to achieve because any styles to the page apply to the *entire* page.

One way of doing this is to use iframes, but these were designed for embedding another page inside your main-page content. As such, this isn't an ideal way to achieve encapsulation. Historically, another problem with attempting to create isolated components is that JavaScript running on the main page has access to the entire DOM, so it has the potential to interfere with the behavior of components included on the page. The Shadow DOM was introduced to solve these encapsulation problems. It provides a way of encapsulating parts of the DOM (known as *DOM sub-trees*) from the main DOM tree. This allows you to create isolated components that you can drop into a page without worrying about their styles or behavior being disrupted by styles or JavaScript included in the main page.

The Shadow DOM is one of four web specifications that, combined, give you the building blocks needed to build Web Components. You can find out more about the web-component specifications at https://webcomponents.org/specs. I'll introduce each of these specifications in chapter 12 and explain how to interact with them from the Aurelia framework.

when the handler is called, it looks up the appropriate method and calls it. This process is depicted in figure 4.11.

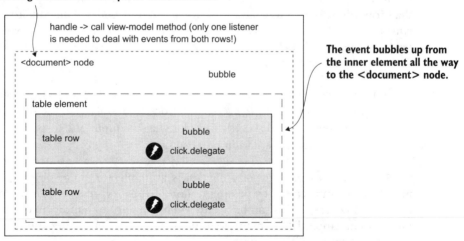

An array of delegated events is mapped at the top level. Aurelia listens for events and effectively routes them to the desired view-model method, reducing the number of required event handlers.

Figure 4.11　The `click.delegate` binding command optimizes event handling in Aurelia by using event bubbling to minimize the number of required handlers. Notice that even though Aurelia receives the click event on any table row, these two `click.delegate` commands are aggregated and handled by the one event handler at the top of the figure.

A good example of the kind of optimization that can be accomplished is the book-list view in which you've already used the delegate binding command to remove books from the list. To refresh your memory, listing 4.15 shows what the relevant part of the view at /src/resources/elements/book-list.html looks like. You've currently got three books in the list, which means if you used the trigger command, Aurelia would need to set up three handlers (one for each of the items in the list). This is OK for a small number of items, but you can imagine the performance impact if you had hundreds or thousands of items in the list. By contrast, because you're using the delegate command, Aurelia will store a reference to three different event targets in its internal map and call the appropriate handler that corresponds to the target.

Listing 4.15 Demonstrating the delegate command (book-list.html)

```
<li class="list-group-item" repeat.for="book of books">
    <div class="col-10">${book.title}</div>
    <div class="col-1">
        <span class="remove-button"
              click.delegate="removeBook($index)"           ⊲───┐
              tooltip="title.bind:'Remove book from list';
                       placement.bind:'right'">
              <i class="fa fa-trash" aria-hidden="true"></i>
        </span>
    </div>
</li>
```

**Attaches a click-event handler to the
removeBook view-model method
using a delegate command**

NOTE By default, Aurelia always calls preventDefault on any event handled with a delegate or trigger binding to cancel the event, if it's cancellable, without any further delegation. If you've used other SPA frameworks in the past that don't do this, you'll be aware of the amount of boilerplate code that this cuts down on. In the 1% of cases where you don't want this, however, you can override the default behavior by passing true to the event-handler function, for example, addBook(true).

A simple rule of thumb for when to use delegate versus when to use trigger is to use delegate unless it's one of those events that doesn't bubble, like the ones mentioned earlier (change, submit, and so on). This rule has a couple of exceptions, so it's best to check the Aurelia documentation if in doubt.

NOTE The contextual property $event is available for these binding commands. You can access it by passing it along in the expression (for example, addBook($event)). This can be useful when you want to handle an event that bubbles and apply DOM manipulation such as only changing the element style on the target of the event.

4.6 *my-books project status*

You've made one minor adjustment to the my-books application in this chapter: add-ing a `disabled` binding to control when users can click the Add button, as shown in figure 4.12.

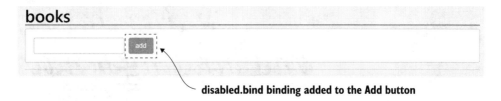

disabled.bind binding added to the Add button

Figure 4.12 The book-management page modified to control when users can click the Add button

You can download the completed chapter 4 my-books project from GitHub at https://github.com/freshcutdevelopment/Aurelia-in-Action.git using the `git clone` command.

Coming up in chapter 5, we'll spice up my-books' views with the addition of value converters and binding behaviors. These tools from Aurelia's binding toolkit put you in control of how your view-model data is rendered on the view, what's sent back to the view-model, and how your bindings behave.

Summary

- Template conditionals allow you to conditionally show or hide fragments of the view, making the UX more intuitive by only revealing what they need to see at a given point in their journey.
- Repeaters can be used to iterate over collections such as ranges, arrays, or sets and are useful when you need to render a collection from the view-model to the view.
- You can handle DOM events, such as `input change` or `button click`, using the `delegate` and `trigger` binding commands, which connect an event from the view to a view-model method.

Value converters
and binding behaviors

This chapter covers
- Creating and using simple value converters
- Exploring advanced value converters with parameters
- Understanding value-converter composition
- Using Aurelia's built-in binding behaviors

So far, the binding expressions that we've looked at have taken a value from the view-model and rendered it out to the view. But what happens if the value in the view-model isn't suitable for display? For example, if you've got a UTC date in your view-model, you'd most likely want to transform this in some way so that it would be suitable to display in the view. Conversely, you might want to transform a local date entered by the user back to UTC format on the way back into the view-model.

Value converters are Aurelia view resources responsible for doing this. What if you need to control when a binding notification is delivered from the view to the view-model? For example, imagine you have an input field bound to a view-model property, and you want only the view-model property to be updated when the user has finished typing in the field? *Binding behaviors* allow you to hook into the Aurelia binding system and change the way bindings behave to suit your needs, in a plethora of scenarios. In this chapter, you'll learn how to use value converters and binding behaviors to gain ultimate control over your Aurelia views.

5.1 Creating a value converter

Let's explore the basic semantics of value converters by implementing a `BookStatus-ValueConverter` capable of converting from a book-status string such as `'good'` to a Font Awesome icon name such as `'fa-smile-o'`. When you're finished with this value converter, you'll end up with happiness-indicator icons next to each of your books, as shown in figure 5.1.

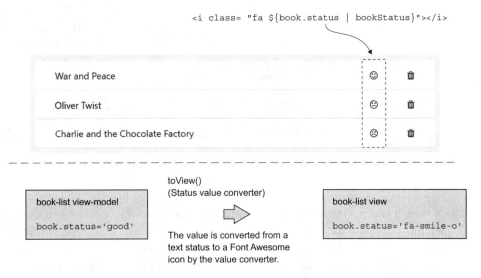

Figure 5.1 The book-list.html view enhanced with a value converter that transforms the book status text from a value like 'good' to the corresponding Font Awesome icon

Before you create a value converter to take a value from the view-model and transform it for display in the view (and vice versa), it's a good idea to know the process, which follows:

1 Create a new view-model class named `ValueConverterNameValueConverter` (for example, `DateFormatValueConverter`).

2 Define a `toView(value)` method that takes a value, transforms it, and returns it to the view. This value will likely be a property value on your view-model. Alternatively, create a `fromView(value)` method that takes a value from the view and transforms it before it's updated on the view-model.

3 Require the value converter into the view using the `<require from="../attri-butes/attributename"` syntax.

4 Use the value converter in a binding expression with the pipe syntax (|), for example, `${readDate | dateFormat}`.

Start by creating a new JavaScript file, /src/resources/value-converters/book-status.js, and add the implementation of the `BookStatusValueConverter` class, as shown in listing 5.1. The implementation for this first value converter is basic. You're implementing the `toView` method to take the `status` value on the `book` object and return the corresponding icon. The `BookStatusValueConverter` class name is the name of the value converter with a suffix of `ValueConverter` to indicate the kind of view resource this class represents.

Listing 5.1   Creating the `BookStatusValueConverter` view-model (book-status.js)

```
export class BookStatusValueConverter{
  toView(value) {                        Implements the toView(value)
                                         method to transform the value
    switch(value){                       from the view-model
        case 'bad':
            return 'fa-frown-o';         Switch statement to get
        case 'good':                     the corresponding icon
            return 'fa-smile-o';         for a given status string
        case 'ok':
            return 'fa-meh-o';
    }

  }
}
```

Now that you've defined the value converter, the next step is to use it in the view. Modify the view at /src/resources/elements/book-list.html, as shown in listing 5.2, to transform the value of each `book.status` value using the new value converter. First, you'll need to require the new value converter resource into the view. With this in place, add a new span to the view to display the status (good, bad, or OK) against each book. Finally, apply the value converter using the pipe syntax to transform the value into an icon (fa ${book.status | bookStatus}).

Listing 5.2   Including the `book-status` value converter (book-list.html)

```
<template>
  <require from="../attributes/tooltip"></require>         Requires the
  <require from="../value-converters/book-status"></require>  new book-status
  <ul class="books list-group list-group-flush">              value converter
      <li class="list-group-item" repeat.for="book of books">  into the view
          <div class="col-10">${book.title}</div>
        <span class="col-1">                              Adds the Font
            <i class="fa ${book.status | bookStatus}"       Awesome icon and
                    aria-hidden="true"></i>                 uses the new value
        </span>                                             converter in the
            ..                                              binding expression
        </div>                                              to render the icon
      </li>
  </ul>
</template>
```

If you reload the browser, instead of the raw status-string values, you'll see the relevant Font Awesome icon that corresponds to the status of each book. Now that you're familiar with the basics, let's take it one step further by looking at some of the more advanced scenarios that value converters make possible. In addition to simple values, value converters can also be applied to collections. In the next section, you'll add client-side filtering to your book list, and in doing so, explore some of the more advanced scenarios enabled by value converters.

5.2 Applying value converters to lists

Value converters can be applied to Aurelia repeaters using the same syntax that you used to apply the value converter to the book's `repeat.for='item of items | value-Converter'` status property. In this case, the difference is that the value converter's `toView` method takes the collection the repeater is applied to as its first parameter, `toView(collection, parameter2,..)`.

Imagine that you have an array of numbers `[1,2,3,4]` in your view-model, but you only want to render the even numbers to the view. You could pass your array through an `evens` value converter, which would filter out any of the odd numbers, delivering only even values `[2,4]` to the view, as depicted in figure 5.2.

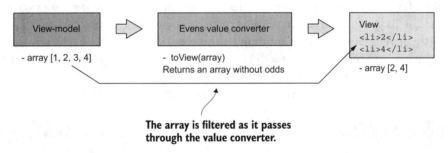

Figure 5.2   You can apply a value converter to an array of numbers so only the even numbers are rendered to the view.

To demonstrate how value converters can be applied to collections in the context of the my-books application, you'll add a new feature to allow users to filter their list of books by typing the book's title into a search term input field. To achieve this, add two new value converters:

- `FilterValueConverter`—This value converter takes the array of books and filters out any results where the book's `title` doesn't match the value of the `searchTerm` view-model property.
- `SearchBoldValueConverter`—This value converter takes the book's `title` as input, highlighting any fragments of the title that match the search term.

When you add these new value converters, the updated `book-list` view will look like figure 5.3.

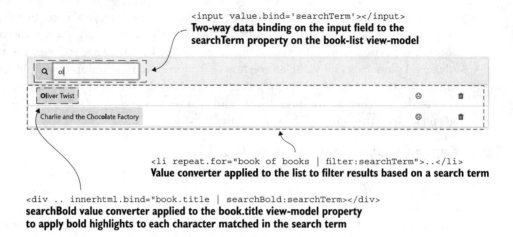

```
<input value.bind='searchTerm'></input>
```
**Two-way data binding on the input field to the
searchTerm property on the book-list view-model**

```
<li repeat.for="book of books | filter:searchTerm">..</li>
```
Value converter applied to the list to filter results based on a search term

```
<div .. innerhtml.bind="book.title | searchBold:searchTerm"></div>
```
**searchBold value converter applied to the book.title view-model property
to apply bold highlights to each character matched in the search term**

**Figure 5.3   Filter and bold-highlight value converters have been added to the `book-list` view to
enable users to filter their list of books by typing in the search box.**

To begin with, create a `FilterValueConverter`. This value converter's `toView` method
takes the books array to filter as its first parameter, and a *converter parameter*, search-
Term, as its second parameter. Converter parameters are values that are passed to a
value converter in the view's binding expression. These can be literal values or values
that are bound from the view-model (as is the case with the search term). Use the `array`
`.filter` function to filter out any books where the `title` doesn't match the `searchTerm`.
Create the new value converter in the ./src/resources/value-converters/filter.js file.

Listing 5.3   Adding the new filter value converter (filter.js)

```
export class FilterValueConverter{
  toView(array, searchTerm) {                    ◁── toView() function takes
    return array.filter((item) => {                  the array to filter and the
      return searchTerm                              searchTerm to filter by
              && searchTerm.length > 0          ◁──
                  ? this.itemMaches(searchTerm,item): true;    array.filter()
    });                                                        function used to
  }                                                            filter out any books
                                                               that don't match
  itemMaches(searchTerm, value){
    let itemValue = value.title;          ◁──   Matches against the
                                                book.title property
    if(!itemValue) return false;

    return itemValue.toUpperCase()
            .indexOf(searchTerm.toUpperCase()) !== -1;
  }
}
```

With this value converter in place, create the `search-bold` value converter in order to add a bold-highlight style to any of the book title characters that match the search term. As with the preceding value converter, you also take the `searchTerm` as a converter parameter in this case. Add the ./src/resources/value-converters/search-bold.js value converter as shown next.

Listing 5.4   Adding the new bold-highlight value converter (search-bold.js)

```
export class SearchBoldValueConverter{          Takes the searchTerm
    toView(value, searchTerm) {                 converter parameter
        if(!searchTerm) return value;
        return value.replace(new RegExp(searchTerm, 'gi'), `<b>$&</b>`);
    }
}                                               Applies the bold highlight
```

The last step required to implement your new feature is to use the two new value converters in the view. Add a new search panel to the `book-list` component to allow the user to filter book titles. You'll do this by wrapping the book list in a container div, `<div class='card'>`, and adding a new search input field with two-way binding to the `searchTerm` view-model property, `value.bind='searchTerm'`. You can pass parameters to value converters using the `.bind='valueExpression | valueConverter:param1:param2...'` syntax. Apply the filter value converter to the repeat `.for='book of books | filter:searchTerm'` books array. Next, use the `innerhtml` custom attribute provided by the Aurelia framework to bind the inner HTML of the book title div to the `book.title` value returned from the `search-bold` value converter, `innerhtml.bind="book.title | searchBold:searchTerm"`.

Modify the view in the ./src/resources/elements/book-list.html file to use the two new value converters.

Listing 5.5   Using the new value converters in the `book-list` view (book-list.html)

```
<template>
    ...
    <require from="../value-converters/filter"></require>          Requires new
    <require from="../value-converters/search-bold"></require>     value converters
    <div class="card">                                             into the view
        <div class="card-header form-inline">
            <div class="input-group">
                <span class="input-group-addon"
                    id="filter-icon">
                    <i class="fa fa-search"                        Adds a new filter
                        aria-hidden="true">                        panel with a two-
                    </i>                                           way binding on
                </span>                                            the searchTerm
                <input type="text" class="form-control"            input field
                    placeholder="filter"
                    aria-describedby="filter-icon"
                    value.bind="searchTerm">
```

Wraps the book list in a new div-styled "card"

```
                    </div>
                </div>

                <ul class="books list-group list-group-flush">
                    <li class="list-group-item"
                        repeat.for="book of books | filter:searchTerm">
                        <div class="col-10"
                            innerhtml.bind="book.title | searchBold:searchTerm">
                        </div>
                        ...
                    </li>
                </ul>
            </div>
        </template>
```

Runs the books array through the filter value converter, passing the searchTerm parameter →

← **Binds innerhtml of title <div> to book.title with the searchBold value converter applied**

You can see the new user search functionality in action by reloading the browser. To build on this example, what if you wanted to also apply a background highlight to the titles of any books that match the search term? You can do this by composing the search-bold value converter with another value converter using a technique called *value-converter composition.*

5.2.1   *Value-converter composition*

Value-converter composition allows you to pipe the output of one value converter into another to transform the source value in several ways before rendering it on the view or sending it to the view-model. You can achieve this by adding more value-converter expressions to a binding expression, like so: <input value.bind='valueExpression | valueConverter1 | valueConverter2' ...>. The input of the preceding value converter is fed into the next value converter. To see this in action, pass the output of the search-bold value converter into a new highlight value converter in order to apply a background to the title of each matching book. The data flow for this example will look like figure 5.4. The original book title is first passed through the search-bold value converter, and then through the highlight-value converter, before being rendered into the view.

Create the new ./src/resource/value-converters/highlight.js value converter, as shown in the following listing. This converter applies a highlight style to any text containing bold tags.

Listing 5.6   Creating the new highlight value converter (highlight.js)

```
export class HighlightValueConverter{
    toView(value) {
        if(value && value.indexOf("<b>") !== -1){
            return `<span style=
                    'background-color: #eceeef; padding:10px'>
                    ${value}</span>`;
        }
        return value;
    }
}
```

← **Implements the toView() method, passing in the text to convert**

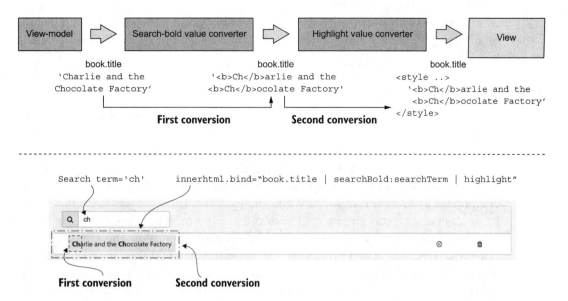

Figure 5.4 The `search-bold` value converter combined with a new `highlight` value converter to highlight the title of each matching book

Next, you'll need to use the new converter in the `book-list` view. Modify the view to require this new value converter and change the `book.title` binding expression to pipe the output of the `searchBold` value converter into the `highlight` value converter.

Listing 5.7 Adding the value-converter composition to `book-list` (book-list.html)

```
<template>
    ...
    <require from="../value-converters/highlight"></require>      ◁─┤ Requires highlight
    ...                                                              value converter
        <ul class="books list-group list-group-flush">             into the view
            <li class="list-group-item"
                repeat.for="book of books | filter:searchTerm">
                <div class="col-10"
                    innerhtml.bind="book.title | searchBold:searchTerm
                                    | highlight">      ◁─┐
                </div>                                   Composes highlight
                ...                                      value converter into the
            </li>                                        binding expression
        </ul>
    </div>
</template>
```

You can see the new user-search functionality in action by reloading the browser.

It's often the little things that can make or break a user's experience with your application. In the next section, we'll look at binding behaviors, a type of view resource that gives you fine-grained control over how the bindings in your Aurelia views behave.

By allowing you to tweak little things, like the frequency of binding notifications, binding-behavior adjustments can make a big difference in application performance, and UX.

5.3   *Binding behaviors*

Imagine you want to implement an autocomplete-style search for books that performs a query against the books API as the user enters the name of the book that they want to add to their bookshelf. In this scenario, it would be useful to be able to ignore some of the keystrokes and perform the query against the server only at certain intervals. This wouldn't impact the UX but would certainly improve the performance of the component by making it less chatty with the backend API. One way to do this would be to observe the property-changed notification as you did with bookTitle. In doing this, you'd need to maintain your own state machine to allow the component to remember how long it had been since the last call. You could then execute a request against the server only if a certain amount of time had elapsed since the previous query. This approach has two major drawbacks, however. First, you need to maintain the new-state-machine code, and second, you're capturing this event quite late in the pipeline, after it has already gone through the entire Aurelia binding system. What if there was a way for this binding to behave so that it doesn't receive a notification unless that time interval has passed?

This is where binding behaviors come in. Binding behaviors are another kind of view resource (like custom elements or custom attributes, but most like value converters). These are one of the core concepts, the basic Lego bricks that make up the Aurelia framework.

Earlier, when we looked at how the Aurelia binding system works, you saw that binding expressions are converted to binding instances to be used in a view. Binding behaviors have complete access to these binding instances throughout their lifecycle. This means that these behaviors can be applied to binding expressions to change the way they behave. Aurelia comes with several binding behaviors out of the box. In this section, you'll tweak bindings applied in the books component by introducing each of these binding behaviors, and look at how the behavior is altered in each scenario. This will give you an idea of how you can tailor the way your bindings work to suit any problem you may encounter when developing Aurelia applications.

For reference purposes, I've included a brief overview in table 5.1 outlining each of the built-in binding behaviors supported at the time of writing.

Table 5.1   The various binding behaviors Aurelia provides out of the box

Name	Where to use it	Example
Throttle	A stream of events in which you only care about a fraction (for example, 1 in 100).	`<div mousemove.delegate ="mouseMove($event)& throttle:100">`

Table 5.1 The various binding behaviors Aurelia provides out of the box *(continued)*

Name	Where to use it	Example
Debounce	A stream of events in which you only care about the last one (for example, when a user stops typing).	`<input value.bind="searchTerm & debounce">`
Update trigger	You want to trigger a binding update based on a nonconventional event.	`<h1 value.bind="title &updateTrigger:'blur'">`
Signal	You want to trigger a binding update based on a configurable expression.	`<h1 value.bind="title & signal: 'should-refresh'">`

5.3.1 Throttle and debounce binding behaviors

The `throttle` and `debounce` binding behaviors give you an easy way to limit how frequently a binding updates. These behaviors are particularly useful when you don't need to know every single time a value updates, for example, if you were performing an action based on a mouse-hover event, or if you were performing a server-side query based on the value in an input box. In these kinds of scenarios, limiting the number of events that fire a notification can give you a nice performance boost.

The `throttle` binding behavior limits either the frequency at which view-model property updates are fixed in two-way binding expressions, or the frequency that the view is updated in the case of a one-way binding expression.

The syntax for the throttle binding behavior is as follows:

```
value.bind="expression & throttle"
```

By default, this limits the notification frequency to 200 milliseconds, but you can change this by specifying the optional parameter as a final argument to the expression, like so:

```
value.bind="expression & throttle:500"
```

This limits the update interval to the millisecond value specified (in this case, 500 ms). Try modifying the `book-title` input binding expression to throttle the frequency at which you're notified of changes to the `bookTitle` property. Then you can observe the results in Chrome Developer Tools. Modify the `input` binding expression in the /src/resources/elements/books.html file to apply the `throttle` binding behavior.

Listing 5.8 Including the `throttle` binding behavior in books view (books.html)

```
<template>
  ...
              <input class="form-control"
                     value.bind="bookTitle & throttle:850"    ⟵┐ Introduces the
                     id="book-title"                              throttle-binding
                     type="text">                                 behavior with
                                                                  an interval of
  ...                                                             850 ms
</template>
```

After making this change, reload the view in the browser and try typing in a book title to see how the applied behavior affects what's logged to the console.

As shown in figure 5.5, you now receive a notification and log to the console only when the value has changed to abc, because the second character was skipped by the throttle binding behavior.

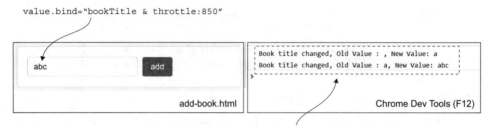

Applying the throttle binding behavior to the input binding means you're only notified of changes every 850 milliseconds.

Figure 5.5   Now, with the throttle binding behavior applied, only notifications for keystrokes occurring on the given throttle interval are received.

The debounce binding behavior is applied in a way comparable to the throttle behavior in that it also limits the notification frequency. In this case, however, the notification frequency is calculated based on the amount of time that has passed since the value last changed. As you can imagine, this is useful for scenarios like an autocomplete-style search, where you want to fire off a request to the server only when the user has paused or stopped typing. The syntax for the debounce binding behavior is as follows:

```
value.bind="expression & debounce"
```

This behavior also has an optional final parameter to allow you to control the notification interval. Try updating the input binding expression to use the debounce binding behavior instead. You should see results comparable to figure 5.5. The modified code should look like the following listing.

Listing 5.9   Adding the debounce binding behavior to books view (books.html)

```
<template>
  ..
            <input class="form-control"
                value.bind="bookTitle & debounce:850"     ⟵  Binding expression
                id="book-title"                               modified to include
                type="text">                                  the debounce
  ..                                                           binding behavior
</template>
```

Although this sample is somewhat contrived, you'll see a more relevant use of this behavior when you implement the star-rating component to allow users to apply ratings to their books in chapter 6.

5.3.2 *updateTrigger binding behavior*

When we looked at how the Aurelia binding system worked end-to-end, I mentioned that the events used to notify a view-model that changes have taken place in a bound element in the view are determined by an Aurelia convention. This convention wires up the event handlers that you're most likely to need by default, so that you don't need to specify them each time. You saw, for example, that in the case of an `<input>` element, you were notified on the change and input events.

But what if you want to be notified of a different event? For example, when applying validation to a form, it's often desirable not to apply the validation message until the blur event is fired, signifying that the user has clicked or tabbed out of that element. Well, it turns out you're in luck. The `updateTrigger` binding behavior allows you to control which events fire a notification. The syntax for this trigger is `value .bind="expression & updateTrigger:blur"`. Try modifying the input element to instead use an `updateTrigger` so that the `bookTitle` is updated only when the user navigates away from the input element. Modify the binding expression as shown in the following listing.

> **Listing 5.10   Adding the `updateTrigger` binding behavior to `books` (books.html)**

```
<template>
  ..
                <input class="form-control"
    value.bind="bookTitle & updateTrigger:'blur'"     ◁──
                id="book-title"
                type="text">
  ..
</template>
```

Binding expression modified to include the updateTrigger binding behavior

If you reload this view in the browser, you should see two differences. First, the `disabled` state isn't removed from the button until you click or tab out of the `input` field, as shown in figure 5.6.

`value.bind="bookTitle & updateTrigger:'blur'"`

Applying the updateTrigger binding behavior to the value binding means you don't receive an update notification until the user clicks or tabs out of the input and triggers a blur event.

Figure 5.6   The `disabled` state isn't updated until the user tabs or clicks away from the field because it's now configured to notify you of a change only on the `blur` event. Also, you receive a console log only on blur, meaning you don't see anything until the full `abc` value is specified.

What if you wanted to also handle the change event in addition to blur? You can do this by adding each of the events that you want update triggers on, separated by a colon (:); for example, `value.bind="bookTitle & updateTrigger:'blur':'change'"`.

5.3.3 *signal binding behavior*

The `signal` binding behavior is useful when you need a binding expression to be updated based on a certain event occurring in your application. For example, say you have a field that shows the current time, which you want to keep up to date within one minute. One way to implement this is to set a timer in the background that fires an event every minute, calling the signal each time. This ensures that you're only rerendering this fragment of the view when you need to, rather than setting up a constant loop to update the value, when you need to rerender it only once per minute. The syntax for this trigger is `value.bind="expression & signal:'literal-signal-name'"`.

Modify the `bookTitle` input element to use a `BindingBehavior` signal. Start by modifying the view at /src/resources/elements/books.html view to include this behavior.

Listing 5.11   Adding the `signal` binding behavior to books (books.html)

```
<template>
...

            <input class="form-control"
                blur.trigger="refreshSignal()"        ◁──┐  Adds a blur trigger to
                value.bind="bookTitle"          ◁─┐      fire the new signal when
                id="book-title"                   │      the user tabs away
                type="text">                      │
                                            Changes the value.bind
                                            expression back to the
            <input class="btn btn-success tap-right"   basic two-way binding
                type="submit" value="add"
                disabled.bind="canAdd() & signal: 'can-add-signal'">  ◁──┐
...                                         Wires up the canAdd binding expression
</template>                                 to signal based on the 'can-add-signal'
```

Next, you need to implement the signal in your view-model. Modify the `Books` view-model temporarily, as shown in listing 5.12, to implement this signal. In this alternative implementation of the `Books` component, import the `BindingSignaler`, which allows you to signal the `canAdd` binding to update as a result of calling the `refreshSignal` method. The `bindingSignaler.signal` method takes the name of the signal, which is then referenced in the view (in this case, `'can-add-signal'`). This name doesn't need to follow any conventions because Aurelia will look for a literal reference to this signal name and connect the signal raised with what's referenced from the view-model. This signal type is most useful in combination with value converters.

Listing 5.12 Adding the `signal` binding behavior to `books` (books.js)

Imports the Binding-Signaler class →

```
import {bindable, observable, inject} from 'aurelia-framework';
import {BindingSignaler} from 'aurelia-templating-resources';
import {BookApi} from '../../services/book-api';

@inject(BookApi, BindingSignaler)
export class Books {

    ...
    constructor(bookApi, bindingSignaler){
        this.books = [];
        this.bookApi = bookApi;
        this.bindingSignaler = bindingSignaler;
    }
    ..
    canAdd(){
        return this.bookTitle.length === 0;
    }

    refreshSignal(){
        this.bindingSignaler.signal('can-add-signal');
    }
    ..
}
```

Removes the @computed decorator import because it's not required in this implementation

Injects the Binding-Signaler class from the Aurelia DI container

Takes an instance of the BindingSignaler singleton

Removes the @computedFrom decorator and changes this into a regular method

Fires a 'can-add-signal' whenever the refreshSignal method is called

In this section, we've covered a variety of different binding behaviors that Aurelia includes out of the box. With these behaviors under your belt, you should be able to tailor the way bindings behave to match most of the different binding scenarios that you run into during an Aurelia development lifecycle. What happens, though, if you run into a scenario where none of these behaviors fits perfectly? In that case, it's possible to create your own custom binding behaviors. We'll cover how to create custom binding behaviors in chapter 13.

5.4 *my-books project status*

You've added two new features to the my-books book-management page. Books can now be filtered using a value converter applied to the books array, with the value-converter composition used to combine two more bindings to highlight the filtered values. You've also used another value converter to transform the boring string-status text on books into a Font Awesome icon to display in the view. The end state of the project in chapter 5 is depicted in figure 5.7.

You can download the completed project from GitHub at https://github.com/freshcutdevelopment/Aurelia-in-Action.git using the `git clone` command.

Real-world Aurelia applications are built by composing many well-encapsulated components. In chapter 6, you'll learn how to manage the complexities that come with building an application in this componentized style, using intercomponent communication techniques such as the Event Aggregator and custom events.

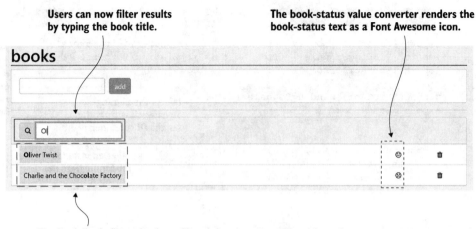

Users can now filter results by typing the book title.

The book-status value converter renders the book-status text as a Font Awesome icon.

The book list is filtered using a filter value converter. Filtered results are highlighted by composing search-bold and highlight value converters

Figure 5.7   The my-books book management page state at the end of chapter 5

Summary

- Sometimes the data in your view-model isn't fit to display in the view, and vice versa.
- Value converters give you the flexibility to control how your view-model data is rendered for best usability.
- Value converters can be composed together in a variety of ways by passing the output of one value converter into another.
- You can hook into Aurelia's binding system using built-in binding behaviors. This is a terrific way of tweaking settings, such as binding notification frequency, to improve the performance of your components.

Intercomponent communication

This chapter covers

- Getting to know the Aurelia component lifecycle
- Exploring intercomponent data flow and binding
- Understanding how and when to use the Event Aggregator
- Determining how and when to use custom events
- Extending my-books with more-advanced intercomponent communication scenarios

Aurelia applications are built by combining many fine-grained components. This allows you to focus on creating or maintaining one component in isolation without needing to consider the context of the entire application. This development style leads to an application that's easy to create, reason about, test, and maintain. In chapter 2, we looked at a basic method of sharing data between components via data binding. This approach is perfect when you want to pass data down the component hierarchy from parent to child but can cause problems when you attempt to expand its use to send data up or across the hierarchy. Attempting to use data binding in these scenarios causes intercomponent coupling. This coupling—created by the introduction of a shared state between components—can undo the reasonability, testability, and maintainability you sought to introduce by componentizing the application in the first place.

6.1   Aurelia components

Though this chapter focuses mainly on how components communicate, it's worth getting a brief recap of the various kinds of components available in the Aurelia framework to put this discussion into context:

- *Custom elements*—Allow you to create custom HTML elements that typically have a view and corresponding view-model; see chapter 3. These are generally the first things that come to mind when you mention Aurelia components. Our discussion of intercomponent communication focuses on custom elements.
- *Custom attributes*—Allow you to create custom HTML attributes; see chapter 3.
- *Value converters*—Allow you to convert values coming to the view from the view-model and vice versa; see chapter 4.
- *Binding behaviors*—Allow you to alter the way bindings behave; see chapter 5.
- *View-engine hooks*—We haven't covered these yet, but they allow you to hook into the Aurelia binding system. One use case is if you have static data that you want to add to your Aurelia view. One way to do this is to create a view-engine hook to inject the static array of values into the binding context in a `beforeBind` hook. You then require the binding behavior into the view, and use the array defined in the view-engine hook.

You can see an overview of Aurelia's components in figure 6.1.

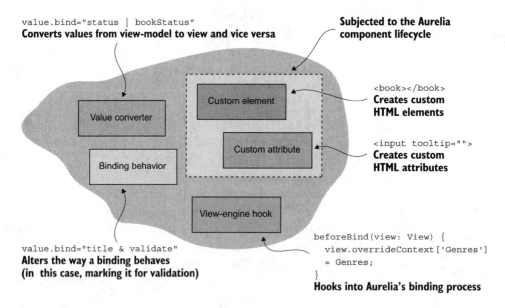

Figure 6.1   Overview of Aurelia's component types, including value converters, binding behaviors, custom elements and attributes, and view-engine hooks

Of Aurelia's component types, custom elements and custom attributes are subject to the component lifecycle, which we first touched on in chapters 1 and 2. To refresh your memory: The component lifecycle is a set of optional hooks available to components. Implementing these hooks in your view-model lets you inject behaviors at various points in Aurelia's templating and binding process, from when the view-model is constructed to when the view is detached from the DOM and unbound. By understanding these hooks, you can make the best decision about when and where you should perform various kinds of actions in your view-models. This knowledge will allow you to prevent all sorts of difficult issues, from an HTTP call not loading data when you expect, to a third-party JavaScript control throwing errors rather than rendering to your view.

6.1.1 The component lifecycle

Custom elements and attributes follow a set component lifecycle depicted in figure 6.2. Let's review when Aurelia calls each of these callback methods, and the kinds of operations suited to each.

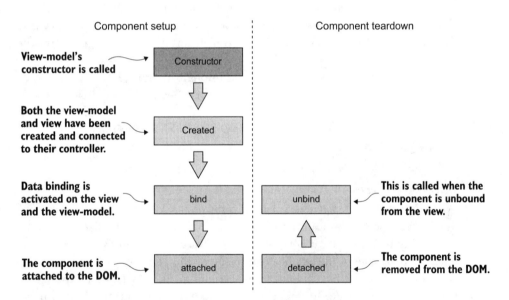

Figure 6.2 The Aurelia component lifecycle, from component creation to cleanup

COMPONENT SETUP

The component lifecycle is initiated from the view-model's constructor. After constructing the view-model, Aurelia then creates the view and the controller, and connects them together. Controllers are responsible for connecting views to view-models. For the most part, they can be considered a private implementation detail, used behind the scenes to automate dynamic component creation. At this point, you can hook into the created(owningView, myView) callback, which takes the owning-View parent (or owning) view and the connected view as arguments. For example, in the my-books project, the owning view of the book-list component is the books view. You'll want to use the created callback when you have data to load before the data binding occurs.

After the component has been created, data binding is activated on the view and view-model, and Aurelia calls the bind(bindingContext, overrideContext) callback. The combination of the bindingContext and overrideContext arguments is called the *scope*. The bindingContext consists of the view-model instance, and by default it doesn't inherit the parent context (except in the case of dynamic composition, which we'll cover in chapter 11). The overrideContext consists of additional contextual properties (for example, the repeater contextual properties, like $index, that we covered in chapter 4) or overrides to values in the bindingContext. One of the ways to add properties to an overrideContext is to use view-engine hooks. For the most part, you won't need to access these variables explicitly. Aurelia uses them to make the view-model's properties and methods available to the corresponding template. This callback is a suitable place to load view-model data that depends on values sent to the view-model using data binding. An example is loading an object with a specific id from an HTTP endpoint where the id is bound from the parent component.

Once data binding is finished, the component is attached to the DOM, triggering the attached callback. You can also use the attached callback to load view-model data, as long as you don't need this data until the data binding has completed. Most commonly, however, you use this callback to perform DOM manipulation, such as initializing a jQuery plugin on an element (as you did with the tooltip custom attribute in chapter 3).

COMPONENT TEARDOWN

When I was first using Aurelia, I built a simple view-model that initiated an interval as part of the component setup process. What I didn't realize was that, without something to explicitly remove the timer, I was creating a new one each time I navigated to that page of the application. Because this timer was tied to charts, the problem became obvious as the values represented by the charts grew exponentially each time I visited the page. In fact, this is a fundamental difference between traditional server-side applications and SPAs. In a traditional web application, the entire page state is refreshed each time you navigate to a different area of your application. In contrast, SPAs maintain the state of JavaScript applications; unfortunately, this also means you need to be more diligent in cleaning up resources used in your components. You can achieve this cleanup in Aurelia using the teardown part of the component lifecycle.

The first method called in this process is the detached hook, called when your component is removed from the DOM. You should use this callback to reverse any

DOM manipulations your component is responsible for, or destroy any jQuery plugin resources that you may have initialized in the `attached` hook.

After the view has been detached from the DOM, it's unbound (the binding context is removed). This is generally where you'd clean up any resources, such as timers or event handlers, you may have set up in the `bind` callback.

With this understanding of the process Aurelia uses to manage its components, and how you can hook into this process to inject your own behavior, you're now in a perfect position to enhance my-books by introducing more fine-grained components and looking at the best way to communicate between them.

6.2 Enhancing my-books

Aurelia provides several techniques that enable you to communicate between components without introducing coupling and shared state. These techniques let you maintain these desirable attributes as your application grows. Such techniques include custom events and the Event Aggregator. In this chapter, we'll look at each of the intercomponent-communication techniques available in Aurelia, exploring how to use them and when they're appropriate.

You'll combine these techniques to expand the functionality of my-books, adding the ability to rate books, edit their details, and mark them as read. In doing so, you'll extend my-books to include the following functionalities:

- Mark a book as read
- Edit book titles and descriptions
- Rate books using a new star-rating component

By the end of this chapter, the application should look something like figure 6.3. To achieve this look, you'll use a combination of techniques.

6.2.1 Aurelia's three core intercomponent-communication techniques

Aurelia has three core intercomponent-communication techniques. Each technique is suited for use in different situations, which are described at a high level in the following subsections.

BINDING

This technique uses Aurelia's templating and binding engine to pass state between components. It works best for communicating down a component hierarchy. It's useful for scenarios where you want to pass a reference from a parent custom element to a child custom element, as you did between the `app` and `book` components in chapter 3.

EVENT AGGREGATOR

The Aurelia Event Aggregator is an Aurelia module that implements the *Event Aggregator pattern* (discussed in section 6.4). This module allows you to set up a one-to-many

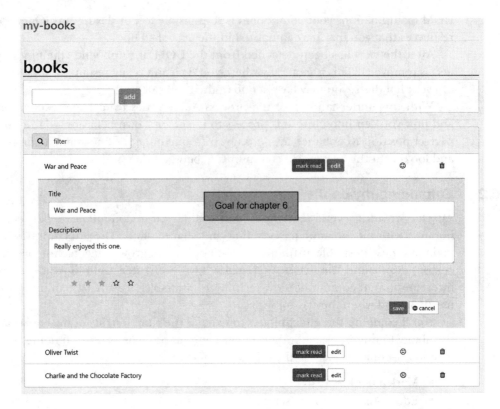

Figure 6.3   The my-books application extended with the ability to edit books, rate them, and mark them as read. This is the desired state of the application you were working toward in chapter 4.

relationship between objects in your application, such as custom elements or standard JavaScript classes. Events are published from a source object to a central Event Aggregator object that forwards them on to one or more registered subscribers. This is great for any of the more complex intercomponent interactions in your application, like notifying a parent component of a change on a child component further down in the component hierarchy. Useful scenarios include, but aren't limited to, the following:

- Communicating changes from a child custom element back up to a parent. Although you could also achieve this with two-way binding, that can lead to component relationships that are difficult to reason about and to debug when issues arise. Because of this, two-way binding isn't recommended for these scenarios.
- Communicating between sibling components.

CUSTOM EVENTS

Custom events allow you to create your own native DOM events that work like the events you're familiar with using as part of your development process, such as `click` and `blur`. As with standard DOM events, you can also trigger these events on DOM nodes. Custom events are available via the custom-events API, a relatively recent addition to the standard web-development toolset. This API is available on modern browsers. Custom events are useful in Aurelia for the following scenarios:

- When you don't want to take a dependency on the Event Aggregator
- When the component that you're creating has a more general purpose, such as an autocomplete list, an upload control, or an image widget that you may want to share between other applications that may or may not use Aurelia

---

State management with the aurelia-store library

No discussion of intercomponent communication is complete without at least mentioning state-management libraries such as Redux (https://redux.js.org/introduction) and Flux (https://facebook.github.io/flux). These libraries are known as *state containers*, and they make it easy to implement unidirectional data-flow concepts by adding more structure than what comes out of the box in most JavaScript frameworks today.

State containers are particularly useful when you have multiple components with shared state that don't have a direct relationship, or in the case of global components that stay around for the lifetime of your application. aurelia-store is a native Aurelia library built on top of RxJS (http://reactivex.io/rxjs) that lets you easily adopt a state-container-based approach to intercomponent communication within your Aurelia application.

Regretfully, I can't cover the ins and outs of state management here. If you're interested in finding out more, I strongly recommend checking out the great documentation by Vildan Softic in the projects GitHub repository (https://sean-hunter.io/aurelia-store-github).

Let's start by reviewing the intercomponent communication you've set up in my-books using data binding.

6.3 *Passing data to child components with data binding*

In chapter 2, you set up a parent-child relationship between the `books` component and the `book-list` component, as shown in figure 6.4.

This is the stereotypical use case where data binding is used to pass data down the component hierarchy. The one drawback of this approach in the context of the my-books functionality at this point is that you're leaning on the fact that the `book-list` view-model and the `books` view-model hold a reference to the same books array. When you remove items from the list, this change is perceived immediately in the `books` view. This breaks a rule of thumb that you should follow when creating Aurelia applications: *data down, actions up*. This mantra emerged from the Ember.js community to provide developers with guidance for how to organize data flow in Ember.js applications. Ember.js is like Aurelia in that it also supports two-way data binding; as with Aurelia, you can run into problems if you attempt to use this binding in scenarios that

The books[] array is initialized in the books parent view-model and bound to the book-list child view-model using one-way data binding.

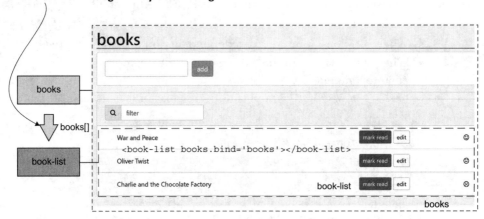

Figure 6.4   The books **array bound from parent component** books **to child component** book-list **via one-way data binding**

it's not suited for. In a nutshell, the idea is that you should pass data down the component tree using one-way data binding and use actions (or events) to communicate changes back up the component hierarchy. The data-down, actions-up pattern is depicted in figure 6.5.

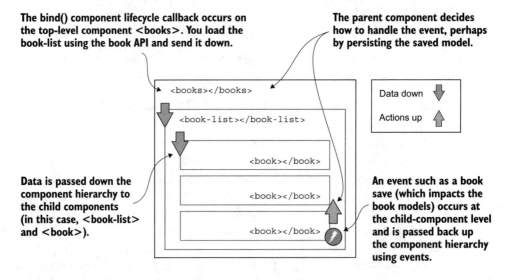

Figure 6.5   Depiction of what a data-down, actions-up approach looks like in the context of the my-books application. On the top left, you can see the books **array is passed down the component tree, a process initiated within the** bind() **component-lifecycle callback. On the bottom right, you can see an event (such as a click) is used to percolate changes back up to the root component.**

Thinking about how the my-books component interactions are structured now, you followed the first part of this convention correctly by using one-way data binding to pass the books array down from the books component to the book-list component. On the other hand, you violated the second half of this convention by directly mutating the books array when the user clicks the remove-book button.

Even though you aren't using two-way data binding, because the child component holds a reference to the books array from the parent component, it's able to modify the parents object directly, rather than notifying the parent that a change has occurred and allowing it to update its own list. But, all is not lost. You can redeem yourself by introducing another Aurelia module called the Event Aggregator. In section 6.5, you'll learn how to use the Event Aggregator pattern to decouple event publishers and subscribers. You'll also review the API and features available in Aurelia's Event Aggregator module and use this module to clean up the data flow for the book-removal feature.

6.4 Event Aggregator to the rescue

Before you can ask the EventAggregator object to rescue you from the current data-flow predicament, you need to become better acquainted with its background. What is this pattern, and where does it come from?

6.4.1 The Event Aggregator pattern

The Event Aggregator pattern is originally from the enterprise architecture world and is easy to understand. In its most basic form, this pattern provides you with a level of indirection between an object creating an event and the object or objects subscribing to the event. This is done by registering a singleton Event Aggregator object with all event publishers and event consumers. Publishers publish events on the Event Aggregator object. The Event Aggregator performs some optional transformations on the events if needed (for example, to generalize the event so that subscribers don't need to listen for as many different event types), and then passes the event on to each of the subscribers. The architecture is depicted in figure 6.6.

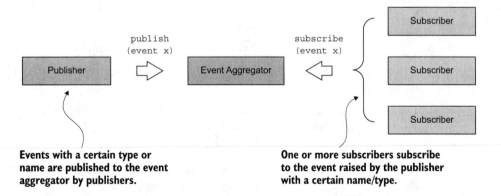

Figure 6.6 Events are published by publisher objects. Subscribers then subscribe to events on the Event Aggregator rather than needing to have a connection to each publisher object.

If you're interested in reading more about the Event Aggregator in general, Martin Fowler's article about it is worth a look: https://martinfowler.com/eaaDev/Event-Aggregator.html.

WHAT'S IT GREAT AT DOING?

The Event Aggregator pattern is great for when you have a complex graph of objects that need to communicate with each other. Instead of each object needing a reference to every other object in the graph, you can centralize these connections in the Event Aggregator object, greatly reducing the level of coupling in the system.

How different does this use case sound from the component hierarchy present in Aurelia applications? Not much at all, so it's also a great solution for reducing coupling within an Aurelia application, which is fundamentally a tree of components. In fact, the Aurelia core team had this idea and implemented this pattern in a framework module called the *Aurelia Event Aggregator.*

6.4.2   *The Aurelia Event Aggregator*

The Aurelia Event Aggregator is a module within the Aurelia framework that implements the Event Aggregator pattern (described in section 6.4.1) to communicate between components without introducing coupling between them. The API for the Event Aggregator is simple, with only three public methods:

- publish(event, data *[optional]*)—Used by the event-source objects (publishers) to notify subscribers of an event. The mandatory parameter event can either be a string name for the event (for example 'remove-book')—often referred to as a channel—or a message type. The second (optional) parameter is the data for that event and can be any type (for example, {bookToRemoveIndex : 5}).

- subscribe(event, callbackFunction)—Used by objects or components that need to perform a kind of action in relation to an event (for example, removing a book from the list of books). Again, the first parameter is the name of the event, which should be the same as the channel name or message type of the corresponding event raised by the publisher. The second parameter is a callback function that describes the action that needs to be taken when the event is received.

- subscribeOnce(event, callbackFunction)—The same as the subscribe method but disposes of the subscription and stops listening for events after the first event is received.

If the Event Aggregator isn't installed in your project, you'll need to install it first. When it's installed, follow the remaining steps beginning at step 2 to learn how to use it:

1 Install the Event Aggregator in your project if it isn't already installed using the au install aurelia-event-aggregator command. In your case, you can skip this step because this is installed and configured as part of the Aurelia CLI setup.

2 Import the `aurelia-event-aggregator` module into the view-model that you want to serve as an event publisher using the following import declaration:

```
import {EventAggregator} from 'aurelia-event-aggregator';
```

3 Inject the event aggregator into your `publisher` object using the `@inject` decorator or the `@inject(EventAggregator)` static `inject` function and take a singleton instance of it in your `constructor(eventAggregator)` constructor.

4 Publish an event of a specific type or channel using the `publish` method: `this.eventAggregator.publish('channel-name', data)`.

5 Perform steps 2 and 3 again on the `subscriber` object to bring a reference to the Event Aggregator into your subscriber.

6 Modify the `attached` or `bind` component-lifecycle callback by adding the subscription to the channel or type: `this.subscription = this.eventAggregator.subscribe('channel-name', data => {})`.

7 Dispose of the subscription in the `detached` component-lifecycle method to ensure that the subscription doesn't linger when the component is no longer active.

Now that you've got an idea of what the Event Aggregator is and the process required to use it in your Aurelia application, let's put this knowledge into practice. In section 6.4.3, you'll fix the data flow issue between the `books` and `book-list` components with the aid of the Event Aggregator.

6.4.3 Fixing book removal with the Event Aggregator

By introducing the Event Aggregator in this scenario, you hope to remove the coupling between the `book` and `book-list` components and ensure that you're following the data-down, actions-up convention. The data flow you're working toward is depicted in figure 6.7.

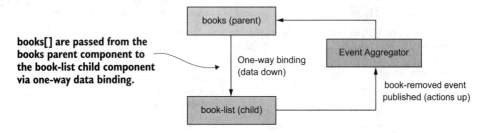

Figure 6.7 Following the data-down, actions-up approach, use one-way data binding to pass the `books` array to the `book-list` (as you're doing already), and then use the Event Aggregator to publish the `book-removed` event back up to the `book` component so that it can update the array.

To achieve this vision, you'll need to take the following steps:

1 Publish the event: add the Event Aggregator to the `book-list` component and publish an event when the `remove-book` button is clicked rather than removing it directly.

2 Subscribe to the event: add the Event Aggregator to the `books` view-model and subscribe to the `book-removed` event. When it occurs, remove the book from the array.

The application will be structured as shown in figure 6.8 after these steps have been completed.

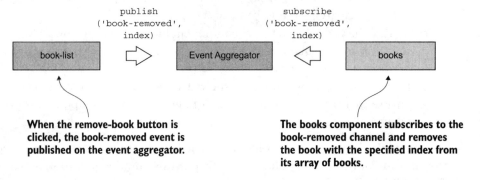

Figure 6.8   Book-removed events are published from the `book-list` component on the `EventAggregator`. The `Books` component subscribes to these events and removes the relevant book from its array.

STEP 1: PUBLISHING THE EVENT

Start by modifying the `book-list` component, replacing the code in the `BookList` view-model file, ./resources/elements/book-list.js, with the contents of the following listing.

Listing 6.1   Add `EventAggregator` to `BookList` view-model—book-list.js

```
import {bindable, inject} from 'aurelia-framework';
import {EventAggregator} from 'aurelia-event-aggregator';      ◁─── Imports the EventAggregator module

@inject(EventAggregator)          ◁─── Injects the EventAggregator instance
export class BookList {
  @bindable books;

  constructor(eventAggregator) {          ◁─── Takes an instance of the eventAggregator in the constructor
    this.eventAggregator = eventAggregator;
  }

  removeBook(index) {
      this.eventAggregator.publish('book-removed', index);      ◁─── Publishes a 'book-removed' event any time the remove-book button is clicked
  }
```

```
    //removed function                                Removes the now-redundant
}                                                     book locator function set up
                                                      in chapter 5
```

With a few minor adjustments to the `book-list` component, you've completed step 1 of the Event Aggregator setup. You're now using DI to take an instance of the Event Aggregator object in the constructor of the `BookList` view-model. The Event Aggregator is then used to publish a `'book-removed'` event in response to a user clicking the `remove-book` button. The next step is to subscribe to this channel and implement the handler function for removing a book in the `Books` view-model.

STEP 2: SUBSCRIBING TO THE EVENT

Next, you'll modify the `Books` view-model to take an instance of the `EventAggregator` object via DI. You'll then hook into the `attached` component-lifecycle callback (called by the Aurelia framework after an instance of the `Books` view has been created and attached to the DOM) and use this instance to subscribe to events in the `'book-removed'` channel. When you receive an event on this channel, call the `removeBook` callback, which is supplied with the `bookIndex` data parameter.

The `removeBook` method removes the book with the specified index from its `books` array. This `books` array is then pushed back down to the `book-list` component via one-way data binding, causing the updated list to be rerendered. A key point to note here is that you keep a copy of the subscription returned from the `subscribe` method, and then use this later to dispose of the subscription. This is important, because unless the subscription is cleaned up by calling the `dispose` method before the component is removed from the DOM or deactivated (in the case of a routeable component) the subscription will continue to receive events. This means that new subscriptions will be created each time this component is reattached or reactivated, which in turn causes memory leaks. Subscribe to events published on the Event Aggregator's `book-removed` channel by modifying the view-model at ./resources/elements/books.js.

Listing 6.2 Subscribe to the `book-removed` channel—books.js

```
import {bindable, inject, computedFrom} from 'aurelia-framework';
import {BookApi} from '../../services/book-api';
import {EventAggregator} from 'aurelia-event-aggregator';      ◁─── Imports the
                                                                   EventAggregator
@inject(BookApi, EventAggregator)          ◁─── Injects the          module
export class Books {                            EventAggregator
                                                instance
  constructor(bookApi, eventAggregator){   ◁───┐
    this.bookTitle = "";                        │
    this.books = [];                            Takes an instance of
    this.bookApi = bookApi;                     the eventAggregator
    this.eventAggregator = eventAggregator;     in the constructor
  }
```

```
addBook () {
  this.books.push({title : this.bookTitle});
  this.bookTitle = "";
}

removeBook(bookIndex){
  this.books.splice(bookIndex, 1);
}

bind(){
  this.bookApi.getBooks()
            .then(savedBooks =>
                 this.books = savedBooks);
}
```

> **Hooks into the attached()
> component-lifecycle
> callback method**

```
attached(){
  this.bookRemovedSubscription = this.eventAggregator
.subscribe('book-removed',
bookIndex => this.removeBook(bookIndex));
  }
```

> **Subscribes to the
> 'book-removed'
> channel and handles to
> book-removed event**

```
  @computedFrom('bookTitle.length')
  get canAdd(){
      return this.bookTitle.length === 0;
  }

  detached(){
    this.bookRemovedSubscription.dispose();
  }
}
```

> **Hooks into the detached
> component-lifecycle callback
> method and disposes of the
> 'book-removed' channel
> subscription**

As a rule, it's best to dispose of any active subscriptions using one of the following component-lifecycle or routing-lifecycle methods:

- Unbound *(component lifecycle)*—Called when the bindings are removed from the component.
- Detached *(component lifecycle)*—Called by the Aurelia framework when the component is removed from the DOM.
- Deactivate *(route-screen-activation lifecycle)*—Called when the view-model is navigated away from.

You've now resolved the issues with the previous implementation of the book-removal functionality by introducing a data-down, actions-up approach using the Aurelia Event Aggregator. But what you've achieved so far isn't too exciting; you've got the same behavior as before, albeit implemented in a cleaner way. In section 6.6, we'll expand on the use of the Event Aggregator with the addition of some more interesting components.

6.5 Extending my-books

In this section, you'll extend the books page, adding several new components. These components will follow the approach that you've now established of passing data down using one-way data binding, and passing actions up using the Event Aggregator. The components to be added are as follows:

- book—Displays book-summary details; allows books to be marked as read or deleted
- edit-book—Displays more detailed book information and allows metadata to be edited

The steps required to implement these new components are as follows:

1. Install the required modules.
2. Create the required date-format value converter.
3. Add the ability to the BookApi to save books.
4. Create a new book view and view-model.
5. Create a new edit-book view and view-model.
6. Modify book-list to use the new book component rather than including the book-summary details inline.
7. Modify the books component to enable communication with the book and edit-book components.

By the end of this section, the my-books book-management page should look like figure 6.9.

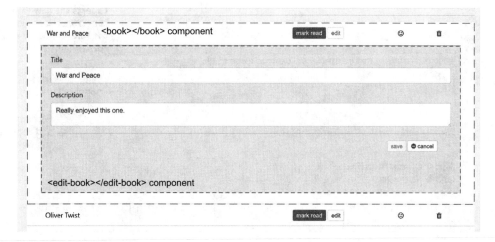

Figure 6.9 Two new custom-element components added as subcomponents to the `<books>` components: `<book>` and `<edit-book>`

6.5.1   *Step 1: Installing the required modules*

Some of these changes rely on a third-party library that you haven't installed yet, called Lodash. Lodash is a JavaScript utility library that provides many convenient methods that can be used across any type of JavaScript application. You can find out more about Lodash here: https://lodash.com/. You'll also need Moment.js, because you'll use it to render a nicely formatted book-read date to the edit-book view using a value converter. You can find out more about Moment.js on the project's website at https://momentjs.com/. Start by navigating to the my-books root directory and run the following Aurelia CLI commands to download and install Lodash and Moment.js from npm and configure them for bundling in the Aurelia.json file:

```
au install lodash
au install moment
```

6.5.2   *Step 2: Adding the date-format value converter*

One of the features of the book component is the ability to mark a book as *read*. Doing this also stamps the book with the date that the book was read. To display this date on the edit form (which you'll come to in step 5), you'll need to create a new value converter capable of taking the JavaScript date object and converting it into a localized, human-readable date to display in the view. Create this value converter in a new JavaScript file at ./src/resources/value-converters/date-format.js with the code shown in the following listing.

Listing 6.3   Creating the date-format value converter—date-format.js

```
import moment from 'moment';          ⟵  Imports the moment module for date formatting

export class DateFormatValueConverter {     ⟵  Exports the new value-converter class following the ValueConverter naming convention
  toView(value) {                           ⟵  This is a toView value converter (from the view-model to the view).
    if(!value) return '';

    return moment(value).format('MM/DD/YYYY h:mm:ss a');   ⟵  Formats the date and returns it to the view
  }
}
```

Skips the formatting if you don't have a value

With this value converter in place, you've got all the requirements to start adding the new custom elements.

6.5.3   *Step 3: Enhancing the book API*

In this step, you'll enhance the book API, adding a method to save books. For now, this method will simulate saving to a backend store by creating and resolving a promise to add an artificial element of latency. (In chapter 8, you'll modify this function to

save the book into a MongoDB database using the `aurelia-fetch-client` module.)
Edit the ./services/book-api.js file to add a new `saveBook` method.

Listing 6.4 Including the `addBook` method in the `BookApi` service—book-api.js

```
import {HttpClient} from 'aurelia-fetch-client';
import {inject} from 'aurelia-framework';

@inject(HttpClient)
export class BookApi{

  ...

  saveBook(book){                          Adds the new
    return new Promise(resolve => {        saveBook method
      setTimeout(() => {
        resolve(book);                     Resolves the
      }, 1000);                            promise manually
    });                                    for now with the
  }              Includes a 1000           existing book
}                ms timeout for
                 simulated latency
```

With these changes in place, you can proceed to step 4 and create the new book
component.

6.5.4 Step 4: Creating the book component

Where the books component is responsible for managing a library of books, the new
book component will be responsible for managing an individual book. To start with,
this will include basics like marking a book as *read* or changing the title or description,
but this will be expanded on in chapter 7 when you'll add more-interesting form elements. To start with, create a new view-model file, ./src/resources/elements/book.js,
and add the contents of listing 6.5.

This view-model has a few interesting points, which we'll explore. To start, import
the Event Aggregator, which serves two purposes:

- Allows you to subscribe to `editMode` changed events that will be raised by a
  child component, `editBooks`. This is done so that when you're editing a book,
  you can mark the Edit button as disabled, indicating to the user that the book is
  already in an editable state.
- Allows you to raise an event to notify the books component when a `removeBook`
  button is clicked to indicate that book should be removed from the list.

You'll also implement a new `markRead` method, which marks the book as *read* and
stamps it with the current time. In chapter 7, you'll extend this functionality by allowing the user to select the date that they read the book from a data-picker control.

Next, you'll move the implementation of the `removeBook` method from the book-
list component to the book component. This method raises an event on the Event

Aggregator that a specific book has been removed. Following this, you'll create a method to toggle the edit mode to be called when the Edit button from the view is clicked. Finally, you'll set up the relevant event subscription and event-cleanup behavior in the subscribeToEvents and unbind methods.

Listing 6.5   Creating the new book view-model—book.js

```
import {bindable, inject} from 'aurelia-framework';
import {EventAggregator} from 'aurelia-event-aggregator';        ◁─┐  Imports the
                                                                     EventAggregator
                                                                     module
@inject(EventAggregator)
export class Book{
                                        bindable book and
    @bindable book;                     searchTerm properties to
    @bindable searchTerm;               receive data from a parent

    constructor(eventAggregator){
        this.eventAggregator = eventAggregator;      editMode property
        this.editMode = false;          ◁─────────   initialized to false
    }
                                              Marks a book as
    markRead(){                        ◁──    read and stamps it
        this.book.readDate = new Date();      with a readDate
        this.book.read = true;
    }
                                                   Triggers a book-removed
                                                   event to be picked up by a
                                                   parent component
    removeBook(){                             ◁───
        this.eventAggregator.publish('book-removed', this.book);
    }
                                              Receives an edit-mode-
    toggleEditMode(event){             ◁──    changed event from the view
        this.editMode = !this.editMode;       and changes the edit mode
    }
                                    Subscribes to events using
    bind(){                    ◁─│  the Event Aggregator
        this.subscribeToEvents();
    }
                                              Implementation of Event
    subscribeToEvents(){           ◁──┘       Aggregator subscriptions
        this.editModeChangedSubscription =
     this.eventAggregator.subscribe('edit-mode-changed', mode => {
            this.editMode = mode;
        });
    }
                                              Cleanup of Event
                                              Aggregator subscriptions
    unbind(){                          ◁──┘
        this.editModeChangedSubscription.dispose();
    }
}
```

With the `book` view-model in place, you need to implement the corresponding `book` view as follows:

1 The `book` component has an `edit-book` child component (to be created in the next step). Import this child component so that you can use it later in the view.

2 Following this, set up a string-interpolation binding on the class attribute of the `li` element with the `class="${book.read ? 'read-book': ''}"` expression. This is one of the most suitable use cases for string-interpolation binding and allows you to style the book differently based on whether it has been read.

3 After that, set a one-way string interpolation on the book `title`. This has been refactored out of the `<book-list>` component.

4 Next, set up a template conditional on the `mark-read` button. This follows the principle introduced in chapter 3 of making the next available steps obvious to the user. This template conditional hides the button when the book has already been marked as *read*, because it makes sense to enable the user to do this only once.

5 The next interesting part is the `mark-read` button. In this case, use the `click.delegate` binding command to delegate the click event to the `markRead` method on the `book` view-model.

6 Add an `edit-mode` button. This button is delegated to the `toggleEditMode` method, which then fires a notification to signal to the child `edit-mode` component when it's time to open. This button will include a disabled binding on the `editMode` property to prevent the user from trying to edit the book when it's already in the edit state.

7 Next, move the `book-status` value converter and `removeBook` buttons from the `book-list` view into the `book` view to make the functionality for editing a book more self-contained.

8 Finally, reference the `edit-book` component (to be created in the next step) and pass the `book` and `editMode` values to the child component via one-way data binding.

Create a new book view file at ./src/resources/elements/book.html, and add the contents shown in the following listing.

Listing 6.6 Creating the new book view—book.html

```html
<template>
    <require from="./edit-book"></require>          ◁┘  Imports the edit-book
    <require from="../value-converters/book-status"></require>   child component
    <require from="../value-converters/search-bold"></require>
    <require from="../value-converters/highlight"></require>
    <li class="${book.read ? 'read-book' : ''} list-group-item">   ◁─┐
        <div class="book col-12">
            <div class="book-options form-inline">      One-way string interpolation
                <div class="col-lg-7 col-md-2"           on class attribute based on
                                                          the book-read status
```

```
        innerhtml.bind="book.title
        | searchBold:searchTerm | highlight">
```
⟵ **innerHTML binding on book title property**

```
                </div>
                <div class="col-lg-3 col-md-5">
                    <button class="read-button btn btn-success btn-sm"
                            if.bind="!book.read"
                            click.delegate="markRead()">
                        <span class="hover-display">
                            <i class="fa fa-check"
                                aria-hidden="true"></i>
                        </span>
                        mark read
                    </button>
```

Hides markRead button if the book has already been read ⟶

⟵ **Marks the book as read**

```
                    <button class="btn btn-secondary btn-sm edit-button"
                            click.delegate="toggleEditMode()"
                            disabled.bind="editMode">
                        edit
                    </button>
                </div>
```

Toggles the edit mode (opens the edit form) ⟶

⟵ **Disables the edit-mode toggle if user is already editing**

```
                <span class="col-1">
                    <i class="fa ${book.status | bookStatus}"
                        aria-hidden="true"></i>
                </span>
                <div class="col-1">
                    <span class="remove-button"
                    click.delegate="removeBook()">
                        <i class="fa fa-trash" aria-hidden="true"></i>
                    </span>
                </div>
            </div>
            <edit-book book.bind="book"
                    containerless
                    edit-mode.bind="editMode">
            </edit-book>
        </div>
    </li>
</template>
```

Delegates the click event to the removeBook view-model method ⟶

Edit-book Custom Element has no wrapping element (container) ⟶

One-way data binding to pass the book down to the edit-book child component ⟵

One-way data binding to pass the editMode down to the edit-book child component ⟵

With the new book component in place, the next step is to add the edit-book component to allow the user to modify book details.

6.5.5   *Step 5: Creating the edit-book component*

Following the usual pattern, begin by importing the Event Aggregator module to allow you to publish events (actions up) that the books and book components will subscribe to. Import the Lodash utilities module, allowing you to check the two different versions of the book object (before and after edits). Declare two bindable properties to allow the editMode and book objects to be passed down from the book component via one-way data binding. Figure 6.10 shows the new edit-book component.

Two way data-binding is configured on the book.title and book.description view-model properties.

The user clicks the Edit button to initiate changes on the edit-book form.

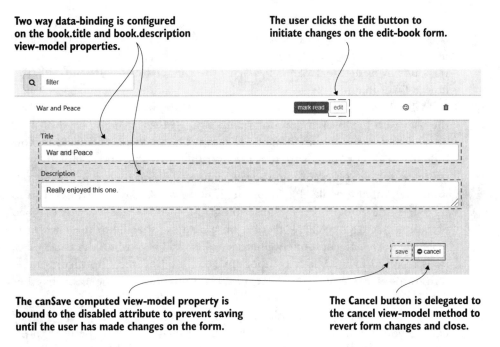

The canSave computed view-model property is bound to the disabled attribute to prevent saving until the user has made changes on the form.

The Cancel button is delegated to the cancel view-model method to revert form changes and close.

Figure 6.10 The `edit-book` **component, which captures user input using a combination of two-way binding and event delegation**

The user interacts with the `edit-book` component by clicking the Edit button on the `book` component. Set up one-way binding from the `edit-book` component to the `edit-Mode` property on the `book` component. This means that when the user clicks the Edit button, the `edit-book` component is notified that it's time to open. Once the form is opened, users can edit the `title` and `description` properties on the bound book. One of the features provided by the `edit-book` component is the ability to undo edits on a given book. Implement this feature by saving the book passed to you via data binding from the parent component into a temporary variable called `temporaryBook`, `this.temporaryBook = Object.assign({}, this.book)`. The value of the temporary book is reset within the Aurelia `bind` component-lifecycle hook (called by the framework when the binding process has started). This ensures that each time the edit form is opened, you get a fresh copy of the temporary book.

This component will also have some smarts around when users can save changes. Add a `canSave` method, computed from the `title` and `description` on the temporary book, allowing you to disable the Save button until one of these values has been edited.

Users can also cancel edits (implemented by the `cancel` method). This reverts all changes by resetting the temporary book back to the unmodified value (`this.temporaryBook = this.book`) and closes the edit form by publishing an event that the editMode has been changed. Alternatively, if the user wants to save edits, they can click the save button. The Save button (delegated to the save method in this view-model) triggers an event that informs the parent (books) component, which then responds by using the BookApi to persist the change to the backend API (though, for now, it fakes that part).

A loading state (implemented via the loading property) will be used to provide the user with feedback that a potentially slow API call is being fired off in the background that may take some time to respond. The tricky part arises when you need to hide the loading indicator to show the user that the API call is complete.

Because you're publishing an event when the Save button is clicked rather than implementing the book API call inline, how do you know when the API call has completed? You'll achieve this by subscribing to the book-save-complete (`book-save-complete-${this.book.Id}`) event on a channel specific to the current book's ID from the attached component-lifecycle callback. Then, when the BookApi call promise is resolved in the books component (modified in step 7 to incorporate this subscription), it can notify the edit-book component that the book has been saved successfully.

The astute reader may notice that this is a break from the data-down, actions-up pattern you've followed so far. The Event Aggregator can also be used to pass events down or across the component hierarchy. It's useful in this case, because the child component has a question it needs answered from the parent component, which is inconvenient to answer with data binding (namely, "Can you let me know when the save has completed so that I can refresh my state?").

The edit-book component is a child component of the book component. To add this component, start by creating a new edit-book view-model at ./src/resources/ elements/edit-book.js with the contents of the following listing.

Listing 6.7 Creating the edit-book view-model—edit-book.js

```
import {bindable, inject, computedFrom} from 'aurelia-framework';
import {EventAggregator} from 'aurelia-event-aggregator';        Imports the lodash
import _ from 'lodash';                                           utilities module for
                                                                  the isEqual method
@inject(EventAggregator)         Imports the Event Aggregator to
export class EditBook{           notify and subscribe to events

                                                                 editMode passed from
    @bindable editMode;                                          the parent component
    @bindable book;                                              using one-way binding

    constructor(eventAggregator){           Book passed from the parent
        this.resetTempBook();               component using one-way binding
        this.eventAggregator = eventAggregator;
    }

    bind(){                                 Resets the book value to the
        this.resetTempBook();               temporary value to undo changes
    }
```

```
editModeChanged(editModeNew, editModeOld){
    if(editModeNew) this.resetTempBook();
}
```
Watches for the edit-mode change and resets the temporary book

Books can be saved if they have been edited.
```
@computedFrom('temporaryBook.title', 'temporaryBook.description')
get canSave(){
    return this.temporaryBook &&
            !_.isEqual(this.temporaryBook, this.book);
}
```
canSave computed property binds via one-way binding to the edit-book view

canSave book calculation

Resets the temporary book ready for the next edit
```
resetTempBook(){
    this.temporaryBook = Object.assign({}, this.book);
}
```

```
cancel(){
    this.temporaryBook = this.book;
    this.toggleEditMode();
}
```
Cancels the delegate method, reverts changes on the book, and closes the edit form

Saves delegate method to be called from the button on the view
```
save(){
    this.loading = true;
    this.publishBookSavedEvent();
}
```
Sets the loading state on the form prior to initializing the async task

Publishes the book-saved event to be picked up by the parent component

Method to be called when the book has been saved
```
bookSaveComplete(){
    this.loading = false;
    this.saved = true;
    setTimeout(() => {
        this.resetTempBook();
        this.saved = false;
        this.toggleEditMode();
    }, 500);
}
```
Removes the loading status

Sets the saved status temporarily to show a tick when saved

Hides the success-indicator icon (tick) by toggling the saved state, and closes the edit form

Publishes the save-book event to be picked up by the parent
```
publishBookSavedEvent(){
    this.eventAggregator.publish('save-book', this.temporaryBook);
}
```

```
attached(){
    this.bookSaveCompleteSubscription
        = this.eventAggregator
        .subscribe(`book-save-complete-${this.book.Id}`,
            () => this.bookSaveComplete());
}
```
Listens for the book-save-complete event on the Event Aggregator

Toggles the edit mode to close the form when edits are complete
```
toggleEditMode(){
    this.eventAggregator.publish('edit-mode-changed', !this.editMode );
}
```

```
detached(){
    this.bookSaveCompleteSubscription.dispose();
}
```
Cleans up the Event Aggregator subscriptions

```
}
```

With the backing view-model in place, create the corresponding `edit-book` view. This view will make use of your `date-format` value converter to transform the `readDate` into a format suitable for display using the combination of a one-way string-interpolation binding and the `toView` value converter, `${book.readDate | dateFormat}`.

You'll control the edit form's visibility with the `editMode` received from the parent view (book). This allows you to only show the form after the user has clicked the Edit button.

The view-model currently has two editable properties, `title` and `description`. Two-way data bindings are set up between the view and view-model for each of these fields to ensure that the view-model is notified of any edits: `value.bind="temporary-Book.title"`. A calculated property is used to control whether the book edits can be saved by using a `disabled` binding on the Save button to prevent this action if no changes have been made: `disabled.bind="!canSave"`. As a pattern, this is a useful way of preventing a user from proceeding to the next step of a UI workflow until they've completed the required steps.

You'll also add visual feedback to indicate to the user that there could be a potential delay when they click the Save button due to the backend HTTP call using a Font Awesome loading icon. This icon is conditionally displayed (using a template conditional) based on the current loading state, `show.bind="loading"`. The Cancel button delegates to the `cancel` method on the `edit-book` view-model, `click.delegate="cancel()"`, which reverts any pending edits on the current book, as you saw in listing 6.7, and closes the edit form.

Create a new `edit-book` view file at ./src/resources/elements/edit-book.html with the following code.

Listing 6.8 Creating the `edit-book` view—edit-book.html

Imports the date-format value converter

```
<template>
    <require from='../value-converters/date-format'></require>    ⟵
    <div
        class="edit-book ${editMode ? 'visible': 'hidden'} }">        Conditionally
            transformable">                                          shows the
        <div class="wrapper">                                        component
            <div class="row">                                        based on
                <span class="col-3 offset-md-10">                    editMode
                    <small class="text-muted">
                        ${book.readDate | dateFormat}    ⟵       Applies the
                    </small>                                      date-format
                </span>                                           value converter
            </div>                                                to readDate
            <form>
                <div class="form-group row">
                    <label for="title">Title</label>
                    <input type="text"
                        class="form-control"
                        id="title"
```

```
                                        value.bind="temporaryBook.title"
                                        placeholder="book title">
                        </div>
                        <div class="form-group row">
                            <label for="description">Description</label>
                            <textarea class="form-control"
                                    id="description"
                                    value.bind="temporaryBook.description"
                                    placeholder="book description">
                            </textarea>
                        </div>
                        <hr/>

                        <div class="form-inline col-3 offset-lg-10 col-sm-12">

                            <div class="custom-control" show.bind="loading">
                                <i class="fa fa-spinner fa-pulse fa-fw"></i>
                                <span class="sr-only">Loading...</span>
                            </div>
                            <div class="custom-control brand-highlight"
                                show.bind="saved">
                                <i class="fa fa-check" aria-hidden="true"></i>
                            </div>
                            <button class="btn btn-secondary btn-sm padded"
                                    click.delegate="save()"
                                    disabled.bind="!canSave"> save
                            </button>
                            <button class="btn btn-secondary btn-sm"
                                    click.delegate="cancel()">
                                <span class="cancel">
                                    <i class="fa fa-minus-circle"></i>
                                </span> cancel
                            </button>
                        </div>

                </form>
            </div>
        </div>
    </template>
```

Annotations (left margin):
- **Two-way binding between the input field and the temporary title** → `value.bind="temporaryBook.title"`
- **Two-way binding between the input field and the temporary description** → `value.bind="temporaryBook.description"`
- **Loader to indicate a slow API call** → `<div class="custom-control" show.bind="loading">`
- **Save button click event is delegated to the save method on the view-model** → `click.delegate="save()"`
- **Save button is disabled if the book hasn't been edited** → `disabled.bind="!canSave"`
- **Cancel button is delegated to cancel the view-model method** → `click.delegate="cancel()"`

6.5.6 *Step 6: Modifying the book-list component*

In this step, clean up the book-list view by delegating the book-management functionality for individual books to the book custom-element component, which you'll require into the view, `<require from="./book"></require>`. Then apply the containerless attribute provided by the Aurelia framework to the `<book containerless>` book element. This attribute ensures that, when rendered to the browser, the element will be injected with a top-level element of `<li>` rather than `<book>` so that Bootstrap styles are applied correctly. The book object is passed down to the book component with the same data-down approach to data flow.

Modify the book-list component to use the new book component rather than implementing this functionality inline. Change the view at ./src/resources/elements/book-list.html, replacing the contents as shown in the following listing.

Listing 6.9   Adding the `book` custom element to the `book-list` view—book-list.html

```
<template>
    <require from="../attributes/tooltip"></require>
    <require from="./book"></require>                              Imports the new book
    <require from="../value-converters/filter"></require>         custom element
    <div class="card">
        ...
        <ul class="books list-group list-group-flush">           Sets the book as
            <book                                                 containerless so that
                                                                  Bootstrap styles work
                containerless                                     correctly
                repeat.for="book of books | filter:searchTerm"
                book.bind="book"                                  Passes the book
                search-term.bind="searchTerm">                    in the current
            </book>                                               iteration to the
        </ul>                                                     book component
    </div>

</template>
```

References the book element → `<book`

6.5.7   Step 7: Modifying the books component

Now that you've got the required components in place, it's time to modify the `books` component to enable orchestration for the new events that will be received from and sent to the child components via the Event Aggregator. This is the last step in the process, and it closes off this new functionality.

The `removeBook` implementation will be switched out to remove books by a specific ID rather than taking the `index` of the book in the `book-list` repeater, as it did earlier. This makes it more flexible and decouples it from the `book-list` component.

Following the same pattern for subscribing to events on the Event Aggregator that you used with both the `book` and `edit-book` view models, hook into the `attached` callback to subscribe to events raised by the `book` and `edit-book` child components. The `books` view-model will subscribe to two events from the Event Aggregator: `'book-removed'` (indicates that a book should be removed from the list by ID) and `'save-book'` (indicates that the specified book should be saved). These two events lay the groundwork for the HTTP interactions for saving and deleting books via the backend API that we'll cover in chapter 8.

Use the Event Aggregator to notify the `edit-book` component when the save has been completed, `this.eventAggregator.publish(`book-save-complete-${saved-Book.Id}`)`, so that it knows when to change the state on the loading widget and inform the user that the save has been successful.

Again, following the same pattern as with the `book` and `edit-book` view-models, you can clean up any active subscriptions on the Event Aggregator when the component is removed from the DOM by hooking into the `detached` component-lifecycle callback.

Modify the `books` view-model at ./src/resources/elements/books.js as shown in the following listing.

Listing 6.10 Incorporating `book` and `edit-book` component interactions—books.js

```
import {bindable, inject, computedFrom} from 'aurelia-framework';
import {BookApi} from '../../services/book-api';
import {EventAggregator} from 'aurelia-event-aggregator';
import _ from 'lodash';

@inject(BookApi, EventAggregator)
export class Books {
```

> Removes the @observable bookTitle property from above the constructor

```
  constructor(...){
    ...
  }
```

> Swaps the implementation of remove book to use an ID rather than an index

```
  removeBook(toRemove){

    let bookIndex = _.findIndex(this.books, book => {
      return book.Id === toRemove.Id;
    });

    this.books.splice(bookIndex, 1);
  }

  ...
  attached(){
    this.subscribeToEvents();
  }
```

> Subscribes to the Event Aggregator events in attached callback

```
  ...
  subscribeToEvents(){
      this.bookRemovedSubscription =
          this.eventAggregator.subscribe('book-removed',
                      bookIndex => this.removeBook(bookIndex));
```

> Subscribes to the book-removed event to remove a book from the array

> Subscribes to the save-book event to notify subscribers a book has been modified

```
      this.bookSavedSubscription =
      this.eventAggregator.subscribe('save-book',
                          book => this.bookSaved(book));
  }
  ...
  bookSaved(updatedBook){
      let index = this.books.findIndex(book => book.Id == updatedBook.Id);
          Object.assign(this.books[index], updatedBook);
      this.bookApi
          .saveBook(updatedBook)
          .then((savedBook) =>
          this.eventAggregator.publish(
          `book-save-complete-${savedBook.Id}`));
  }
```

> Saves the book using the book API

> Publishes a save-book-complete event for a specific book

```
  ...

  detached(){
    this.bookRemovedSubscription.dispose();
    this.bookSavedSubscription.dispose();
  }
}
```

> Cleans up the Event Aggregator subscriptions in a detached callback

With the two new components in place, let's review the overall communication flow between each of the book-management components:

1   The `books` array is passed from the `books` component to the `book-list` using one-way data binding.

2   Individual books are then bound from the `book-list` (via the repeater) onto `book` component instances.

3   `Book` instances are then passed down to the `edit-book` component, along with the `editMode` of the form.

4   Clicking the Save button on the `edit-book` view delegates to a view-model method that publishes an event on the `save-book` Event Aggregator channel.

5   The `books` component subscribes to this event and responds by saving the book, using the `BookApi` service.

Because the `saveBook` method is an asynchronous call, the `edit-book` component shows a loading dialog whenever a book is saved, and as such, needs to know when the save operation has been completed. The `books` component does this by publishing an event on the Event Aggregator channel, which the `edit-book` component subscribes to, so it can update its status when the save operation has been completed. After the book is saved or canceled using the edit form on the `edit-book` component, an event is published on the `edit-mode-changed` Event Aggregator channel, indicating to the `book` component (a subscriber of this event) that the form should be closed. Apart from one exception with the `book-save-complete` event, this data flow follows the data-down, actions-up approach. This data flow is depicted in figure 6.11.

If you reload the browser, the book-management page should now incorporate the new components, as shown in figure 6.12.

Now that you can edit book details, it's time to get a bit fancier and add a star-rating component to allow users to rate books they've read. In section 6.6, we'll implement a new `star-rating` custom element component with the aid of custom events.

6.6   *Custom events*

Whether it's clicking a button or receiving input-validation feedback, users interact with web applications via DOM events. Responding to such events is a piece of cake. But when it comes to custom controls, there are various techniques available for handling events. These techniques vary based on the framework author and differ from responses to native browser events such as `click`. Custom events allow you to create your own events that can be fired on native DOM elements. These events can be handled in the same way that you'd handle a regular DOM event. This is useful as a component author, because it makes it easier for other developers to learn and use your component. Custom events are also great for intercomponent-communication scenarios where you don't want to take a dependency on the Event Aggregator. A good example of this is a custom control such as an enhanced select list element. In such a

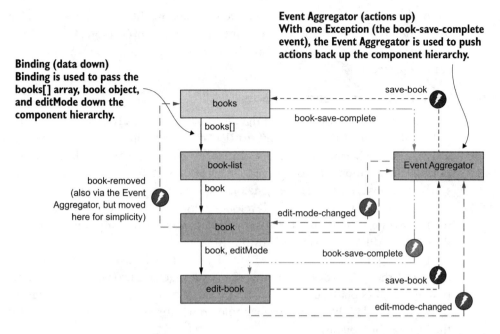

Figure 6.11 **Intercomponent communication flow between the two new components,** `book` **and** `edit-book`, **and the existing components,** `book` **and** `book-list`. **One-way data binding is used to pass data down the component hierarchy. A number of events (such as** `edit-mode-changed` **and** `save-book`) **are pushed through to the EventAggregator, which routes them up the** `books` **component hierarchy to the destination components.**

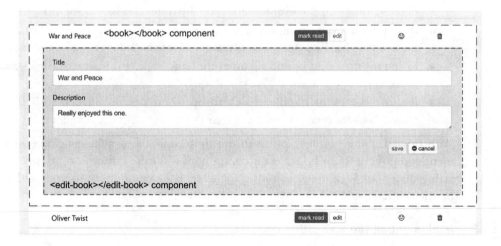

Figure 6.12 **Book-management page modified to incorporate the two new components:** `book` **and** `edit-book`

control, custom events could be created for actions like select-value-changed to allow the consumer to easily wire it into their own application. Custom events also minimize the Aurelia-specific code in a control, making it more portable to non-Aurelia projects.

6.6.1   *Browser support for custom events*

Custom events are supported in Edge, Firefox 11, Safari 11, and Chrome 15. You can polyfill if you need to support IE9 to IE11 by using a library like custom-elements-polyfill, which can be found at https://www.npmjs.com/package/custom-event-polyfill. Basic support is also present in Firefox 6, IE 9, and Safari 5.1 (533.3). Basic support means a more verbose syntax is required to use custom events in these browsers. This article on the Mozilla developer network is a good resource if you want to further explore the syntax for basic support: https://developer.mozilla.org/en-US/docs/Web/API/CustomEvent/CustomEvent.

The good news is that, by using Aurelia, you'll get a custom-event polyfill included as part of the pal-browser package. This package is a browser-specific implementation of Aurelia's platform-abstraction layer, which gives you a platform-agnostic way to work with Aurelia's libraries. For example, some Aurelia libraries can be used in either the browser or Node.js.

6.6.2   *Using custom events*

You can use custom events in your JavaScript applications by following these five steps:

1 Import the DOM class from the aurelia-framework package.
2 Create the new custom event using the createCustomEvent method; for example, DOM.createCustomEvent('change'). You can optionally pass additional details along with the event as additional parameters to this method.
3 Dispatch the event using the dispatchEvent method on the element you want the event to be fired on, this.element.dispatchEvent(changeEvent);.
4 Listen for the event by adding an event handler, this.listener = e => handle-Event();.
5 Remove the event handler to clean up when you're finished with the event this.element.removeEventListener('change', this.listener);.

With this taken care of, let's put it to use by adding a new star-rating custom element component to my-books. This component will raise custom events any time the rating on a book is changed, allowing the edit-book component to update the status on the relevant book.

6.6.3   *Implementing the star-rating component*

Start by adding a new star-rating view-model file at ./src/resources/elements/star-rating.js and adding the contents of listing 6.11. This view-model has a lot of code, but don't worry, it's all very simple.

Most of this listing is pure JavaScript, so we won't go into all of it in great detail. That said, from an Aurelia perspective, this example provides some interesting take-aways. To begin with, the DOM element that this custom element view-model is associated with is injected using the `@inject` decorator `@inject(Element)`. Store a reference to this element in the constructor, so that you can then fire the `change` custom event on this element when the new rating is selected.

Use the `bind` component-lifecycle callback again in this view-model. This time, take the rating value (1 to 5) passed from the parent component (`edit-book`) and use it to highlight the relevant number of stars. For example, if a book has a rating of 3, you highlight three stars because of the value applied in the `bind()` method.

The `rate()` method is bound to the `click.delegate` binding command on the `star-rating` view. This method applies the star rating to the component based on the index of the star clicked and then raises a custom event to inform the `edit-book` component of the new rating.

The `raiseChangedEvent` performs the second and third steps in the custom-event-management process mentioned in section 6.6.2 (create the custom event, dispatch the event). A new event named `'change'` is created using the `createCustomEvent` method, passing along the star rating. This event is then dispatched on the custom element that you saved a reference to in the constructor.

Listing 6.11 A new star-rating custom element view-model—star-rating.js

```
import {inject, bindable, DOM} from 'aurelia-framework';

@inject(Element)                          Injects a reference to
export class StarRating{                  the current element

    @bindable rating;                     Declares a bindable
                                          rating property
    constructor(element){
                                          Takes the current element
        this.element = element;           in the constructor
        this.stars = [
                        { type: '-o', displayType: '-o', rated : false },
                        { type: '-o', displayType: '-o', rated : false },
                        { type: '-o', displayType: '-o', rated : false },
                        { type: '-o', displayType: '-o', rated : false },
                        { type: '-o', displayType: '-o', rated : false }
                     ];

        this.hovered = false;             Defaults the star
    }                                     hovered state to false

    bind(){
        this.applyRating(this.rating);    Applies the rating
    }                                     bound from the
                                          parent on bind()
```

Declares the star-rating default data

Applies the rating on each of the stars

```
applyRating(rating){
    this.stars.forEach((star, index) =>
                          this.rateStar(star, rating, index));
}
```

Applies the rating for an individual star

```
rateStar(star, rating, index){

    if(index < rating) this.toggleOn(star);
    else {
        this.toggleOff(star);
    }

}
```

Toggles a star to 'rated'

```
toggleOn(star){
    star.displayType = '';
    star.type = '';
    star.rated = true;
}
```

Toggles a star to 'unrated'

```
toggleOff(star){
    star.displayType = '-o';
    star.type = '-o';
    star.rated = false;
}
```

Calculates the star rating based on the stars index

```
ratingFromIndex(index, star){

    if(index === 0 && star.rated) return 0;

    return index + 1;

}
```

Rates a star with a given index

```
rate(index){

    let rating = this.ratingFromIndex(index, this.stars[0]);

    this.rating = rating;

    this.applyRating(rating);

    this.raiseChangedEvent();

}
```

Handles the mouse-out exit from a star

```
mouseOut(hoverIndex){

    if(!this.hovered) return;

    this.hovered = false;

    this.applyHoverState(hoverIndex);
}
```

```
applyHoverState(hoverIndex){
    this.stars.forEach((star, index) =>{
        if(!this.shouldApplyHover(index, hoverIndex, star)) return;

        if(this.hovered){
            this.toggleDisplayOn(star);
        }
        else{
            this.toggleDisplayOff(star);
        }
    });
}
mouseOver(hoverIndex){
    if(this.hovered) return;

    this.hovered = true;

    this.applyHoverState(hoverIndex);
}
toggleDisplayOff(star){
    star.displayType = star.type;
}

toggleDisplayOn(star){
    star.displayType = '';
}

shouldApplyHover(starIndex, hoverIndex, star){
    return starIndex <= hoverIndex && !star.rated;
}

raiseChangedEvent(){
    let changeEvent =
    DOM.createCustomEvent('change', {detail:{rating: this.rating}});
    this.element.dispatchEvent(changeEvent);
}
}
```

Applies the hovered state to a star

Handles the mouse-over event on a star

Toggles the star-displayed status to off

Toggles the star-displayed status to on

Calculates whether a hover state should be applied to a star

Raises a custom 'change' event to be handled by other components

Dispatches the rating-changed custom event

Creates the custom event, passing along the star rating

Now that you have the view-model in place, you need to create the corresponding view to complete the star-rating custom-element component. For a small snippet of code, listing 6.12 has quite a lot happening in it. To begin, use the repeat.for template repeater to render a <li> element for each of the stars. The click event on these elements is delegated to the rate method on the view-model, which allows a rating to be applied when a star is clicked. The $index contextual-repeater property is passed to the rate() method to indicate the rating value to apply. The mouseover and mouseout events are also delegated to view-model methods. These are used to change the hover state on stars, highlighting them if they don't have a rating applied yet.

The debounce binding behavior is applied to both the mouseover and mouseout events to limit the frequency at which you update the hover state. The rating stars are represented using the fa fa-star Font Awesome icon. This icon is wrapped in a span to allow the color to be changed to a highlight yellow when a star has a rating applied. String interpolation bindings are used to apply both the span class and the Font Awesome icon type based on values on the star-rating view-model.

Create a new star-rating view file at ./src/resources/elements/star-rating.html, and add the contents shown in the following listing.

Listing 6.12   Creating a `star-rating` custom element view—star-rating.html

```
<template>
  <ul class="ratings">
    <li repeat.for="star of stars"          ◁— Renders a li for each star
        click.delegate="rate($index)"        ◁— Delegates the click event on a star to the rate() method passing the $index
        mouseover.delegate="mouseOver($index)
          & debounce:100"
        mouseout.delegate="mouseOut($index)   ◁— Delegates the mouseOut event to the view-model method
          & debounce:100">
      <span
        class="star ${star.displayType === '' ? 'rated' : ''}">   ◁—
        <i class="fa fa-star${star.displayType}" ></i>   ◁—
      </span>                                String interpolation star class
    </li>
  </ul>
</template>
```

Delegates the mouseOver event to the view-model method

Applies the debounce binding behavior to limit event frequency

Applies the debounce binding behavior to limit event frequency

String interpolation binding on the Font Awesome star icon

With the star-rating element completed, you finally get to make use of it by including it and subscribing to rating-changed events on the edit-book view-model. Modify the edit-book view-model file, ./src/resources/elements/edit-book.js, to listen for custom events raised from the star-rating component.

Listing 6.13   Using the `star-rating` component—edit-book.js

```
...
export class EditBook{

  ...

  constructor(eventAggregator){          ◁— Creates a handler method for rating-changed events
    ...
    this.ratingChangedListener =
      e => this.temporaryBook.rating = e.rating;
  }

  bind(){                                 Adds a listener on the rating element to handle changed events
    this.resetTempBook();
    this.ratingElement
      .addEventListener("change", this.ratingChangedListener);   ◁—
  }
  ...
  @computedFrom('temporaryBook.title',
               'temporaryBook.description',   ◁— Modifies the @computedFrom expression to include rating-change detection
               'temporaryBook.rating')
```

```
get canSave(){
    return this.temporaryBook
        && !_.isEqual(this.temporaryBook, this.book);
}

...

cancel(){

    this.temporaryBook = this.book;
    this.starRatingViewModel
        .applyRating(this.temporaryBook.rating);      Undoes any rating
    this.toggleEditMode();                            changes on cancel
}
...
                                                      Removes the
                                                      change-event
detached(){                                           listener to cleanup
    this.bookSaveCompleteSubscription.dispose();
    this.ratingElement
        .removeEventListener('change', this.ratingChangedListener);
}
}
```

Consuming the `star-rating` component from the `edit-book` view-model is a trivial process. Hook into the `bind` component-lifecycle event, adding a listener to the change event on the `ratingElement`. This property value is bound from the `edit-book` view using the `ref="ratingElement"` expression, as shown in listing 6.14.

On receiving this event, run the `ratingChangedListener` handler created in the `edit-book` constructor and apply the rating that you received in the `change` event to the temporary book. If the book is saved, the new rating is applied to the book linked to the edit form. If the user clicks Cancel, the rating is reverted to its pre-edit value. If the user cancels their edits, revert the star-rating value on the `star-rating` component. You do this by taking a reference on the view-model using the `view-model.ref` view-template expression (listing 6.14) and then calling the `applyRating` method on this view-model to set the star rating back to the pre-edit value. Lastly, clean up by hooking into the `detached` component-lifecycle callback and removing the `change` star-rating handler before the view is removed from the DOM.

With event management in place, finalize the `star-rating` component implementation by using it in the `edit-book` view. Modify the `edit-book` view at ./src/resources/elements/edit-book.html to make use of the `star-rating` custom-element component.

Listing 6.14 Using the `star-rating` component—edit-book.html

```
<template>                                          Requires the star-
    ...                                             rating custom element
    <require from='./star-rating'></require>        into the view
    ......
    <div ref="editFormDiv" class="edit-book         Gets a reference to
        ${editMode ? 'visible' : 'hidden'} transformable">   the edit form div for
                                                    use in the view-model
```

```
<div class="wrapper">
    <div class="row">
        <span class="col-3 offset-md-10">...</span>
    </div>
    <form>
        ...
        <hr/>
        <star-rating
            view-model.ref="starRatingViewModel"
            ref="ratingElement"
            rating.bind="temporaryBook.rating">
        </star-rating>
        ...
</template>
```

References the star-rating element

Creates a view-model reference to the starRating view-model

Makes the ratingElement available to the edit-book view-model

Binds the rating on the star-book component to the book's rating

In listing 6.14, you pass a reference to the `star-rating` element itself to the `EditBook` view-model using the `ref="ratingElement"` template expression. The `ref=ELEMENT _NAME` template expression creates a property on the view-model to hold the DOM element named in the expression. In this, it allows you to attach an event handler for the `'change'` to the DOM element of the `star-rating` custom element and respond to this event by calling the `ratingChangedListener` method.

With the `star-rating` custom element in place, run the `au run --watch` command to reinitialize the my-books application, and navigate to http://localhost:9000 to view the results in your browser. It should look something like figure 6.13. You can download the completed project from GitHub at https://github.com/freshcutdevelopment/Aurelia-in-Action.git using the `git clone` command.

Figure 6.13   Book-management functionality extended to include the new `star-rating` component

With the additional functionality enabled by the Aurelia Event Aggregator and custom events, my-books is starting to take the shape of a more realistic SPA. In the next chapter, you'll enhance it further, adding more-advanced form components such as check boxes and drop-down lists. You'll also add validation to the form using the Aurelia validation plugin. In doing so, you'll become familiar with the variety of observer types that make up Aurelia's powerful binding engine.

Summary

- Aurelia has three main intercomponent communication techniques: binding, the Event Aggregator, and custom events.
- Binding is useful in scenarios when you need to pass data from a parent component down the component hierarchy.
- Binding breaks down when you attempt to use it to communicate back up or across a component hierarchy due to the intercomponent coupling created by shared state.
- A good convention to follow with intercomponent communication is data down, actions up. This can be achieved by using binding to pass data down the component hierarchy, and then using either the Event Aggregator or custom events to pass actions up.
- The Event Aggregator is your go-to tool for communicating between various levels of the component hierarchy, including child-to-parent and child-to-sibling relationships.
- Custom events are great for when you don't want to take a dependency on the Aurelia Event Aggregator, or when you have a more general component that you may want to use outside of your Aurelia application.

Working with forms

Forms are one of the primary ways that users interact with your website. Well-implemented forms make users happy. Conversely, poorly implemented forms can slow down or stop user activity on your site. You can address two of the main aspects of well-built forms using Aurelia's binding and validation components. Binding can be used to provide rapid feedback, guiding the user on the correct form journey by making their next action obvious. Validation can be used to show users the feedback they need to submit the form in a way that's unobtrusive and avoids breaking user flow. In this chapter, you'll learn how to use the main HTML form elements that you're used to, such as check boxes, radio elements, select controls, and text input, with Aurelia's binding system. You'll then learn how to add validation to your Aurelia forms using Aurelia's validation plugin.

7.1 *Working with forms in my-books*

You'll expand on the work that you started in chapter 4, enhancing the book-management functionality in my-books to allow for more-comprehensive edits on book metadata. These enhancements will include the following:

- *Users can add or edit book genres*—To be implemented with a select element binding
- *Users can allocate books to a specific book shelf (a way of grouping books into certain preset buckets)*—To be implemented using a multiple-select binding
- *Users can specify whether they own a book*—To be implemented with an `input` `checked` binding
- *Users can specify the number of times they've read a book*—To be implemented using a two-way binding, combined with the Aurelia validation plugin to ensure that the value entered is a valid integer

By the end of this chapter, the updated edit-book form should look like figure 7.1.

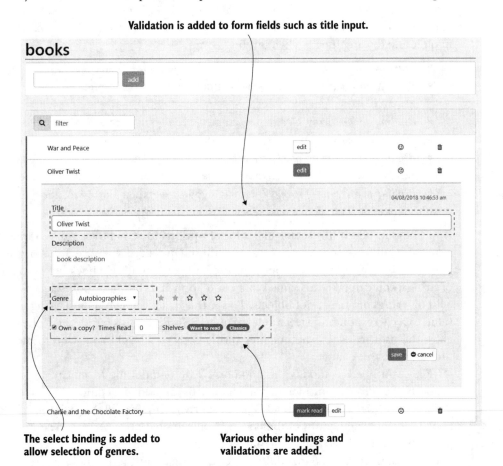

Figure 7.1   The my-books book-management page modified to support more-comprehensive edits on book metadata and form validation

With our vision laid out for where we want to go with the edit-book form, let's dive right in and start making the required changes. In the next section, you'll initiate these changes by adding the `own-a-copy` check-box binding.

Before you get started, you'll need to update your ./books.json seed file with the contents of the chapter 5 version of this file from GitHub at http://mng.bz/y21e. New fields have been added to the book models to support the examples in chapter 5.

7.2   *Check boxes*

Check boxes in Aurelia behave like you'd expect in a standard HTML page. In Aurelia, it's far simpler to keep the state of the value or an array of checked values on the view-model in sync with the corresponding `input checked` value or values in the view. Aurelia achieves this by subscribing to changes on the element and corresponding view-model property using a *checked observer*. The checked observer listens for value changes on each of the checked input elements bound to properties on the view-model. This is a two-way binding, and it's set up by applying the `checked` binding command to one or more `input` elements on the view. The following scenarios can be implemented using the `checked` binding command:

- *Binding to a Boolean value*—`<input type='checkbox' checked.bind='readBook' >`
- *Binding to an array of numbers*—`<input model.bind='genreId' checked.bind ='genreIds' type='checkbox'>`
- *Binding to an array of objects*—`<input type='checkbox' model.bind='genre' checked.bind='genres' >`
- *Binding to an array of objects with a matcher*—`<input type='checkbox' model .bind='genre' checked.bind='genres' matcher.bind='genreMatcher' >`
- *Binding to an array of strings*—`<input type='checkbox' value.bind='genreName' checked.bind='genreNames'>`

Don't be daunted if this seems like a lot of options to remember. Aurelia follows the same conventions for binding to each of these types across several kinds of form elements. This means that once you learn the syntax for binding check boxes to an array of strings, you can take this same syntax and apply it to binding multiselect controls to a list of strings or an array of objects. To see this in action, you'll bind a single checked value to a corresponding view-model property. You'll do this by adding a check box to allow the user to select whether they own a copy of a book. You need to modify two files to make this change.

First, you need to modify the edit-book.js view-model file to make use of the new property. To refresh your memory, in chapter 6, you added a computed property, `canSave`, to the `EditBook` view-model. This property calculates whether the user can save a book based on whether any of the book's properties have been edited. The value of this property is recalculated each time one of the properties included in the `@computedFrom` decorator has its value changed. Because you'll be adding a new field to the form, you need to add the new metadata property, `ownACopy`, to the `computedFrom` listing to ensure that the canSave value is recalculated when the corresponding check box on the view is checked or unchecked. Modify the view-model in the ./src/resources/elements/edit-book.js file as shown in the following listing to incorporate this property.

Listing 7.1 Using the ownACopy book property in the view-model (edit-book.js)

```
...
    constructor(eventAggregator ){
        this.resetTempBook();

        this.eventAggregator = eventAggregator;
        this.ratingChangedListener =
                        e => this.temporaryBook.rating = e.rating;
    }

@inject(EventAggregator, BookApi )
export class EditBook{


    @computedFrom('temporaryBook.title',
                  'temporaryBook.description',       ownACopy book property
                  'temporaryBook.rating',            included in canSave
                  'temporaryBook.ownACopy')   ◁──┘   computed property
    get canSave(){
        return this.temporaryBook
        && !_.isEqual(this.temporaryBook, this.book);
    }
    ...
```

With the required view-model changes in places, let's update the edit-book.html view file to add a new check box to the form. To do this, add a new input element of the checkbox type. Because the input type is set to checkbox, you can use the checked binding command to bind the temporaryBook.ownACopy view-model property to the checked value on the input element. As with the other input elements you've looked at so far, this binding is two-way by default. Modify the ./src/resources/elements/edit-book.html view file to include the new input element.

Listing 7.2 Using the ownACopy book property in the view (edit-book.html)

```
<template>
    <require from='./star-rating'></require>
    <require from='../value-converters/date-format'></require>
    <div ref="editFormDiv"
         class="edit-book ${editMode ? 'visible': 'hidden'} transformable">
        <div class="wrapper">
            ...
            <form>
            ...
                <hr/>
                <div class="form-inline row">
                    <star-rating
                        ...
```

Bootstrap styles on the check box with added spacing

Bootstrap styles on the label

Bootstrap styles on the input

Adds a new form styled with the Bootstrap form-inline class

Checked binding command is applied to check-box input element

```
            </star-rating>
        </div>
        <hr/>
        <div class="form-inline row">
            <div class="form-check mb-2 mr-sm-2 mb-sm-0">
                <label class="form-check-label">
                    <input class="form-check-input"
                        type="checkbox"
                        checked.bind="temporaryBook.ownACopy"/>
                    Own a copy?
                </label>
            </div>
        </div>
        <hr/>
        <div class="form-inline col-3 offset-lg-10 col-sm-12">
            ...
        </div>
        </form>
    </div>
  </div>
</template>
```

Reloading the browser, the page should look something like figure 7.2.

This isn't an exhaustive list of check-box binding scenarios. If you want to read more about the syntax required for several other scenarios (for example, binding to an array

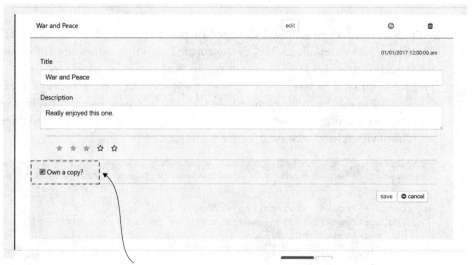

The checked.bind binding command is applied to an input check box bound to the temporaryBook.ownACopy property.

Figure 7.2   Check box added using the `checked.bind` binding command to create a two-way data binding between the check box on the view and the `temporaryBook.ownACopy` view-model property

of numbers) check out the Aurelia site at http://aurelia.io/docs/binding/checkboxes. Next, we'll look at the options available for binding to radio elements and add the ability to select a book's genre.

7.3 Radio elements

Like check boxes, radio elements in Aurelia are also used in the way that you'd be familiar with from standard HTML, but with two main differences:

- You'll typically use a template repeater to render each of the available options (in your case, the set of available genres). Input elements of the radio type with the same name are grouped together into a radio-button-group, where only one element in the group can be selected. You can define the value of each of these elements using the model property.
- These elements can be bound to a single selectedItem view-model property with two-way data binding using the checked binding command. As with the check box, this uses a checked observer to listen for change events on the input element and subscribe to changes on the bound view-model property to keep the view and view-model in sync. The difference between the checkbox and the radio element is that radio elements can be bound only to a view-model property with a single value, such as a number or string, whereas check boxes are bound to an array of values (except in the case of binding to a single Boolean value).

The following scenarios can be implemented using the checked binding command on an input element of the radio type:

- *Binding to a Boolean value*—<input type='radio' checked.bind='readBook'>
- *Binding to a number*—<input type='radio' model.bind='genreId' checked .bind='selectedGenreId'>
- *Binding to an object*—<input type='radio' model.bind='genre' checked.bind ='selectedGenre'>
- *Binding to an array of objects with a matcher*—<input model.bind="{ id: 2, genre: 'Art' }" matcher.bind="genreMatcher' checked.bind='selectedGenre'>
- *Binding to a string*—<input type='radio' value.bind='genreName' checked .bind='genreNames'>

Let's see the radio functionality in action and use it to implement an initial version of a genre-selection control in the edit-book form, as shown in figure 7.3.

To add the genres radio box, you'll first need to modify your BookApi service class to include the functionality for loading a list of genres and book shelves (not for immediate use, but we'll come back to them shortly). This change allows you to retrieve the list of genres to be rendered as radio input elements. Once you've made the required BookApi changes, modify the Books view-model to load genres and

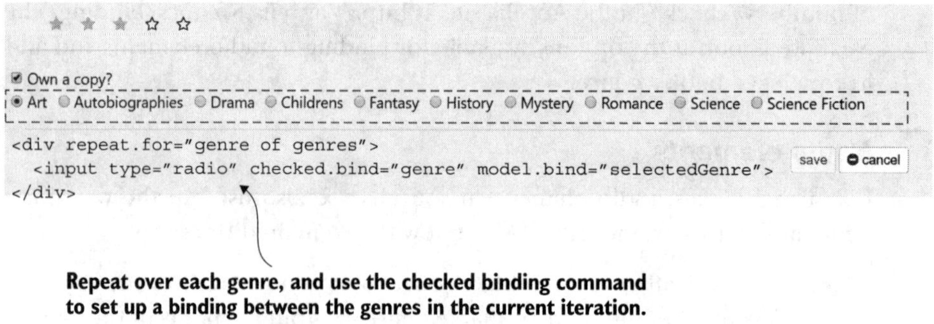

```
<div repeat.for="genre of genres">
  <input type="radio" checked.bind="genre" model.bind="selectedGenre">
</div>
```

Repeat over each genre, and use the checked binding command to set up a binding between the genres in the current iteration.

Figure 7.3   The edit-book form modified to include a radio control to allow users to select a book's genre. This uses a `Checked` binding command and a repeater to render and bind an input field for each genre in the `genres` array on the `EditBook` view-model.

shelves and pass these down to the edit-book component via one-way data binding. This modification involves the following steps:

1   Modify the book API to return hardcoded genre and shelf arrays.
2   Modify the Books view-model to load shelves and genres.
3   Pass the genre and shelf arrays down the component hierarchy to the EditBook view-model via one-way binding.
4   Modify the EditBook view-model, adding the two new bindable properties.
5   Modify the edit-book.html view file to render the list of genres and selected genre using the combination of an Aurelia template repeater, the checked binding command, and input fields of the radio type.

7.3.1   *Step 1: Modifying the book API*

The updated version of the edit-book form requires the addition of two new methods to the BookApi class: getGenres and getShelves. These methods will return a hard-coded array of values for now, which you'll swap out for real backend calls in chapter 8. In the initial implementation of this API, the saveBook functionality simulated the latency of a backend API call using the setTimeout function. In this example, refactor this logic into a simulateFetch method so that you can use it for the two new methods, getGenres and getShelves, as well. Modify the ./src/services/book-api.js file to incorporate these changes.

Listing 7.3   `BookApi` modified to include loading genres and shelves (book-api.js)

```
import {HttpClient} from 'aurelia-fetch-client';
import {inject} from 'aurelia-framework';

@inject(HttpClient)
export class BookApi{
```

```
    constructor(http){
        this.http = http;
        this.simulatedLatency = 500;          ◄─┐  Simulated latency
    }                                              lifted to a class field


    getBooks(){

    ...
    }                              New method to
                                   retrieve a preset list
                                   of book shelves
getShelves(){                  ◄─┘

    let shelves = [
                    'Classics',
                    'Want to read',
                    'Research',
                    'For the kids',
                ];


    return this.simulateFetch(shelves);


}                                 New method to
                                  retrieve a preset
                                  list of genres
getGenres(){                  ◄─┘

        let genres = [
                        {id: 1,   name:'Art'},
                        {id: 2,   name:'Autobiographies'},
                        {id: 3,   name:'Drama'},
                        {id: 4,   name:'Childrens'},
                        {id: 5,   name:'Fantasy'},
                        {id: 6,   name:'History'},
                        {id: 7,   name:'Mystery'},
                        {id: 8,   name:'Romance'},
                        {id: 9, name:'Science'},
                        {id: 10, name:'Science Fiction'},
                    ];

                                          saveBook
    return this.simulateFetch(genres);    refactored to use a
}                                         new simulateFetch
                                          method
    saveBook(book){                   ◄─┘
        return this.simulateFetch(book);
    }


    simulateFetch(fetchResult){       ◄─┐  Latency simulation
        return new Promise(resolve => {    refactored into its
            setTimeout(() => {             own method
                resolve(fetchResult);
            }, this.simulatedLatency);
        });
    }
}
```

7.3.2 *Step 2: Modifying the Books view-model*

Now that your book API has support for retrieving genres and shelves, you need to consume these in the books component, passing them down the component hierarchy using the data-down pattern covered in chapter 6.

First, modify the Books view-model to retrieve these values from the API using the new loadGenres() and loadShelves() methods, which means importing the BookApi service class into the view-model. The loadGenres() method calls the async API, receives a promise response, and then unwraps the promise result, storing the savedBooks and genres retrieved in the view-model properties.

> **Listing 7.4   Retrieving shelves and genres (books.js)**

```
...

@inject(BookApi, EventAggregator)
export class Books {
  ...

  bind(){
    this.loadBooks();          ⟵ Loads books,
    this.loadGenres();           genres, and shelves
    this.loadShelves();
  }

    loadGenres(){
      this.bookApi.getGenres()
        .then(genres =>{
            this.genres = genres;
        });
  }

  loadShelves(){
      this.bookApi.getShelves()
        .then(shelves => {
            this.shelves = shelves;
        });
  }

   loadBooks(){
      this.bookApi.getBooks()
                .then(savedBooks =>
                        this.books = savedBooks);
  }                                               ⟵ Includes an empty
  addBook () {                                       array of shelves and
    this.books                                       genres for new books
        .push({title : this.bookTitle, shelves : [], genres : []});
    this.bookTitle = "";
  }
  ...
}
```

7.3.3 Step 3: Passing the genres and shelf arrays down the component hierarchy

Modify the books view to bind the shelves and genres down from the books component, through the book-list and book components, to the edit-book component, using one-way binding as you previously did with the books[] array, as shown in the following five listings.

Listing 7.5 Binding genres and shelves down to the books view (books.html)

```
<template>
    ...
    <book-list if.bind="books.length > 0
                 && genres.length > 0
                 && shelves.length > 0"
        shelves.bind="shelves"
        genres.bind="genres"
        books.bind="books">
    </book-list>
</template>
```

Loads the book-list component only if the genres and shelves are present

Listing 7.6 Adding bindable properties to the BookList view-model (book-list.js)

```
...
@inject(EventAggregator)
export class BookList {
    @bindable books;
    @bindable shelves;
    @bindable genres;

    //-- removed redundant function --
}
```

Adds the new shelves and genres bindable properties

removeBook function removed, now handled in book component

Listing 7.7 Adding bindings for shelves and genres (book-list.html)

```
<template>
    <require from="../attributes/tooltip"></require>
    <require from="./book"></require>
    <require from="../value-converters/filter"></require>
    ...
    <ul class="books list-group list-group-flush">
        <book containerless
            ...
            shelves.bind="shelves"
            genres.bind="genres"
            search-term.bind="searchTerm"></book>
    </ul>
</template>
```

Binds the shelves and genres down to the book component

Listing 7.8 Adding shelves and genres to the Book view-model (book.js)

```
@inject(EventAggregator)
export class Book{
```

```
    @bindable book;
    @bindable genres;                    Adds the new shelves
    @bindable shelves;                   and genres bindable
    @bindable searchTerm;                properties
    ...
}
```

Listing 7.9   Binding `genres` and `shelves` to `edit-book` (book.html)

```
<template>
    ...
        <edit-book book.bind="book"
    genres.bind="genres"                 Binds the shelves and
    shelves.bind="shelves"               genres down to the
    containerless edit-mode.bind="editMode">    edit-book component
</edit-book>
    ...
</template>
```

7.3.4   Step 4: Modifying the EditBooks view-model

To make use of the values loaded and passed down from the `books` component, you need to add two new bindable properties to the view-model (`shelves` and `genres`). Next, subscribe to changed events on the new `@bindable selectedGenre` property, updating the temporary-books genre ID based on the value the user selects. You do this by following the `propertyNameChanged(newValue, oldValue)` convention, which is available for any bindable property on a view-model. In this case, the method is `selectedGenreChanged`. The book's genre is then added to the `canSave` computed-property listing to ensure that the disabled status of the Save button correctly accounts for when the user selects a genre. Modify the ./src/resources/elements/edit-book.js view-model to incorporate genre selection.

Listing 7.10   Modifying `EditBook` to include genre support (edit-book.js)

```
import {bindable, inject, computedFrom} from 'aurelia-framework';
import {EventAggregator} from 'aurelia-event-aggregator';
import _ from 'lodash';

@inject(EventAggregator, BookApi)
export class EditBook{

    ...
    @bindable selectedGenre;
    @bindable genres;
    @bindable shelves;
    temporaryBook = {};

    constructor(eventAggregator){
        ...
        this.saved = false;
    }
```

```
bind(){
    ...
```

Sets selected shelves based on book-model values

```
    this.selectedShelves =
        this.shelves.filter(shelf =>
                this.temporaryBook
                    .shelves.indexOf(shelf) !== -1);

    this.selectedGenre = this.genres
                    .find(g => g.id == this.book.genre);
}
```

Sets selected genre based on book-model value

```
toggleEditShelves(){
    this.editingShelves = !this.editingShelves;
}
```

Toggles edit mode on shelves to enable select control

```
unToggleEditShelves(){
    this.temporaryBook.shelves = this.selectedShelves;
    this.editingShelves = !this.editingShelves;
}
```

Untoggles edit mode on shelves to disable select control

```
selectedGenreChanged(newValue, oldValue){
    if(!newValue) return;
    this.temporaryBook.genre = newValue.id;
}

...
```

Subscribes to selected-genre change and updates the temporary book as needed

```
@computedFrom('temporaryBook.title',
            'temporaryBook.description',
            'temporaryBook.ownACopy',
            'temporaryBook.genre',
            'saved',
            'temporaryBook.shelves')
get canSave(){

    let clean = this.temporaryBook.title == this.book.title &&
            this.temporaryBook.genre == this.book.genre &&
            this.temporaryBook.ownACopy == this.book.ownACopy &&
            this.temporaryBook.description == this.book.description &&
            this.temporaryBook.shelves == this.book.shelves;

    return !clean;
}
...
```

Modifies computedFrom to use a dirty check on the view-model properties and incorporate added fields

7.3.5 Step 5: Modifying the edit-book view

With the genres loaded and the selectedGenre property in place in the EditBook view-model, you're now able to add the new genre-selection control to the edit-book.html view file. Because you're using Bootstrap 4, you need to add a little boilerplate around each radio input element to style it correctly as a Bootstrap form element. The Bootstrap 4 styling includes a div wrapper, followed by an optional label and an input element. The `form-check-inline` class lays out the radio boxes horizontally rather than stacking them vertically. To render a radio box for each genre, you need to add an Aurelia repeater to this `div` wrapper. Then, you need to define each input element's value using the `model.bind` binding command.

Next, use the `checked` binding command to set up a two-way binding to the `selectedGenre` view-model property. All input elements are given the name `genre` to indicate that these should be grouped into the `radio-button-group`. Because of this, the `selectedGenre` property is updated as you click different radio buttons on the page.

Finally, use a string-interpolation binding to render the genre name as the ${genre .name} label value. Modify the view at ./src/resources/elements/edit-book.html to add the genre-selection radio control.

Listing 7.11   Modifying `edit-book` to include genre support (edit-book.html)

```
<template>
    <require from='./star-rating'></require>
    <require from='../value-converters/date-format'></require>
    <div ref="editFormDiv" ... >
        <div class="wrapper">
            ...
            <form>
                <div class="form-inline row">
                    <div class="form-check mb-2 mr-sm-2 mb-sm-0">
                        <label class="form-check-label">
                            <input class="form-check-input"
type="check box"
checked.bind="temporaryBook.ownACopy">
Own a copy?
                        </label>
                    </div>
                    <div class="form-group">
                        <div class="form-check form-check-inline
                                mb-2 mr-sm-2 mb-sm-0"
                             repeat.for="genre of genres" >
                            <label class="form-check-label">
                                <input class="form-check-input"
                                    type="radio"
                                    name="genre"
                                    model.bind="genre"
                                    checked.bind="selectedGenre">
                                ${genre.name}
                            </label>
                        </div>
                    </div>
                    ....
            </form>
        </div>
    </div>
</template>
```

Annotations:
- **Repeats over each of the genres on the EditBook view-model** → `repeat.for="genre of genres"`
- **Sets the input type as radio** → `type="radio"`
- **Binds the genre in the current repeater iteration to each input element** → `model.bind="genre"`
- **Renders the name of the current genre model** → `${genre.name}`
- **Checked binding command is applied to the selectedGenre view-model property** → `checked.bind="selectedGenre"`

7.4 Select controls

Select controls in Aurelia follow the same pattern that you've seen for both check boxes and radio elements. They can be used to bind one selected item to a corresponding view-model property, or multiple selected items to a selected array of values on the view-model. You can bind numbers, Booleans, objects, and strings. The steps required to implement an Aurelia select are as follows:

1 Add a `<select>` element to the view and indicate whether it's a multiselect control using the `multiple` attribute.

2 Bind the `value` attribute of the `<select>` element to a view-model property representing either a single value or an array of values (in the case of a `multiple` select).

3 Declare the `<option>` element that represents each of the `select` items. This can either be done manually or via a repeater (as you saw with the `radio` input element type). Typically, you'd only use a repeater where the model value you're binding to has more than two possible states, or if you have a list of possible states in your view-model that you want to bind to. In the genre example, you have a list of genres to bind to in your view-model, so it makes sense to use a repeater to render each of the possible states. But for a `select` with only two values, such as Yes and No, it's simpler and clearer to manually add each of the options in your view template.

4 Bind the `value` of each option using either the `model.bind` or `value.bind` binding commands. They behave in a comparable way, but the `value` binding command coerces anything that it's assigned to be a string. For example, an integer value of `1` becomes `'1.'`

5 Optionally, use string interpolation to render the value of selected items into each `select` option; for example, `<option> ${genre.name} </option>`.

Aurelia `select` element bindings support the following scenarios:

- *Binding to a Boolean value*—`<select value.bind='ownACopy' ><option model .bind='true'></option>... </select>`
- *Binding to a number*—`<select value.bind='selectedGenreId' ><option model .bind='genre.id'>{genre.name}</option>... </select>`
- *Binding to an object*—`<select value.bind='selectedGenre' ><option model .bind='genre'>{genre.name}</option>... </select>`
- *Binding to an array of objects with a matcher*—`<select value.bind= matcher.bind ="genreMatcher" ><option model.bind='genre'>{genre.name}</option> ...</select>`
- *Binding to a string*—`<select value.bind='selectedGenreName' ><option model .bind='genre.name'>{genre.name}</option>... </select>`

The initial implementation for genre selection using a `radio` element works so long as you only have a limited number of genres, but as you add more genres to the system, you'll run out of horizontal real estate to render new genres to the page. A better approach is to use a `select` element so that you can add any number of genres without a problem.

7.4.1 *Single-value select binding*

In this section, you'll make the genre-selection control more flexible by switching the `radio` element out for a `select` element, exploring how to use the `select` element to bind to a single view-model property. After you've completed these changes, the edit-book form should look like figure 7.4.

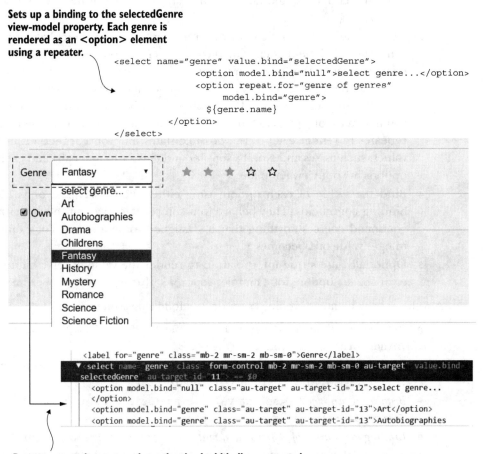

Sets up a binding to the selectedGenre view-model property. Each genre is rendered as an <option> element using a repeater.

```
<select name="genre" value.bind="selectedGenre">
            <option model.bind="null">select genre...</option>
            <option repeat.for="genre of genres"
                model.bind="genre">
              ${genre.name}
          </option>
      </select>
```

```
<label for="genre" class="mb-2 mr-sm-2 mb-sm-0">Genre</label>
▼<select name= genre  class= form-control mb-2 mr-sm-2 mb-sm-0 au-target  value.bind=
    selectedGenre  au-target-id= 11  > == $0
  <option model.bind="null" class="au-target" au-target-id="12">select genre...
  </option>
  <option model.bind="genre" class="au-target" au-target-id="13">Art</option>
  <option model.bind="genre" class="au-target" au-target-id="13">Autobiographies
```

Repeat over each genre, and use the checked binding command to set up a binding between the genre in the current iteration.

Figure 7.4 Edit-book form modified to use a `select` control for genre selection rather than radio elements. This is done using the combination of the `select` value binding command, a repeater (to render each option), a `model` binding command (to bind each option value), and a string interpolation to render each genre name.

The `EditBook` view-model already has everything you need to support switching out the `radio` for a `select` element. All that's required is to remove the `radio` from the `edit-book.html` view file and add the new `select` element in its place. Place the new `select` element ahead of the `star-rating` element in the view. This change involves the following steps:

1 Remove the `<input type='radio'>` element and `div` wrapping.

2 Add the new `<select>` element. This is a single select, so you don't need to add the `multiple` attribute.

3 Bind the value of the `select` element to the `selectedGenre` view-model property: `value.bind="selectedGenre"`. Because you've already wired up the `selected-GenreChanged` subscription, the view-model will be notified when the user selects a new genre, and the `disable` state on the `canSave` button will automatically update.

4 Add a single `option` manually (outside of the repeater), and bind it to `null`: `value.bind="selectedGenre"`. Genre selection is optional, so you don't want to force the user to select one.

5 Add another option with a `repeat.for` binding command to render an option for each genre, binding the value of each genre to the corresponding option element: `value.bind="genre"`.

6 Use string interpolation to render the genre name into the `${genre.name}` option content.

Modify the view in the `./src/resources/elements/edit-book.html` file to add the new select element.

Listing 7.12 Modifying `edit-book` to use a `select` control (edit-book.html)

```
<template>
    <require from='./star-rating'></require>
    <require from='../value-converters/date-format'></require>
    <div ref="editFormDiv" ... >
        <div class="wrapper">
            ...
            <form>
                <div class="form-group row">
                    <label for="description">Description</label>
                    ...
                </div>
                <hr/>
                <div class="form-inline row">                    Label for the genre-
                    <div class="form-group">                     selection control
                        <label for="genre"                    ←
                               class="mb-2 mr-sm-2 mb-sm-0">
                            Genre
                        </label>
                        <select name="genre"
                                class="form-control mb-2 mr-sm-2 mb-sm-0"
                                value.bind="selectedGenre">
```

Binds the value of the select element to the selectedGenre property ⟶

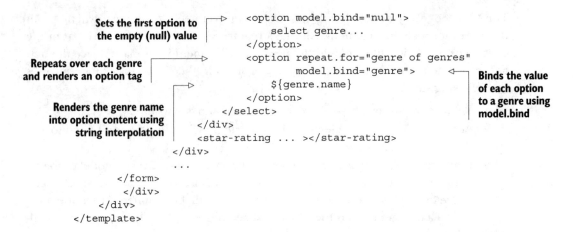

Sets the first option to the empty (null) value

Repeats over each genre and renders an option tag

Renders the genre name into option content using string interpolation

Binds the value of each option to a genre using model.bind

```
<option model.bind="null">
    select genre...
</option>
<option repeat.for="genre of genres"
        model.bind="genre">
    ${genre.name}
</option>
    </select>
  </div>
  <star-rating ... ></star-rating>
</div>
...

      </form>
    </div>
  </div>
</template>
```

7.4.2   *Multiple-value select binding*

The next feature that you want to implement in my-books is a control that allows you to allocate books to one or more shelves. This feature is a perfect fit for the multiple `select` element used to bind to an array of selected values on a view-model. Because a multiselect control is a little unwieldy to display all the time on your minimal edit-book form, add a template conditional to show this control on demand (when a user clicks the Edit button). The finished feature should look like figure 7.5.

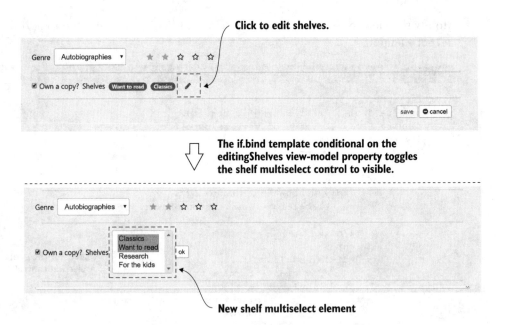

Click to edit shelves.

The if.bind template conditional on the editingShelves view-model property toggles the shelf multiselect control to visible.

New shelf multiselect element

Figure 7.5   Edit-book form modified to include new shelf multiselect element. The user can toggle the shelf controls' edit mode using the pencil-icon control and the OK button.

Before modifying the view to reflect figure 7.5, you need to initialize a new edit-Shelves Boolean field in the constructor to indicate whether the multiselect control should be displayed.

Listing 7.13   Modifying EditBook to work with shelves (edit-book.js)

```
...

@inject(EventAggregator, BookApi )
export class EditBook{

    @bindable editMode;
    @bindable book;
    @bindable selectedGenre;

    constructor(eventAggregator, bookApi ){
        ...
        this.bookApi = bookApi;          Initializes editingShelves
        this.editingShelves = false;   ◁— property to false to hide
    }                                     the shelf select control

}
```

Now that the EditBook view-model supports shelf management, you can modify the edit-book.html view file to support the new multiselect genre control. To begin with, you need to add the new select element with the multiple attribute set: <select multiple ...>. To differentiate between *edit-shelf-list* mode and *selected-shelves* mode, hide this control when the user isn't editing the list. In its place, show a label for each of the selected shelves. You can do this by applying the show.bind binding command to the <select> element, binding it to the editingShelves view-model property.

Add an edit-shelves icon control and delegate its click event to the toggleEdit-Shelves method on the view-model. This allows the user to edit the shelves by selecting one or more options from the select element. The select element will be bound to the temporaryBook.shelves array property on the view-model, value.bind="temporaryBook.shelves", which preselects selected shelves specified in the books .json seed file returned from the book API.

Render an option for each of these shelves using a repeater, repeat.for="shelf of shelves", and bind the value of each option to the shelf value in the iteration. To display the shelf name, use a string-interpolation binding, rendering the shelf into the ${shelf} option content. When the editingShelves option is toggled off, render a label for each for the selected shelves using a <span repeat.for="shelf ...> repeater. Modify the view at ./src/resources/elements/edit-book.html to include the shelf-management controls.

Listing 7.14   Adding shelf management to the edit-book view (edit-books.html)

```
<template>
    <require from='./star-rating'></require>
```

```
<require from='../value-converters/date-format'></require>
<div ref="editFormDiv" ... >
    <div class="wrapper">
        ...
        <form>
            <div class="form-group row">
                <label for="description">Description</label>
                ...
            </div>
            <hr/>
            <div class="form-inline row">

                <star-rating ... ></star-rating>
            </div>
            <hr/>
            <div class="form-inline row">
                <div id="own-a-copy"
                    class="form-check mb-2 mr-sm-2 mb-sm-0">
                    ...
            </div>
            <div class="form-group">
                <label for="shelves"
                        class="mb-2 mr-sm-2 mb-sm-0">
                    Shelves
                </label>

                <select show.bind="editingShelves"
                        name="shelves"
                        class="form-control
                                mb-1
                                mr-sm-1
                                mb-sm-0"
                        multiple
                        value.bind="temporaryBook.shelves">
                    <option repeat.for="shelf of shelves"
                            value.bind="shelf">
                        ${shelf}
                    </option>
                </select>
                <button show.bind="editingShelves"
                        click.delegate="toggleEditShelves()"
                        class="btn btn-secondary btn-sm">
                    ok
                </button>
                <div class="mb-2 mr-sm-2 mb-sm-0"
                    show.bind="!editingShelves">
                    <span repeat.for="shelf
                                    of temporaryBook.shelves"
                        class="badge badge-pill
                                badge-default
                                mb-2 mr-sm-2
                                mb-sm-0">
                        ${shelf}
                    </span>
                    <span class="icon-button"
```

Label for the
shelves select
element

Binds visibility of
shelves select to the
editingShelves view-
model property

Binds the value of the
temporaryBook shelves
array to the select value

Renders each
shelf option

Binds the shelf model
in the current iteration
to the option value

Renders the current shelf
into the option content
using string interpolation

Toggles the editingShelves
view-model property when
the OK button is clicked

Repeats over
each shelf

Multiple-select control
to allow user to select
multiple shelves

Hides the OK button
when you're not in
editingShelves mode

Shows the list of shelf
labels when you're not
in editingShelves mode

Renders the shelf
name to each
shelf label

```
                                   click.delegate="toggleEditShelves()">
                                <i class="fa fa-pencil"
                                   aria-hidden="true"></i>
                          </span>
                      </div>
                  </div>
                  ...
              </form>
          </div>
      </div>
</template>
```

Toggles the editingShelves mode when the pencil-icon control is clicked (label pointing to the `click.delegate="toggleEditShelves()"` line)

You should now be able to reload the updated my-books application to review your much-improved form.

You've finished touring the various form bindings supported by the Aurelia framework. Aurelia supports binding to any kind of form element available, from simple input fields to check boxes, radio elements, and select controls. Each of these controls can be bound to simple values such as numbers, strings, or objects. Depending on the type of element you can bind to, bind either a single form value to a view-model property or multiple form values to an array view-model property. You can see a complete listing of the form element bindings supported by Aurelia on the Aurelia Hub.

Giving users the ability to add data to the my-books application is great, but trusting user input without verifying it first is a terrific way to end up with a chaotic dataset. Form validation allows you to catch issues with user input before it even makes it to the server. Aurelia's validation system ties neatly into its binding and templating engine, allowing you to easily add validation to your form elements without muddying your view's markup. In section 7.5, we'll take our first look at the `aurelia-validation` plugin, adding validation to the edit-books form.

7.5 *Validation*

Imagine you want to create a user-registration form, where the user needs to enter a valid email address, a password that complies with your complexity requirements, and other relevant details. One of the most critical parts of such a form is ensuring that the business requirements for what constitutes a valid user registration are satisfied. Validation is typically applied on both the frontend (JavaScript, HTML, and CSS) and the backend (server-side business logic) to both give the user immediate feedback when constraints aren't met so that they can correct it and verify that the data being sent back to the server is valid (in the case of a direct post to the backend web API or a user with JavaScript disabled in their browser).

Before using SPA technologies, I used to implement the client-side validation with a jQuery validation plugin. This plugin allowed me to apply attributes to an element that should be validated. I then had to hook up validation to fire on a certain form event (such as a field blur or form submit), and the plugin would take care of displaying the appropriate error-response details to the user. If you're familiar with this kind of process, the Aurelia validation system should feel comfortable to you. If not, don't worry; we'll cover how Aurelia's validation system works from the ground up, exploring all the key concepts. By the end of this section, you'll have everything you need to build validation into your own forms.

7.5.1   *The Aurelia validation plugin*

The Aurelia validation plugin allows you to apply validation to view-model fields bound to input elements in the view. It's built with the Aurelia architecture in mind, and because of this, it fits perfectly with Aurelia's binding and templating engine. You can choose from the many different validation libraries out there, and if you have a favorite library, it's easy enough to wire it in. The advantage you get with the Aurelia validation plugin is its ease of use within the Aurelia framework.

In this section, you'll add validation to two fields in the my-books edit-book form. Do this by combining Aurelia's validation plugin (allowing you to create and apply validation rules to input fields) with Bootstrap 4 to display user-friendly validation results with success and error styling. Add the following fields:

- *Book title*—This is required. Add a required validation rule to this field to ensure that a title is provided.
- *Times read*—Add a new input element to capture the number of times that users have read a book. This will require a custom validation rule, to ensure that the user enters a positive integer value.

By the end of this section, the edit-book form validation output should look like figure 7.6.

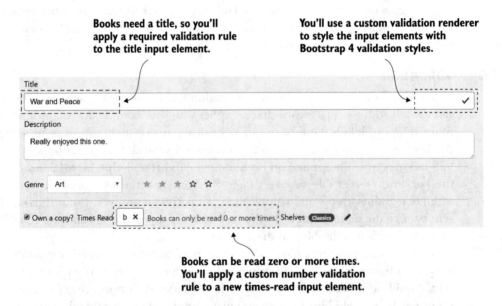

Figure 7.6   Edit-book form modified to include the required validation rule on the `title` property and the custom integer validation rule on the `timesRead` view-model property. Output is displayed using Bootstrap 4 validation styles.

Before we dive into the specifics of implementing the new validation functionality, it's useful to understand the Aurelia validation plugin. This will give you a good bird's-eye view of the moving parts and how you can put them together to meet the validation requirements of your Aurelia applications.

7.5.2 *Aurelia validation overview*

The Aurelia validation system consists of several components that combine to create validation rules, apply the validation rules to a model, and render the validation results to the view (figure 7.7).

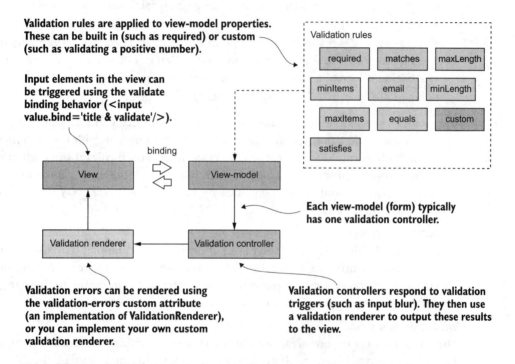

Validation rules are applied to view-model properties. These can be built in (such as required) or custom (such as validating a positive number).

Input elements in the view can be triggered using the validate binding behavior (<input value.bind='title & validate'/>).

Validation errors can be rendered using the validation-errors custom attribute (an implementation of ValidationRenderer), or you can implement your own custom validation renderer.

Each view-model (form) typically has one validation controller.

Validation controllers respond to validation triggers (such as input blur). They then use a validation renderer to output these results to the view.

Figure 7.7   Overview of the major components that play a part in Aurelia's validation architecture

With this picture in mind, let's dig into the various components in Aurelia's validation architecture.

VIEW-MODEL
Validation can be applied to either view-model properties or a custom object on the view-model, which is then marked for validation via the validation controller. Properties are validated by applying various *validation rules*.

VALIDATION RULES
Validation rules allow you to apply various constraints to view-model properties. They can be applied either to simple values (such as a string) or to an entire object. Several

validation rules come built-in with the Aurelia framework, which at the time of writing includes the following:

- `required()`—Ensures that a value is provided
- `email()`—Verifies that the user has provided a valid email address
- `matches(regex)`—Validates the value against a regex
- `minLength(length)`—Ensures the string property value has a minimum length
- `maxLength(length)`—Ensures that a string property value doesn't exceed a maximum length
- `minItems()`—Ensures that an array has a given minimum number of items
- `maxItems()`—Ensures that an array has a given maximum number of items
- `satisfies(function (value, object) -> returns a promise)`—Validates using a custom function that returns a promise, which is useful when validating against a backend service, as you'll see in chapter 8
- `equals(expectedValue)`—Checks this against a given expected value.

Because they're flexible, the built-in validation rules are likely to take you most of the way. But what if you come across a validation requirement that can't be implemented using the built-in rule set? You can create custom validation rules if the built-in rules don't meet your requirements. You'll see this when you implement validation on the times-read form element. Validation rules are executed by a *validation controller* referenced by your view-model.

VALIDATION CONTROLLER

Each view-model that requires validation has one or more mapped validation controllers. Validation controllers are orchestrators that are responsible for receiving validation triggers (such as an input change or blur event) and responding to these triggers by applying the relevant validation feedback to the view via a *validation renderer.*

VALIDATION RENDERER

The validation renderer is responsible for rendering validation results to the view. The plugin provides an implementation of this component out of the box: the `validation-errors` attribute. This custom attribute can be applied to an element and makes all validation errors associated with the element available to both the element and its descendants.

You can then use markup in the view to display validation results to users. Alternatively, you can implement a custom validation renderer. This is useful if you want to avoid muddying the view markup with validation display code and when you have a specific style that should be applied. For example, you can implement a Bootstrap renderer to show validation results in a Bootstrap style, or a materialize validation renderer to show validation results in a Material Design style (an alternative to Bootstrap that follows design guidelines developed by Google), and so on. This is my preferred approach to validation because it keeps the validation display code separated from the main view.

VIEW

You can mark view elements for validation using the `validate` binding behavior provided by the Aurelia validation plugin. For example, applying validation to an `input` element is a simple matter of `<input value.bind='title & validate'/>`, which applies the `validate` binding behavior to the `input` value binding.

From there, the view can take as large a role as you want in the validation process. You can use either the `validation-errors` renderer, which means more validation markup in your view, or a custom validation renderer, which incurs little or no involvement from the view in deciding how the validation results should be displayed to the user.

Now that you understand the components that make up the Aurelia validation system, the next step is to see how they interact. Do this by importing the validation plugin into the my-books application and using it to add validation to the edit-books form.

7.5.3 Adding validation to the edit-books form

Adding validation to an Aurelia application is achieved using the following steps:

1 Create a custom validation renderer (optional).
2 Add a validation controller to your view-model.
3 Set up your validation rules.
4 Enlist any require-input elements in your view for validation.

STEP 1: CREATING THE CUSTOM RENDERER (OPTIONAL)

Because you want the edit-book form to use Bootstrap 4 styling without the need for additional validation markup in the view, you need to implement a custom validation renderer. In case you're wondering why you focus on the renderer first, this component is configured during validation-controller implementation on the view-model (step 2). You don't need to have this in place before starting step 2, but in this case, it saves you circling back to it later. The implementation details for this renderer aren't important at the moment, so you can take a shortcut by adding a validation renderer provided by the Aurelia core team on the Aurelia Hub: http://aurelia.io/docs/plugins/validation#validator. I've taken the Bootstrap 3 validation renderer provided in the documentation and modified it to work with Bootstrap 4 styles.

Let's get started. Create a directory, ./src/renderers, to contain the renderer file, and then create a new file called bootstrap-form-renderer.js in this directory. With this file created, copy the contents of the file from the Aurelia in Action GitHub repository at http://mng.bz/31Z6 into the new bootstrap-validation-renderer.js file that you created.

> **TIP** If you've currently got the `au run` command running in watch mode, you may receive a gulp error when you add this file to your project. Stopping and rerunning this command should resolve the error by forcing a clean build of your app and vendor bundles.

STEP 2: ADDING A VALIDATION CONTROLLER TO YOUR VIEW-MODEL

The second key validation component you need to set up is the validation controller. This will allow you to receive validation triggers from the `title` and `times-read` input elements in the view, execute any configured validation rules, and surface the validation results via the validation renderer you created in step 1. To use a validation controller, you first need to import it from the `aurelia-validation` module, and then make an instance of it available to the view-model.

You can get a new instance of the validation controller in one of two ways: the `New-Instance` class and the `ValidationControllerFactory`. The `NewInstance` class is injected into the view and allows you to create a new instance of the validation controller class as part of the `@inject` decorator. You can then take the `@inject` decorator as a dependency in the view-model constructor. This is the approach you'll take here.

> ### Validation-controller instances
>
> View-models that require validation need one or more validation-controller instances. Aurelia's default convention is a singleton instance per container (where each component has its own container). In this case, however, you need one or more instances to ensure that validation applies only to the form at hand rather than other forms, which are also part of the same container. You have two choices for overriding this convention.
>
> The first method is to use the `NewInstance` class, available as a part of the `aurelia-framework` package. You can use it by calling the `NewInstance` class constructor as part of the `@inject` decorator for your `@inject(NewInstance.of(Validation-Controller))` view-model. The instance of this class is then made available to your view-model via the `constructor(validationController){...}` standard constructor DI semantics.
>
> The second method for generating a new validation-controller instance is the `ValidationControllerFactory` class, available from the `aurelia-validation` package. To use this class, inject an instance of it into your class with `@inject(ValidationControllerFactory)`. You can then use it to generate any number of controllers that you need using the `createForCurrentScope()` method: `this.controller = controllerFactory.createForCurrentScope();`.
>
> You can learn more about each of these injection methods in the Aurelia Hub validation article at http://aurelia.io/docs/plugins/validation#introduction.

With the validation controller available in the constructor, you can start wiring up the validation. Any configuration you need to apply to the validation controller can be done as part of the view-model constructor. In this case, all you need to do is set the validation renderer for the controller to be the `BootstrapFormRenderer` that you created in step 1, `this.controller.addRenderer(new BootstrapFormRenderer())`.

Aurelia validation rules are applied to a model, which can be either the view-model or a nested object. Because you want to apply validation to a nested object, `temporary-Book`, rather than the view-model, you need to create a class to represent the object you

want to validate. In this case, create an instance of a new `Book` class, and assign it to the
`temporaryBook` view-model property, `temporaryBook = new Book()`. This is in contrast
to the previous implementation, where the temporary `book` model was an object literal. The `resetTempBook` method also needs to be modified to make use of the `book`
model supplied from the parent component. This copies all properties from the supplied `book` model to corresponding properties on the `temporaryBook` model.

The validation controller will execute any defined validation rules automatically
based on validation triggers that you configure in the view, but in certain cases you
may want to force the validation rules to execute outside of this process. This interaction is depicted in figure 7.8.

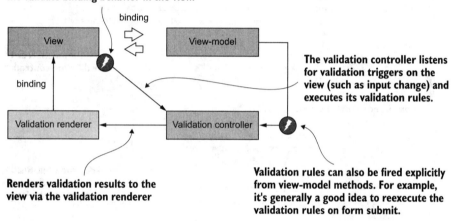

**Figure 7.8   Validation events can be triggered in Aurelia either by using validation triggers in the
view or by explicitly running validation rules from the view-model.**

The most common use case for this is on form submit or save. You can do this by calling the `validate` method on the controller, `this.controller.validate()`. In your
case, validate the temporary book in the `save` method. The `validate` method returns
a promise, because some validation rules may require a long-running operation such
as an HTTP request. As such, they're treated asynchronously as a group. Check the
validation result and continue saving the book only in the event that the validation
result is `valid`. Modify the `./src/resources/elements/edit-book.js` view-model file
to configure the new validation controller instance, as shown in the following listing.

Listing 7.15   Adding a validation controller to `EditBook` (edit-book.js)

```
import {bindable, inject, computedFrom, NewInstance} from 'aurelia-
    framework';
import {EventAggregator} from 'aurelia-event-aggregator';
import {BootstrapFormRenderer}
```

◁─┐ **Imports the NewInstance
   class from the aurelia-
   framework package**

Injects a new
instance of
the Validation-
Controller
into the
view-model

Imports the
BootstrapForm-
Renderer

Imports the ValidationRules
and ValidationController
classes from the aurelia-
validation package

```
        from '../../renderers/bootstrap-form-renderer';
import {ValidationRules, ValidationController}
        from 'aurelia-validation';
import _ from 'lodash';


@inject(EventAggregator,
        NewInstance.of(ValidationController) )
export class EditBook{
```

Adds the
validation
controller
dependency to
the constructor

Sets the
validation
controller in a
view-model field

Creates a new instance of the
Book class and assigns it to a
temporaryBook property

Adds the
BootstrapFormRenderer to
the validation controller

```
    @bindable editMode;
    @bindable book;
    @bindable selectedGenre;
    temporaryBook = new Book();

    constructor(eventAggregator, bookApi, validationController ){
        this.validationController = validationController ;
        this.controller.addRenderer(new BootstrapFormRenderer());
        ...
    }

    ...

    @computedFrom('temporaryBook.title',
                  'temporaryBook.description',
                  'temporaryBook.rating',
                  'temporaryBook.ownACopy',
                  'temporaryBook.genre',
                  'saved',
                  'temporaryBook.shelves',
                  'temporaryBook.timesRead')
    get canSave(){
        if(!this.temporaryBook.Id) return false;

        return this.isDirty();
    }

    ...

    save(){
        this.controller.validate()
                        .then(result => {
                            if (result.valid) {
                                this.loading = true;
                                this.publishBookSavedEvent();
                            }
                        });
    }   ...
}
export class Book {
    title='';
    description='';
}
```

Adds the timesRead
property to the canSave
computed calculation

Executes
validation rules
on save

Checks if the
validation result is
valid; if it is, continues
saving the book

Unwraps the
validation
promise

Adds a new Book
class to run validation
against

TIP If you run into any bundle compilation errors after adding validation to this view-model, it's likely that a step from the appendix has been missed. Please try adding the validation dependencies as detailed in the appendix. If you have any further problems, try cloning the latest project version from GitHub: http://mng.bz/Astu.

STEP 3: SETTING UP THE VALIDATION RULES

Now that your view-model's validation controller is configured, you need to configure the validation rules that you want to execute and apply them to your Book model class created in step 2. To refresh your memory, you need to verify two constraints:

- Users must enter a book title.
- Users must supply a value for the number of times they've read a book as either zero or a positive integer.

The first validation rule that you'll set up will ensure that the user enters an integer greater than or equal to zero in the times-read input element. Implement this using a new custom validation rule called 'zeroOrPositiveInteger'. Custom validation rules are created using the customRule method on the ValidationRules class that you imported from the aurelia-validation package. This method takes three parameters:

- The first parameter is the rule name, in this case 'zeroOrPositiveInteger'.
- The second parameter is a validation function that takes the value to be validated, the object the rule is being run against, and any additional optional parameters that need to be passed along to the rule.
- The third parameter is the validation result message.

Custom validation rules should return a Boolean, where true represents validation success and false represents validation failure. They should also follow the single-responsibility principle, doing only one thing well. The 'zeroOrPositiveInteger' validation rule function is as follows:

```
(value, obj) => value === null || value === undefined
    || (Number.isInteger(value) || value >= 0)
```

In this case, you allow null or undefined values in this rule and reject only cases where the user has specified an invalid value. This means that you can combine the zeroOrPositiveInteger rule with a required() rule, with each rule performing the validation that it's responsible for. This also allows you to make the validation-result messages specific, telling the user exactly what they need to fix in each scenario. If you checked three or four different conditions in your validation rule, the message would need to cover each of these cases, making it unclear to the user which validation constraint they violated.

The second validation rule to set up is the title required validation rule. To implement this rule, you can use the standard required validation rule available from the aurelia-validation-package. To apply these two validation rules to the model, use the `ensure()` method. This method can take either a function that returns a property value or the name of the property to validate. Choose the former option, using an arrow function to specify that the `title` property is required, `ValidationRules` `.ensure(a => a.title).required()`. You'll also apply a `required()` validation rule to the `timesRead` property.

To apply the custom validation rule, `zeroOrPositiveInteger`, you need to use the `satisfiesRule` method, which takes the name of the custom validation rule to execute: `satisfiesRule('zeroOrPositiveInteger')`. To complete the validation-rule configuration, you need to specify the class or instance the rules should be applied to, using the `ValidationRules.on()` method.

Listing 7.16   Setting up validation rules in `EditBook` (edit-book.js)

```
. . .

@inject(EventAggregator,
          NewInstance.of(ValidationController) )          ◁──  Injects a new
export class EditBook{                                          instance of the
                                                               validation controller

. . .
                                                     Defines a new custom
                                                     validation rule and         Allows for null or
                                                     gives the validation        undefined numbers
                                                     rule a name                 and verifies that the
ValidationRules.customRule(                                                      input value is an
  'zeroOrPositiveInteger',                                                       integer >= 0
  (value, obj) => value === null || value === undefined
    || (Number.isInteger(value) || value >= 0),
  'Books can only be read 0 or more times. '
);
                                                Applies a required
                                                validation rule to the
ValidationRules                                 Book title property
  .ensure(a => a.title).required()    ◁──
  .ensure(a => a.timesRead)                     ◁──          Initiates validation
  .required()                                    ◁──         rule setup for the
  .satisfiesRule('zeroOrPositiveInteger')    ◁──             timesRead property
  .on(Book);    ◁──
}              Applies the        Adds the             Adds the required
               validation rules   positiveInteger custom   validation rule to the
               to the Book class  validation rule to the   timesRead property
                                  timesRead property
```

Now that the validation controller, validation rules, and renderer are in place, it's time to make use of the validation setup from the edit-book.html view file.

STEP 4: MARKING INPUT ELEMENTS FOR VALIDATION

The last step of the validation setup process is to mark the `title` and `times-read` input fields for validation. First, add the new `times-read` input field with a two-way binding to the `timesRead` property on the `temporaryBook` model. With this in place, you can apply the `validate` binding behavior to the `value.bind="temporary-Book.title & validate"` and `value.bind="temporaryBook.timesRead & validate"/>`

binding expressions. The validate binding behavior generates validation triggers (such as input change and blur) that the validation controller (set up in step 2) responds to.

Listing 7.17 Marking the books view fields for validation (edit-book.html)

```
<template>
    ...
    <div ref="editFormDiv" ... >
        <div class="wrapper">
            ...
            <form>
                <div class="form-group row">
                    <label for="title">Title</label>
                    <input type="text"
                        class="form-control"
                        id="title"
                        value.bind="temporaryBook.title
                            & validate"                     <——   Marks the
                        placeholder="book title">                 temporaryBook.title
                </div>                                            property value for
                ...                                               validation using validate
                <div class="form-inline row">                     binding behavior
                    <div id='own-a-copy'... >
                        ...
                    </div>
                    <div class="form-group">
                        <label for="times-read"
                            class="mb-2 mr-sm-2 mb-sm-0">
                            Times Read
                        </label>
                        <input name="times-read"
                            class="form-control
                                number
                                mb-2 mr-sm-2
                                mb-sm-0"
                            placeholder="0"
                            value.bind="temporaryBook.timesRead
                                & validate"/>               <——
                    </div>                                        Enlists the time-read
                </div>                                            field for validation
            </form>                                               using validate
        </div>                                                    binding behavior
    </div>
</template>
```

Adds the new timesRead field

Run the au run --watch command to load the latest version of the application in your browser. If you navigate to the browser, the validation rules should be applied as you interact with the form, displaying Bootstrap validation styles against the title and times-read input elements, as shown in figure 7.9.

After setting up validation on the edit-books form, you should understand the core components that make up Aurelia's validation system. These components can be

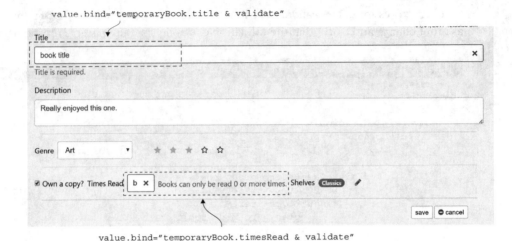

value.bind="temporaryBook.title & validate"

value.bind="temporaryBook.timesRead & validate"

Figure 7.9   Title and Times Read input fields marked for validation using the validate binding behavior

combined in numerous ways to implement any validation requirements you might come across. The `aurelia-validation` package is powerful.

So far, you've managed to prototype out the main book-management section of the my-books application with the help of the simple books.json seed file to serve as the fake backend. In the next chapter, we'll take my-books to the next level, hooking it in to the my-books REST API using a combination of the `aurelia-fetch-client` and `aurelia-http-client` modules. In doing so, you'll learn how to GET, PUT, POST, and DELETE data from an API endpoint in Aurelia.

Summary

- Forms are created in Aurelia using standard HTML elements and a combination of one-way and two-way binding.
- All the standard input elements, such as check boxes, `radio` elements, and `select` controls, are supported by Aurelia's binding system.
- You can bind to simple values such as strings, Booleans, numbers, or objects.
- Some elements, such as the `select` element, support multiple selected items, and these bind to an array property on the view-model, rather than a single value.
- Repeaters are used in cases where users need to select between multiple input options, such as with check boxes, `select` elements, and `radio` elements.
- You can set up form validation with Aurelia's validation plugin.
- The Aurelia validation plugin is built to work seamlessly with Aurelia's architecture, so it's generally an excellent choice for Aurelia applications over third-party validation libraries.

- Aurelia's validation architecture consists of five main components: the validation controller, validation renderers, validation rules, the view-model, and the view.
- Validation controllers orchestrate Aurelia's validation system, responding to validation triggers and outputting validation results via validation renderers.
- Validation renderers are responsible for applying validation results to the view.
- Validation rules allow you to place constraints on view-model properties. Several validation rules are provided by the framework, and you can create your own using custom validation rules.
- Custom validation rules should have a single responsibility, allowing them to be combined in numerous ways, and ensuring specific and meaningful validation error messages.

Working with HTTP

In the real world, no SPA lives in isolation. SPAs are typically part of an ecosystem that involves a multitude of components, such as REST APIs and other dependencies, both internal to your application and external. The first Aurelia application I built integrated with a backend REST API to fetch application data and statistics, the Octopus Deploy REST API to retrieve a list of servers that we were interested in, and other APIs with information pertinent to the application. Integrating with these kinds of external dependencies brings your application to life.

With the growing popularity of serverless architectures, it's increasingly common to host a simple SPA and use it to knit together a suite of external utilities—from cloud databases to SaaS (software as a service) offerings like Salesforce. The technology required to build these kinds of applications has existed for quite some time, starting with Microsoft's invention of AJAX, back in 2000. The built-in browser API for working with AJAX, the XMLHttpRequest API, is beginning to show its age, and developers are starting to expect a cleaner and more modern HTTP browser API. Because of this, libraries like jQuery have created higher-level APIs to make it easier to work with HTTP requests in general, and AJAX specifically.

Recently, a more modern native API has started making its way into browsers. It's called the Fetch API and makes working with HTTP much simpler. It provides built-in support for concepts such as CORS- and HTTP-origin header semantics, which were not on the radar when the XMLHttpRequest API was invented. Aurelia provides two packages, `aurelia-http-client` and `aurelia-fetch-client` (which uses the new Fetch API under the hood), that simplify HTTP communication by providing a higher-level API on top of Fetch. The `aurelia-fetch-client` makes it significantly easier to use the Fetch API as part of the Aurelia application architecture due to its support for DI.

In this chapter, you'll learn how to build HTTP interactions into your Aurelia applications, connecting the my-books SPA to the my-books REST API by means of the `aurelia-fetch-client` and `aurelia-http-client` packages.

8.1 Overview of the Aurelia HTTP toolkit

The `fetch-client` and `http-client` plugins have a lot of overlap in terms of core functionality, each providing support for all HTTP verbs. The differentiating factor is the browser API that they're built on. `aurelia-http-client` aims to provide a simple-to-use abstraction over the traditional `XMLHttpRequest` object, which has been in browsers since 2000. This is the object that existing utilities, such as jQuery's AJAX library, are built on.

Because it was created so long ago, many things that we've come to expect from a modern HTTP client API aren't supported. Further, the functionality that is supported is verbose and requires a lot of boilerplate code. In contrast, the `aurelia-fetch-client` plugin is built on the recent Fetch API and provides access to some of the more recent browser APIs, such as service workers and the Cache API. It also provides support for concepts such as CORS.

The recommendation from the Aurelia core team is to use `aurelia-fetch-client` where possible and fall back to `aurelia-http-client` in cases where the functionality you need isn't supported. An example of this is if you require download progress or request cancelation.

Both Aurelia HTTP clients can be globally configured, avoiding the need to repeatedly specify options such as the base URL and credentials that should be applied to every request. Both clients also support *request interception*. Request interception is used to hook into an HTTP request on its way out to an HTTP endpoint (for header manipulation or request logging) and on its way back. Interception provides flexibility in the way HTTP requests are handled in your SPA. An overview of the Aurelia HTTP toolkit can be seen in figure 8.1.

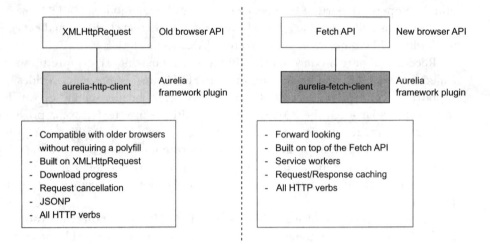

Figure 8.1   Overview of the Aurelia HTTP toolkit. This consists of `aurelia-http-client`, which is built on the XMLHttpRequest API, and `aurelia-fetch-client`, which is built on the Fetch API.

8.2   Using aurelia-fetch-client

`aurelia-fetch-client` is a wrapper over the browser's native Fetch API. This article on the Mozilla Developer Network is a great resource if you're interested in learning more about the Fetch API: https://developer.mozilla.org/en/docs/Web/API/Fetch_API. `aurelia-fetch-client` supports the same methods as the native Fetch API, but it also provides the following advantages:

- *Request tracking*—Every request sent from `aurelia-fetch-client` is tracked, giving you an overview of the HTTP interaction across your application.
- *HTTP interception*—You can intercept and optionally manipulate requests coming in and going out of your application. This is useful for cross-cutting tasks, such as logging or providing feedback to the user, when your application is performing HTTP communication.
- *Injection*—This module is injectable into the services and view-models across your Aurelia application.
- *Default value configuration*—You can set default values, such as a base URL for your API, request headers, or credentials, which are then applied to every request.

8.2.1   Adding fetch to my-books

In the previous chapters, you emulated HTTP interaction in my-books using the combination of an HTTP request to a seed JSON file and simulated backend calls to the `BookApi` service that return hardcoded data. In this section, swap out this fake backend for a simple REST API built using Node.js, Express.js, and MongoDB. This REST API has the following endpoints:

- `/BOOKS (GET)`—Retrieves a list of books
- `/BOOKS (POST)`—Creates a new book
- `/BOOK/ID (GET)`—Retrieves a specific book by ID
- `/BOOK/ID (DELETE)`—Deletes a book by ID
- `/BOOK/ID (PUT)`—Updates a book by ID
- `/GENRES (GET)`—Lists all genres
- `/SHELVES (GET)`—Lists all shelves

The updated architecture of the my-books application encapsulates HTTP calls to the my-books REST API within the `BookApi` class, which depends on `aurelia-fetch-client`. You can see an overview of this architecture in figure 8.2.

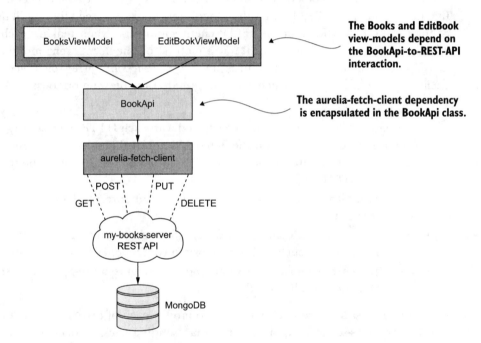

Figure 8.2 The my-books application modified to communicate with the my-books-server REST API via `aurelia-fetch-client`

Before making any changes to my-books, you need to set up the my-books-server, which is available from GitHub. Instructions for how to do this can be found in the appendix and in the GitHub repository at https://github.com/freshcutdevelopment/my-books-server. This is a simple Node.js-based REST API with a MongoDB backend. We won't cover how this server was built because it's outside the scope of this

book. But if you're interested, you can read more on this topic in Simon Holmes' terrific book, *Getting MEAN* (Manning, 2015) at http://mng.bz/87FF.

> **TIP**   The Fetch API is a relatively recent addition to browsers. If you need to
> support users on Internet Explorer (any version other than Edge), or browser
> versions lower than Edge version 14, Firefox version 39, Chrome version 42,
> or Safari version 10.1, you'll need to use a polyfill to patch the missing func-
> tionality for these browsers. The polyfill fetch library from GitHub is a good
> option: https://github.com/github/fetch.

Now that you've set up the my-books-server REST API and have it running at http://
localhost:8333/api, modify the `BookApi` class to make use of the new endpoints. To
begin, import two modules from the `aurelia-fetch-client` package: the `HttpClient`
module (which you'll use for HTTP communication) and the `json` module (which
allows you to serialize book objects to JSON before they're sent to the backend). With
the transition to a REST API rather than the simple books.json seed file, you'll need to
configure the base URL that the HTTP client should use when making each of its
requests. This is done using the `configure` method on the `HttpClient` module. This
method takes a function that returns an `HttpClientConfiguration` object, `http`
`.configure(config => {})`, which you configure to the following options:

- `config.withDefaults ({credentials:...}, {headers...})`—Allows you to
  configure default parameters to be passed with each HTTP request. Any configuration options available on the Fetch API are configurable here. This is most
  useful when you have headers or credential options that need to be the same
  with every HTTP request you send.
- `config.withBaseUrl (url)`—Allows you to configure the base URL used for
  HTTP requests.
- `config.useStandardConfiguration()`—Sets up reasonable defaults on the
  `httpClient` object, such as the same-origin CORS policy for credentials.
- `config.withIntercepter()`—Allows you to configure a pre-/post-request interceptor function. We'll cover this shortly.

After configuring the base URL, you need to modify each of the `BookApi` methods to
call the my-books-server endpoints rather than sending back hardcoded values. The
pattern is similar in each case. Use the `this.http.fetch(URL)` method to make the
HTTP call, unwrap the promise, and deserialize the JSON message into an object with
the `response.json()` method, returning the resulting value as a POJO to the caller.
The HTTP GET verb is used by default when you call `httpClient.fetch()`, so in the
cases where you're deleting, updating, or creating data, you need to specify the relevant verb (method) as a part of the fetch options.

  Additionally, when creating or updating items, you need to serialize the message
body using the `json` method. You'll also perform a little housekeeping, removing all
simulated latency from the service, because you're no longer working with mock data.

Connecting to a real HTTP API introduces a chance for errors. To handle this, add a catch block to trap errors on each HTTP call, logging the error details to the console. Modify the ./src/services/book-api.js service class as shown in the following listing.

Listing 8.1 Using the my-books-server REST API in `BookApi` (book-api.js)

```
import {HttpClient, json} from 'aurelia-fetch-client';        ◁─┐
import {inject} from 'aurelia-framework';                       │  Imports the
                                                                │  HttpClient and JSON
                                                                │  modules, and injects
@inject(HttpClient)                                           ◁┤  the http client into
export class BookApi{                                           │  the BookApi class via
                                                                │  constructor injection
    constructor(http){                                        ◁─┘
        this.http = http;

        const baseUrl = 'http://localhost:8333/api/';         ◁─┐
                                                                │  Configures the base
        http.configure(config => {                             │  URL of the REST API
            config.withBaseUrl(baseUrl);                      ◁─┘
        })
    }

    getBooks(){                                                     Switches the getBooks
                                                                    method to fetch from
        return this.http.fetch('books')                   ◁──┘   the API endpoint
                .then(response => response.json())
                .then(books => {
                    return books;
                })
                .catch(error => {
                    console.log('Error retrieving books.');
                    return [];
                });

    }

    getShelves(){                                                   Switches the getShelves
                                                                    method to fetch from
        return this.http.fetch('shelves')                 ◁──┘   the API endpoint
                .then(response => response.json())
                .then(shelves => {
                    return shelves;
                })
                .catch(error => {
                    console.log('Error retrieving shelves.');
                    return [];
                });
    }

    getGenres(){                                                    Switches the getGenres
                                                                    method to fetch from
        return this.http.fetch('genres')                  ◁──┘   the API endpoint
                .then(response => response.json())
                .then(genres => {
```

```
            return genres;
        }).
        .catch(error => {
            console.log('Error retrieving genres.');
            return [];
        });
}


addBook(book){
    return this.http.fetch('books', {
        method: 'post',
        body: json(book)
        })
        .then(response => response.json())
        .then(createdBook => {
            return createdBook;
        })
          .catch(error => {
              console.log('Error adding book.');
        });

}


deleteBook(book){
    return this.http.fetch(`book/${book._id}`, {
            method: 'delete'
            })
            .then(response => response.json())
            .then(responseMessage => {
                return responseMessage;
            })
              .catch(error => {
                  console.log('Error deleting book.');
              });


}


saveBook(book){
    return this.http.fetch(`book/${book._id}`, {
            method: 'put',
            body: json(book)
            })
            .then(response => response.json())
            .then(savedBook => {
                return savedBook;
                })
                .catch(error => {
                    console.log('Error saving book.');
            });


}
}
```

Configures the addBook method with the HTTP POST verb

Configures the addBook method with the HTTP DELETE verb

Configures the saveBook method with the HTTP PUT verb

Catches errors and logs to console

TIP In this case, you've handled errors by catching them and logging an error message to the console. By contrast, in a real-world application, you'd want to notify the user that there was an issue connecting to the backend service and potentially retry the request. One way to implement this kind of error notification is to use the Aurelia Event Aggregator to raise an error event, passing along the error message. You can then listen for error events in a component higher up in the hierarchy and add global error-notification logic via an error-notification component or similar. You could also transmit the error to an error-tracking and reporting service, such as TrackJS or Raygun, to give you visibility into errors encountered by users.

With the `BookApi` changes in place, you need to modify the components in the application to work with the slightly revised data structure returned from the REST API and MongoDB. The revision to this structure incorporates the MongoDB database ID format (`"_id": "5991713f95fd5759604ffb7b"`) and refers to genres by ID reference rather than name (`"genre": "5991713f95fd5759604ffb70"`). Because the concepts in the following section have been covered already, feel free to skip these steps and download the complete version from chapter 7 at https://github.com/freshcut-development/Aurelia-in-Action. The changes you'll need to make are as follows:

- Modify the `EditBook` view-model to use the new books data structure.
- Modify the `edit-book.html` view to make use of the new books data structure.
- Modify the `Books` view-model to make use of the new books data structure.

STEP 1: MODIFY EDITBOOK VIEW-MODEL
Modify the contents of the `EditBook` view-model, `./src/resources/elements/edit-book.js`.

Listing 8.2 Modifying `EditBook` to use the new data structure (edit-book.js)

```
...
export class EditBook{
    ...
    bind(){
        ...
        this.selectedGenre = this.genres
                        .find(g => g._id == this.book.genre);      // Replaces ID with _id to use the database ID returned from MongoDB

        this.selectedShelves = this.shelves
                        .filter(shelf =>
                            this.temporaryBook
                                .shelves
                                .indexOf(shelf.name) !== -1);      // Populates the selectedShelves array; these are now objects rather than strings
    }
    selectedGenreChanged(newValue, oldValue){
        if(!newValue) return;
        this.temporaryBook.genre = newValue._id;                   // Replaces ID with _id to use the database ID returned from MongoDB
    }
```

```
  attached(){
      this.bookSaveCompleteSubscription =
          this.eventAggregator
          .subscribe(`book-save-complete-${this.book._id}`,    ◁────┐
                  () => this.bookSaveComplete());
  }
  ...
                                        Replaces ID with _id to
}                                        use the database ID
...                                      returned from MongoDB
```

STEP 2: MODIFY EDIT-BOOK VIEW

Modify the contents of the edit-book view, ./src/resources/elements/edit-book.html.

Listing 8.3   Modifying edit-book to use the new data structure (edit-book.html)

```
...
<label for="shelves" class="mb-2 mr-sm-2 mb-sm-0">Shelves</label>
<select show.bind="editingShelves"         ◁─┐
      name="shelves"                          │
      class="form-control mb-1 mr-sm-1 mb-sm-0"   Uses object-based
      multiple                                    multiselect binding
      value.bind="selectedShelves">      ◁──────  rather than string-
    <option repeat.for="shelf of shelves"         based
          model.bind="shelf">            ◁──┘
        ${shelf.name}
    </option>
</select>
<button show.bind="editingShelves"...>ok</button>
...
```

STEP 3: MODIFY BOOKS VIEW-MODEL

Modify the contents of the Books view-model, ./src/resources/elements/books.js.

Listing 8.4   Modifying the Books view-model (books.js)

```
...
export class Books {              Modifies the addBook method
...                               to call book-api to POST book
  addBook () {                ◁──┘
    this.bookApi.addBook({title : this.bookTitle}).then(createdBook => {
        this.books.push(createdBook);
        this.bookTitle = "";
    });
  }

  removeBook(toRemove){
                                              Modifies the
    this.bookApi.deleteBook(toRemove).then(() => {    ◁──  removeBook method to
      let bookIndex = _.findIndex(this.books, book => {     hit the API endpoint
        return book._id === toRemove._id;        ◁──  and updates the books
      });                                             array with the result
```

```
        this.books.splice(bookIndex, 1);
    });
  }
  ...
  bookSaved(updatedBook){
      this.bookApi
        .saveBook(updatedBook)
        .then((savedBook) => {
            let index = this.books
                          .findIndex(book =>
                              book._id == savedBook._id);

            Object.assign(this.books[index], savedBook);

            this.eventAggregator
                .publish(`book-save-complete-${savedBook._id}`);
        });
  }
  ...
}
```

> **Modifies the bookSaved callback method to hit the API PUT endpoint and updates the books array with the result**

With this housekeeping taken care of, the application should look the same as it did before, but if you lift the hood and take a look, you can see that the data is now retrieved from the REST API, as shown in figure 8.3.

By adding `aurelia-fetch-client` to my-books, you've seen how a default configuration can be configured on the `httpClient` object and used for each request. You used this default configuration to minimize duplicate code across the HTTP calls, isolating the base URL so that you could define it in one place. You've also seen how to modify the HTTP verb on requests, which allows you to easily create, delete, and update data on any REST API you want to use.

Next, we'll look at another configuration option available on `aurelia-fetch-client`: *interceptors*. You'll use interceptors to log each of the HTTP interactions that you've added to the Aurelia application and observe the requests being made under the hood.

8.2.2 *Intercepting and manipulating requests*

Interceptors give you a straightforward way to manipulate requests coming to and from your Aurelia application via `aurelia-fetch-client`. You can think of a interceptor like a middleman for your requests, allowing you to take the request or response and modify it in any way (including swapping it out and replacing it with a new request/response entirely, if that suits your purpose). Most commonly, interceptors are used for tasks such as appending request headers and logging. The interceptor flow is depicted in figure 8.4.

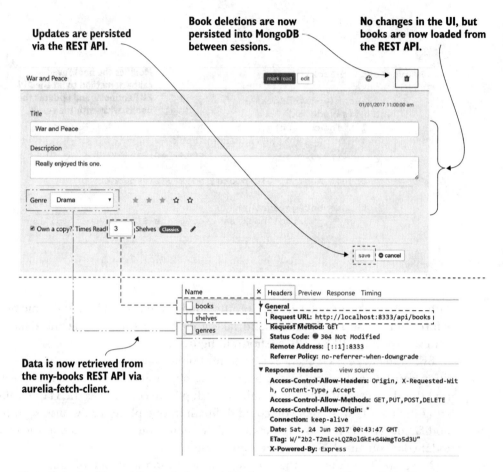

Figure 8.3   Fetching, adding, updating, and deleting books is now achieved via REST calls to the my-books-server API using `aurelia-fetch-client`.

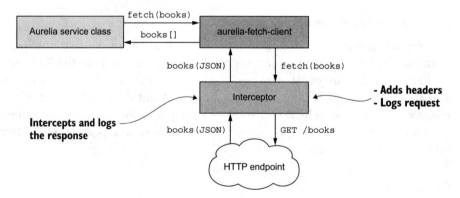

Figure 8.4   Requests made via `aurelia-fetch-client` can be intercepted and manipulated.

To see it in action, modify the `BookApi` class to intercept and log all my-books HTTP interactions. Modify the ./src/services/book-api.js class.

Listing 8.5 Logging HTTP requests from `BookApi` (book-api.js)

```
...
export class BookApi{

    constructor(http){
        this.http = http;

        const baseUrl = 'http://localhost:8333/api/';

        http.configure(config => {                          Adds an interceptor
            config.withBaseUrl(baseUrl)                     to the http client
                .withInterceptor({                          configuration
                    request(request) {
                        console.log("request", request);
                        return request;
                    },
                    response(response) {
                        console.log("response", response);
                        return response;
                    }
                });
        });
    }
    ...
}
```

Adds a callback request to log the content of each request → `request(request)`

Adds a callback response to log the content of each response → `response(response)`

Refresh the browser, and then you should see the request and response bodies logged into the Chrome Developer Tools (F12). In this example (figure 8.5), I reloaded the page, causing the initial set of books, genres, and shelves to be loaded. I then deleted and created a book. The pertinent details of the requests are logged, including the type (CORS, in this case, because of calling an HTTP endpoint with a different URL than the Aurelia site), the request URL, the method (or HTTP verb), and, in the case of the response, a status code and a Boolean value to indicate whether the request was redirected. Figure 8.5 depicts a log of each of these interactions.

Aside from using them to analyze and debug HTTP communications in your Aurelia application, you can use interceptors to manipulate HTTP requests. For example, say you wanted to add an `awesome` custom header to each request. One option is to include it in the base configuration, but the drawback is that it would then be included in every request. What if you wanted to include the header only on a POST? Easy, let's give it a try. To do this, conditionally add a header to the awesome-custom-header HTTP requests, but only when the method is of the POST type. Modify the interceptor in ./src/services/book-api.js and add a custom header for POST requests only.

The interceptor logs each request and corresponding response.

Initial load: books, genres, and shelves are fetched from the API.

```
INFO [aurelia] Aurelia Started                       vendor-bundle.js:14034
request                                                       book-api.js:16
▶ Request {method: "GET", url: "http://localhost:8333/api/books",
  headers: Headers, referrer: "about:client", referrerPolicy: ""…}
request                                                       book-api.js:16
▶ Request {method: "GET", url: "http://localhost:8333/api/shelves",
  headers: Headers, referrer: "about:client", referrerPolicy: ""…}
request                                                       book-api.js:16
▶ Request {method: "GET", url: "http://localhost:8333/api/genres",
  headers: Headers, referrer: "about:client", referrerPolicy: ""…}
response                                                      book-api.js:20
▶ Response {type: "cors", url: "http://localhost:8333/api/books",
  redirected: false, status: 200, ok: true…}
response                                                      book-api.js:20
▶ Response {type: "cors", url: "http://localhost:8333/api/shelves",
  redirected: false, status: 200, ok: true…}
response                                                      book-api.js:20
▶ Response {type: "cors", url: "http://localhost:8333/api/genres",
  redirected: false, status: 200, ok: true…}
request                                                       book-api.js:16
  Request {method: "DELETE", url:
▶ "http://localhost:8333/api/book/594624d25964fc3280b866d4",
  headers: Headers, referrer: "about:client", referrerPolicy: ""…}
response                                                      book-api.js:20
  Response {type: "cors", url:
▶ "http://localhost:8333/api/book/594624d25964fc3280b866d4",
  redirected: false, status: 200, ok: true…}
request                                                       book-api.js:16
▶ Request {method: "POST", url: "http://localhost:8333/api/books",
  headers: Headers, referrer: "about:client", referrerPolicy: ""…}
response                                                      book-api.js:20
▶ Response {type: "cors", url: "http://localhost:8333/api/books",
  redirected: false, status: 200, ok: true…}
>
```

A DELETE request is logged when a book is deleted.

A POST request is logged when a new book is added.

Figure 8.5   Intercepting and logging requests between the my-books Aurelia client and the Node.js server

---

Listing 8.6   Adding a custom header to POST requests (book-api.js)

```
export class BookApi{

    constructor(http){
        this.http = http;

        const baseUrl = 'http://localhost:8333/api/';

        http.configure(config => {
            config.withBaseUrl(baseUrl)
                .withInterceptor({
                    request(request) {
```

```
                                            if(request.method == 'POST'){
  Adds custom  ┌──▷             request
  header for                    .headers['awesome-custom-header']
  POST requests │                   = 'aurelia-in-action';
               │               }
                               console.log("request", request);
                               return request;
                            },
                            response(response) {
                               console.log("response", response);
                               return response;
                            }
                         });
                    });
               }
               ...
          }
```

You can use the logging that you set up to see this new interception logic in action. Navigate back to the browser, add and delete a book, and check the developer console log. You'll see that the custom header is applied only for the POST request, as shown in figure 8.6.

8.3 Working with aurelia-http-client

`aurelia-fetch-client` solves most of the HTTP communication requirements that you'll come across in your Aurelia development, but you may run into the occasional scenario where the functionality that you need hasn't made it into the Fetch API browser yet. In these cases, you'll need to fall back to the `aurelia-http-client` package. As mentioned earlier, a common case for this is if you need to communicate with a JSONP API.

JSONP provides a mechanism for sharing data between different domains, so it's a common requirement of third-party REST APIs. This makes it a useful tool to keep in your back pocket. To see how this can be used in practice, add a new service class to my-books that retrieves the books API using a JSONP request. Then, add a reference to this new service in the `Books` view-model class to log the results.

Begin by importing the `HttpClient` and configuring the base URL, as you did with the `fetch-client` example. The difference in this case is that you import the module from the `aurelia-http-client` package instead of the `aurelia-fetch-client` package. Then, in a new method, `getBooksJsonp`, make a JSONP call using the `jsonp` method on the `HttpClient` class, `this.http.jsonp('booksjsonp')`. This method takes a URL and a callback-parameter name—the name of the URL parameter that specifies the function used to wrap the JSONP response (which, in your case, is set to `'callback'` in the my-books-server response). If you're interested in learning more about cross-site requests and JSONP, I recommend checking out *CORS in Action* by Monsur Hossain (Manning, 2014), which delves into these concepts in much greater depth, at http://mng.bz/BASc.

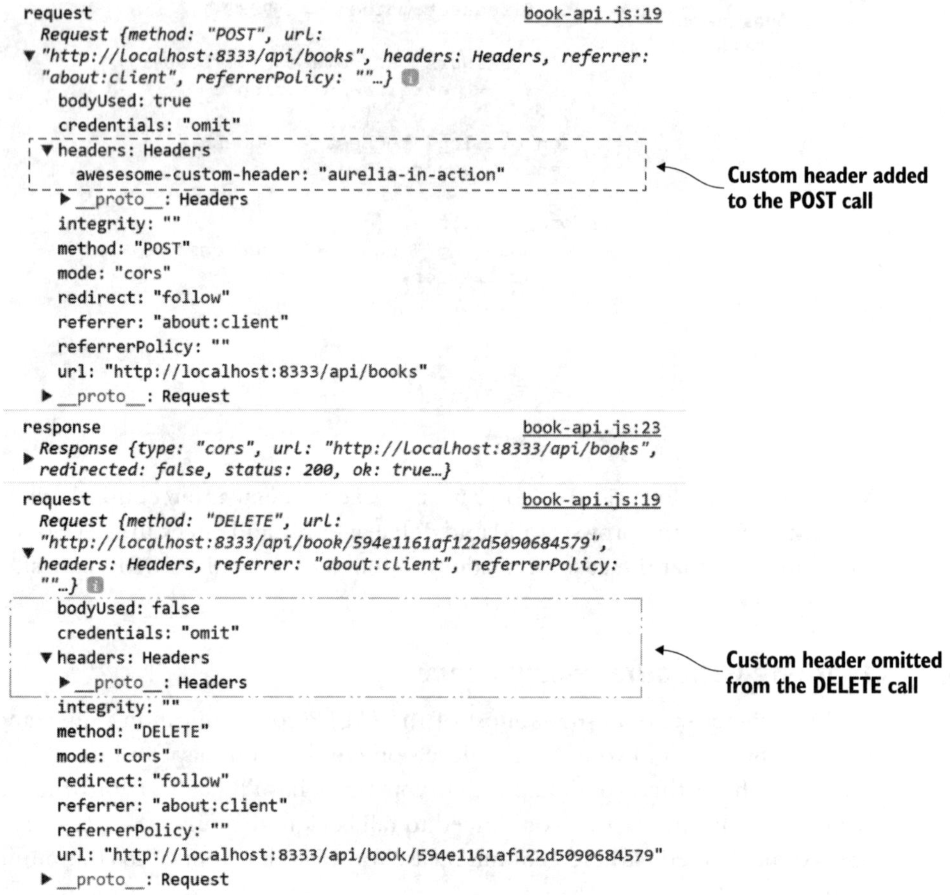

```
request                                          book-api.js:19
  Request {method: "POST", url:
▼ "http://localhost:8333/api/books", headers: Headers, referrer:
  "about:client", referrerPolicy: ""…} 🔵
    bodyUsed: true
    credentials: "omit"
  ▼ headers: Headers
      awesesome-custom-header: "aurelia-in-action"        ◄─── Custom header added
    ▶ __proto__: Headers                                       to the POST call
    integrity: ""
    method: "POST"
    mode: "cors"
    redirect: "follow"
    referrer: "about:client"
    referrerPolicy: ""
    url: "http://localhost:8333/api/books"
  ▶ __proto__: Request
response                                          book-api.js:23
  Response {type: "cors", url: "http://localhost:8333/api/books",
▶ redirected: false, status: 200, ok: true…}
request                                          book-api.js:19
  Request {method: "DELETE", url:
▼ "http://localhost:8333/api/book/594e1161af122d5090684579",
  headers: Headers, referrer: "about:client", referrerPolicy:
  ""…} 🔵
    bodyUsed: false
    credentials: "omit"
  ▼ headers: Headers                                        ◄─── Custom header omitted
    ▶ __proto__: Headers                                        from the DELETE call
    integrity: ""
    method: "DELETE"
    mode: "cors"
    redirect: "follow"
    referrer: "about:client"
    referrerPolicy: ""
    url: "http://localhost:8333/api/book/594e1161af122d5090684579"
  ▶ __proto__: Request
```

Figure 8.6 Custom headers added to POST requests sent via `aurelia-fetch-client`

The shape of the response object is slightly different than the JSON requests that you
made with `fetch-client`. In this case, the response body is already deserialized into
an array for you, so all you need to do is retrieve the response body from the
`responseMessage.response` message. To implement this change, add a new `BookApi-
JSONP` class under ./src/services/book-api-jsonp.js.

Listing 8.7   Adding the `BookApiJSONP` class (book-api-jsonp.js)

```
import {HttpClient} from 'aurelia-http-client';   ◄─┐  Imports the
import {inject} from 'aurelia-framework';           │  HttpClient class

@inject(HttpClient)
export class BookApiJSONP{
```

```
constructor(http) {
    this.http = http;

    this.baseUrl = 'http://localhost:8333/api/';

    this.http.configure(config => {          ⎤ Configures the
        config.withBaseUrl(this.baseUrl);    ⎦ base URL
    });                                  ◄
}
                                                          ⎤ Makes an HTTP
                                                          │ JSONP call
getBooksJsonp() {                                         │ specifying the URL
    return this.http.jsonp('booksjsonp', 'callback')  ◄──┘ and the callback
        .then(responseMessage => {
            return responseMessage.response;   ◄──┐ Retrieves the
        })                                        ⎦ response body
        .then(books => {
          return books;
        });
    }
}
```

To see the results of this JSONP call, wire up the new service class in the Books view-model and log the response, as shown in the following listing, importing the newly created service and loading the books array from the bind lifecycle callback.

Listing 8.8 Including the JSONP request (books.js)

```
...
import {BookApiJSONP} from '../../services/book-api-jsonp';  ◄─┐
                                                              │ Imports the
@inject(BookApi, EventAggregator, BookApiJSONP)            ◄──┤ BookApiJSONP
export class Books {                                          │ service class
                                                              │
  constructor(bookApi, eventAggregator,bookApiJSONP){    ◄────┘
    ...
    this.bookApiJSONP = bookApiJSONP;
  }
  ...
  bind() {                          ⎤ Loads the books array in
    ...                             │ the bind() component-
    this.loadBooksJsonp();     ◄────┘ lifecycle callback
  }

  loadBooksJsonp() {                                    ⎤ Logs the result
      this.bookApiJSONP.getBooksJsonp()                 ⎦ to the console
              .then(savedBooks => console
                            .log("jsonp books", savedBooks));  ◄─┘
  }
  ...
}
```

Figure 8.7 depicts the JSONP-network request, the autogenerated callback-function name injected into the URL callback parameter, and the wrapped JSONP-network response.

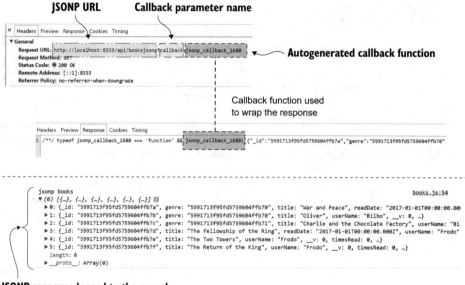

JSONP response logged to the console

Figure 8.7   JSONP-network call with `json_callback_1680` autogenerated callback method used to wrap the network response

This gives you a taste of the functionality available with `aurelia-http-client`. To see the full API and additional configuration options, such as fluent configuration, you can check out the latest documentation on the Aurelia Hub at http://aurelia.io/docs/plugins/http-services.

With an Express.js backend added to your Aurelia project, you're one step closer to creating a real-world, usable web application, but it still has a long way to go. Two major shortcomings are navigation and authentication. Currently, the site consists of two pages—the homepage and the books page—but the user doesn't have a great deal of indication as to which is active. Additionally, the application is devoid of authentication, allowing any Tom, Dick, or Harry to view any book collection. In the next chapter, you'll remedy both shortcomings, adding a navigation bar and a much-needed authentication system to the my-books application. In doing so, you'll become familiar with the ins and outs of Aurelia's router.

Summary

- Two HTTP modules are provided with the Aurelia framework. These modules sit on top of the `XMLHttpRequest` object (`aurelia-http-client`) and the new Fetch API (`aurelia-fetch-client`).
- `aurelia-fetch-client` is a simple wrapper on top of the Fetch API. It's injectable and, though the name may not make it obvious, it supports the full range of HTTP verbs.

- Because `aurelia-fetch-client` is so new, some features, such as JSONP, aren't supported yet, and you'll need to drop down to the alternative HTTP package: `aurelia-http-client`.
- The combination of these two packages gives you the power and flexibility that you need to meet any HTTP-related challenge when developing your own applications.
- If you run into issues and need to diagnose your HTTP logic, interceptors can save the day. These give you visibility into your Aurelia HTTP pipeline, allowing you not only to trace incoming and outgoing requests, but also to manipulate them on the way through.

Routing

9

This chapter covers

- Previewing SPA routing
- Getting started with the Aurelia router
- Understanding Aurelia's routing lifecycle
- Dynamically specifying route modules
- Extending my-books book management with the Aurelia router

Web browsers come with a known set of behaviors that most users are familiar with. Two examples that come to mind are the Back button, which takes the user back to the previous page they were on, and the ability to bookmark a specific page within a website. When the industry first started building SPAs, these behaviors were often overlooked, leading to frustrating user experiences where users would press the Back button only to find themselves at the homepage of the SPA, with the entire state of their browsing session lost. Frameworks have come a long way from those early days, and most now solve this problem by adding support for client-side routing. Client-side routing allows you to achieve the feeling of speed and provides other advantages you get with an SPA while still supporting the standard browser behaviors that users expect. This chapter delves into the details of Aurelia's routing system, allowing you to manage any of the client-side routing requirements you'll come across. To secure an Aurelia application (chapter 10), it's best to have a good grounding of how Aurelia's routing system works; the topics go together like peanut butter and jelly. Because of this, many of the features that you'll develop in this chapter will give you the foundation you'll need for chapter 10.

9.1　Understanding client-side routing

To understand client-side routing with Aurelia, it's worth briefly recapping the differences between the traditional request/response page-routing model and the client-side routing model that we covered in chapter 1.

Traditional request/response applications load the entire page for each request. To illustrate this, imagine you want to implement the my-books website using the server-side routing model (we'll call this Scenario 1). In this case, the initial page request returns the index.html page as the response. Then, when the user clicks a link through to the /books URL, the browser sends another request to the server, which then returns the HTML (and data) representing the book-management page.

In the case of an SPA (Scenario 2), when the user initially navigates to the my-books site, the browser makes a request to the server to retrieve the index.html file (the same as Scenario 1). When the user clicks the /books anchor tag, however, the SPA router (Aurelia's routing module) determines which component should be rendered into the DOM and replaces the contents of the application *shell* with a component. The application shell is the container with common elements that you want to remain consistent across every page of your SPA. The differences between these scenarios are depicted in figure 9.1.

The alternative to using client-side routing is to update the content inside the application without maintaining a history of these state changes using the router. For example, in Scenario 2 you'd still have an application shell that you could then use to slot in various components as the user moves between different application states. The question is, what benefits do you get from introducing client-side routing? It has two main benefits:

- Support for standard web-browser UX patterns such as the Back and Forward buttons
- Deep linking to pages within your SPA

Client-side routing allows you to emulate traditional request/response-style page changes in your SPA by listening for URL changes and swapping the contents of your application shell accordingly. With this in mind, let's explore how you can achieve it with the Aurelia router.

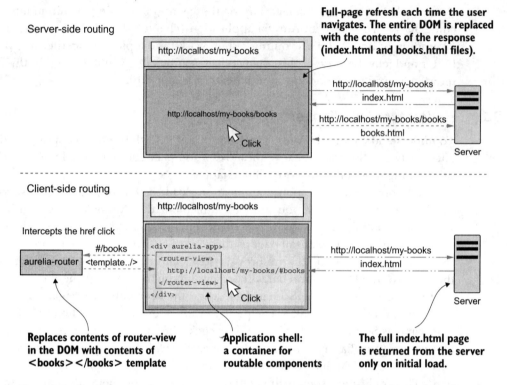

Figure 9.1   The differences between the request/response routing model and the SPA routing model

9.2   *Introducing the Aurelia router*

To understand the problem that the Aurelia router solves, let's first look at what it would take to implement client-side routing without this component. An SPA typically has two major triggers where user interaction causes a state change that you'll want to respond to:

- A URL change; for example, when a user navigates to a page within your application (such as by using the route #/books/edit/1). In this case, you'd need something to listen for, either the hashchange DOM or a history event such as pushstate. You can read more about the hashchange event on MDN at https://developer.mozilla.org/en-US/docs/Web/Events/hashchange.
- The user clicking a link (an anchor tag within your page).

In each of these scenarios, you'd need to configure an event handler to respond by updating the DOM fragment inside your SPA shell to represent the new application state. The Aurelia router abstracts these implementation details, allowing you to configure which routes correspond to which components in your application. It handles both these routing triggers seamlessly, allowing you to focus on the problem at hand; see figure 9.2.

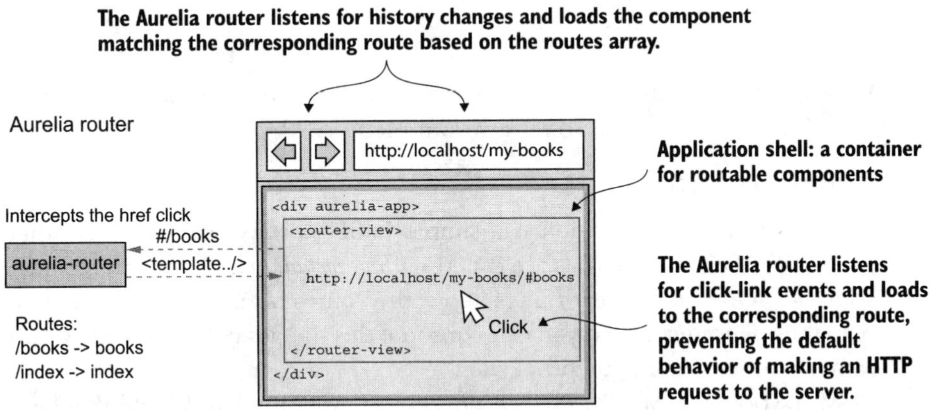

The Aurelia router listens for history changes and loads the component
matching the corresponding route based on the routes array.

Figure 9.2   The Aurelia router abstracts the logic necessary for handling user-route-change triggers
within your application, loading the corresponding route specified in your routing configuration.

As you saw in chapter 2, the router needs to be configured so that it knows which component to load when the user visits a given route. In the next section, we'll briefly recap this configuration and then look at some of the other configuration options used to implement features such as dynamic navigation menus, deep linking, and wildcard routes.

Before beginning the next section, please ensure that you have the latest version of the my-books-server Node.js application and MongoDB up and running, as described in the appendix.

9.2.1 Basic configuration

To refresh your memory, you can configure the router in the App view-model by implementing a configureRouter callback. The current routing configuration for my-books is shown in the following listing.

Listing 9.1   my-books initial routing configuration (app.js)

```
export class App {
  configureRouter(config, router) {
    this.router = router;
    config.title = 'my-books';
    config.map([
      { route: ['', 'home'], name: 'home', moduleId: 'index' },
      {
        route: 'books',
        name: 'books',
        moduleId: './resources/elements/books'
      },
    ]);
```

Defines the route-configuration function

Sets the router on the view-model

Sets the view title

Adds the routes to the router

Defines the home route

Defines the books route

```
    }
}
```

We won't cover the basic configuration in detail here, but you can refer to section 2.6.1, "Configuring the router," to refresh your memory.

9.2.2   *Routing metadata*

Aurelia's route configuration is a simple JavaScript/TypeScript object that exposes properties. These properties are called *routing metadata* and are useful for a variety of scenarios. One of the neat things about the route-configuration metadata is that it's bindable. This means that you can consume this metadata from the view as you would with any other view-model properties.

My favorite use case for this is rendering a navigation bar. Wouldn't it be nice if you didn't need to manually update the navigation bar HTML for each new route added to your Aurelia application? You can achieve this by using the metadata exposed by the routing configuration. To see this in practice, add a navigation bar to the top of the Aurelia view. Once you're done, you should have a new navigation-bar section displayed at the top of the page (right above the `<router-view>` custom element), as shown in figure 9.3.

To create the navigation bar in Aurelia, you'll need to complete the following three steps:

1 Add the new properties to the route configuration.
2 Create the new `nav-bar` HTML custom element to render the nav to the page.
3 Use the new `nav-bar` element in the app view.

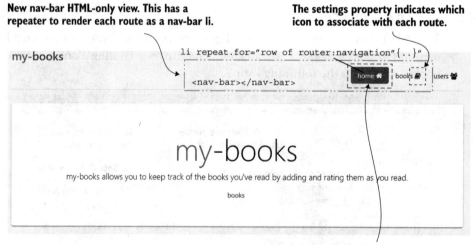

New nav-bar HTML-only view. This has a repeater to render each route as a nav-bar li.

The settings property indicates which icon to associate with each route.

```
li repeat.for="row of router:navigation"{..}"
```

`<nav-bar></nav-bar>`

my-books

my-books

my-books allows you to keep track of the books you've read by adding and rating them as you read.

books

The isActive route-metadata property highlights the current active route: ${row.isActive ? 'active' : }

Figure 9.3   Routing metadata used in combination with Aurelia's binding system to add a new `<nav-bar>` component to the my-books application

Besides the route, name, and moduleId properties (configured in chapter 2), the routing configuration has several more properties available. You'll configure two of these properties now. The title property determines the web-page title shown in the tab (for example, home | my-books). You'll also repurpose this property to display the title of the current route in the navigation view.

The nav property defaults to false, and routes can be marked as navigable by setting this property to true. This value is used by the router.navigation property, which returns a list of the navigable routes (routes enabled for display on the navigation menu). The settings property can be used to provide additional data to your Aurelia route. In this case, use it to indicate an optional Font Awesome icon that should be displayed along with the menu item. To demonstrate this, add a console log message to display a value for this property.

Listing 9.2 nav properties added to the route configuration (app.js)

```
export class App {
  configureRouter(config, router)
  ...
  config.map([
    { route: ['', 'home'], name: 'home', moduleId: 'index',
➡ title:'home', nav:true , settings: {icon:'home'}},
    { route: 'books', name: 'books', moduleId: './resources
➡ /elements/books', title:'books', nav:true, settings: {icon:'book'}},
  ]);
  }
}
```

Reload the browser to see the newly configured routing rules. If you open the developer tools window, you should see the navigable routes exported to the console. Figure 9.4 highlights the isActive, title, and settings properties available in the NavModel object. With the routing in place, the next step is to create a new HTML-only custom element and render the routes to the page.

To render the navigation bar to the screen, you'll need to create a new HTML-only custom element. This custom element will take a bindable router property (passed down from the parent app component). Then, use a repeater to render each of the navigable routes to the repeat.for="row of router.navigation" view. A bonus here is that the isActive property keeps track of the current active route, so you don't maintain this separately. Then, use the row.title and row.href properties to render the URL and link text for each menu item. Create a new view file, ./src/resources/elements/nav-bar.html, and include the contents of listing 9.3.

```
INFO [aurelia] Aurelia Started
▼ [] 🔋
  ▼ 0: NavModel
    ▶ config: Object
    ┌ ─ ─ href: "#/" ─ ─ ─ ─ ─ ─ ─ ─ ┐
    │   isActive: true               │  ◀── You'll use this to highlight
    └ ─ ─ ─ ─ ─ ─ ─ ─ ─ ─ ─ ─ ─ ─ ─ ─┘      the current active route.
        order: 101
        relativeHref: ""
    ▶ router: AppRouter
    ▶ settings: Object                  ◀── Used for the title of the page
    ┌──────────────────────────────┐        and the nav-link-item text
    │   title: "home"              │  ◀──
    └──────────────────────────────┘
    ▶ __observers__: Object
    ▶ get href: function ()
    ▶ set href: function ()
    ▶ get isActive: function ()
    ▶ set isActive: function ()
    ▶ get title: function ()
    ▶ set title: function ()
    ▶ __proto__: Object
  ▼ 1: NavModel
    ▶ config: Object                    ◀── Renders the route URL
    ┌ ─ ─ ─ ─ ─ ─ ─ ─ ─ ─ ─ ─ ─ ─ ─ ─┐      to the nav menu
    │   href: "#/books"              │  ◀──
    └ ─ ─ ─ ─ ─ ─ ─ ─ ─ ─ ─ ─ ─ ─ ─ ─┘
        isActive: false
        order: 102
        relativeHref: "books"
    ▶ router: AppRouter                 ◀── Additional custom route settings.
    ┌ ─ ─▶ settings: Object ─ ─ ─ ─ ─ ┐      You'll use this later to add icons
    │   title: "books"              │        to each nav menu item.
    └ ─ ─ ─ ─ ─ ─ ─ ─ ─ ─ ─ ─ ─ ─ ─ ─┘
    ▶ __observers__: Object
    ▶ get href: function ()
    ▶ set href: function ()
    ▶ get isActive: function ()
    ▶ set isActive: function ()
    ▶ get title: function ()
    ▶ set title: function ()
    ▶ __proto__: Object
      length: 2
  ▶ __array_observer__: ModifyArrayObserver
  ▶ __proto__: Array(0)
> |
```

Navigable routes coming from the router:navigation property

Figure 9.4   Log of the navigable routes defined in the routing configuration

---

Listing 9.3   Creating the `nav-bar` component (nav-bar.html)

```html
<template bindable="router">        ◀─┤ Exposes a bindable
    <nav>                                router property
        <ul class="nav nav-pills float-right">
            <li repeat.for="row of router.navigation"   ◀── Renders a menu item for
                class="nav-item">                            each navigable route
                <a class="nav-link
                    ${row.isActive ? 'active' : ''}"    ◀── Binds the active style
                    href.bind="row.href">                    menu item to the
                    ${row.title}                             row.isActive property
```

Binds the href link to the row.href property

Uses string-interpolation binding to render

```
                    <i if.bind="row.settings.icon"          ◁──┐
      class="fa fa-${row.settings.icon}">                      │
</i>                                                            │
                  </a>                                          │
             </li>                  Conditionally renders a     │
          </ul>                        Font Awesome icon        │
      </nav>                         based on the route data    │
</template>
```

With the new component in place, the last step is to introduce the nav bar into the app view. This is done in the standard way by requiring the custom element (in this case, you need the .html extension as this is an HTML-only view). Then, use the <nav-bar> custom element, passing the router down from the app component using data binding. Modify the view in the ./src/resources/elements/app.html file.

Listing 9.4 Adding `nav-bar` in the `app` view (app.html)

```
<template>
    <require from="bootstrap/css/bootstrap.css"></require>
    <require from="font-awesome.css"></require>
    <require from="styles.css"></require>
    <require from="./resources/elements/nav-bar.html"></require>   ◁──┐  Requires the
                                                                       │  nav bar HTML-
    <div class="container">                                           │  only custom
        <div class="header clearfix">                                  │  element into
        <h3 class="text-muted">                                        │  the app view
            <span class="brand-highlight">my</span>-books
        </h3>
        <nav-bar router.bind="router"></nav-bar>          ◁──┐  Uses the
        </div>                                                │  new nav-bar
        <router-view></router-view>                          │  component
        . . .

    </div>
</template>
```

Reloading the my-books view in the browser, you should now be able to switch between the books and home views using the navigation bar.

This configuration is suitable for basic routing needs (switching between top-level routes), but what about the deep-linking feature that I mentioned at the beginning of the chapter? Most applications require the ability to link to a view passing an identifier for the data that needs to be shown. One example of this is Twitter, which allows you to view a specific tweet by specifying the tweet ID as part of the URL. In the next section, we'll look at how you can use optional or mandatory route parameters to achieve deep linking.

9.3   *Passing route data to components*

In this section, we'll add a basic user-management page to the my-books application and use route parameters to deep link to a specific user. By the end of this section, the application will look like figure 9.5.

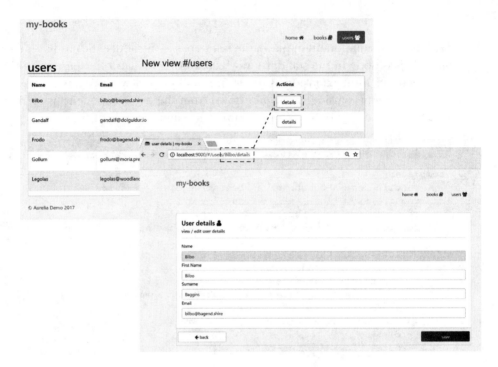

Figure 9.5   User management added to my-books. Route parameters will be used to deep link to a user by username.

9.3.1   *Route option types*

Route parameters are configured in Aurelia by modifying the options specified in the `route` property of your routing configuration map in your `app` view-model. The following variations are available:

- Basic routes
- Routes with query parameters
- Wildcard routes

BASIC ROUTES

In this case, you specify the plain relative URL from the root of your application, for example, `route: 'user/details'`. A basic route also accepts query parameters. For example, you could create a link to the route named `user-detail` from the view by adding a route-href custom attribute to an anchor tag, specifying the route's name: `<a ... route-href="route: user-detail; params.bind: {name: 'Bilbo'}"...>`. This translates to the following URL: http://localhost:9000/#/users/details?name =Bilbo.

PARAMETERIZED ROUTES

An alternative to the user-detail URL is to use required parameters, which use the `route: 'user/:name/details'` syntax, where `:name` is the route parameter that the user needs to specify. Passing route parameters uses the same syntax as with the basic routes: `<a ... route-href="route: user-detail; params.bind: {name: 'Bilbo'}" ...>`. Modifying the route configuration to include the `:name` parameter in your app view-model is enough for the router to translate the URL to the new value of http://localhost:9000/#/users/Bilbo/details rather than http://localhost:9000/#/ users/ details?name=Bilbo. You can specify this in any order you want. For example, an alternative to this route is `route: 'user/details/:name'`, which results in http:// localhost:9000/#/users/details/Bilbo as the URL.

WILDCARD ROUTES

Wildcard routes allow you to match anything after the `/*` character in your route property expression. For example, the `route: 'blog/:id/*'` route expression would match URLs like `route: 'blog/1234/getting-started'` and `route: 'blog/1234/ quick-start'`. In these cases, the `activate()` method is passed an object with the remainder of the URL after the wildcard character, for example, `'getting-started'`. An effective use case for this would be a slug (a descriptive post name) for a blog post, where even though you'll look the post up by ID, having the slug in the URL improves your Google juice.

9.3.2　Adding the user-management pages

With these routing options in mind, let's look at the query-parameter route option to see how this can be used in the context of the new user-management page. The steps for adding user management are as follows:

1　Add the user-api service so you can retrieve a list of users from the REST API.
2　Add a users component to display a list of users.
3　Add a user-details component to view and edit user details.
4　Modify the routing configuration to add the users and user-details routes.

The first step is to add the new user-API service class. As you're already familiar with the implementation details from when you implemented the books-api service, we won't cover it again. Create a new service class at ./src/services/user-api.js and add the contents of the following listing.

Listing 9.5   Creating a new `user-api` service class (user-api.js)

```
import {HttpClient, json} from 'aurelia-fetch-client';
import {inject} from 'aurelia-framework';

@inject(HttpClient)
export class UserApi{

    constructor(http){
        this.http = http;

        const baseUrl = 'http://localhost:8333/api/';

        http.configure(config => {
            config.withBaseUrl(baseUrl);
        });
    }

     getUser(name){
        return this.http.fetch(`users/${name}`)
                .then(response => response.json())
                .then(user => {
                    return user;
                })
                .catch(error => {
                    console.log('Error retrieving user.');
                });

    }

    getUsers(){

        return this.http.fetch('users')
                .then(response => response.json())
                .then(users => {
                    return users;
                })
                .catch(error => {
                    console.log('Error retrieving users.');
                });

    }

    addUser(user){
        return this.http.fetch('users', {
            method: 'post',
            body: json(user)
            })
            .then(response => response.json())
            .then(createdUser => {
                return createdUser;
            })
            .catch(error => {
                console.log('Error adding user');
            });
    }
```

Configures the base URL for all requests in this service

Fetches a user by name (used for the user-details page)

Gets a complete list of users from the API

Adds a user, serializing the passed-in user object to JSON and posting to the API

```
deleteUser(user){
    return this.http.fetch(`users/${user.name}`, {        ◁┐  Deletes a user by calling
            method: 'delete'                                  │  the user's endpoint with
            })                                                │  the DELETE verb
            .then(response => response.json())
            .then(responseMessage => {
                return responseMessage;
            })
            .catch(error => {
                console.log('Error deleting book');
            });
}

saveUser(user){
    return this.http.fetch(`users/${user.name}`, {       ◁┐  Saves a user by
            method: 'put',                                  │  calling the PUT
            body: json(user)                                │  endpoint
        })
        .then(response => response.json())
        .then(savedUser => {
            return savedUser;
        })
        .catch(error => {
            console.log('Error saving book');
        });
    }
}
```

The user component should look familiar to you. You'll create a new custom element by creating a new view/view-model pair. The view-model retrieves the list of users via the UserApi service class, which is then bound to the view and rendered into a table using a templating repeater. Create a new JavaScript file at ./src/resources/elements/users.js and enter the contents of the following listing.

Listing 9.6   Adding the `users` view-model (users.js)

```
import {bindable, inject} from 'aurelia-framework';
import {UserApi} from '../../services/user-api';

@inject(UserApi)
export class Users{                                      Stores the injected
    constructor(userApi){                                API user class on the
        this.userApi = userApi;          ◁──────         current object
    }
                                              Loads the users in
    bind(){                                   the bind() lifecycle
        this.loadUsers();       ◁───────       callback
    }
                                                    Saves the users on the
    loadUsers(){                                    view-model once the
        this.userApi.getUsers().then(users => {     promise returns so they're
            this.users = users;          ◁─────      available for binding
        });
```

```
    }
}
```

Then, create the corresponding view file to display basic user information in a table. Each row in the table includes an Edit button to allow users to click through and view more-detailed user information. This is achieved by using a `route-href` custom attribute. This attribute takes a binding expression that includes the route that should be used to calculate the URL value (`user-detail`) and any parameters that should be passed to the route calculation (`user.name`). Create a new HTML file at ./src/resources/elements/users.html and add the contents of the following listing.

Listing 9.7 Adding the `users` view (users.html)

```html
<template>
    <require from="./heading.html"></require>
    <heading text.bind="'users'"></heading>

    <div class="card">
        <table show.bind="users"
                class="table table-striped table-bordered">
            <thead>
                <tr>
                    <th>Name</th>
                    <th>Email</th>
                    <th>Actions</th>
                </tr>
            </thead>
            <tbody>
                <tr repeat.for="user of users">
                    <td>${user.name}</td>
                    <td>${user.email}</td>
                    <td>
                        <a class="btn btn-secondary"
route-href="route: user-detail;              ◁——  Uses the route-href
params.bind: {name:user.name}" >                    custom attribute to
                        details                       generate a link to the
                    </a>                              user-details page
                </td>
                </tr>
            </tbody>
        </table>
    </div>
</template>
```

The `user-details` component is responsible for retrieving a user by name from the UserApi service and rendering details to a form on the view. The name of the user is pulled from the `params` array, which is passed to the activate-routing-lifecycle callback, `activate(params, routeConfig) {...}`. We'll cover the routing lifecycle in section 9.5. Create the `user-details` view-model file at ./src/resources/elements/user-details.js and add the contents of the following listing.

Listing 9.8 Adding the `user-details` view-model (user-details.js)

```
import {bindable, inject} from 'aurelia-framework';
import {UserApi} from '../../services/user-api';

@inject(UserApi)
export class UserDetails{

    constructor(userApi){
        this.userApi = userApi;
    }

    activate(params, routeConfig) {
        this.loadUser(params.name);
    }

    loadUser(name){
        this.userApi.getUser(name).then(fetchedUser => {
            this.user = fetchedUser;
        });
    }

    saveUser(){
        this.userApi.saveUser(this.user).then(savedUser => {
            alert('Successfully saved user');
        });
    }
}
```

> Loads a user by the name specified in the route params argument during the activate callback

Create the corresponding `user-details` view file at ./src/resources/elements/user-details.html, as shown in the following listing. This is effectively a form that allows users to view and edit user information.

Listing 9.9 Adding the `user-details` view (user-details.html)

```
<template>
    <form if.bind="user" class="form card" submit.trigger="saveUser()">
        <div class="card-block">
            <h4 class="card-title">User details
                <i class="fa fa-user" ></i></h4>
            <h6 class="card-subtitle mb-2 text-muted">
                view / edit user details</h6>
            <hr/>
            <div class="form-group">
                <label for="name">Name</label>
                <input readonly
                        name="name" class="form-control"
                        placeholder='enter a name'
                        value.bind="user.name">
                </input>
                <label for="first_name">First Name</label>
                <input name="first_name" class="form-control"
                        placeholder='enter first name'
```

```
                            value.bind="user.first_name">
                </input>
                <label for="surname">Surname</label>
                <input name="surname" class="form-control"
                        placeholder='enter a surname'
                        value.bind="user.surname">
                </input>
                <label for="email">Email</label>
                <input name="email" class="form-control"
                        placeholder='enter an email address'
                        value.bind="user.email">
                </input>
            </div>
        </div>
        <div class="card-footer">
            <a class="btn btn-secondary col-sm-2"
  route-href="route: users" >
                <i class="fa fa-arrow-left"></i> back
            </a>
            <button type="submit" class="btn btn-primary
  col-sm-2 push-sm-8"
                    disabled.bind="user.name.length == 0">
                save
            </button>
        </div>
    </form>
</template>
```

With the required files in place, the last step is to add the two new routes representing the users and user-details views. The users route uses a basic route configuration, as you saw with the books and index views. The user-details route, however, uses a parameterized route, 'users/:name/details', which allows you to then pass along the username in the query string to deep link to the given user that takes a URL like http://localhost:9000/#/users/Bilbo/details. A user of the my-books application could bookmark or refresh this page and still get the same page state.

Listing 9.10   Adding the user-management routes (app.js)

```
export class App {
    configureRouter(config, router) {
    this.router = router;
    config.title = 'my-books';
    config.map([
        ...
        { route: ['', 'home'], name: 'home', moduleId: 'index', title:'home',
        ➥ nav:true, settings: {icon:'home'} },
        { route: 'books', name: 'books', moduleId: './resources/elements/
        ➥ books', title:'books', nav:true, settings: {icon:'book'}},
        { route: 'users', name: 'users', moduleId: './resources/elements/
        ➥ users', title:'users', nav:true, settings: {icon:'users'}},
```

```
    { route: 'users/:name/details', name: 'user-detail', moduleId: './
 ➡ resources/elements/user-details', title:'user details'},
]);
    ...
```

Reloading your browser, you should now be able to list and edit users using the two new components. We'll look at the user-management section further while adding authentication to my-books in chapter 10. If you run into any problems here, double-check that you've got the my-books-server API and MongoDB instance running as described in the appendix. It would also be worth verifying that each of the new files was added in the expected location. You can cross-check your solution against the complete chapter 10 copy on GitHub at http://mng.bz/qsEg.

9.4 *Specifying route modules dynamically*

The routing configuration that you've seen so far is static in nature. You specify a route expression, which maps to a module with a specific name (like the my-books /users route that maps to the `users` module). In some cases, however, it's useful to be able to determine which module to load at runtime. For example, imagine you have an off-the-shelf web application distributed to a variety of different customers, and you want to load a different component for a given route based on which customer the application is loaded for. Aurelia supports this functionality using a feature called *navigation strategies.*

Navigation strategies are functions that you can add to your route configuration instead of hardcoding the `moduleId` to load. Aurelia executes your navigation strategy function at runtime to determine the desired route. You could implement

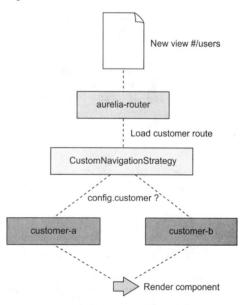

Figure 9.6   Customer-specific navigation strategy used to determine which component to load for the /custom route at runtime

customer-specific modules by adding a new navigation strategy. This strategy, for example, could look at a `config` value to determine which module to load, as shown in figure 9.6.

This can be implemented in the routing configuration, as shown in listing 9.11. In this example, the `config.customer` value is hardcoded to `'b'` (though, for example, this could just as easily be loaded from a configuration file at runtime). Next, instead of explicitly stating the `moduleId` for the customer route, this is calculated using `customNavigationStrategy`, which in this case calculates the model name using the `customer-${this.config.customer}'` expression, based on the value of `config` `.customer`.

Listing 9.11   Dynamic routing module example (app.js)

```
export class App {

  configureRouter(config, router) {
    this.router = router;
    this.config = config;

    config.title = 'Custom Navigation Example';
    config.customer = 'b';                          ◁── Sets the customer value
                                                          from configuration; could
    config.map([{                                         just as easily be a config file
        route: ['', 'home'],
        name: 'home',
        moduleId: 'home' ,
        nav:true
  },
    {                                                         Sets the navigation
        route: [ 'customer'],                                 strategy for the
        name: 'customer',                                     customer route
        navigationStrategy: this.customNavigationStrategy  ◁──┘
      }
    ]);
  }
                                                         Sets the customer module
  customNavigationStrategy = (instruction) => {   ◁──    to load based on the value
      instruction.config.moduleId = `customer-${this.config.customer}`;   defined in config
  }
}
```

Another option is to specify the customer ID as part of the route expression, because route parameters are also available to navigation strategies. In that case, you could use this ID in the navigation strategy. In addition to specifying the `moduleId` in your navigation strategy, you could alternatively specify `viewport` or `redirect` (which we'll cover shortly).

> **TIP**   If you're interested in reading more about dynamically specified routes, head over to the Aurelia Hub article on the topic, http://aurelia.io/docs/ routing/configuration#basic-configuration.

Dynamic routes are a convenient way to inject into the routing process at the point where Aurelia determines which module to load, but what if you want to inject into other points in the process to perform cross-cutting actions like logging or authentication? You can achieve this using another routing feature, called *pipelines*.

9.5 The screen-activation lifecycle and the route pipeline

You can hook into Aurelia's routing system in two different ways. The first is the *screen activation* lifecycle.

> **NOTE** A note on terminology. In Aurelia, a *screen* is the name for a navigable component. For example, the users, user-details, and books components in the my-books application are screens but the edit-book component isn't.

9.5.1 The screen-activation lifecycle

The screen-activation lifecycle is like the component lifecycle in that it also provides optional callbacks that you can add to your component view-models. Aurelia executes these callbacks at various points during its routing process. Because this lifecycle is implemented by the Aurelia router, even if you add these hooks to your view-model, they won't be called unless the component is initialized by the router. Figure 9.7 depicts this lifecycle.

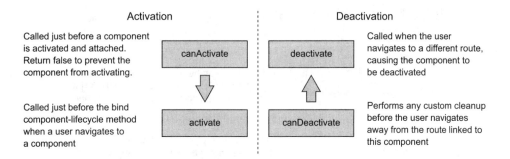

Figure 9.7   Aurelia's screen-activation lifecycle hooks available in navigable component view-models

> **Screen-activation-lifecycle hook methods**
> Here is an explanation of Aurelia's activation-lifecycle hook methods:
> - The canActivate(params, routeConfig, navigationInstruction) hook is called when a user navigates to a route linked to your component. You can return a Boolean value from this method to determine whether this component can be activated, which can be useful for preventing a component from loading. You can optionally return a promise for a Boolean value, in which case the router will wait to bind and attach your component until this result is returned.
> - The activate(params, routeConfig, navigationInstruction) hook is called when a user navigates to a route tied to your component, allowing you to perform any custom logic before it's bound and attached to the DOM. This is a suitable place to retrieve and populate data on your component by returning a promise to indicate the router should wait until your data comes back before proceeding. You should recognize the activate hook from the user-details component, where you used it to retrieve a user based on the name specified in the route parameters.

> **(continued)**
> - The `canDeactivate()` hook is called before the user navigates away from a screen to allow you to prevent navigation. This method returns a Boolean value to indicate whether the user is permitted to navigate away from the screen.
> - The `deactivate()` hook is called when a user navigates to a screen, to allow you to perform custom logic before it's unbound and detached from the DOM. This is a suitable place to add any custom cleanup logic that needs to be called as the user navigates away from the screen.

9.5.2   *Pipeline steps*

When it comes to injecting behavior into Aurelia's route pipeline, *pipeline steps* take up where the screen-activation lifecycle hooks leave off, allowing you to inject behavior into different points (called *slots*) in the route pipeline, as depicted in figure 9.8.

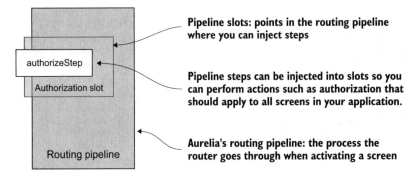

Figure 9.8   How routing slots and steps fit into Aurelia's route pipeline

The advantage of pipeline steps compared to screen-activation lifecycle hooks is that they allow you to define behavior to be applied to every routed view-model in your application. For example, one of the most useful pipeline slots is the `authorize` slot, which is called right before the screen view-model's `canActivate` function is called.

As you can imagine, it would be possible to implement authorization by implementing `canActivate` on every navigable view-model, returning `false` if the user was not authorized, but this would create a lot of duplicate code. In turn, this would mean that you'd need to update the authorization logic in every view-model any time this logic was changed. By contrast, you can achieve the same result by creating a new `authorize` step and adding this into the `authorize` pipeline slot. Pipeline steps are fantastic for cross-cutting behavior that needs to be applied any time a screen is loaded in your application.

The router also has an API for adding steps into each of the predefined slots. For example, the router configuration object has a `config.addAuthorizeStep(step)` method, which adds an authorize step into the corresponding `authorize` pipeline slot.

NOTE   Aurelia has two router classes: the `AppRouter` class, which is the main application router, and the `Router` class that it derives from. The `Router` class is used for child routers. Pipelines are available only for the `AppRouter` class.

Besides `authorize`, the other slots include `preActivate`, `preRender`, and `postRender`.

TIP   Check out this page on the Aurelia Hub if you're interested in reading more about each of Aurelia's pipeline slots: http://aurelia.io/docs/routing/configuration#pipelines.

For now, we'll look at the `preActivate` slot. Let's see what it takes to add a new pre-activate step to Aurelia's route pipeline. You'll then be able to follow the same process to add steps to any of the available pipeline slots in your own applications.

To add a new step to the route pipeline, do the following:

1   Create a new pipeline step. This needs to be an object that contains a function with the `run(navigationInstruction, next)` signature.
2   Add the pipeline step into the corresponding slot using the appropriate API method on the `config.addPreActivateStep(step)` route `config` object.

Try creating and adding the `preActivate` pipeline step to the my-books routing configuration. Add a new step, and then log the results to the console to see when each of the pipeline steps is fired. This log output includes steps from the route pipeline, the screen-activation lifecycle, and the component lifecycle so that you get a complete picture of what happens when the component loads. These steps are illustrated in the following listing.

Listing 9.12   `preActivate` route-pipeline step added to `app` (app.js)

```
export class App {
    configureRouter(config, router) {
        this.router = router;                        Creates the new
        config.title = 'my-books';                   preActivate pipeline step
        var step = {
                                                     Defines the required run
            run: (navigationInstruction, next) => {  function implementing
                console.log("pre-activate for module" the logging behavior
                        ,navigationInstruction.config.moduleId)
                return next()                        Logs the current
            }                                        moduleId on
        };                                           pre-activate
        config.addPreActivateStep(step);     Adds the new
        ...                                  pre-activate step
                                             to the pipeline
```

As you can see in figure 9.9, the screen-activation lifecycle hooks (`pre-activate` and `activate`) are called first, allowing you to perform any setup actions that should be run before data binding is executed or the view is attached to the DOM. You've also added further logging to the `user-details`-view component lifecycle methods to provide a complete picture of the process.

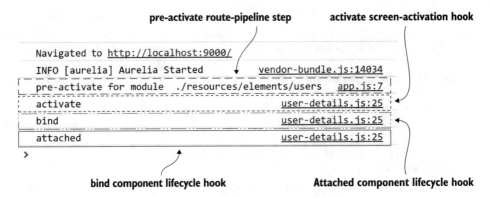

Figure 9.9   Console log output illustrating the pre-activate pipeline step, executed right before the user-details screen is activated

This covers a basic introduction to Aurelia's route pipeline, but we'll come back to the `authorize` slot and corresponding step as a means of securing the routes in chapter 10.

9.6   *Aurelia's 404*

Expect the unexpected. I think that statement is at least as true for web developers as anyone else (if not much more!). As much as you try to think about all the unusual ways that users will interact with your application, they always manage to run into the *one* situation you didn't think of. One of the common interaction patterns is users trying out the URL structure in the nav bar to see if they can discover hidden gems within your application. Fortunately for us, Aurelia provides a straightforward way to deal with this situation.

The router provides a configuration method, `config.mapUnknownRoutes`, which can take either an explicit `moduleId` string (for example, `'index'`) or a function. The function gives you more flexibility when you need it, though most of the time a simple `moduleId` will suffice. Add unknown-route support to my-books. This will give you an overview of how you could use either the static or dynamic unknown-route-handling techniques.

9.6.1   *Handling an unknown route: option 1, moduleId*

To see how this option works, create a new component to display when the user stumbles across a route in my-books that you haven't anticipated. Then, modify the route configuration to map unknown routes to this new component. By the time you're done, the user will receive a friendly message even when they deviously play with the route parameters (see figure 9.10).

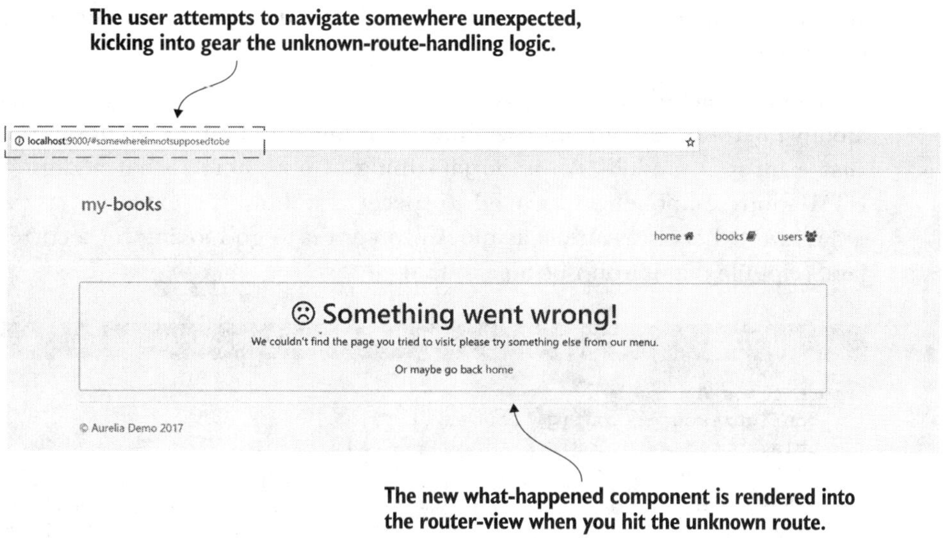

The user attempts to navigate somewhere unexpected, kicking into gear the unknown-route-handling logic.

The new what-happened component is rendered into the router-view when you hit the unknown route.

Figure 9.10 Unknown-route-handling logic added to my-books application, rendering the `what-happened` component into `router-view`

CREATING THE WHAT-HAPPENED COMPONENT

Start by creating a new HTML-only custom element called what-happened. Create a new HTML file at ./src/resources/elements/what-happened.html and add the template shown in the following listing.

Listing 9.13 Creating the `what-happened` HTML template (what-happened.html)

```
<template>
    <div class="card card-outline-warning mb-3 text-center">
    <div class="card-block">
        <h1>
<i class="fa fa-frown-o" ></i> Something went wrong!
        </h1>
        <blockquote class="card-blockquote">
        <p>
           We couldn't find the page you tried to visit,
           please try something else from our menu.
        </p>
        <footer>
           Or maybe go back <a route-href="route: home;">home</a>
        </footer>
        </blockquote>
    </div>
    </div>
</template>
```

With this template in place, you need to modify the route configuration so that it knows to render this view.

MODIFYING THE ROUTE CONFIGURATION

Modify the route configuration as shown in listing 9.14 to map unknown routes to the what-happened module. An important thing to note here is that because this is an HTML-only component, you need to specify the .html file extension as part of the moduleId. Otherwise, Aurelia assumes you want it to go looking for a corresponding JavaScript file that it won't be able to find.

Listing 9.14   Route configuration modified to handle unknown routes (app.js)

```
export class App {
    configureRouter(config, router) {
    this.router = router;
    config.title = 'my-books';
    config.map([
      ...
    ]);
    config.mapUnknownRoutes('./resources/elements/what-happened.html');    ⟵
  ...
```

Renders the what-happened template when the user hits an unknown route

9.6.2   *Handling unknown routes: option 2, a function*

Although option 1 is suitable for most cases, at times you'll need to determine at run-time which component to render when the user attempts to visit an unknown route. For example, you might want to render a different component if the user attempts to visit /admin. In these cases, you can instead pass a function to the mapUnkownRoutes method. The function must return a result matching one of the following conditions:

- A string moduleId
- An object with a moduleId property of the string type
- A route config object
- A promise that returns one of the preceding options

In the next section, you'll implement a function that returns a different moduleId based on whether the user enters /admin or any other route. The resulting view will look like figure 9.11.

The user attempts to navigate to an unknown admin area, kicking off the unknown-route-handling logic.

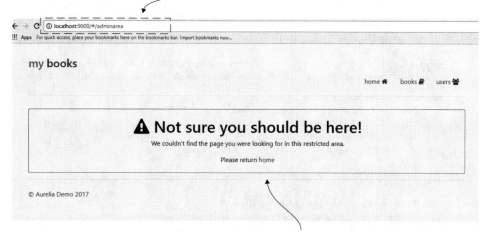

The new admin-unknown-route component is rendered into the router-view when you hit the admin area unknown route.

Figure 9.11 The my-books router-view section renders a new admin-unknown-route view, depending on whether the unknown path belongs in the admin area.

CREATING THE ADMIN-UNKNOWN-ROUTE VIEW

The first step is to create the new admin-unknown-route HTML template file. Create a new file at ./src/resources/elements/admin-unknown-route.html.

Listing 9.15 Creating the `admin-unknown-route` **view (admin-unknown-route.html)**

```
<template>
    <div class="card card-outline-danger mb-3 text-center">
    <div class="card-body">
        <h1>
            <i class="fa fa-exclamation-triangle"></i>
            Not sure you should be here!
        </h1>
        <blockquote class="card-bodyquote">
        <p>
            We couldn't find the page you were
            looking for in this restricted area.
        </p>
        <footer>
            Please return <a route-href="route: home;">home</a>
        </footer>
        </blockquote>
    </div>
    </div>
</template>
```

Now, the next step is to create the new function that determines which module to render based on the route at runtime. Modify the ./src/app.js file as shown in listing 9.16 to add a new `handleUnknownRoutes` function, which takes the routing `instruction` parameter and returns the appropriate `moduleId` based on the path. Then, modify the `mapUnknownRoutes` function to take this function rather than a static `moduleId`.

Listing 9.16   Configuring the unknown-route function (app.js)

```
export class App {
    configureRouter(config, router) {
    this.router = router;
    config.title = 'my-books';
    var handleUnknownRoutes = (instruction) => {

      let path = instruction.fragment.toLowerCase();

      if(path.includes('admin'))
       rcturn './resources/elements/admin-unknown-route.html'

      return './resources/elements/what-happened.html';
    }
    config.map([
      ...
    ]);
    config.mapUnknownRoutes(handleUnknownRoutes);    ⟵┐  Renders the appropriate
  ...                                                    template based on the
                                                         kind of unknown route
```

These two options give you a lot of flexibility in handling the gamut of route variations that users will throw at your applications, by rendering a view to give the user some useful information about what they need to do next. Another option for handling unexpected routes, or routes that may have been refactored out of your application, is to use another routing feature, called *redirects*.

9.7   *Redirecting routes*

Redirects allow you to specify that when a user visits a route, they should be redirected to another route. These are particularly useful for when you want to retire a route in your application without breaking the user's existing bookmarks. You can do this by keeping the old route in your route array (the *from* route) and adding a `redirect` route that should be returned instead (the *to* route).

To see how this is used, modify the my-books route configuration again to add support for a legacy version of the `users` route. Modify the route configuration in the ./src/app.js file to add a new `'legacy-users'` route. This route will have a `redirect: 'URL FRAGMENT'` property that takes the URL fragment you want to redirect to (the users route). The route expression that you'll use here is (route: 'legacy-users', redirect: 'users'). This expression explicitly looks for the route #/legacy-users and redirects it to #/users. You could make this route more flexible and allow it to also handle parameterized routes by adding a wildcard to the route expression (route: 'legacy-users/*'), which would also match URLs like #/legacy-users/bob/details.

```
export class App {
    configureRouter(config, router) {
    ...
    config.map([
      ...
      { route: 'users', name: 'users', moduleId: './resources/elements/
    ➡ users', title:'users', nav:true, settings: {icon:'users'}},
      { route: 'users/:name/details', name: 'user-detail', moduleId: './
    ➡ resources/elements/user-details', title:'user details'},
      { route: 'legacy-users', redirect: 'users'}      ◁──┐
    ]);                                          Redirects the legacy-
    ...                                          users route to the new
                                                 /users URL fragment
```

Now that you're well equipped to handle any kind of routing scenario that you might come across, let's change the pace a little and look at two UI-related routing features that you can use to create a consistent look and feel across your Aurelia application.

9.8 View ports

Imagine you have a classic master-details application for accountants, with transactions in the left panel and transaction details in the right panel. So far, we've handled mapping between routes and modules as one-to-one by mapping a URL fragment to a specific moduleId. But, by using another Aurelia router feature called *view ports*, you can add a new level of flexibility to the UI.

View ports are different regions of a page in your Aurelia application. You can use them by defining one or more named router-view custom elements within the page—for example, transaction-master and transaction-details. Each router-view element has a corresponding view port (you've been using them all along without even realizing it). By naming the view ports, you provide a reference that you can refer to in the routing configuration. You can then specify each of these view ports in the routing configuration and map them to the desired route, for example:

```
/transactions
   viewPorts: {
transaction-master: { moduleId: 'transaction/master' },
transaction-detail: { moduleId: 'transaction/detail' }}.
```

This relationship between the route configuration, view ports, and modules is depicted in figure 9.12.

If you were to implement such a layout, the corresponding HTML would look like listing 9.18.

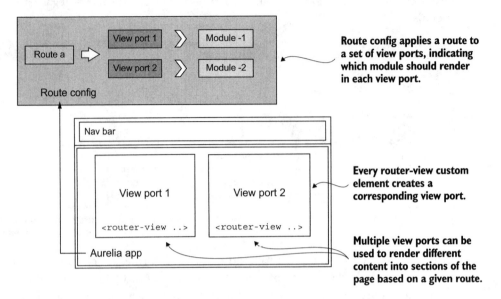

Figure 9.12   You can define multiple view ports in a page within your Aurelia application and map these to a route name in your route configuration.

Listing 9.18   View-port example template (app.html)

Defines the transaction-
master view port

```
<template>
    <router-view name='transaction-master'></router-view>
    <router-view name='transaction-detail'></router-view>
</template>
```

Defines the transaction-
detail view port

We won't bring view ports into the my-books sample application, but you can read more and check the samples available on the Aurelia site for further information. The next layout tool that Aurelia provides is aptly named layouts. We'll explore how you can use layouts to define a different page structure for different sections of your website.

9.9   *Extending my-books with layouts*

In the my-books application, the main application structure is made up of a naviga-tion bar and a content section. This has been suitable up until now, but in the next chapter you'll add an authentication system, which will require some pages to have a different structure. Ideally, you don't want the navigation bar of the application to be displayed at all on the login or register pages. Instead, you want a simplified layout so that you can show the user only what they need to see.

Fortunately, *layouts* make this easy. Layouts allow you to define multiple top-level pages into which views in your application can be rendered. This allows you to design your UI the way that best fits each page in your application. In this section, we'll reorganize the user interface, associating each of the modules with one of the following layouts:

- `main-layout`—This consists of a navigation bar, the content (such as the list of books), and a footer.
- `login-layout`—This consists of a brand-style my-books header and a simple login form.

By the end of this section, you'll be able to visit the new my-books login page using the #/login route of the my-books application, as shown in figure 9.13.

The login route points to a different layout.

login-layout has a simpler design without the navigation bar.

Figure 9.13   Login page layout associated with the new login route

You can create layouts in the same way that you create a standard custom element in Aurelia. You first create the view, and then optionally create the corresponding view-model for any behavior that your layout should perform. These layouts are then mapped to routes in your routing configuration.

So, when the user visits a specific route, Aurelia follows the standard process you've seen so far in this chapter, looking up the `moduleId` mapped to this route.

The router then checks if you've got a layout view or view-model configured for the route. If the router finds a layout, it conceptually renders the layout view inside your `router-view` element, and then renders the view associated with your `moduleId` inside the layout.

Layouts use a shadow DOM feature called *slots* (we'll cover the Shadow DOM in detail in chapter 12) to give you the ability to segment the view into different regions.

> **Shadow DOM slots**
>
> As discussed in chapter 4, the Shadow DOM is a web-component specification currently in the process of being adopted by all modern browsers. It provides a way of encapsulating a part of the DOM (a component) to prevent its styles and behavior from being disrupted by the styles and JavaScript in the main document.
>
> Shadow DOM slots are like holes in the Shadow DOM, into which you can inject markup. These holes, called *slots*, allow you to compose your custom element, declaring parts that can be replaced by the calling code. Imagine, for example, that you had a `book` custom element, which had a `title` and `description`. By defining slots for each of these fields, you could consume and then inject custom markup into each slot. We'll cover this concept in detail in chapter 12.

You define one or more slots in your layout view, and then reference the slots by name in the view associated with your route. To separate the application into the login and main layouts, create a new login screen (module and corresponding route). When the user visits #/login, render the login screen into the `login-layout`. If the user visits any other route (for example, #/users), render that screen into the main layout. Figure 9.14 shows how layout views fit into Aurelia's routing system.

The concept of layouts is easiest to understand with examples. Let's get our hands dirty and restructure the my-books application to make use of layouts. This process involves the following steps:

1 Create two layout views (`main` and `login`).
2 Modify the `app` view to remove template components now in the layout.
3 Create the new `login` component.
4 Modify the routing configuration to add layout support.

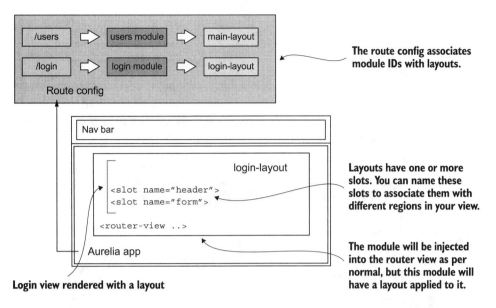

Figure 9.14 A /login route is mapped to a login module (view/view-model pair) and associated with the `login-layout` view. The `login` view is then rendered inside the login layout into the header and form slots.

9.9.1 Creating the layouts

Adding a login page to the project introduces a requirement for a screen without a navigation bar (users shouldn't see any secured routes until they've been authenticated). You could implement this by hiding the `nav-bar` component using binding until the user has been authenticated. But a cleaner way to do this is to split the login screen into its own layout. That way, you can display the login layout (with specific login styles or a navigation bar) until you've successfully authenticated the user.

This keeps the view logic in the main layout much simpler, because it doesn't need to concern itself with the case where a user isn't authenticated. To implement the login page, the first step is to create the two new layouts. The `login-layout` will be a simple view, which defines two slots:

- A `"header"` slot, where you'll render the my-books brand-style header
- A `"form"` slot, where you'll render the login form

You could reuse these same slots later if you decided to apply the same layout to a module with similar requirements (for example, a registration form). Create the new login layout at ./src/login-layout.html and add the contents of the following listing.

Listing 9.19 Creating the login layout (login-layout.html)

```
<template>
    <require from="login-styles.css"></require>
```

```
    <div class="container">
        <slot name="header"></slot>
        <slot name="form"></slot>
    </div>
</template>
```

> Defines the view slots into which content regions will be rendered

Next, you need to create the main layout. This layout takes the router from the parent component via data binding to render the navigation bar at the top of the page. As such, you need to create a corresponding view-model for this view. Create the new main-layout view-model at ./src/main-layout.js.

Listing 9.20 Creating the `main-layout` view-model (main-layout.js)

```
import {inject, bindable} from 'aurelia-framework';
import {Router} from 'aurelia-router';

@inject(Router)
export class Layout{
    @bindable router;                    ⭠  Creates the bindable router
    constructor(router){                     property to allow the router to
        this.router = router;                be bound from the parent view
    }
}
```

The main-layout view exposes only one slot. Because you haven't named the slot in the layout, the router will render the entire contents of any associated views into this slot. If you'd named the slot, you'd also need to reference this slot in the consuming view, so Aurelia knows which slot the corresponding markup should be injected into. You'll see an example of this when you implement the login view. You've also moved the nav-bar component from the app view into this layout because it shouldn't be displayed for the login layout. Create the new main-layout view at ./src/main-layout.html.

Listing 9.21 Creating the `main-layout` view (main-layout.html)

```
<template>
    <require from="./resources/elements/nav-bar.html"></require>    ⭠
    <div class="container">
        <div class="header clearfix">
            <h3 class="text-muted">
        ➥     <span class="brand-highlight">my</span>-books
            </h3>
            <nav-bar router.bind="router"></nav-bar>
        </div>
        <slot></slot>                              ⭠
        <footer class="footer">
            <p>&copy; Aurelia Demo 2017</p>
        </footer>
    </container>
</template>
```

> Requires the nav-bar component into the main layout

> Defines a slot where each screen (such as 'books') will be rendered

The second step involves trimming down the app view to remove any contents that have now been shifted into the main-layout view. Modify the app view as shown in the following listing.

Listing 9.22 Trimming down the app view (app.html)

```
<template>
    <require from="bootstrap/css/bootstrap.css"></require>
    <require from="font-awesome.css"></require>
    <require from="styles.css"></require>
    <router-view></router-view>
</template>
```

Trims down the app view, removing components that have been shifted to layouts

9.9.2 Adding the login view

The login view will be associated with the login-layout in the router. To begin, create an empty view-model, which you'll later flesh out with authentication functionality in chapter 10. Create the new login view-model at ./src/resources/elements/login.js.

Listing 9.23 Adding the login view-model (login.js)

```
export class Login{
    constructor(){
    }
}
```

Creates a minimal login view-model implementation, to be fleshed out in chapter 10

The login view needs to define two slots that correspond to the named slots defined in the login-layout. The content in the div elements for each of these slots will be rendered into the corresponding layout slots, as shown in figure 9.15.

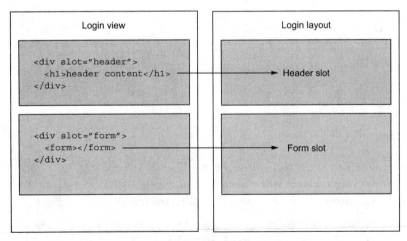

Header markup defined in the view is injected into the header slot in the login layout. The form markup is injected into the form slot.

Figure 9.15 Markup from the login view is injected into the corresponding login layout slots.

Create the new `login` view at ./src/resources/elements/login.html.

Listing 9.24   Adding the `login` view (login.html)

> Declares the HTML header fragment to be rendered into the 'header' layout slot

> Declares the HTML form fragment to be rendered into the 'form' layout slot

```
<template>
    <div slot="header">
        <h1 class="brand-heading">my-books</h1>
    </div>
    <div slot="form" class="container">
        <div class="row justify-content-center align-items-center">
            <div class="card">
                <div class="card-header">
                    <h1>login</h1>
                </div>
                <form class="card-block form-inline">
                    <label class="sr-only"
                    for="userName">user name</label>
                    <div class="input-group mb-2 mr-sm-2 mb-sm-0">
                        <input type="text"
                                class="form-control"
                                id="userName" placeholder="user name">
                    </div>
                    <label class="sr-only" for="password">password</label>
                    <div class="input-group mb-2 mr-sm-2 mb-sm-0">
                        <input type="password"
                                class="form-control"
                                id="password"
                                placeholder="password">
                    </div>
                    <button type="submit"
                            class="btn btn-success">login
                    </button>
                </form>
                <div class="card-footer text-muted">
                    welcome back to my-books
                </div>
            </div>
        </div>
    </div>
</template>
```

To differentiate the login page and give users a warm welcome to the my-books site when they first visit, add a new stylesheet at ./src/login-styles.css and add the contents of the following listing. This stylesheet is applied to only the login layout.

Listing 9.25   Adding the login style sheet (login-styles.css)

```
body{
    background-image: url("/images/background2.jpeg");
    background-repeat: no-repeat;
    background-size: 100% 100%;
}
```

```
h1{
    color: #009688;
}

.brand-heading{
    font-family: 'Shadows Into Light Two', cursive;
    font-size: 100px;
    color:white;
}

html, body {
    height: 100%;
}
.container, .row.justify-content-center.align-items-center {
    height: 90%;
    min-height: 90%;
}

.card, .card-header, .card-footer{
    background: rgba(225, 225, 225, .5);
}

.card-block{
    background: rgba(225, 225, 225, .8);
}
```

9.9.3 *Modifying the routing configuration*

With the required components in place, you need to adjust the routing configuration to make use of the new layouts. The following layout-configuration options are available in the routing configuration:

- `layoutViewModel` *name*—In this case, the router automatically looks for a layout view of the same name by convention and renders it for you. This is used for the main layout.
- `layoutView` *name*—Used if you don't have a corresponding view-model. This is used for the login layout, where you don't require any JavaScript logic in the layout itself.
- `layoutModel` *JSON object*—This allows you to pass some initial seed data to the layout (such as a page heading).

Modify the routing configuration in the app view-model at ./src/app.js to associate the login route with the `login-layout` and every other route with the `main-layout`.

Listing 9.26 Modifying the app routing configuration (app.js)

```
export class App {
    configureRouter(config, router) {
...
    config.map([
        {
          route: ['', 'home'],
```

```
        name: 'home',
        moduleId: 'index',
        title:'home',
        nav:true,
        settings: {icon:'home'},
        layoutViewModel: 'main-layout'         ◁─┐
      },
      {
        route: 'books',
        name: 'books',
        moduleId: './resources/elements/books',
        title:'books', nav:true,
        settings: {icon:'book'},
        layoutViewModel: 'main-layout'          ◁─┤
      },
      {                                              Links all existing
        route: 'users',                              routes to the
        name: 'users',                               main-layout,
        moduleId: './resources/elements/users',      which includes
        title:'users',                               navigation bar
        nav:true,
        settings: {icon:'users'},
        layoutViewModel: 'main-layout'          ◁─┤
      },
      {
        route: 'users/:name/details',
        name: 'user-detail',
        moduleId: './resources/elements/user-details',
        title:'user details',
        layoutViewModel: 'main-layout'          ◁─┘
      },
      {
        route: 'login',
        name: 'login',
        moduleId: './resources/elements/login',
        title:'login',
        layoutView: 'login-layout.html'      ◁─┐ Links the new
      },                                         login route with
                                                 the login-layout
      ...
    }
}
```

As a last step, download the login-page background image from the *Aurelia in Action* GitHub repository (http://mng.bz/cKEa) and copy it to ./images/background.jpg. If you reload the application and visit the login page at http://localhost:9000/#/login, you should see the login form with the newly created layout.

This form isn't functional yet, but we'll flesh out the authentication functionality in chapter 10. Navigating back to the homepage, http://localhost:9000, you should see that the existing pages in the application still conform to the original page layout.

9.10 *my-books project status*

Figure 9.16 highlights the major changes made to the my-books application in this chapter. You added the following features:

- A dynamic navigation bar built using routing metadata
- A user-management section that uses route parameters to allow deep linking to users by name
- A `main-layout` and a `login-layout` that prepare you to implement authentication in chapter 10 by allowing you to specify a separate page look and feel for the newly created login form

In chapter 10, we'll expand on the user-management functionality that we implemented in this chapter. We'll use a combination of the authorization pipeline step with other Aurelia features to implement a JSON Web Token (JWT)–based authentication system and secure my-books.

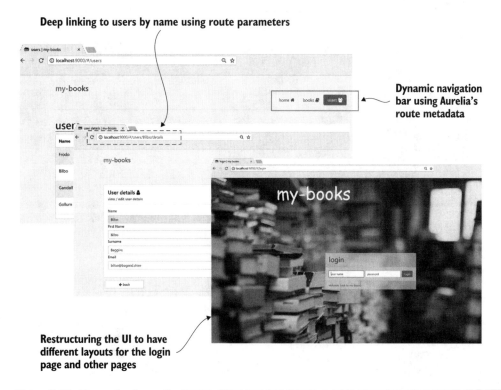

Figure 9.16 The my-books application modified to take advantage of the Aurelia router

Summary

- Client-side routing allows you to create SPAs that feel like real websites with support for the standard browser-interaction patterns that users expect.
- Client-side routing in general is achieved by catching anchor-tag clicks or browser navigation events and pushing them into the browser's history.
- The Aurelia router abstracts the implementation details of client-side routing, allowing you to specify which component to render when a user visits a given URL.
- Aurelia's router can be configured in a plethora of ways to allow you to tailor your application's routing system based on its unique app-navigation requirements.
- The router also provides hooks in the form of the screen-activation lifecycle and pipeline steps. These allow you to inject behavior at different points in the routing and screen-activation processes to implement features such as authorization.
- You can use a combination of view ports and layouts to compose the various segments of your UI in a way that feels consistent across your application.

Authentication

This chapter covers

- Comparing cookie- and token-based authentication
- Securing your Aurelia applications with tokens
- Using value converters, HTTP interceptors, and route-pipeline steps

Although we've assumed only one user account in the my-books application to this point, launching it in the real world would require it to support multiple users in a variety of roles. You're probably already familiar with the concepts of authentication and authorization, so we won't cover these in detail. But SPAs require a nontraditional approach to authentication. Whereas traditional server-side applications are typically secured using cookies and server-side rendered views—where the server has the context of who the user is—SPAs don't have this luxury. Because the application views (such as the navigation bar) are rendered on the client side, you need a new set of tools and techniques: first, to handle what is shown based on a user's authentication status, and then, to render the page appropriately based on the user's authorization level. This chapter demonstrates how you can use a combination of JSON Web Tokens (JWTs), local storage, and Aurelia's routing system to build authentication and authorization into your Aurelia applications.

10.1   *Client-side authentication*

Traditional server-centric applications typically follow a standard approach to authentication using cookies. You're probably already familiar with the authentication flow for a cookie-based approach, but let's quickly break it down so that we can compare it with an alternative approach that fits perfectly with an SPA-style architecture.

We'll call the first approach the *traditional stateful approach*, because it relies on the state (session ID) being saved on the server to be checked on subsequent requests. The authentication workflow for this approach is as follows:

1 The user enters a username and password into a form, which is then posted to the server.

2 The server verifies the credentials and generates a session ID for the user, attaching this to a cookie that's returned to the browser. The session ID is also typically stored in a database to allow it to be retrieved in subsequent requests, regardless of whether these requests return to the same server or a different one.

3 The browser attaches this session cookie on each request, allowing the server to verify the user's identity and respond accordingly.

4 On logout, the session cookie is removed from the browser and deleted from the server-side data store.

With the exploding popularity of SPAs and mobile applications, another approach has arisen, better suited to these application types—the token-based authentication approach. These two approaches are depicted in figure 10.1.

10.1.1   *Token-based authentication*

A token-based approach is stateless, meaning that the server doesn't need to keep track of a session ID between requests. Instead, a token is attached to each request. This token contains all the information that a server needs to verify the request's authenticity. There have been many different token formats, but recently JSON Web Tokens (JWTs) have become the industry-wide default approach. To understand what makes token-based authentication such a great fit for SPAs, let's look at the authentication workflow in a token-based approach, contrasting this with the traditional cookie-based approach:

1 The user logs in with their credentials.

2 The user credentials are sent to an authentication server, which verifies the credentials and generates a signed token.

3 The token is signed with a private key so that it can be verified on subsequent requests.

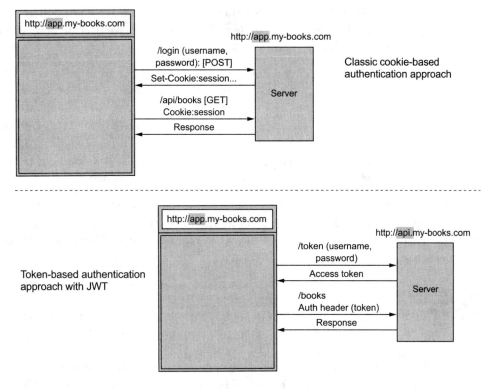

Figure 10.1 **Comparison of the traditional cookie-based workflow with a token-based approach**

4 The token is then stored client-side (typically in local storage, but session- and cookie-based storage also work).

5 The token is then retrieved from local storage and attached to each request to the server. This token is generally sent as an `authorization` header with the `bearer` JWT format, but it can also be transmitted as a part of a `POST` request body or query parameter.

6 The server decodes the JWT, and if the token is valid (based on the private key), the server processes the request and returns.

7 On logout, the token is removed from local storage, with no need to clear up session state on the server.

10.1.2 *Comparing cookie- and token-based authentication approaches*

The traditional cookie-based approach works well when you have a single domain or subdomain, but what if you have a separate API that lives under an entirely different domain? Because cookies are tied to a single domain or subdomain, they don't support a scenario where your application architecture is made up of multiple domains (like most SPAs). Token-based authentication satisfies this requirement, and it offers some additional benefits. The key benefits to a token-based approach, specifically regarding SPA architecture, are as follows:

- *It's stateless.* The backend doesn't need to keep track of users' session IDs. This makes the approach more scalable because you don't have that added footprint as more users log into the system.
- *You can store extra metadata in a JWT, so long as it's valid JSON.* This can be used to eliminate additional round trips to the server to retrieve details such as user roles. This is convenient not only from a client-side-development perspective, but it also brings an opportunity to improve performance.

I've touched only briefly on the ins and outs of cookies versus tokens here. If you're interested in finding out more, you might want to check out this great guide on the Auth0 blog at https://sean-hunter.io/aia-cookies-vs-tokens. With this understanding, let's take a closer look at the JWT format.

10.1.3 JWT format

A JWT is a string composed of a header, a payload, and a signature (see figure 10.2). The *header* describes the kind of token (for example, JWT) and the hashing algorithm used to generate the signature (for example, HMAC-SHA256). The *payload* contains the body of the token, which includes anything you require on the client side to present the user with the correct behavior. In the my-books example, this will include the

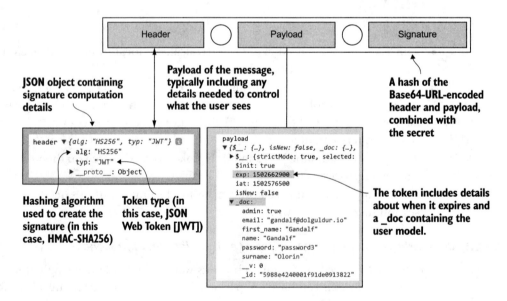

Figure 10.2 **JWTs are strings comprising a header, payload, and signature separated by dot (.) characters.**

user model that you'll use to render the current username to the view and determine whether a user is an admin.

The *signature* is used to check the validity of the token server-side and ensure that it hasn't been tampered with. It's calculated by Base64-URL encoding the header and the payload, concatenating them, and then hashing the result with a secret key on the server, using the hashing algorithm defined in the header. You can think of the secret key as a password for your token, except instead of being used to view the contents of your token (which you can do by decoding it), it's used to verify that the token hasn't been modified by an entity that doesn't know your password.

10.2 Securing my-books

So far, we've treated the my-books application as a single user app. In this chapter, we'll extend this to include support for multiple users with different bookshelves. Users will need to log in when they first visit the site. After logging in, they should see a view of the system restricted to their own bookshelf. We'll also separate the user-management section that you added in chapter 9, restricting it so that only users with the admin flag are able to view and manage the list of my-books users. The functionality to be implemented includes the following:

- A login page for users to enter a username and password. The username and password will be sent to the my-books-server application's /token endpoint. This endpoint returns a token that you'll store in local storage to keep track of the current user's session.
- A filtered navigation bar that shows users only the menu items they're authorized to see.
- A filtered view of the books retrieved from MongoDB, restricted to the current user's bookshelf by sending the user's token with all requests to the backend.

You'll achieve these features by using a set of Aurelia tools that you're already familiar with, including HTTP interceptors, route-pipeline steps, and value converters, and combining them to implement a basic JWT-based client-side authentication system across the my-books application.

> **TIP** Although we've used a custom authentication server in the my-books server for demonstration purposes, in many real-world SPAs, this isn't the best fit for your users. Great third-party services such as Auth0 and Azure Active Directory are designed specifically to solve this piece of the puzzle. They can provide features like single sign-on across several applications in each system or enterprise, and much more. On top of this, they're created by people who write authentication systems for a living. I highly recommend looking at them as part of your own SPA projects.

10.2.1 *Authentication architecture*

The authentication workflow you'll implement in my-books is shown in figure 10.3.

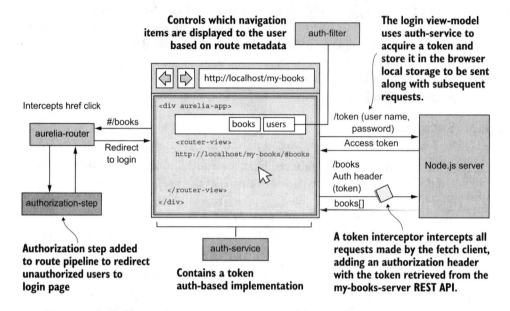

Figure 10.3   **my-books authentication-and-authorization architecture, securing user access using a combination of a route-pipeline step, value converter, service class, route metadata, and an HTTP interceptor**

The my-books authentication flow depicted in figure 10.3 will work as follows:

1 The user logs into the application using the login page (consisting of the `login-layout` that you implemented in chapter 9 and the `login` component). When the user logs in, a new `auth-service` within the my-books SPA sends a request to the my-books /token-server endpoint, which validates the user's credentials and sends back a token identifying the user.

2 On receipt of the token, the login component uses the `auth-service` to save the token into the browser's local storage and redirects the user to the /home page.

3 When the user visits any route that requires an AJAX request (such as the /books route), an HTTP interceptor is used to add a new authorization header to each HTTP request. This header includes the token that was stored in local storage during the login process.

4 The my-books API server verifies the token and returns a list of results linked to the given user account.

5 If the user attempts to visit a page other than the login page without being authenticated, a new router-authorization step will intercept the request, redirecting them back to the login page.

6 The nav-bar will be filtered to ensure that only administrators can view and manage user accounts. This is achieved using a new auth-filter value converter.

7 When the user logs out, the token is cleared from local storage via the auth-service, allowing the user to reinitiate the login process or use a different account.

With this architecture and authentication flow in mind, let's look at the first required component of your auth system—the authentication service.

NOTE Please follow the setup steps in the appendix to enable authentication in the my-books-server sample Node.js application.

10.2.2 *Creating the authentication service*

The authentication service is the principal component of the my-books authentication architecture. Each of the other components uses the AuthService to implement its part of the auth process. To begin, add the login method to be used by the login screen. While you're here, add the logout method (though we'll come back to this later). The login method takes the username and password supplied on the login form and makes an HTTP request to the my-books-server /token endpoint. It then stores the JWT retrieved from the endpoint in the local storage. The logout method removes the token from local storage, clearing the current user's session. Create a new service at ./src/services/auth-service.js.

Listing 10.1 Creating a new authentication service (auth-service.js)

```
import {HttpClient, json} from 'aurelia-fetch-client';
import {inject} from 'aurelia-framework';

@inject(HttpClient)
export class AuthService{

    constructor(http){
        this.http = http;
    }

    logIn(userName, password){

        return this.http.fetch('token', {
                method: 'post',
                body: json({name: userName, password : password})
            })
            .then(response => response.json())
            .then(tokenResult => {
                if(tokenResult.success)
                    window.localStorage.setItem("token", tokenResult.token);
                return tokenResult;
            })
            .catch(error => {
                console.log('Error retrieving token');
```

Posts the username and password as a JSON body to the token endpoint

Stores the retrieved token in local storage

```
        });
    }
    logOut(){
        window.localStorage.removeItem("token");     ◁──┘
    }
}
```

Removes the token from
local storage to log out

With the required service in place, the next step is to flesh out the `login` component that you added in chapter 9, making the `auth-service` associate a token with the given user.

10.2.3 *Implementing login*

The `login` view-model uses the `auth-service` to acquire a token for the user. Once the user has been logged in, the router is used to redirect the user to the homepage using the router's `navigateToRoute` method. By the end of this section, you'll have a functional login page capable of authenticating a user and acquiring a JWT, as shown in figure 10.4.

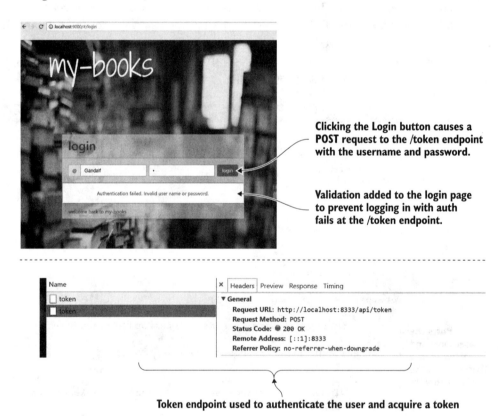

Figure 10.4   Login page modified to add support for logging in a user and acquiring a JWT

Modify the login view-model at ./src/resources/elements/login.js as follows.

Listing 10.2 Modifying the login view-model to add user login (login.js)

```javascript
import {inject} from 'aurelia-framework';
import {AuthService} from '../../services/auth-service';
import {Router} from 'aurelia-router';

@inject(Router,AuthService)
export class Login{

    constructor(router, authService){
        this.authService = authService;
        this.router = router;
    }

    logIn(){
        this.authService.logIn(this.userName,
                               this.password)
            .then(tokenResult => {
              if(tokenResult.success){
                  this.errorMessage = "";
                  this.router.navigateToRoute('home');
              }
              else{
                  this.errorMessage = tokenResult.message;
              }
          });
    }
}
```

- Passes the username and password from the form down to the auth service
- Navigates to the homepage on login success
- Sets a bindable error message property based on login failure

The login view you implemented in chapter 9 was minimal and didn't include functionality to display validation errors. Let's add basic login and validation functionality to the view. Hook into the login form-submit using the submit.trigger="logIn()", calling the logIn view-model method. The username and password fields are bound to the corresponding view-model properties. You also need to add a disabled binding on the Login button to prevent the user from proceeding until they've provided a username and password. Adding a disabled binding like this is a simple but effective way to give the user a clue to the next step in the login process. Modify the login view at ./src/resources/elements/login.html.

Listing 10.3 Modifying the login view to support login (login.html)

```html
<template>
    <div slot="header"><h1 class="brand-heading">my-books</h1></div>
    <div slot="form" class="container">
        <div class="row justify-content-center align-items-center">
            <div class="card">
                <div class="card-header">
                    <h1>login</h1>
                </div>
```

```
                      <form class="card-block
 Login on     ┌ ─ ▷      form-inline" submit.trigger="logIn()">
 form-submit  │         <label class="sr-only" for="userName">user name</label>
              │         <div class="input-group mb-2 mr-sm-2 mb-sm-0">
                            <input type="text"
                                   class="form-control"
                                   id="userName"
                     ┌ ─ ▷       value.bind="userName"
                     │           placeholder="username">
                     │     </div>
     Binds the      │
   username and     │       <label class="sr-only" for="password">password</label>
 password input     │       <div class="input-group mb-2 mr-sm-2 mb-sm-0">
    fields to the   │           <input type="password"
    view-model      │                  class="form-control"
                    │                  id="password"
                    └ ─ ▷            value.bind="password"
                                     placeholder="password">
                          </div>
                          <button type="submit" class="btn btn-success"
                                  disabled.bind="!(userName.length > 0
                 ┌ ─ ▷            && password.length > 0)">
 Disables login until the      login
 username and password    </button>
    are provided   │
                         </form>
                         <div class="card card-outline-danger text-center"
                               show.bind="errorMessage.length > 0">
                           <div class="card-block  login-error">
                               ${errorMessage}                    ◁ ─┐  Shows an error
                           </div>                                     │  message on
                         </div>                                       │  login failure
                         <div class="card-footer text-muted">
                             welcome back to my-books
                         </div>
                 </div>
             </div>
             </div>
        </template>
```

In the next section, we'll look at how to apply authentication to user requests by attaching the JWT from local storage using an HTTP interceptor.

10.2.4 *Intercepting HTTP requests*

In chapter 8, you learned about Aurelia's HTTP interceptor feature, which allows you to inject logic into Aurelia's HTTP pipeline. The my-books-server application looks for an authorization header on each request structured like 'authorization bearer {TOKEN}'. The server verifies this token using a private key and extracts the user details from the request. If the token isn't present in the request, the service returns an HTTP 403 response message to indicate that the user needs to log in before they can access the requested resource. If the service can successfully extract the user details from the token, then the results (such as the list of books) are filtered based on the user making the request.

Modify ./src/services/auth-service.js as shown in the following listing. This code adds an interceptor that will retrieve the token from local storage and attach a new authorization header containing this token to each request using the `request.headers.append` method.

Listing 10.4 Modifying `auth-service` to include http interceptor (auth-service.js)

```
import {HttpClient, json} from 'aurelia-fetch-client';
import {inject} from 'aurelia-framework';

@inject(HttpClient)
export class AuthService{

    ...
    getToken(){
        return window.localStorage.getItem("token");      ⟵ Retrieves the token
    }                                                         from local-storage

    get tokenInterceptor(){
        let auth = this;                                   ⟵ Sets auth to the
        return {                                              current this context
            request(request) {                             ⟵ Hooks into the
                let token = auth.getToken();                  FetchClient
                if(token){                                    requests
                    request.headers
                        .append('authorization', `bearer ${token}`);   ⟵
                }                                          Appends the token
                return request;                            as an authorize
            }                                              request header
        };
    }
}
```

Gets the token from local storage

To add this interceptor into the HTTP pipeline across the application, you need to add it to the base `HttpClient` configuration defined in the app view-model using the `HttpClient withInterceptor` method. Modify the ./src/app.js file, configuring the `HttpClient` to use the auth interceptor as shown in the following listing.

Listing 10.5 Modifying the `app` view-model to use `auth http` interceptor (app.js)

```
import { AuthService } from "./services/auth-service";
import { inject } from "aurelia-framework";
import { HttpClient } from "aurelia-fetch-client";

@inject(AuthService, HttpClient)
export class App {
  constructor(authService, http) {
    this.authService = authService;
```

```
const baseUrl = "http://localhost:8333/api/";

http.configure(config => {          ◁——┐  Adds the auth HTTP
  config                                │  interceptor to the base
    .withBaseUrl(baseUrl)               │  HttpClient configuration
    .withInterceptor(this.authService.tokenInterceptor);
});
}


...
  }
}
```

With the `auth` interceptor in place, you can now see a new authorization header sent with each request.

On relaunching the project, you can use any of the seed users set up by the my-books-server initialization procedure. You can see a full list of user credentials in the appendix, but for now you can log in as the Gandalf administrator with *Gandalf* as the username and *password3* as the password. If you inspect the local storage using the F12 developer tools, you'll see a new token key-value pair stored, as shown in figure 10.5.

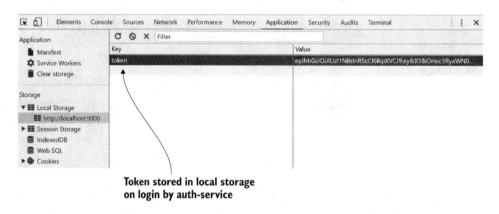

Figure 10.5   The JWT stored in local storage on login

Exercise: Cleaning up the configuration

With the changes you've made to the `app` view-model to globally configure the `Http-Client`, you no longer need to configure it in the `user-api` and `book-api` view-model constructors. Refactor these classes, removing the now redundant configuration. To see the version where this housekeeping has been done, you can jump to Chapter-10-Complete on the *Aurelia in Action* GitHub repository (https://github.com/freshcut-development/Aurelia-in-Action).

Navigate to the /books route, and then open the F12 developer tools to see the header in action, as shown in figure 10.6.

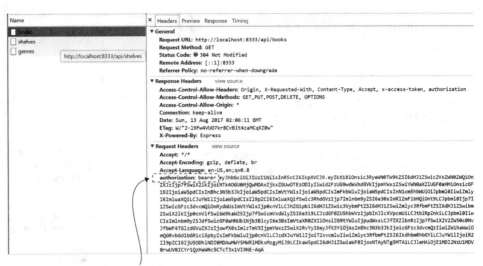

auth HTTP interceptor used to append an authorization
header containing the JWT value to each request

Figure 10.6 `auth` **interceptor used to automatically intercept HTTP requests across the my-books application and append an authorization header containing the JWT**

10.2.5 *Routing redirection*

Certain routes in your application are public, some are available only to authenticated users, and some are available only to users with an authorization level (for example, administrators). Route redirection is about detecting which route a user has requested (for example, by navigating to a URL inside your application) and either allowing the user to visit the route if they're authorized to do so or redirecting the user to an appropriate page if they're not. In Aurelia, you can achieve this using an authorization route-pipeline step. To refresh your memory, in chapter 9 you learned that route pipeline steps are behaviors that you can inject into slots in Aurelia's route pipeline to intercept and manipulate the user's request to a given route.

In the my-books application, you'll create an authorization step that exports a run function, run(navigationInstruction, next), where navigationInstruction contains details about the current route and the next function passes control to the next step in the route pipeline. First, you'll check whether the user is attempting to visit a secured route by checking the route metadata for any routes containing auth properties using the getAllInstructions() method on the current navigationInstruction. If the route is secured and the user is unauthorized, you'll cancel the next step in the route pipeline and instead redirect the user to the login screen. Add a new authorization step at ./src/router-steps/authorization-step.js and add the contents of the following listing.

Listing 10.6 Creating the authentication route-pipeline step (authorization-step.js)

```
import {Redirect} from 'aurelia-router';

export class AuthorizeStep {          ⟵  Declares a new
                                          authorization-
  constructor(authService){              pipeline step
    this.authService = authService;
  }

  run(navigationInstruction, next) {                          Checks whether the
    if (navigationInstruction.getAllInstructions()            requested route is
        .some(i => i.config.settings.auth)) {     ⟵          authenticated

      if (!this.authService.isLoggedIn()) {              ⟵   Checks whether the
        return next.cancel(new Redirect('login'));   ⟵         user is logged in
      }
    }                                                      Redirects
                                                           unauthenticated users
    return next();    ⟵  Continues to the next             to the login page
  }                       step in the pipeline if the
}                         user is authenticated
```

To make use of the authorization step, you also need to modify the route configuration defined in the app view-model. In chapter 9, you added navigation-menu icons by setting an icon-setting value for each route. You'll extend these settings further here, adding two new values to indicate which routes are secured and which are admin only. For example, you could restrict the user's endpoint to be accessible only to authenticated users with the admin role. You also need to modify the app view-model to instantiate the new authorization step and add it to the route pipeline. Modify the app view-model at ./src/app.js as shown in the following listing.

Listing 10.7 Modifying app to add the authorization routing config (app.js)

```
import { AuthService } from "./services/auth-service";
import { inject } from "aurelia-framework";
import { HttpClient } from "aurelia-fetch-client";
import { AuthorizeStep } from "./router-steps/authorization-step";

@inject(AuthService, HttpClient)
export class App {
  ...

  configureRouter(config, router) {
    this.router = router;
    ...
```

```
let step = new AuthorizeStep(this.authService);          ◁┐ Instantiates the
                                                            authorization
                                                            routing step and
config.addAuthorizeStep(step);                           ◁┘ adds it to pipeline

config.map([
  {
    route: ["", "home"],
    name: "home",
    moduleId: "index",
    title: "home",
    nav: true,
    settings: { icon: "home", auth: true},          ◁┐
    layoutViewModel: "main-layout"
  },                                                        Tags secured routes to
  {                                                         inform the route step
    route: "books",                                         and nav-bar filter
    name: "books",                                          about which routes
    moduleId: "./resources/elements/books",                 require authentication
    title: "books",
    nav: true,
    settings: { icon: "book", auth: true },         ◁┘
    layoutViewModel: "main-layout"
  },
  {
    route: "users",
    name: "users",
    moduleId: "./resources/elements/users",
    title: "users",
    nav: true,
    settings: { icon: "users", auth: true, admin:true },  ◁┐
    layoutViewModel: "main-layout"
  },
  {
    route: "users/:name/details",                               Tags admin-
    name: "user-detail",                                        only routes
    moduleId: "./resources/elements/user-details",
    title: "user details",
    settings: { auth: true, admin:true },                 ◁┘
    layoutViewModel: "main-layout"
  },
  {
    route: "login",
    name: "login",
    moduleId: "./resources/elements/login",
    title: "login",
    layoutView: "login-layout.html"
  },
  {
    route: "legacy-users",
    redirect: "users"
  }
]);
```

```
        config.mapUnknownRoutes(handleUnknownRoutes);
    }
}
```

With route interception in place, users will be redirected if they attempt to access a route they don't have permission for, but wouldn't it be better if they didn't even see the option to navigate to that route in the first place? Next, add a filter to the navigation bar to ensure that users see only navigation menu options relevant to them.

10.2.6   *Filtering the navigation bar*

In this section, you'll enhance the navigation bar with the following features:

- Users will only see relevant menu options, based on their role.
- Users can see the username they're logged in under.
- Users can log out of the current session.

By the end of this section, you'll be able to log in as a non-administrative user (such as Bilbo/password1) to see a non-admin view of the navigation bar and log out of the application, as shown in figure 10.7.

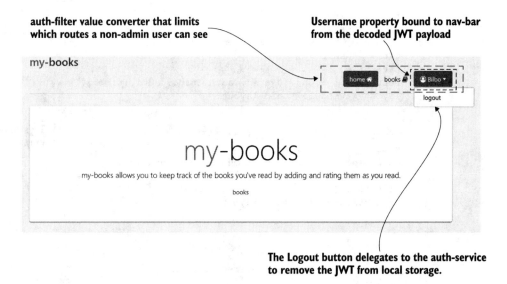

Figure 10.7   The auth-filter, user details, and Logout button added to the navigation bar

Implement the filter logic using a value converter (we'll come to that next), but first you need to modify the auth-service to add support for retrieving the current user from the token. JWTs are Base64-encoded strings, so you'll need to retrieve the token, Base64 decode it, and return the value of the user saved in the token body.

Modify the ./src/services/auth-service.js file, as shown in the following listing, to extend the auth API.

```
import {HttpClient, json} from 'aurelia-fetch-client';
import {inject} from 'aurelia-framework';

@inject(HttpClient)
export class AuthService{

    constructor(http){
        this.http = http;
    }

    ...

    isLoggedIn(){
        let token = this.getToken();

        if(token) return true;

        return false;
    }

    getToken(){
        return window.localStorage.getItem("token");
    }

    getUser(){
        let token = this.decodeToken();
        return token._doc;
    }

    decodeToken(token){

        token = token || this.getToken();

        if(!token) return;

        try {
            return JSON.parse(atob(token.split('.')[1]));
        }
        catch (e) {
            return null;
        }
    }
}
```

Checks if the user is logged in based on the presence of the token

Retrieves the token from local storage

Gets the user from the token

Decodes the JWT so that you can extract the user with Base64 decode

Value converters are one of the core features in Aurelia. They're so versatile that even after you've been using the framework for months, you still find new and interesting use cases for them. In this case, you've effectively got an array (the application routes) that you need to perform a transformation on (filtering out the routes that the user shouldn't see) before they're rendered as nav-bar menu items in the view. This is a perfect use case for a value converter. The value converter's toView method will take the array of routes that you need to convert, toView(routes), and then filter the returned routes based on whether the user is logged in and whether they're an admin. Create a new value converter called auth-filter at ./src/resources/value-converters/auth-filter.js.

Listing 10.9   Creating a new auth-filter value converter (auth-filter.js)

```
import {AuthService} from '../../services/auth-service';
import {inject} from 'aurelia-framework';

@inject(AuthService)
export class AuthFilterValueConverter {

  constructor(authService){
    this.authService = authService;
  }

  toView(routes) {

    let isAuthenticated = this.authService.isLoggedIn();
    let isAdmin = isAuthenticated && this.authService.getUser().admin;

    return routes.filter(r => r.settings.auth === undefined
                  || (r.settings.auth === isAuthenticated
                      && (!r.settings.admin || isAdmin)));
  }
}
```

Annotations:
- Takes the routes collection as input
- Checks whether the user is logged in using the auth service
- Checks whether the user is an admin using the auth service
- Returns only routes the user has access to, checking route metadata against the auth status

Until now, the nav-bar component requirements have been simple, so you've gotten away with an HTML-only custom element. But with the new requirements, this component now needs access to the auth-service to display the logged-in username and support user logout. To enable these functions, implement a new view-model for the nav-bar component. This view-model will implement the bind callback, retrieving the user's name via the auth-service. You'll also implement a logOut method, which will call on the auth-service to clear the current user's token from local storage and redirect them to the login page. Add a new view-model at ./src/resources/elements/nav-bar.js.

Listing 10.10   Adding a new nav-bar view-model (nav-bar.js)

```
import {inject} from 'aurelia-framework';
import {AuthService} from '../../services/auth-service';
import {Router} from 'aurelia-router';
```

```
@inject(Router,AuthService)
export class NavBar{

    constructor(router, authService){
        this.authService = authService;
        this.router = router;
    }

    bind(){
        this.user = this.authService.getUser();
    }

    logOut(){
        this.authService.logOut();
        this.router.navigateToRoute('login');
    }
}
```

Hooks into the bind component-lifecycle callback and sets the current user for display

Logs the user out, clearing their token and redirecting them to the login page

Putting it all together, you'll add authorization filtering and logout features to the nav-bar view. First, you need to require the auth-filter value converter into the view and apply it to the route repeater. This will filter the list of available menu items. You'll also add a new section to the navigation menu to show the current user's name once they're logged in and add a click delegate to allow the user to log out of the app. Modify the nav-bar view at ./src/resources/elements/nav-bar.html, as shown next.

Listing 10.11 Modifying `nav-bar` to support authorization (nav-bar.html)

Requires the auth-filter value converter into the view

```
<template>
    <require from="../value-converters/auth-filter"></require>
    <nav>
        <ul class="nav nav-pills float-right">
            <li repeat.for="row of router.navigation | authFilter"
                class="nav-item">
                <a class="nav-link
                    ${row.isActive ? 'active' : ''}" href.bind="row.href">
                    ${row.title}
                    <i if.bind="row.settings.icon"
                        class="fa fa-${row.settings.icon}">
                    </i>
                </a>
            </li>

            <li class="nav-item dropdown">
                <a class="nav-link dropdown-toggle"
                    data-toggle="dropdown" href="#"
                    role="button"
                    aria-haspopup="true" aria-expanded="false">
                    <i class="fa fa-user-circle-o" aria-hidden="true">
                    </i> ${user.name}
                </a>
```

Filters out routes the user shouldn't see

Renders the username (retrieved from decoded JWT)

```
            <div class="dropdown-menu">
                <a class="dropdown-item" href="#"
                    click.delegate="logOut()"> logout
                </a>
            </div>
        </li>
    </ul>
</nav>
</template>
```

Delegates the logout method to log the user out of the application

You also need to make a minor change to the ./src/main.html file, now that you've changed the nav-bar from an HTML-only custom element to a regular custom element. Remove the .html extension from the nav-bar require statement.

Listing 10.12   Updating the `nav-bar require` statement (main-layout.html)

```
<template>
    <require from="./resources/elements/nav-bar"></require>
    ...
</template>
```

Removes the .html extension from the nav-bar-component require statement

10.3   *my-books project status*

In this chapter, you added the following features to the my-books application:

- Users can log in and receive a filtered view of the application based on what they're authorized to see.
- Users can log out of the application.
- Users only see books that belong to their bookshelf.

Figure 10.8 highlights the major changes made to the my-books application in this chapter.

In chapter 11, we'll look at a new Aurelia-framework feature you haven't seen yet—dynamic composition—which allows you to control the way Aurelia pages are composed at runtime to create truly flexible SPAs.

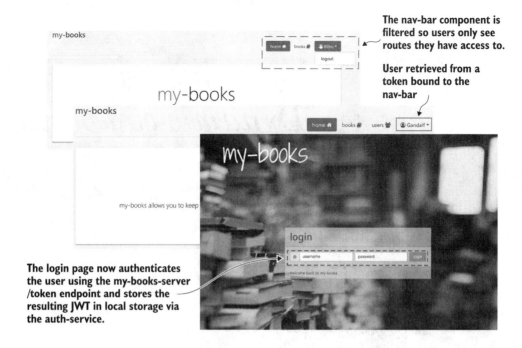

The nav-bar component is filtered so users only see routes they have access to.

User retrieved from a token bound to the nav-bar

The login page now authenticates the user using the my-books-server /token endpoint and stores the resulting JWT in local storage via the auth-service.

Figure 10.8 The my-books application modified to add authentication and authorization

Summary

- SPA architecture imposes different requirements on authentication systems from traditional client-server-based web applications. Because of these requirements, token-based authentication is a better fit for this architecture than the classic cookie-based auth system.
- JWTs are a token format convenient for encoding user details in a way that can be verified by the server.
- By combining a token-based authentication model with standard Aurelia building blocks such as services, route-pipeline steps, and HTTP interceptors, you can secure your Aurelia applications, allowing users to see only the resources they're authorized to use.

Dynamic composition

Imagine you're tasked with building an application that would help grocery stores manage their products. One page in this application would let users look up products by key fields. Some key fields should contain only a few discrete values (for example, product category, like fruit and vegetables, or cleaning products), so standard drop-down lists would be the best fit. Other key fields, like product name, contain potentially hundreds of values, and in these cases an autocomplete style of control would work better. Based on what you've learned so far, you can achieve this by creating a new form and using custom elements to represent each of the various kinds of fields the user needs to search on. But what if the customer needs the ability to configure the application, adding their own search fields based on properties in their database, and they want to be able to choose the type of field they use (autocomplete, check-box, text-area)? In scenarios like these, you don't know which components should make up the view until runtime. This means that the standard approach that we've covered so far, using custom elements, doesn't work. Fortunately, Aurelia provides a feature called *dynamic composition*. Dynamic composition allows you to control which components to load at runtime rather than hardcoding the component types into your view. This feature makes building this style of flexible UI a breeze.

11.1 Static vs. dynamic composition

So far, you've created pages by including top-level custom-element components with nested child components. We'll call this approach *static composition*. This is the recommended default approach when creating pages, and it's the one you'll use the most. But there's a second approach, called *dynamic composition*, which is the perfect fit to solve the kind of application requirements described in the imaginary grocery-store scenario. With dynamic composition, you use an Aurelia custom element, `<compose>`, which allows you to specify which view or view-model to load at runtime (after the page has loaded) rather than hardcoding them. This is very abstract, so let's look at a concrete example to put this in context.

Say you have to create a new Aurelia form that contains a text area (implemented using an `au-textarea` custom element) and an input field (implemented with an `au-textbox` custom element). Figure 11.1 contrasts the static- and dynamic-composition approaches.

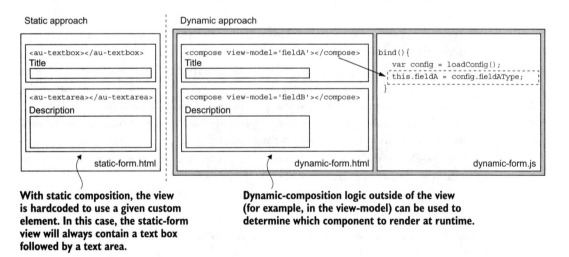

Figure 11.1 A comparison of the static versus dynamic view composition approaches to creating a form

In the static-composition approach, you'd `require` these two custom elements into the view, and add them to the `<au-textarea ... >` form. In the dynamic-composition approach, you'd instead use the `compose` custom element, passing in the view-model to load: `<compose view-model="au-textarea"`. If you were to specify the view-model explicitly like this, however, it somewhat defeats the purpose of dynamic composition, because you're still *statically* telling the view which component to load inside the `compose` element. But where this feature gets cool is when you can instead use a binding expression to specify which component to load: `<compose view-model="./ ${controlType}"`.

With this change, the decision for which component to load has been taken out of the hands of the parent view, and instead placed in the hands of the parent view-model. This means that you can determine which child component to load based on logic, such as loading the control configuration from a config file.

11.2   *The <compose> custom element*

Now that you've got a basic understanding of the dynamic-view-composition approach and how it differs from the way that you've previously created your views in Aurelia, let's take a closer look at the `<compose>` custom element, which makes it all possible.

The `compose` element can be configured using the following options:

- `view-model`—Pass the view-model name of the child component, for example, `<compose view-model="au-textarea">`. This is great once you've determined which component to load dynamically.
- `containerless`—Attach the `containerless` custom attribute to a `compose` element to render the child component without the `<compose>` container element (such as a surrounding `<div>` element), for example, `<compose containerless view-model="au-textarea">`. This is particularly useful if you have styling that depends on a specific DOM structure.
- `view`—Pass the view filename of the child component, for example, `<compose view="./heading.html ">`. This is great for creating partial views, because the view context is inherited from the parent component. In the case of a heading partial, you could initialize a `headingText` property in the parent view-model, which would then be available in the `heading` child view.
- `model`—Pass data to your dynamic components using the `model` option, for example, `<compose view-model="..." model="fields">`. Data passed in the model property is available as an argument to the `activate` lifecycle hook: `activate(model){this.fields=model}`.

The `compose` custom element enables two main scenarios: partial views and dynamic child components. In the next section, you'll implement a sample form to see both scenarios in action.

11.3   *Dynamically composed views*

Because this example doesn't make sense in the context of the my-books application, we'll take a detour here, and instead implement the form in a gist. Dynamic composition is useful for solving certain kinds of problems, such as partial views and views made up of dynamic components, which we'll cover in this chapter. Although these scenarios aren't applicable to the my-books application—hence, the detour into a sample gist—it's important to understand that dynamic composition exists. That way, when you run into either of these problems in your own projects, you'll have the best tool at hand to solve them. You can get started by visiting the following gist run at https://sean-hunter.io/aia-dynamic-composition-start. This gist has the shell of a dynamic `book-edit` form, which we'll flesh out throughout the chapter. If you'd like to see the completed version, check out this gist: https://sean-hunter.io/aia-dynamic-composition-complete. Figure 11.2 shows an overview of what the form will look like when we've completed this chapter.

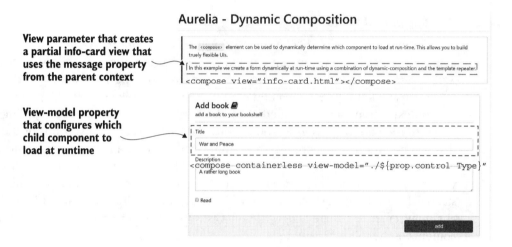

Figure 11.2   Completed add-book form, which uses dynamic composition to load child components (`info-card`, `au-textbox`, and more) at runtime

Start by creating a new app shell, a bare-bones view/view-model pair, as shown in the following two listings. This app shell will host the new dynamically composed form. The files are already in place for you on GistRun, so all you need to do is fill out the contents.

Listing 11.1   Creating the `app` view (app.html)

```html
<template>
  <link rel="stylesheet" type="text/css" href="style.css">
  <h1>${message}</h1>
  <hr/>
</template>
```

Creates new
app-shell view

With the shell in place, you can start fleshing out the form. The first feature you'll implement is an `info-card` partial view to provide the user with some information about what the form is for.

Listing 11.2   Creating the `app` view-model (app.js)

```
import {bindable} from 'aurelia-framework';
export class App {                              ◁─┐  Creates new app-
                                                   │  shell view-model
  constructor(){
    this.message = 'Aurelia - Dynamic Composition';
  }

}
```

11.3.1 Creating partial views

The composition feature is convenient for creating *partial views* within your Aurelia application. Partial views, in the context of Aurelia, are a way of splitting out lightweight subviews without the need to create a corresponding view-model. As opposed to custom elements, where the child binding context is isolated from the parent binding context, components included using the `compose` element share the binding context with the parent. This gives you a lightweight way to split out sections of the view that you might want to reuse. As an example, you'll create a new `info-card` view and include it in the app parent view using `compose`. It's important to note that although you're using this view with `compose`, there's nothing to stop you from also using it as a standard custom element elsewhere in the application, where you might have different requirements. Create a new file on GistRun called info-card.html and copy the contents of the following listing.

Listing 11.3   Creating the new `info-card` view (info-card.html)

```
<template>                               ◁─┐  Creates a new
  <section  class="card info">              │  Bootstrap card view
    <p>
      The <code>&lt;compose&gt;</code>  element can be
      used to dynamically determine
      which component to load at runtime. This allows
      you to build truely flexible UIs.
    </p>                                        Binds description
    <p>                                         from inherited parent-
      ${description}                    ◁────── component context
    </p>
  </section>
</template>
```

Next, add a new `compose` element to your app view, specifying the `info-card` view file path to load it as a child component, `<compose view="info-card.html">`. The `compose` element will inject the contents of the `info-card` view at runtime.

Listing 11.4 Modifying the `app` view to use the `info-card` view (app.html)

```
<template>
  ...
  <compose view="info-card.html"></compose>
</template>
```
Creates a partial view using the compose custom element

The GistRun display has now been updated to show the new `info-card` view, as shown in figure 11.3. You can jump to this step by navigating to the following gist in your browser: https://sean-hunter.io/aia-dynamic-composition-info-card.

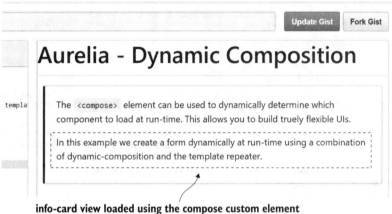

info-card view loaded using the compose custom element

Figure 11.3 The `info-card` partial view injected into the main app view using the compose element

11.3.2 Creating a configurable form with dynamic composition

The second and most powerful scenario for the `compose` element is using it to dynamically load child components without needing to explicitly state which component should be loaded in the parent view. To demonstrate this scenario, you'll implement a new form for adding books. You can configure it by specifying field metadata in the `form` view-model and using a repeater in the `form` view to loop over these metadata fields at runtime, rendering the component that corresponds to each field. Figure 11.4 illustrates how this form will work.

The first component to create in this example is the `form` itself. Begin by creating a new `au-form` custom-element component. The view-model will declare a set of fields, allowing you to configure relevant field metadata, such as the name, placeholder, and, more importantly, the component used to render this field: `this.fields = [{ controlType: "au-text-box" ...}]`. Create the AuForm view-model by adding a new `au-form.js` file to the gist with the contents of listing 11.5.

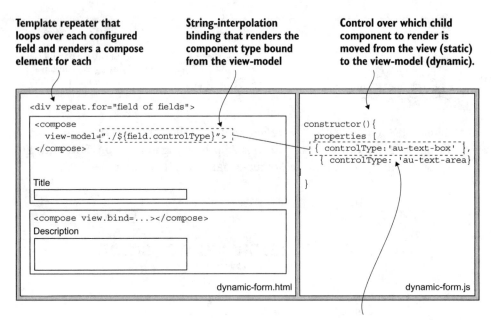

Figure 11.4 The `au-form` fields are composed using a combination of the `compose` element, data binding, and the template repeater.

Listing 11.5 Creating the `form` view-model (au-form.js)

```
import {inject, bindable} from 'aurelia-framework';

export class AuForm{                    ◁——| Creates the new configurable
                                            | form parent component

  constructor(){
    this.fields = [                     ◁——| Creates an array of
      {                                     | properties to represent
                                            | the form fields
        name : "Title",
        value : "War and Peace",
        controlType: "au-text-box",
        placeholder:'Enter a title'},
      {
        name : "Description",
        value : "A rather long book",
        controlType: "au-text-area"},
      {
        name : "Read",
        value: true,
        controlType: "au-checkbox"
      }
    ];
  }
}
```

The name of the field

The default value of the field (could be loaded from API)

The Aurelia component name to render for this field

Optional field placeholder

```
addBook(){
  alert(`book added with title ${this.fields[0].value} `);
}

}
```

The `AuForm` view-model exposes a bindable property called `fields` that includes metadata for the fields to be rendered to the `form` view. To use this metadata, create a new au-form view. This form will repeat over the `repeat.for="field of fields"` field, rendering each of them using the `compose` custom element, `<compose view-model="./${field.controlType}" ...>`. Aurelia will interpret the `compose` view-model expression, loading the component referenced by each field (for example, `au-textarea` for the text-area field). You'll also bind the field model to the component to pass metadata such as the field name and placeholder, which Aurelia will use when rendering the child components. To implement the new form, add a new au-form.html file to the GistRun gist, adding the contents of the following listing.

Listing 11.6 Creating the `form` view (au-form.html)

```
<template>
  <form class="form card" submit.trigger="addBook()">          Adds the book
    <div class="card-block">                                   data from the
      <h4 class="card-title">Add book                          form on submit
          <i class="fa fa-book"></i>
      </h4>
        <h6 class="card-subtitle mb-2 text-muted">
          add a book to your bookshelf
          </h6>                                                 Composes a
        <hr/>                                                   component at
         <div class="form-group">                              runtime
           <div repeat.for="field of fields">
              <compose                                          Renders the component
                  containerless                                 without the <compose>
                  view-model="./${field.controlType}"          container element
                  model.bind="field"></compose>                Passes the field
          </div>                                                object down to the
        </div>                                                  child component
      </form>                                                   using data binding
    </div>                                                      on model property
    <div class="card-footer">
      <button type="submit" class="btn btn-primary col-sm-3 push-sm-9"
              disabled.bind="fields[0].value.length == 0">
        add
      </button>
    </div>
  </div>
</template>
```

Binds the component view-model from the control-type value of the field

---

With this dynamic component-loading infrastructure in place, you need to create the view/view-model pair for each of the field components. The view-models for these components implement the `activate` lifecycle hook, allowing the parent au-form component to pass down the current field metadata. Create the three new field components by adding the au-textbox, au-text-area, and au-checkbox, as shown in the following six listings. After creating these components, you should have six new files in your GistRun gist. You can jump directly there using this link: https://sean-hunter.io/aia-dynamic-composition-textbox.

Listing 11.7 Creating the `textbox-component` view-model (au-text-box.js)

```
export class AuTextBox{

  activate(model) {                    ◁──── Model passed in, activates
    this.field = model;                       the lifecycle callback
  }                                ◁──── Sets the field backing
                                         this component from
}                                        the model
```

As you can see in listing 11.8, each of the field components takes their metadata, such as name, label text, placeholder, and default value, from the au-form parent component. For example, the textbox-field binding expression is implemented using two string-interpolation bindings to the relevant field properties, <label for="${field.name}">${ field.name}</label>.

Listing 11.8 Creating the `textbox-component` view (au-text-box.html)

```
<template>
    <div class="form-group">
        <label for="${field.name}">${ field.name}</label>
        <input name="${field.name}"
            class="form-control"                       Binds values on
            type="text"                                the component
            placeholder="${field.placeholder}"         from the field
            value.bind="field.value">                  configuration
    </div>
</template>
```

Listing 11.9 Creating the `textarea-component` view-model (au-text-area.js)

```
export class AuTextArea{          Model passed to the
                                  activate lifecycle callback
  activate(model) {        ◁────
    this.field = model;
  }                        ◁──── Sets the field backing this
                                 component from the model
}
```

Listing 11.10 Creating the `textarea-component` view (au-text-area.html)

```
<template>
  <div class="form-group">
    <label for="${field.name}">${ field.name}</label>
    <textarea class="form-control"
              id="${field.name}"
              rows="3"
              value.bind=" field.value">
    </textarea>
  </div>
</template>
```

Binds values on the component from the field configuration

Listing 11.11 Creating the `checkbox-component` view-model (au-checkbox.js)

```
import {bindable} from 'aurelia-framework';

export class AuCheckbox{
  activate(model) {
    this.field = model;
  }
}
```

Model passed to the activate lifecycle callback

Sets the field backing this component from the model

Listing 11.12 Creating the `checkbox-component` view (au-checkbox.html)

```
<template>
  <div class="form-check">
    <label class="form-check-label">
      <input class="form-check-input"
             type="checkbox"
             value.bind="field.value">
      ${field.name}
    </label>
  </div>
</template>
```

Binds values on the component from the field configuration

The last step to implement the new dynamic form is to add the new au-form custom element to the `<au-form></au-form>` app view. Modify the app.html view file to use the new custom element.

Listing 11.13 Modifying the `app` view to use the new `form` component (app.html)

```
<template>
  <require from="./au-form"></require>
  <link rel="stylesheet" type="text/css" href="style.css">
  <h1>${message}</h1>
  <hr/>
  <compose view="info-card.html"></compose>
  <hr/>
  <div class="container">
    <au-form></au-form>
  </div>
</template>
```

Requires form into the app view

Uses the new form custom element

After updating the app component, the gist will refresh to show the dynamic form. You can add any number of new fields by adding values to the au-form fields array. The completed form will look like figure 11.5. You can skip directly to this point in the GistRun by following this link: https://sean-hunter.io/aia-dynamic-composition-complete.

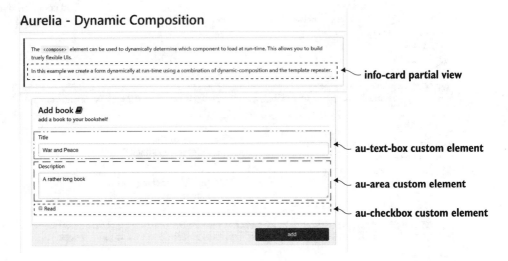

Figure 11.5   The completed dynamic au-form component, which uses dynamic composition to render fields specified in the au-form view-model at runtime

This chapter has been a reminder of the key role that components play in Aurelia's application model. So far, we've covered how to create Aurelia components statically (using custom elements and attributes) and dynamically (using the compose element). We've also noted that Aurelia's component system works well with the Web Component Specification. In chapter 12, we'll look at what the Web Component Specification is, and how to use standard features such as HTML templates and the Shadow DOM in Aurelia projects.

Summary

- Aurelia has two ways to compose views: static and dynamic.
- Static composition is useful when you have one or more preset custom elements that should make up your view, as will usually be the case in your Aurelia projects.
- Dynamic composition is used rarely but is a perfect fit for two scenarios: partial views (due to the shared binding context between the parent and child components) and when you need the flexibility to determine which components to load at runtime.

Web Components
and Aurelia

This chapter covers

- Introducing Web Components
- Exploring how Aurelia uses the Web Component APIs
- Using the Shadow DOM with Aurelia

Web Components are encapsulated UI widgets (generally, custom elements) that you can easily drop into your web applications without the need for modifications to your application or third-party libraries like jQuery. For example, one option for embedding Google Maps in a website is to import the Google Maps Web Component, which includes all the dependencies needed to render a map to your page. Web Components are built on a set of relatively new APIs called the Web Components APIs, which are supported in most modern browsers. These APIs are an implementation of the Web Component Specifications established by the W3C. The Web Component Specifications aim to establish a framework-agnostic way of implementing common features that Web Components require, such as HTML templating and imports. In this chapter, we'll explore what Web Components are, why you should care, and how you can use the Web Component APIs within your Aurelia applications.

12.1 *Introducing Web Components*

When I started building websites, around 2005, there were a few cutting-edge technologies that made it possible to develop UI widgets that could be created once and then dropped into any website to enhance functionality. At the time, this collection of technologies consisted of Flash, Java applets, and Silverlight. In 2005, these technologies were great. They closed the gap between what was possible in the browser natively, and what we as developers wanted to deliver to our end users on the web. Common use cases included things like video players or file-upload controls. These technologies worked by providing a plugin model, where users would install an application on their PC (for example, Adobe Flash), which would then plug into the browser. You could then create applications that ran within this sandboxed environment, where the creators of the plugin systems could establish APIs that filled the gaps in what the browser provided. These technologies helped solve two problems:

- *Encapsulation*—Due to the nature of the plugin model, widgets created in these technologies were encapsulated from the rest of the page, meaning that styles and behavior from the rest of the page didn't leak into the controls. This made it easy to drop a control created for one site into another and have it work.
- *Bridging the feature gap*—Although it's easy to forget today, back in 2005 there were things that you couldn't do with native-browser technologies. Period. The new technologies solved this problem by adding features that weren't supported by native-browser APIs.

Though these technologies were essential at the time, events have transpired that have made them as extinct as dinosaurs. Two key events led to this development:

- *The advent of smartphones and tablets (primarily the iPhone) that refused to enable plugins.* This meant that an increasing segment of users couldn't be reached using these technologies.
- *Browser technologies got much, much better.* Among the changes, we got ES2015+ and HTML5, which allow us to build the kind of rich components in our web applications that previously were impossible with the browser APIs alone.

Recently, a new collection of technologies has evolved to help solve the problem of creating encapsulated components for the web. These technologies consist of four web specifications designed to make it easy to build encapsulated UI blocks that you can write once and drop into other websites without modifying either the component block or the destination site.

These specifications are in the process of being implemented by the various browser vendors as APIs. The four specifications are as follows:

- *HTML Imports*—Allow you to load HTML documents into other HTML documents.
- *The Shadow DOM*—Provides encapsulation of styles and markup. This is the key to creating components that you can seamlessly drop into any website. You can

achieve some of the same benefits with iframes, but whereas iframes are targeted at loading external pages into your website and coincidentally provide encapsulation, the Shadow DOM is designed with encapsulation in mind, and has features created for this purpose.

- *HTML Templates*—Provide a way of including snippets of markup within a page that aren't executed when the page loads. This means, for example, that if you include an image within an `<img>` tag, it won't be retrieved from the server and rendered until you choose to initiate the template using the JavaScript API.

- *Custom elements*—Provide the building blocks to create custom DOM elements that behave like the DOM elements you use every day. For example, you could create an `<info-card> </info-card>` custom element with child nodes, styling, and custom events that would behave like an out-of-the-box element, like the `<p>` tag.

In the next section, we'll explore the HTML Imports API, introducing the problems that it solves and how you can use it in Aurelia projects.

12.2 HTML Imports

HTML Imports define a method for loading external HTML documents into a parent document. This is useful in the context of Web Components when you begin to think of a page as a hierarchy of bite-sized UI widgets. The following are the main benefits of HTML Imports:

- *Web-native loading system*—Although there are many other mechanisms for achieving a similar result for JavaScript dependencies (such as RequireJS), the HTML Imports API is in the process of being adopted by browsers (so far only Chrome, Opera, and Firefox with a feature flag). This means that soon it should be possible to import components via HTML Imports without bringing in any third-party dependencies.

- *Dependency management*—Dependent components are loaded in the order you expect. For example, if you import the `google-map` component, which imports a `map-renderer`, then the `map-renderer` should be loaded first to set up the dependencies. Further, because you're importing the entire HTML file, this process also captures any JavaScript or CSS dependencies as a byproduct.

- *Native HTML parsing*—Instead of needing a third-party API for parsing component HTML, this is done by the browser, increasing the performance related to initializing a Web Component on the page.

- *Deduplication of dependencies*—If you imagine a dependency graph where two parent components rely on the same child component, the child component will be loaded only once.

You can use HTML Imports by adding a `rel="import"`-link tag in the page head, as shown in the following listing, where you import an `info-card` component into the page. One of the neat things about HTML Imports is that you can include everything that the component needs inside the referenced HTML page. This provides consumers of your component with a straightforward way to bring it into the application.

Listing 12.1   Using the HTML Imports API (index.html)

```html
<html>
  <head>
    <link rel="import" href="info-card.html">        ◁─┐  Imports the info-
  </head>                                               │  card.html file into
  <body>                                                │  the index.html file
  </body>
</html>
```

For example, Google provides a Google Maps Polymer component that makes it trivial to add Google Maps to your website without an iframe. All that's required is to include an HTML import statement to load the Web Component:

```
<link rel="import" href="google-map.html">
```

> **TIP** No discussion of Web Components is complete without Polymer. Polymer is an open source JavaScript library created by Google that provides higher-level abstractions to make building Web Components easier. You can find out more at the Polymer project website: www.polymer-project.org.

This is all well and good, but how does it apply to Aurelia? Like many subsystems within the Aurelia framework, Aurelia's template-loading system uses a plugin model. A base template loader, called `loader`, defines the common template-loading interface. Other loaders, including `text-template-loader`, `aurelia-webpack-loader`, and `html-import-template-loader`, each implement this standard interface, as shown in figure 12.1.

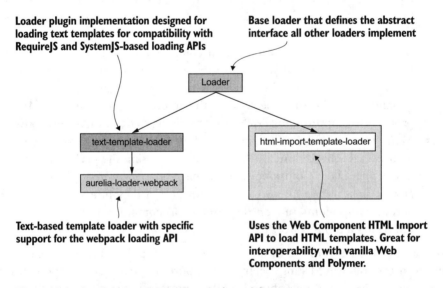

Figure 12.1   Aurelia's template-loading-plugin model

As you can see, Aurelia supports an `html-import-template-loader` that's specifically designed to allow you to include vanilla and Polymer Web Components easily within your Aurelia applications. This loader works by creating a new `rel='import'` link element, as you saw in the `google-map` component example, and asynchronously loads the target HTML component.

Using this loader within your Aurelia application is a matter of adding the plugin to Aurelia's bootstrap process in the main.js file, as shown in the following listing.

Listing 12.2 Modifying the `main` module to include the HTML template (main.js)

```
export function configure(aurelia) {
  aurelia.use
    .standardConfiguration()
    .developmentLogging();

  aurelia.use.plugin('aurelia-html-import-template-loader');   ◁─┐  Adds the HTML
                                                                 │  import-loader
  aurelia.start().then(a => a.setRoot());                          plugin
```

TIP If you're interested in learning more about using Polymer components, check out this great guide on the Aurelia Hub: http://aurelia.io/docs/integration/polymer, which takes you through a step-by-step process of adding Polymer components to an Aurelia project with the aid of `aurelia-html-import-template-loader`.

12.3 HTML Templates

Regardless of which SPA frameworks you use, one of the fundamental requirements involves taking a snippet of HTML (often called a *template*), injecting variable values, and then rendering it to the DOM. Taking the Backbone.js style template (listing 12.3) as an example, this template would be rendered by implementing a Backbone.js view, which looks up the template by ID using jQuery and renders it using the Underscore.js templating engine. You can read more about Underscore.js at the framework's website: http://underscorejs.org.

Listing 12.3 Overloading-script-template with Backbone.js (greetings.html)

```
<script type="text/template" id="greeting-template">   ◁─┐  text/type script type
  hello <%= name %>                                        tells the browser not
</script>                                                  to execute the script
```

NOTE Backbone.js is an alternative SPA framework that was extremely popular from 2012 to 2013. This framework follows a Model-View-Controller (MVC) architecture, where views are typically defined using templates defined within the script tags.

This method (overloading the HTML script tag) was pioneered by John Resig in his Micro-Templating utility in 2008. This approach is great for the most part. Because the `script` tag is set to `display:none` by default, nothing is rendered when the template is loaded. It doesn't get rendered until you choose to do this with JavaScript; the browser doesn't parse this script as content. Further, the template is *inert*; the browser doesn't attempt to process the text as JavaScript because the type is set to something other than `text/javascript`. But this approach comes with a downside. It can potentially lead to cross-site scripting (XSS) vulnerabilities if you're not careful about the way you handle user input. As long as you're aware of these vulnerabilities, it's not a problem, but ideally there would be a standard approach that circumvents it all together. The *HTML Templates* standard introduced as a part of the Web Components Specifications solves this problem.

HTML Templates provide a standard for creating snippets of markup that aren't rendered when the page is loaded but are instead loaded at runtime with JavaScript. These work in much the same way as the *overloaded-JavaScript* approach but don't have the drawback of potential XSS vulnerabilities. You can see a sample HTML template in listing 12.4, which shows a simple `info-card` HTML template. Using templates is as simple as declaring a new `<template>` element with some content. This syntax should look familiar to you. Because Aurelia uses standard HTML Templates, the `<info-card>` template shown in the following listing is also a valid Aurelia view.

Listing 12.4   Basic HTML template (info-card.html)

```
<template id="info-card">          ◁──┐   HTML Templates
  <div class="info-card">                defined using the
    <p>Basic info card.</p>              <template> tag
  </div>
</template>
```

After declaring the `template` element, you need to do the following:

1   Query it from the DOM: `document.querySelector('#info-card')`.
2   Clone the node, creating a new copy of the DOM fragment from the template so that it can be included in the current document.
3   Append the cloned node to the current document, shown in the following listing.

Listing 12.5   Using the `info-card` template (info-card.js)

```
                                                            Gets the info-card
                                                            and body DOM
let infoCard         = document.querySelector('#info-card');  elements
let bodyElement      = document.querySelector('body');
let infoCardInstance = document.importNode(infoCard.content, true);   ◁──┐

bodyElement.appendChild(infoCardInstance);   ◁──┐          Imports the contents of
                                                          the info-card element
               Appends the new info-card                  into a new DOM node
               DOM node to the body element
```

12.3.1 Using HTML Templates in Aurelia

As you've seen throughout the code samples in previous chapters, Aurelia views are created using HTML Templates. To make it clear how close the template syntax is, let's look at the same info-card view template in Aurelia. The only difference here is you're using a one-way string binding to render the card's message to the (${message}) DOM, as shown in the following listing. The string binding can be thought of as a little bit of extra syntactic sugar Aurelia adds to the template to make it easier to render data from your JavaScript model to your view.

> **Listing 12.6** info-card **HTML template converted to an Aurelia view (info-card.html)**

```
<template>
  <div class="info-card">
    <p>${message}</p>          Aurelia one-way
  </div>                       data binding used to
</template>                    render the message
```

12.4 Custom elements

For assorted reasons (primarily, performance), the Aurelia team created a framework-specific implementation of custom elements, rather than using the vanilla Web Components option. Having said this, custom-element structure is quite similar between the two, meaning that if you're familiar with creating custom elements in vanilla Web Components, it should be relatively easy to carry this knowledge over to Aurelia, and vice versa.

To illustrate this, I've prepared an example to create a vanilla custom element. This is done by defining a class that extends the HTMLTemplate. This class defines how the custom element builds its HTML. The class is then registered with the browser against a specific tag name. Then, when you include an element with the registered name (for example, <x-info-tag>) in your HTML file, the browser knows to render the element using your custom-element definition, rather than including the element text verbatim.

You can also define callbacks (like Aurelia's component lifecycle hooks), to be called by the browser at various points in the custom element's lifecycle. Listing 12.7 shows a vanilla Web Component's x-info-card custom-element implementation. In this class, you hook into the attributeChangedCallback lifecycle method, setting the textContent of the element to the value of the message attribute. Not quite as elegant as the syntax that we've grown to know and love with Aurelia, but it gets the job done.

In this listing, you begin by registering the x-info-card element with the browser so that it will be interpreted as a custom element using the customElements.define method. This method takes the name of the element and the class definition that implements the element. This class needs to extend the HTMLElement type (the base element that other DOM elements derive from). You then create a getter function to observe changes to the message attribute, which for now only occurs when you declare the attribute in your HTML file. Finally, you hook into the `attributeChangedCallback`-lifecycle method, setting the text content of the element based on the `'message'` attribute value.

Listing 12.7   Vanilla Web Components `info-card` implementation (x-info-card.js)

```
customElements.define('x-info-card',                          Defines the
  class XInfoCard extends HTMLElement {                        custom element
    static get observedAttributes() {return ['message']; }

    attributeChangedCallback(attr, oldValue, newValue) {       Observes
      if (attr == 'message') {                                 changes on
        this.textContent = newValue;                           the message
      }                           Sets the element's           attribute
    }                             textContent on
  }                               change
});
```

You may be wondering how the browser knows to interpret this as a custom element. This is done using the new `customElements.define` method, which takes the name of the custom element and the custom element class definition as input. Once you've defined an element, you can use it in the DOM as you'd expect: `<x-info-card message="info-card">`.

> **NOTE**   The x- prefix on custom elements used to be the more common convention, but now component vendors tend to prefix their components with something that signifies which library the components come from, for example, `polymer-` for Polymer components and `au-` for Aurelia components. We'll use the x- in this case to indicate these are our custom elements and to differentiate them from the Aurelia custom elements defined later in the chapter.

> **NOTE**   At the time of writing, the custom-element API is only supported in browsers with a minimum version of Chrome 49.0, Opera 43.0, or Safari 10.1. Polyfills are available to fill the gaps in the browser API and are covered in a later section on Web Component polyfills.

The combination of custom elements and HTML Templates defines a standard way of creating Web Components, but doesn't provide any features around encapsulation. Next, we'll look at the Shadow DOM API to see how to create components that are truly isolated from the styles and JavaScript DOM interactions of the host page.

12.5   *The Shadow DOM*

Imagine the following scenario. You've found a third-party control you want to drop into your page. The documentation for the component displays a nicely laid-out control, with a color scheme that would fit perfectly into your application. With a feeling of anticipation, you eagerly install the component with npm and include it into your page layout. The problem is that, when you reload the page, you realize that the styles of a different third-party library happen to conflict with the component you've added, pushing the margins and padding way off to the side of the page. If that wasn't bad enough, as you start typing into the control, you realize that none of the key-down events are registering because that same bad neighbor happens to control this as well.

Wouldn't it be nice if you had a way of encapsulating each of the components to ensure a predictable result when including them on your page? Further, if you put yourself in the shoes of the component author, wouldn't it be nice if you could publish that component without facing the inevitable barrage of GitHub issues reporting the weird and wonderful ways that developers have found to break your beautiful component with the important directives littered throughout their 10-year-old CMS?

You're in luck. The Shadow DOM was introduced to solve these encapsulation problems. It provides a way of encapsulating parts of the DOM (DOM subtrees) from the main DOM tree. This allows you to create isolated components that you can drop into a page without worrying about their styles or behavior being disrupted by the styles or JavaScript included in the main page. The following section assumes a working knowledge of the Shadow DOM. If concepts such as Shadow DOM slots and scoped CSS sound like science fiction to you, I recommend checking out my blog post on the topic: https://sean-hunter.io/aia-the-shadow-dom. This post will get you up to speed, walking you through the process of using the vanilla Shadow DOM outside of Aurelia. With that out of the way, let's get started using the Shadow DOM with Aurelia.

12.5.1 Using the Shadow DOM with Aurelia

Aurelia provides four key features that allow you to use the Shadow DOM in your projects: the CSS as="scoped" require option, the @useShadowDOM decorator, Shadow DOM slots, and layouts. In this section, we'll review the kinds of problems that each of these features helps to solve. In the next section, you'll apply what you've learned to introduce a reusable ux-card component to the my-books application.

SCOPED CSS AND THE AS="SCOPED" ATTRIBUTE

CSS scoping in Web Components is a hot, and much-debated, topic. Scoped CSS has two requirements:

- Avoid applying outside styles to your component.
- Avoid leaking styles from within your component to the outside.

You can meet the first requirement in Aurelia by decorating your view-model using the @useShadowDOM decorator. You'll see a demonstration of this soon. The second requirement can be met in two ways. The following listing shows one way: by adding the as="scoped" option to your stylesheet's require statement. The problem with this approach is that it relies on an API that's currently supported only in Firefox, so the applications are limited.

Listing 12.8   How to use scoped CSS (scoped-css.html)

```
<template>
  <require from="./card-styles.css" as="scoped"></require>          ◁────┐
    <template id="info-card">
        <div class="card-content">
            <slot name="header">To be replaced with header</slot>
            <div class="card-body">
                <slot name="body"><p>To be replaced with body </p></slot>
            </div>
        </div>                                        Card styles are imported
    </template>                                       as scoped to restrict the
</template>                                               CSS to this component
```

The second way to confine styles to only your component is to include the styles inline within the Web Components template, and then use the Shadow DOM to encapsulate the component under a shadow root node.

> **TIP**   It's becoming more popular to apply a build tool such as PostCSS to translate your CSS, and optionally scope it to a particular component. This is outside of the scope of this discussion, but if you're interested in finding out more, I recommend checking out the PostCSS website: https://github.com/ postcss/postcss.

USING THE @USESHADOWDOM DECORATOR

To have an Aurelia component inject its contents inside a shadow root node, you need to add the @useShadowDOM decorator to the view-model class declaration. The following listing imports this decorator from the aurelia-framework package and uses it to indicate that the info-card component should be injected under a shadow root node.

Listing 12.9   Using the Shadow DOM in a view-model (info-card.js)

```
import {useShadowDOM} from 'aurelia-framework';          ◁────┐   Imports the
@useShadowDOM()            ◁────┐                                useShadowDOM
export class InfoCard{          Applies the decorator to         decorator
}                               inject this custom element
                                under a shadow root node
```

To complete this component, you'll also create a simple info-card view template, as shown in listing 12.10. To see this component in action, you can run it live in GistRun: https://sean-hunter.io/aia-listing-12-10. It's worth noting that these styles are scoped to the info-card component because you're using the @useShadowDOM decorator. Using this decorator prevents any styles that you declare within the info-card view template from leaking outside.

Listing 12.10   The info-card view template (info-card.html)

```
<template>
    <style>                         Inline styles encapsulated within
        .card-content {    ◁────    the info-card view template
```

```
            border:1px solid grey;
            width: 500px;
            height: 150px;
            margin-bottom:10px;
            padding:20px;
            color: #777;
            background-color: #F7F7F7;
            font-family: 'Source Sans Pro',
                Helvetica, 'Open Sans', sans-serif;
        }

        .card-body{
            background-color:white;
            padding:10px;
            padding-bottom: 30px;
        }
    </style>

    <div class="card-content">
        <p>info card content</p>
    </div>

</template>
```

Now that we've covered how to use the basic Shadow DOM functionality in Aurelia, let's take it one step further and see how you can use Shadow DOM slots to create templated reusable components.

SHADOW DOM SLOTS

Aurelia's Shadow DOM slot syntax is identical to vanilla Web Components. But by using Aurelia's lightweight binding syntax, you can bind content into the different slots, giving it a distinct advantage. For example, to bind content into the header and body slots from the info-card vanilla Web Component example, it's a simple matter of using one-way string interpolation binding. In the following listing (a sample root app.html view file), you've used two info-card elements, and you're binding the header and body content from the app.js view-model values, ${card1Header}. These could easily come from a repeater if you wanted to render the cards in a list.

Listing 12.11 Using Shadow DOM slots in an Aurelia view (app.html)

```
<template>
    <require from='./info-card.html'>          ← Imports the info-card HTML-
    <info-card>                                   only custom element
        <span slot="header">
            <h1>${card1Header}</h1>            ← One-way binding used to
        </span>                                   inject a custom-header
        <span slot="body">                        DOM fragment
            <span>${card1Body}</span>          ← One-way binding used to
        </span>                                   inject a custom-body
    </info-card>                                  DOM fragment
```

```
        <info-card>
            <span slot="header">
                    <h1>${card2Header}</h1>
            </span>
            <span slot="body">
                    <span>${card2Body}</span>
            </span>
        </info-card>
    <info-card>
</template>
```

Shadow DOM slots are useful for creating templated components, but that's not all you can use them for. They can also be used to define content in Aurelia's layouts, as you saw in chapter 9.

Layouts

We covered layouts in detail in chapter 9, but I want to revisit them briefly in the context of the Shadow DOM. To refresh your memory, layouts allow you to define multiple top-level pages into which views in your application can be rendered. This allows you to design your UI the way that best fits each page in your application. You can project custom HTML into different regions of the layout using Shadow DOM slots. This is another example of Aurelia using the basic building blocks provided by the web platform rather than reinventing the wheel.

Now that you've got a grounding in what the Web Component APIs are and how you can use them as a part of your Aurelia projects, let's put this knowledge into practice. In the next section, we'll use Shadow DOM slots to create a templated component.

12.6   *Creating the my-books share-book component*

Imagine a scenario where—due to a growing my-books user base—you've started to receive requests for a social sharing feature that allows users to share details about the books they're reading, on their social networks. In this section, we'll create this feature, using some of the Web Component functionality covered throughout this chapter (but without posting to a social network).

The Shadow DOM is useful for creating encapsulated components that are easily transferable between different Aurelia projects. In this section, you'll create a templated Bootstrap 4 `card` component with slots for the header, an image, content, and a footer. You'll then create a `share-book-card` component that will use the `ux-card`, injecting book-specific content (such as the book-cover image, title, and description) into slots defined by the `ux-card` component. To indicate that these are reusable components, prefix them with a `ux-` dash and place them in a new /components directory. By the end of this section, users will be able to share books by clicking the Share button on a specific book row, as shown in figure 12.2.

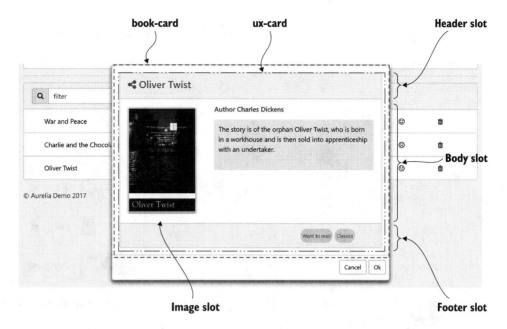

Figure 12.2 A new `ux-card` component that contains Shadow DOM slots to allow you to inject custom DOM fragments into the relevant sections

The book-sharing component will live inside another Aurelia component called the *Aurelia dialog*. This is a general-purpose modal-dialog component installed via the `aurelia-dialog` plugin (npm package). The steps required to add the book-sharing component are as follows:

1 Modify the `book` component to include a new Share button. When the user clicks this button, you'll launch the `share-book` dialog component.

2 Create the `ux-card` component. This is a new, general-purpose component, which you'll then extend, adding HTML fragments specific to sharing books.

3 Create the subcomponents. The `ux-card` component includes three subcomponents: the `ux-text-area` component (to allow users to modify the book description before sharing), the `ux-tags` component (to show the shelves that a book is assigned to), and the `ux-thumbnail-image` component (a thumbnail image with a backing link).

4 Create the parent `book-card` view, which extends the `ux-card` view, injecting book-specific content into the relevant blocks.

5 When the user clicks the OK button to share the book, you'll use a new `ux-font-block` component to show an icon to indicate that the book has been shared successfully, as shown in figure 12.3.

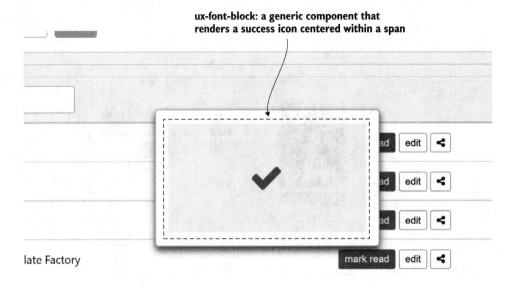

ux-font-block: a generic component that
renders a success icon centered within a span

Figure 12.3   The new ux-font-block component renders a success icon when the book has been successfully shared.

TIP   If you haven't already, be sure that you've installed the aurelia-dialog component and pulled down the latest version of the my-books companion stylesheet (section A.7 of the appendix). With these requirements in place, you're all set to start adding the new features.

12.6.1 Adding the Share button

Users interact with the sharing feature by clicking a new Share button that will be added to the book component. Let's start by modifying the book view to include the new button. This button will delegate to a new share method on the book view-model to launch the dialog. Modify the ./src/resources/elements/book.html view template as shown in the following listing to add the new button.

Listing 12.12   Add the Share button to the books view (book.html)

```
<template>
    ...

    <li ...>
        <div class="book col-12">
            <div class="book-options form-inline">
                ...
                <div class="col-lg-3 col-md-5">
                    <button class="read-button btn btn-success btn-sm"
                            if.bind="!book.read"
                            click.delegate="markRead()">
                        <span class="hover-display">
```

```
                                        <i class="fa fa-check"></i>
                                   </span> mark read
                              </button>
                              <button class="btn btn-secondary btn-sm edit-button"
                                     click.delegate="toggleEditMode()"
                                     disabled.bind="editMode">
                                   edit
                              </button>
                              <button class="btn btn-secondary btn-sm edit-button"
                                     click.delegate="share()" >
                                   <i class="fa fa-share-alt"
                                      "aria-hidden=true"></i>
                              </button>
                        </div>
                        ...
            </li>
</template>
```

Adds the new Share button, which delegates to the share() view-model method ⊳ (points to the share button block)

Next, you need to modify the `books.js` view-model to show the `share-books` dialog when the button is clicked. The Aurelia dialog component can be initialized from a view-model by importing the `DialogService` from the `aurelia-dialog` module and injecting it into the view-model. This dialog service can then be used to open a new dialog using the `dialogService.open` method, which takes the view-model that represents the component that should be rendered into the dialog. You can think of the dialog like a simple wrapper without any content. This gives you the flexibility to inject any kind of content you want into the modal by creating a new component, as shown in figure 12.4. In this case, you'll create a new `ShareBook` component.

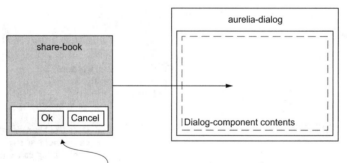

The aurelia-dialog can be used to show a modal pop-up. The contents of the pop-up are determined by the component specified in the dialogService.open method (view or view-model).

Figure 12.4 Customizing the contents of Aurelia modal dialogs by creating a component, which will then be injected into the modal-dialog container element

When opening the modal dialog, you'll also supply a `model` parameter. This is a plain JavaScript object containing the data the dialog needs. In this case, you'll pass the book to share. When the dialog is opened, you also wire up the whenClosed callback. This is a suitable place to inject any cleanup or finalization behavior that needs to be executed when the dialog is closed. An implementation isn't included in this case, because you don't want to share the books on a social network.

You can pass the result of the dialog edits to this method. The whenClosed method would be useful, for example, if you were asking a user a question or requesting input that you then needed in the parent dialog once the modal had been closed. Modify the book view-model to add the new share-book handler at ./src/resources/elements/book.js.

Listing 12.13 Modifying the books view-model to include book sharing (book.js)

```
import {bindable, inject} from 'aurelia-framework';
import {EventAggregator} from 'aurelia-event-aggregator';
import {DialogService} from 'aurelia-dialog';
import {ShareBook} from './share-book';

@inject(EventAggregator, DialogService)
export class Book{

    @bindable book;
    @bindable genres;
    @bindable shelves;
    @bindable searchTerm;

    constructor(eventAggregator, dialogService){
        this.eventAggregator = eventAggregator;
        this.editMode = false;
        this.dialogService = dialogService;
    }

    ...

    share(){
        this.dialogService.open(
        {
            viewModel: ShareBook,
            model: this.book
        })
        .whenClosed(response => {});
    }

    ...
}
```

Imports the dialog service from the aurelia-dialog plugin

Imports the ShareBook component (to be implemented next)—the view for the share-book dialog

Injects the dialog service and saves it on the class

Opens the share-book dialog when the Share button is clicked

Uses the ShareBook component as the share-book dialog content

Passes the current book to the dialog

Any empty handler included for demonstration purposes

Next, you need to create the sharing component to be used by the dialog. This will serve as the container for the share-book card and allow the user to either share the book by clicking the OK button or close the dialog by clicking Cancel. Create a new ShareBook view-model at ./src/resources/elements/share-book.js.

Listing 12.14   The new `share-book` view-model (share-book.js)

```
import {inject} from 'aurelia-framework';
import {DialogController} from 'aurelia-dialog';        ←⎺⎤

                                                             Imports the
@inject(DialogController)                               ←⎺⎤  dialog controller
export class ShareBook{                                      from the aurelia-
                                                             dialog plugin
    completedFont  = "fa fa-check fa-3x";                    and injects it
    completedStyle = "color:#27ae60";
    loadingFont    = "fa fa-spinner fa-pulse fa-3x fa-fw";

    constructor(dialogController){
        this.controller = dialogController;           ←⎺⎤
        this.state = "sharing";
    }                                    ⎡ Implements the activate()
                                         ⎢ hook method and saves
    activate(book){                 ←⎺⎤  the book model
        this.book = book;
    }
                                        ⎡ Sets the dialog into a
    ok(book){                           ⎢ loading state when users
        this.state = "loading";    ←⎺⎤  click the OK button
        this.font  = this.loadingFont;
        setTimeout(_ => this.complete(book) , 500);
    }
                                        ⎡ Sets the dialog into
    complete(book){                ←⎺⎤  the completed state
        this.state = "complete";        ⎢ and closes
        this.font  = this.completedFont;
        this.fontColor = this.completedStyle;
        setTimeout(_ => this.controller.ok(book) , 800);
    }
}
```

Next, create the corresponding share-book view file at ./src/resources/elements/
share-book.html. This is a standard, custom-element template, so you shouldn't see
anything shocking here. One thing to note is that you call the cancel method
exposed by the DialogController to close the dialog when a user clicks the Cancel
button.

Listing 12.15   The new `share-book` view (share-book.html)

```
                          ⎡ Dialog wrapping
                          ⎢ element
<template>
    <ux-dialog>        ←⎺⎤      ⎡ Dialog body
        <ux-dialog-body>  ←⎺⎤                        ⎡ Closes the dialog
        </ux-dialog-body>          ⎡ Dialog footer   ⎢ when the Cancel
        <ux-dialog-footer>  ←⎺⎤                      ⎢ button is clicked
            <button click.trigger="controller.cancel()">  ←⎺⎤
                Cancel
            </button>
```

```
                    <button click.trigger="ok(book)">
                        Ok
                    </button>
                </ux-dialog-footer>
            </ux-dialog>
        </template>
```

⟵ Delegates the OK button-click event to the OK method, passing in the current book

As shown in figure 12.5, if you run the `au-run --watch` command at your terminal and navigate to the /books route, you'll see the new Share button. Clicking this button will initialize an empty dialog with the Cancel and OK buttons.

Clicking the Share button now initializes a basic empty dialog.

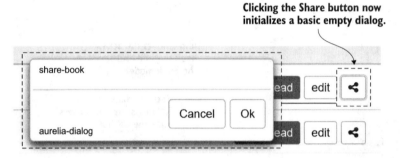

Figure 12.5 Basic `share-book` modal dialog, initiated by clicking the `share-book` button

With the basic modal dialog infrastructure in place, you're ready to create the `ux-card` component that provides the bulk of the book-sharing UI functionality.

12.6.2 *Creating the ux-card component*

You can think of the `ux-card` component as a blueprint for creating more-specific kinds of card components. As shown in figure 12.6, you'll use Shadow DOM slots in the `ux-card` component to define sections that can be replaced by custom HTML.

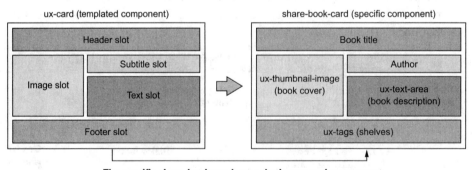

The specific share-book-card extends the ux-card component, projecting book details such as the title into the relevant slots.

Figure 12.6 The `ux-card` component can be used as a blueprint to create more-specific kinds of cards.

In this case, you'll create a share-book-card component that will replace content in the header slot with the book title, and so on. This approach is powerful because you could also use this same ux-card blueprint to create other kinds of cards. For example, imagine you needed to create a user-profile feature, which would allow users to view the profiles of other my-books users. One way to implement this is to create a user-profile card where the header slot was used for the username, the image slot was used for the user's avatar image, and so on.

You'll now put into practice the basic Shadow DOM templating techniques we covered earlier in the chapter. This is an HTML-only custom element because you don't require any non-view-related behavior. In this template, you define several named Shadow DOM slots that the user can optionally replace (for example, the title slot, <slot name="title">Title</slot>). Create the ux-card component at ./src/resources/components/ux-card.html as shown in the following listing. You'll need to create a new components directory under the resources directory to house this component.

Listing 12.16 Creating the new ux-card component (ux-card.html)

```
<template>
    <style>
        h4      { color:#26a69a; }
        .card { width: 40rem; }
    </style>
    <div class="card">
    <h4 class="card-header">
        <slot name="title">Title</slot>            ⟵  Defines slots for header,
    </h4>                                              image, and so on, templating
    <div class="card-block row">                       out the view structure
        <div class="col-md-4" >
            <slot name="card-image"></slot>
        </div>
        <div class="col-md-8">
            <h6 class="card-subtitle mb-2 text-muted">
                <slot name="sub-title">Subtitle</slot>
            </h6>
            <div class="card-text">
                <slot name="card-text">
                    content
                </slot>
            </div>
        </div>
    </div>
    <div class="card-footer">
        <slot name="card-footer">
            footer
        </slot>
    </div>
    </div>
</template>
```

In the next step, you'll create the subcomponents to be projected into each of the slots defined in the ux-card blueprint.

12.6.3 Creating the subcomponents

The share-book-card component will be a specific implementation of the blueprint defined in the previous step. Before you create this component, you need to create the subcomponents that it relies on: the ux-text-area, ux-thumbnail-image, and ux-tags components. The layout of these components is depicted in figure 12.7.

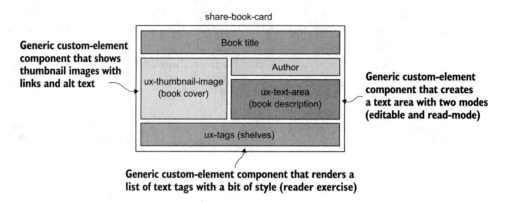

Figure 12.7 Layout and responsibilities of the `share-book-card` subcomponents, including the `ux-text-area`, `ux-thumbnail`, and `ux-tags` components

You'll create the ux-text-area component first. As you saw with the basic Shadow DOM examples earlier in the chapter, this component uses the @useShadowDOM() decorator to indicate to Aurelia that the custom-element template should be injected under a new shadow root node to encapsulate the styles and behavior. The user interaction flow for this component is depicted in figure 12.8.

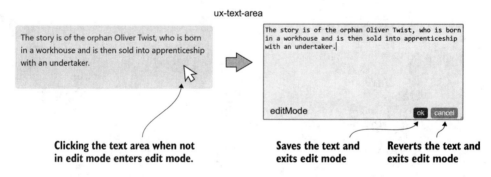

Figure 12.8 The `ux-text-area` component transitions between read mode and edit mode

Initialize this component in read mode and transition it to editMode when clicked. You'll notice that you set focus on the text-area element within a setTimeout function. By applying the focus in this way, you queue the DOM interaction to be executed after the binding has executed and the text area is displayed. This ensures the element has transitioned to the visible state by the time you try to set its focused state. Create the new ux-text-area component in the ./src/resources/components/ux-text-area.js file as follows.

Listing 12.17   Create the ux-text-area view-model (ux-text-area.js)

```
import { useShadowDOM, bindable } from "aurelia-framework";   ⊲─┐ Encapsulates the
                                                                 │ component within a
@useShadowDOM()                                              ⊲─┘ Shadow DOM node
export class UxTextArea {
  @bindable textContent;          ⊲─┐ textContent used to
  @bindable rows;                   │ represent the content
                                    │ of the text-area
  constructor() {
    this.editMode = false;        ⊲─┐ Initializes the text-area
  }                                 │ in read mode

  bind(){
      this.textContentTemp = this.textContent;   ⊲─┐ Saves pre-edit text
  }                                                 │ content in case the
                                                    │ user cancels
  edit() {
    this.editMode = true;                    ⊲──────┐
                                                     │ Switches the text-area to edit
    setTimeout(_ => {this.element.focus();}, 1);   │ mode and switches focus to
  }                                                  │ the current element

  ok() {                          ⊲─┤ Saves the temporary
    this.editMode = false;           │ text for the text-area
    this.textContent = this.textContentTemp;
  }

  cancel() {                      ⊲─┤ Undoes the text changes by
    this.editMode = false;           │ reverting to the temporary text
    this.textContentTemp = this.textContent;
  }
}
```

Number of rows in the text area ──▷ @bindable rows;

Next, you need to create the corresponding view template. A key point here is that because this template is injected under a new shadow root, you need to define styles specific to this component. Styles such as the button color aren't inherited from the parent page, as shown in figure 12.9.

Create the ux-text-area view at ./src/resources/components/ux-text-area.html.

text-area HTML fragment
injected under a new
shadow root node

Styles are defined
under the shadow root
because they aren't
inherited from the
host page.

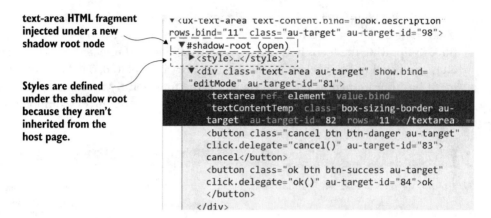

Figure 12.9   DOM fragment for the `ux-text-area` component injected under a shadow root node

---

Listing 12.18   Creating the `ux-text-area` view (ux-text-area.html)

```
<template>
    <style>
        .text-area {                          ◁── Only shows the underlying
            position: relative;                  textarea element if the
        }                                        component is in edit mode

        .text-area button {
            position: absolute;
            bottom: 8px;
        }

        .text-area button.cancel {
            right: 10px;
        }

        .text-area button.ok {
            right: 68px;
        }

        .text-area textarea {
            margin-top: 10px;
            background-color: #f5f5f5;
            width: 100%;
        }

        .text-block {
            background-color: rgba(158, 158, 158, 0.18);
            height: 100px;
            padding: 10px;
            border-right-width: .25rem;
            border-radius: .25rem;
        }
```

```
        .text-block:hover {
            cursor: pointer;
            background-color: rgba(158, 158, 158, 0.44);
        }

        .btn {
            border: 1px solid transparent;
            line-height: 1.25;
            border-radius: .25rem;
            transition: all .15s ease-in-out;
        }

        .btn-success {
            color: white;
            background-color: #009688;
        }

        .btn-success:hover {
            background-color: #4DB6AC;
        }

        .btn-danger {
            color: white;
            background-color: #BDBDBD;
        }

        .btn-danger:hover {
            background-color: #E0E0E0;
        }

        .box-sizing-border{
            -webkit-box-sizing: border-box;
            -moz-box-sizing: border-box;
            box-sizing: border-box;
        }
    </style>
    <div class="text-area" show.bind="editMode">
        <textarea ref="element"
                rows="${rows}"
                value.bind="textContentTemp"
                class="box-sizing-border">
        </textarea>
        <button class="cancel btn btn-danger" click.delegate="cancel()">
            cancel
        </button>
        <button class="ok btn btn-success" click.delegate="ok()">
            ok
        </button>
    </div>

    <p class="text-block"
        click.delegate="edit()"
        show.bind="!editMode">
```

Only shows the underlying textarea element if the component is in edit mode

Exposes a reference to the textarea element to the view-model

Specifies the number of textarea rows

Binds the textarea value to the temporary text

Undoes the temporary text when the user clicks the Cancel button

Saves the temporary text when the user clicks the OK button

Enables edit mode when the Edit button is clicked

Only shows the read-mode view of the text-area when the user isn't editing

```
        ${textContent}              ◁─┐   Renders the text content
    </p>                              │   to the read-mode <p>
</template>                           │   element body
```

Next, you'll create the `ux-thumbnail` image component. This is a generic component responsible for showing a thumbnail image for a given source URL (provided by data binding from the parent component). You can also pass an image HREF, which is a link to an external resource related to the image, an image caption, and whether the image should use absolute positioning.

In this scenario, you'll use the component to render a thumbnail image for the book cover. If the user clicks the image (following the bound image HREF), their browser will navigate to the Wikipedia page for the book. This component also uses the `@useShadowDOM` decorator for encapsulation. As you can imagine, this component has broad applications. For example, you could use it to display an avatar for users that links to the user's Twitter profile. Because this is a generic component that could potentially be used in other Aurelia projects, you'll create it under the components directory as well. Create the `ux-thumbnail` image view-model at ./src/resources/components/ux-thumbnail-image.js as follows.

Listing 12.19   Creating the `ux-thumbnail-image` view-model (ux-thumbnail-image.js)

```
import {bindable, useShadowDOM} from 'aurelia-framework';     ◁─┐   Encapsulates the
                                                                │   component within a
@useShadowDOM()                                               ◁─┘   Shadow DOM node
export class UxThumbnailImage{
    @bindable imgSrc;                    ┐   Makes the image
    @bindable imgHref;                   │   source href and
    @bindable imgCap;                    ┘   caption configurable
    @bindable positionAbsolute = false;  ◁─┐
}                                          │   Defaults the component to
                                           │   use relative positioning
```

Let's create the corresponding view template, which uses data-bound parameters, such as the image URL, from the parent component. Create the `ux-thumbnail-image` view template at ./src/resources/components/ux-thumbnail-image.html.

Listing 12.20   Creating the `ux-thumbnail-image` view (ux-thumbnail-image.html)

```
<template>
    <style>                        ◁─┐   Inline styles encapsulated
        img {                        │   within the custom element's
            padding: 3px;            │   shadow root node
            background-color: #E0E0E0;
            border-radius: .25rem;
            width: 160px;
            height: 244px;
            -webkit-box-shadow: 0 2px 2px 0 rgba(0, 0, 0, 0.14),
                                0 1px 5px 0 rgba(0, 0, 0, 0.12),
                                0 3px 1px -2px rgba(0, 0, 0, 0.2);
```

```
        box-shadow: 0 2px 2px 0 rgba(0, 0, 0, 0.14),
                    0 1px 5px 0 rgba(0, 0, 0, 0.12),
                    0 3px 1px -2px rgba(0, 0, 0, 0.2)
    }
    .thumbnail-image {
        width: 100%;
    }
    .thumbnail-image:hover {
        background-color: white;
        opacity: 0.7;
    }
</style>
<style if.bind="positionAbsolute">              ◁── Declares absolute styling
    img {                                            based on the component
        position: absolute;                          user's preference
        left: 32px;
        top: 15px;
    }
</style>
<a class="thumbnail-image"
    href.bind="imgHref">           ┐  Binds the image HREF,
    <img                           │  source, and caption passed
        src.bind="imgSrc"          │  from parent component
        alt="imgCap">              ┘
</a>
</template>
```

Exercise: Create a tags component

Create the new ux-tags component that's used in the share-book dialog. This component is rendered in the footer slot of the ux-card to show a list of the bookshelves that the shared book is assigned to.

In listing 12.21 in the next section, add the ux-tags component import and component reference. You can find one possible implementation for this component in the *Aurelia in Action* GitHub repository under the components directory (http://mng.bz/Yxmv).

The required subcomponents are now in place. Next, you'll create the share-book-card component, which you can think of as an instance of the ux-card blueprint.

12.6.4 *Creating the share-book-card component*

Now you can create the share-book-card, projecting the book-cover image into the image slot (ux-thumbnail-image), the book title into the header slot, the author into the subtitle slot, the book description (editable using the ux-text-area component) into the text slot, and the shelves into the footer slot, as shown in figure 12.10.

Create the share-book-card HTML-only custom element view, as shown in listing 12.21. The book to render in this component is passed down from the parent component. This is achieved by adding the bindable attribute to the template element,

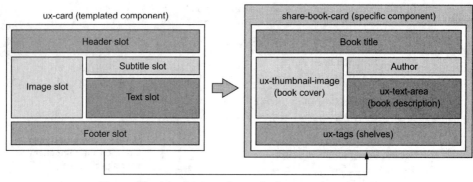

The specific share-book-card extends the ux-card component,
projecting book details such as the title into the relevant slots.

Figure 12.10 `share-book-card` as an instance of the `ux-card` blueprint with book details
projected into each of the available Shadow DOM slots

template bindable="book". This is created under the usual ./src/resources/elements
directory, because it's not expected to be reusable in other Aurelia projects.

Listing 12.21   Creating the `book-card` view (share-book-card.html)

```
<template bindable="book">
  <require from="../components/ux-card.html"></require>
  <require from="../components/ux-thumbnail-image"></require>
  <require from="../components/ux-text-area"></require>
  <!- Add ux-tags component import -->

  <ux-card class="ux-card">
      <div slot="card-image">
          <ux-thumbnail-image
              img-src.bind="book.imageUrl"
              img-href.bind="book.url">
          </ux-thumbnail-image>
      </div>
      <h4 slot="title">
        <i class="fa fa-share-alt" aria-hidden="true"></i> ${book.title}
      </h4>
      <h6 slot="sub-title">Author
          <a href.bind="book.authorBioUrl"> ${book.author} </a>
      </h6>
      <div slot="card-text">
          <ux-text-area
              text-content.bind="book.description" rows.bind="11">
          </ux-text-area>
      </div>
      <div slot="card-footer" class="row">
          <!- Add ux-tags component reference -->
      </div>
  </ux-card>
</template>
```

- Imports the subcomponents
- Uses the ux-card component
- Projects a ux-thumbnail image of the book's cover image into the card-image slot
- Projects the book's title into the title slot
- Projects the author's name into the author slot
- Projects a ux-text-area with the book's description into the card-text slot
- Exercise content

The share-book-card component is now in place, and you're almost ready to see it in action. The last step is to wire it into the share-book dialog to render the book details when the user clicks the Share button.

12.6.5 Tying it all together

The last step in creating the share-book dialog is to tie it all together by including the share-book-card component into the dialog component. The component has three states: sharing, loading, and complete, as shown in figure 12.11. When the user clicks the OK button, the sharing process is initialized, and a loading dialog is shown. Once the share has been completed, the dialog moves into the completed state.

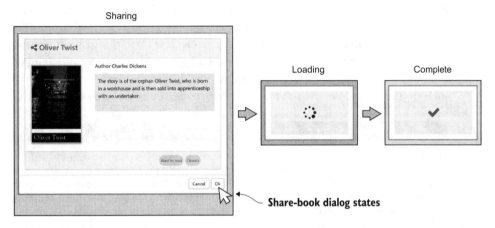

Figure 12.11 Three different states of the share-book **dialog. The user initiates this process by clicking the OK button, causing the dialog to transition through to the loading state, and then the complete state.**

To represent the loading and complete states, you'll need to create one last simple component, the ux-font-block. The ux-font-block component is responsible for rendering a Font Awesome icon within a square. Again, because this component has uses outside of the current context, create it in the components directory and give it a ux- prefix. The Font Awesome font and the color are bound from the parent component. Because this is an HTML-only custom element, you'll pass these through using the bindable attribute on the template, template bindable="font, color". Create the ux-font-block component at ./src/resources/components/ux-font-block.html.

Listing 12.22 Creating the new ux-font-block **view (ux-font-block.html)**

```
<template bindable="font, color">
    <style>                              ◁─┐  Web Component–
        .font-block {                        specific styles
            width: 280px;
            height: 150px;
            padding: 50px;
```

```
        background-color: #f5f5f5;
        display: flex;
        align-items: center;
        justify-content: center;
    }
  </style>
  <div class="font-block">
    <span css.bind="color">
        <i class="${font}"></i>
    </span>
  </div>
</template>
```

Binds the span's
CSS to the bindable
color property

Renders the font
icon (for example, a
loading indicator)

Finally, you can modify the share-book dialog to include the ux-font-block and
share-book-card components. The state variable is used to determine which of
these components should be shown at a given time. You'll add both components to
the ux-dialog-body section of the dialog, leaving the footer section unchanged. Modify
the share-book dialog view template at ./src/resources/elements/share-book.html to
include the share-book-card and ux-font-block components.

Listing 12.23   Adding new subcomponents to share-book dialog (share-book.html)

```
<template>
    <require from="./share-book-card"></require>
    <require from="../components/ux-font-block.html"></require>
    <ux-dialog>
        <ux-dialog-body>
            <ux-font-block
                    show.bind="state != 'sharing'"
                    color.bind="fontColor"
                    font.bind="font">
            </ux-font-block>
            <share-book-card
                    show.bind="state == 'sharing'"
                    book.bind="book">
            </share-book-card>
        </ux-dialog-body>
        <ux-dialog-footer
                show.bind="state == 'sharing'">
            <button click.trigger="controller.cancel()">
                Cancel
            </button>
            <button click.trigger="ok(book)">
                Ok
            </button>
        </ux-dialog-footer>
    </ux-dialog>
</template>
```

Imports the
subcomponents

Adds the ux-font-block
component to show the
loading and complete states

Adds the share-book-
card component and
only shows in the
sharing state

Hides the footer once
the user clicks OK to
complete the share

You can now reload the project to view the changes to the share-book dialog with the
addition of these subcomponents.

Exporting Aurelia components as standard web components

No SPA framework is an island. Within your company, it's likely that you have several web applications developed on varying technology stacks. Wouldn't it be convenient if you could export selected Aurelia components as standard web components for use across the applications in your organization?

The Aurelia web components library allows you to do just that. This can be extremely useful for cross-cutting types of components like auto-complete controls, or other standard UI widgets that scream out to be shared beyond the boundaries of your Aurelia applications. If this excites you, you can find out more about the Aurelia web components library at www.npmjs.com/package/aurelia-web-components.

12.7 *my-books project status*

In this chapter, you added a new book-sharing feature to the my-books application that uses a combination of the `aurelia-dialog` plugin and Shadow DOM slots, as shown in figure 12.12. You can download the completed project from GitHub at https://github.com/freshcutdevelopment/Aurelia-in-Action.git using the `git clone` command.

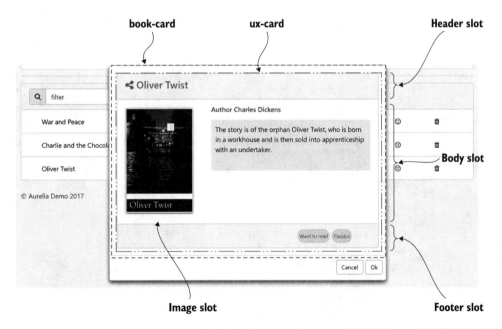

Figure 12.12   The my-books book-management page state at the end of chapter 12

Keeping with the component theme, in the next chapter we'll delve deeper into Aurelia's component APIs. You'll learn how to create custom binding behaviors and advanced custom attributes, and how you can override some of Aurelia's default conventions to fit specific requirements of your application.

Summary

- Web Components are a set of four specifications: HTML Imports, HTML Templates, custom elements, and the Shadow DOM. These specifications aim to provide the building blocks for creating reusable widgets for the web.
- By making use of the standard Web Components APIs, you can build reusable UI widgets that you can easily share between projects or even different frameworks.
- Aurelia uses HTML Imports and HTML Templates under the hood. By using Aurelia, you're already using Web Components.
- You can also use the Shadow DOM in your Aurelia projects if you want to create encapsulated components that control their own styles and are isolated from the host application.
- Shadow DOM slots can be used to create view blueprints with replaceable parts into which you can inject custom HTML. This feature lets you create truly reusable components.

Extending Aurelia

13

This chapter covers

- Getting unconventional with convention overrides
- Looking at custom binding behaviors
- Creating advanced custom attributes with dynamic options

This is the chapter that I was most looking forward to writing, because it gives me the opportunity to show you some of the amazing extensibility points Aurelia has on offer. When building applications with Aurelia, most of the time you'll be well served by following Aurelia's default conventions, but there will come a time when your application's requirements will diverge from what comes out of the box.

One of the remarkable things about Aurelia is that although the initial starting point is simple, it provides you with several power-ups that allow you to move beyond the basics and create applications that solve even the thorniest problems. Some of these power-ups include convention overrides, custom binding behaviors, and custom attributes with dynamic options. In this chapter, we'll explore how you can use each of these power-ups to solve the trickier problems you'll run into when building complex Aurelia applications.

13.1 *Overriding Aurelia's default conventions*

Because Aurelia's conventions are what you'd choose yourself, most of the time it's the right choice to use the defaults. But there are times when it's useful to get unconventional by overriding Aurelia's default conventions. Aurelia is equipped with several decorators that provide a convenient way of doing this. As a rule, by adding these decorators to your view-model (either a custom attribute or custom element), you can change Aurelia's default behavior. In this section, we'll review the following decorators: @useView, @noView, @inlineView, @containerLess, @customAttribute, and @customElement, as shown in figure 13.1. You can see each of the examples from this section in action on this GitHub gist: https://sean-hunter.io/aurelia-convention-overrides.

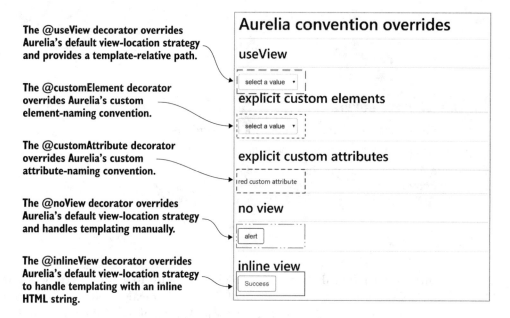

The @useView decorator overrides Aurelia's default view-location strategy and provides a template-relative path.

The @customElement decorator overrides Aurelia's custom element-naming convention.

The @customAttribute decorator overrides Aurelia's custom attribute-naming convention.

The @noView decorator overrides Aurelia's default view-location strategy and handles templating manually.

The @inlineView decorator overrides Aurelia's default view-location strategy to handle templating with an inline HTML string.

Figure 13.1   A collection of decorators that can be used to override Aurelia's conventions

13.1.1 *Specifying a view template relative path with @useView*

Aurelia provides several approaches that allow you to change the way views are selected corresponding to your view model. The first approach we'll look at is the @useView decorator. This decorator (and the others that we'll look at throughout the chapter) is in the decorators module of Aurelia's templating package. If you're interested in looking at how these decorators are implemented, I recommend checking out the source code on GitHub: https://sean-hunter.io/aurelia-decorators.

Aurelia uses a strategy pattern to determine which route should be loaded into the view. It does this by first checking whether the view-model class has a decorator that explicitly specifies a view strategy (such as useView). If no view strategy is specified, it uses the fallback strategy (the conventional view strategy). If a view-strategy decorator is present, it will defer to this strategy to locate the view template. Aurelia's view-strategy anatomy is depicted in figure 13.2.

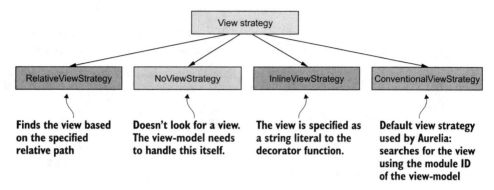

Figure 13.2   The anatomy of Aurelia's view-strategy system

The useView decorator is a shortcut for the relative view strategy depicted in figure 13.2. It's particularly useful if you want to organize your project differently. For example, imagine you have a group of view templates that you'd prefer to reference from a ./src/templates directory. You could achieve this using the useView decorator. The example view-model in listing 13.1 uses this decorator to override the conventional view strategy for the bootstrap-select view-model. Instead of looking for a bootstrap-select.html view template, it will find the view at ./my-select.html. It does this by looking at the relative path passed to the useView decorator.

Listing 13.1   `bootstrap-select` view-model (bootstrap-select.js)

```
import {useView, bindable} from 'aurelia-framework';          Imports the
                                                              useView decorator

@useView('./my-select.html')              Explicit relative
export class BootstrapSelect{             path specified to
  @bindable options;                      the view template
}
```

For completeness, I've also included the corresponding my-select view template in the following listing. As you can see, there's nothing special about this template to indicate that it isn't using the conventional view strategy, because this is entirely controlled by the view-model.

Listing 13.2   `bootstrap-select` view (my-select.html)

```
<template>
    <div class="form-inline">              Simple select
      <select class="form-control">        list view
        <option value="">select a value</option>
```

```
    <option repeat.for="option of options"
            model.bind="option">${option}</option>
    </select>
  </div>
</template>
```

To use a component using an unconventional view strategy, follow the standard process of requiring the view-model into the view, as shown in the following listing.

Listing 13.3   Using the `my-select` custom element (app.html)

```
<template>
    <require from="style.css"></require>
    <require from="bootstrap-select"></require>        ◁─┐ Requires the
                                                          bootstrap-select view-
    <section>                                             model module ID
        <h1>${message}</h1>
        <hr/>

        <h2>useView</h2>
        <hr/>
        <bootstrap-select options.bind="selectOptions">  ◁─┐ Uses the
        </bootstrap-select>                                  bootstrap-select
                                                             custom element
    </section>

</template>
```

Although the `RelativeViewStrategy` is useful for altering the logic Aurelia uses to find the view template, what if you want to skip the template part of the process entirely and control the HTML yourself? Next, we'll look at how you can use the `NoViewStrategy` to do just that.

13.1.2   Handling custom-element views manually with @noView

In the same way that you can use the `useView` decorator as a shortcut to tell Aurelia to use the relative view strategy, you can use the `@noView` decorator to switch a view-model to a no-view strategy. This is typically used when you want to take over fine-grained rendering control. Listing 13.4 shows how you could use this decorator to create an `alerter` component (a simple button that shows a native-web-browser alert) using a view-model without a corresponding view template. In this component, hook into the `attached` component-lifecycle callback, manually append an Alert button to the DOM, and attach an event listener. The event listener is then wired up when the view is detached.

Listing 13.4   Creating the `alerter` view-model (alerter.js)

```
import {noView, inject} from 'aurelia-framework';         ◁─┐ Imports the
                                                             noView decorator
@noView()              ◁─┐ Uses the noView decorator
                          (no parameters required)
```

```
@inject(Element)
export class Alerter{            ◄──┐  Injects the parent
                                    │  element to append
    constructor(element){           │  the button to
      this.element = element;
      this.alerter = _ => {
        alert("hello world");
      };                                 Manually attaches the
    }                                     button to the parent
                                          node in the DOM
    attached(){                     ◄──┘
        this.button = document.createElement("button");
        this.button.className += "btn btn-outline-primary";
        let content = document.createTextNode("alert");

        this.button.appendChild(content);

        this.element.appendChild(this.button);

        this.button.addEventListener('click', this.alerter, false);
    }

    detached(){
      this.button.removeEventListener('click', this.alerter, false);
    }
}
```

As you saw with the component that used the useView decorator, components without a view template are also required into a view using the view-model's module ID.

Listing 13.5 Using the `alerter` view-model (app.html)

```
<template>
  ...
  <require from="alerter"></require>    ◄──┐  Requires the alerter
  <section>                                │  into the view
      ...
      <hr/>                           Uses the alerter
      <alerter></alerter>         ◄──┘ custom element
  </section>
</template>
```

Although it's unlikely that you'll need to use this decorator in your own project development, you may come across it when using Aurelia UI frameworks. As such, it's worth having a basic understanding of how it works. Next, we'll look at a view strategy that you're likely to come across more frequently in your day-to-day development: the inline view strategy.

13.1.3 *Specifying views as template strings with @inlineView*

The inline view strategy allows you to specify your view markup in a string literal that Aurelia should use when creating the view instance, rather than loading it from a view template, as it would when using the conventional view strategy. You can create an inline view by decorating your class with the @inlineView decorator and passing in the literal view-template string, as shown in the following listing. All the usual features that you'd expect from an Aurelia view are available here, such as binding and loading dependent view resources like CSS files using the require statement. Inline views are particularly useful when you have a tiny amount of view markup.

Listing 13.6 Creating the `alerter-inline` view-model (alerter-inline.js)

```
import {inlineView} from 'aurelia-framework';

@inlineView(`<template>
            <button type="button" class="btn btn-outline-success"
                    click.delegate="showAlert()">Success
            </button>
            </template>`)
export class AlerterInline{

    showAlert(){
      alert("hello world");
    }
}
```

⟵ Passes the literal markup string to the inlineView decorator

As with the preceding examples, components that use the inline view strategy can be deployed within other Aurelia views using the standard method (shown as follows).

Listing 13.7 Using the `alerter` inline view-model (app.html)

```
<template>
    ...
    <require from="alerter-inline"></require>

    <section>
    ...
        <hr/>
        <h2>inline view</h2>
        <alerter-inline></alerter-inline>
    </section>

</template>
```

You've seen how view strategy decorators can be used to change how Aurelia locates and creates the view instance for a view-model, but what if you want to change the name of a component as it's referred to in the view? In the next two sections, we'll look at how you can use the @customElement and @customAttribute decorators to override the default component-naming behavior for custom elements and attributes.

13.1.4 *Explicitly naming custom elements with @customElement*

By applying the @customElement decorator to a class, you can indicate that the decorated class is a custom element, regardless of the class name. You can pass the desired name of the custom element to this decorator to control how the element should be used in the view. For example, decorating the BootstrapSelectCustomElement class with @customElement('select-custom-element') allows you to use the custom element by that name in the view, ('select-custom-element'), as seen in the following two listings.

> **Listing 13.8 Creating the view-model (bootstrap-select-custom-element.js)**

```
import {customElement, bindable} from 'aurelia-framework';

@customElement('select-custom-element')          ◁──┐  Explicitly sets the
export class BootstrapSelectCustomElement{            element name using the
  @bindable options;                                  customElement decorator
}
```

The corresponding view template is created, as usual, with no knowledge of the element name.

> **Listing 13.9 Creating the corresponding view (bootstrap-select-custom-element.html)**

```
<template>
    <div class="form-inline">
      <select class="form-control">
        <option value="">select a value</option>
        <option repeat.for="option of options"
                model.bind="option">${option}</option>
      </select>
    </div>
 </template>
```

In this case, you still need to require the view with the module name of the view-model. This changes the name of the element itself, not the corresponding module, as shown in the following listing.

> **Listing 13.10 Using the explicitly named custom element (app.html)**

```
<template>
    <require from="style.css"></require>

    <require from="bootstrap-select"></require>
    <require from="bootstrap-select-custom-element"></require>

    <section>
        ...
        <bootstrap-select options.bind="selectOptions"></bootstrap-select>

        <h2>explicit custom elements</h2>
        <hr/>
```

```
        <select-custom-element options.bind="selectOptions">
        </select-custom-element>

        <hr/>
    </section>
  </template>
```

You've seen how to override Aurelia's custom-element-naming conventions. Aurelia also allows you to apply the same technique to custom attributes using the @custom-Attribute decorator.

13.1.5 *Explicitly naming custom attributes with @customAttribute*

As you may have guessed, you can also explicitly name custom attributes using the @customAttribute decorator. This decorator can be used in basically the same way as the custom-element decorator (pass in the name that you want the attribute to use). You can also pass in additional metadata, including the default binding mode (1 for one-way or 2 for two-way) and any aliases for the attribute. For example, in listing 13.11 you create a custom attribute named red. Aurelia knows to interpret this as a custom attribute rather than using the default convention (to load it as a custom element), even though it doesn't follow conventional naming: RedCustomAttribute. You could also specify a default binding mode and aliases for this attribute like @custom-Attribute('red', 1, ['red', 'hot', 'spicy']). The aliases could then be applied to an element instead, causing the same red-custom-attribute view-model to be initialized, for example, <span hot>.

> **Listing 13.11   Creating the `red` custom attribute (red.js)**

```
import {customAttribute, inject} from 'aurelia-framework';

@customAttribute('red')      ⟵─┐   Decorates the class,
@inject(Element)                │   specifying the attribute
export class Red{               │   name as 'red'
  constructor(element){
    this.element = element;
    this.element.style.color = 'red';
  }
}
```

As with custom elements, you still need to use the module name rather than the attribute name when requiring the attribute into the view. In this case, however, they happen to be the same, as shown in the following listing.

> **Listing 13.12   Using the `red` custom attribute (app.html)**

```
<template>
    ...
    <require from="red"></require>      ⟵─┐   Uses the 'red' custom
                                              attribute in the app view
```

```
    <section>
        ...
        <hr/>
        <h2>explicit custom attributes</h2>
        <hr/>
        <span red>red custom attribute</span>
        <hr/>
    </section>

</template>
```

With this power-up under your belt, you've got what you need to move beyond Aurelia's default conventions. The next power-up we'll look at will provide you with a lens that you can use to explore the inner workings of Aurelia's binding system, and even change it on the fly.

13.2 *Creating an inspect custom binding behavior*

In chapter 5, I introduced the concept of *binding behaviors*. I'll refresh your memory: Binding behaviors are like value converters in that they're declaratively applied to a binding, using the & behavior-name syntax. What makes binding behaviors different is that they have access to the binding instance throughout its lifecycle, as opposed to value converters, which have access to only the value as it's intercepted between the view and view-model. Some built-in examples of these include the throttle and debounce behaviors, which allow you to control the frequency at which binding notifications are fired. In this section, we'll look under the covers of binding behaviors to learn how they work, and what's required to create one yourself. Although you'll seldom need to create your own, like anything, knowing how they work will allow you to use them much more effectively.

The binding behavior that you'll create can be applied to bindings to collect metadata such as the binding mode and target. This metadata is then added to the override-binding context of the current component's scope to allow you to display the metadata in a table on the view, as shown in figure 13.3. You can see this binding behavior in action on GistRun: https://sean-hunter.io/inspector-binding-behavior.

You can create custom binding behaviors by creating a class with the {Name}Binding-Behavior naming convention. This class needs to implement the bind(binding, scope, [...args]), and unbind(binding, scope) methods, as shown in listing 13.13. The bind method takes the binding to operate on, the scope that the binding is applied to, and an optional set of arguments. Arguments are passed to a binding behavior using the & behaviorName:arguments syntax shown in chapter 5. The bind method should be used to either alter the binding (for example, the throttle binding behavior that replaces the binding method with a throttled version), or observe and report on the binding internals (as is the case for the inspect binding behavior). The unbind method is then used to return the binding to its original state (before the behavior was applied) to prevent memory leaks. In the case of the throttle binding

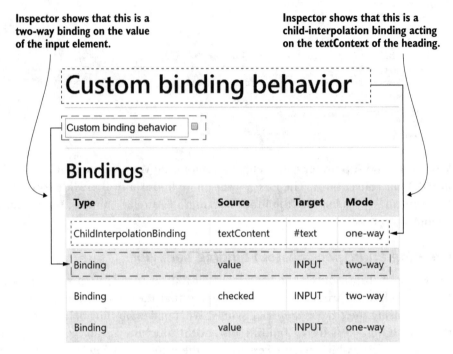

Inspector shows that this is a two-way binding on the value of the input element.

Inspector shows that this is a child-interpolation binding acting on the textContext of the heading.

Custom binding behavior

Custom binding behavior

Bindings

Type	Source	Target	Mode
ChildInterpolationBinding	textContent	#text	one-way
Binding	value	INPUT	two-way
Binding	checked	INPUT	two-way
Binding	value	INPUT	one-way

Figure 13.3   The result of applying the `'inspect'` custom binding behavior to the heading, input, and checkbox elements to provide details about each binding expression, such as the binding type and mode

behavior, the throttled version of the method is replaced again with the original unthrottled version and clears the `timeout` object used internally to implement the throttling. In the case of the `inspect` binding behavior, you're clearing the array of bindings that you populated on the context during the `bind` method.

The `inspect` binding behavior intercepts the binding object, pulling out the observer type (for example, a child-interpolation binding used for string interpolation like `${message}`), the binding source (for example, the element value), the target (for example, an `input` element), and the binding mode (one-way or two-way). This binding metadata is then stored in the overriding context for the current scope. To refresh your memory: the overriding context is like an overlay on top of the current binding context, where values in the overriding context take precedence over values in the binding context. Adding the bindings to this context makes them accessible in the view.

Listing 13.13   Create the inspect-binding behavior (inspect-binding-behavior.js)

```
export class InspectBindingBehavior {
  bind(binding, scope) {
```

◁── **Implements the required bind method to save the binding metadata**

```
                let name = binding.targetObserver ?                        ◁─┐ Gets the
                         binding.targetObserver.constructor.name             │ binding type
                                : binding.constructor.name;

Gets the    ┌─▷ let currentBindings = scope.overrideContext["bindings"] || [];
current     │
bindings    │   currentBindings.push({                                       ◁──┐
array from  │                           "type" : name,                          │
the override-│                          "source" : binding.targetProperty,      │ Stores the
Context     │                           "target": binding.target.nodeName,      │ binding
            │                           "mode" : binding.mode                   │ metadata
            │                         });                                       │
                                                                               │
                scope.overrideContext["bindings"]  =  currentBindings    ◁──────┘

            }
                                                          Restores the binding
            unbind(binding, scope) {                  ◁─┐ scope to its original
               delete scope.overrideContext["bindings"]; │ state on unbind
            }
        }
```

To round up the `inspect-binding-behavior` example: binding behaviors can be required into the view by name, as shown in listing 13.14. Unlike the `toView` and `from-View` value-converter methods, the `bind` and `unbind` methods on a custom binding behavior are called only once (when the corresponding `bind` and `unbind` component-lifecycle methods are called), rather than each time the value this binding is applied to changes. With this binding behavior, you can now inspect the bindings applied to elements in the view like this: `<input value.bind="message & inspect"></input>`. Any bindings that you inspect appear in the bindings table at the bottom of the view.

Listing 13.14 Using the inspect-binding behavior (app.html)

```
<template>
  <require from="./inspect-binding-behavior"></require>        ◁─┐ Imports the
  <require from="./style.css"></require>                          │ custom binding
                                                                  │ behavior
  <section>
  <h1>${message & inspect}</h1>                                ┐

  <hr/>                                                        │ Applies the
                                                               │ binding behavior
  <input value.bind="message & inspect"></input>              │ to inspect each
  <input type="checkbox" checked.bind="checked & inspect"     │ of the view's
    value.one-way="isChecked & inspect">                      │ bindings
  <hr/>                                                        ┘

  <h2>Bindings</h2>
  <table class="table table-striped table-bordered">
    <tr>
      <th>Type</th>
      <th>Source</th>
      <th>Target</th>
```

```
      <th>Mode</th>
    </tr>
    <tr repeat.for="binding of bindings">          ◁—  Renders the inspected
      <td>${binding.type}</td>                          binding metadata to
      <td>${binding.source}</td>                         the view
      <td>${binding.target}</td>
      <td>${binding.mode == 1 ? "one-way" : "two-way" }</td>

    </tr>
  </table>
  </section>
</template>
```

Binding behaviors can be daunting, but if you take the time to understand them, you'll add a degree of control and flexibility to the way you work with Aurelia that you may not have seen otherwise. The next power-up we'll look at is custom attributes with dynamic options, and to understand them, you'll create a jQuery Selectize wrapper that may be useful in your future Aurelia projects.

13.3 *Creating a Selectize.js custom attribute*

Selectize is a useful jQuery plugin that allows you to create a hybrid control that combines a `textbox` and a `<select>` element. This means that you can have a select list that also allows the user to get type-ahead-style autocomplete responses when entering values into the field. Use this control to add a country picker to my-books using a new `au-selectize` custom attribute. This control allows users to select their country using an autocomplete-style drop-down list. This custom attribute goes beyond what we covered in chapter 3, using the `@dynamicOptions` decorator to allow additional bindable properties to be added without the need to declare each individually. Figure 13.4 shows the `user-details` page modified to include the new country picker.

> **NOTE**   If you haven't done so already, please follow the steps in section A.9 of the appendix before you get started with the implementation steps.

Using the `@dynamicOptions` decorator is convenient for the use case of wrapping an external jQuery dependency where you may not want to explicitly map all the properties that you support as bindable properties on the custom-attribute view-model. You can listen for changes on these properties by implementing the `property-Changed(name, newValue, oldValue)` method on your custom attribute view-model and responding based on the name of the changed attribute. They're also useful in cases where the name of the bindable property isn't known when creating the attribute. In this case, you'll use four dynamic properties:

- URL—Applicable only if the `selectize` custom attribute is set to run against a remote endpoint rather than from a local list. This will be set to the `/countries` endpoint. Because this custom attribute uses the singleton `HttpClient` instance, it will take the base URL that you configured up front in the `app` view-model, so all you need here is the relative endpoint used to retrieve the country list.

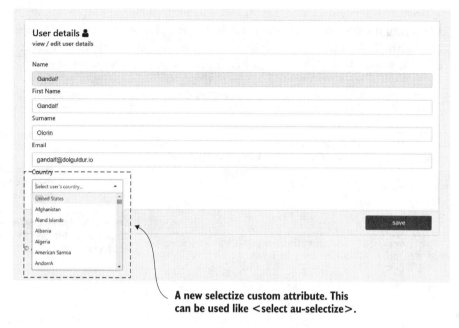

A new selectize custom attribute. This can be used like <select au-selectize>.

Figure 13.4 The new `selectize` custom attribute, which allows users to select their country via an autocomplete-style select list.

- *The* `valueField` *property*—Indicates which property on the object returned from the remote endpoint should represent the select-option value. You'll set this to the `country-code` property.
- *The* `labelField` *property*—Used to indicate which property on the object returned from the remote endpoint should be used as the select-item label. You'll set this to the country name.
- *The* `searchField` *property*—Used to indicate which property on the object returned from the remote endpoint should be searched over. This will also be set to the country name.

In this custom attribute, hook into the `attached` component-lifecycle callback and either initialize a remote `selectize` element (one that gets its values from a remote web API) if you have a URL, or a client `selectize` element (one that expects its values to be specified as `option` child nodes to the `select` element). We'll focus on the remote implementation because this is what you'll use for the user-details page. Activate the Selectize jQuery plugin by calling the `selectize` method. This performs some DOM manipulation, hiding the original `select` element, and replacing it with an `input` and a collection of `<div>` elements to represent each select option.

Because this element needs to pull a list of countries from the my-books-server API, hook into the `selectizeElement load` callback using the `HttpClient` module to fetch the matching countries.

Because the consumer of this custom element (the user-details page) needs to know when the user picks a different country, you'll also handle the 'change' selectize method, forwarding that event on to the select element. The user-details component can then respond to this change by assigning the new country to the user.

Listing 13.15 Creating the `selectize` custom attribute (au-selectize.js)

```
import selectize from 'selectize';                                 Imports the
import {dynamicOptions, inject} from 'aurelia-framework';          selectize module
import {HttpClient} from 'aurelia-fetch-client';
                                                                   Imports the
                                                                   dynamic options
@dynamicOptions                                                    decorator
@inject(Element, HttpClient)
export class AuSelectizeCustomAttribute{
                                                      Applies the dynamic options
                                                      decorator to the custom
    constructor(element, http){                       attribute class
        this.element = element;
        this.http = http;
        this.selected = {};               Injects the current select
    }                                     element that the jQuery
                                          plugin should be applied to
Initializes the
selected value
to an empty     attached(){
object              if(this.url) this.initializeRemoteSelectize();    Initializes the jQuery
                    else{                                             plugin once the view
                        this.initializeClientSelectize();             has been attached to
                    }                                                 the DOM
                }

    initializeClientSelectize(){
        this.selectizeElement = $(this.element).selectize()[0];
    }
                                                                      Creates the
                                                                      selectize control,
    initializeRemoteSelectize(){                                      taking the
        this.selectizeElement = $(this.element).selectize({          configuration
Preloads the data      valueField:  this.valueField,                 from dynamic
from the backend       labelField:  this.labelField,                 properties
API (this could also   searchField: this.searchField,
be an option)          preload: true,
                       options: [],
Implements the         load: (query, callback) => {
load method,               this.http.fetch(this.url).then(response => response.json())
delegating the             .then(data => {
remote call to                 callback(data);
the Aurelia                })
HttpClient             .catch(error => {
                           callback();
                       });                        Delegates the selectize-
                   }                              control change events to
        })[0];                                    the original select element

        this.selectizeElement.selectize.on('change', () => {
            let notice = new Event('change', {bubbles: true});
```

```
        $(this.element)[0].dispatchEvent(notice);
    });
  }

  unbind(){
      this.selectizeElement.selectize.destroy();
  }
}
```

Cleans up the selectize element when the component is unbound

The syntax for binding dynamic options to a custom attribute is the same as you saw with the static options back in chapter 3. For example, to specify the URL dynamic option on the `au-selectize` attribute, you use the `au-selectize="url: countries"` expression, where `countries` is a literal string. The other parts to note from listing 13.16 are that you're listening for the `change` event on the `select` element (which, as you saw, is delegated from the `selectize` attribute) and calling the `countryChanged` view-model method to assign the new country to the user. You're also initializing the select control with the current country assigned to the user. Modify the ./src/resources/elements/user-details.html view template as follows.

Listing 13.16 Adding country-select to the `user-details` view (user-details.html)

Imports the selectize custom attribute

```
<template>
    <require from="../attributes/au-selectize"></require>
    <require from="selectize/dist/css/selectize.default.css"></require>
    ...
                <label for="email">Email</label>
                <input name="email" class="form-control"
                       placeholder='enter an email address'
                       value.bind="user.email">
                </input>
                <label for="select-country">Country</label>
                <div class="row no-gutter">
                    <div class="col-md-3">
                        <select id="select-country" if.bind="selected"
                            au-selectize="url: countries;
                                          valueField: code;
                                          labelField:name;
                                          searchField:name;
                                          selected.bind : selected"
                            class="demo-default"
                            placeholder="Select user's country..."
                            change.delegate="countryChanged($event)">
                        <option value.bind="selected.code">
                            ${selected.name}
                        </option>
                        </select>
                    </div>
                </div>
            </div>
        </div>
```

Imports the default selectize styles from the node-modules folder

Passes the dynamic options to the custom attribute

Delegates the select change event to the countryChanged method

Initializes the select control with the user's current country

```
        . . .
    </form>
</template>
```

Before you see the new `user-details` page in action, you'll need to make a minor adjustment to the `user-details` view-model. The user's country is stored as a country code, but the select control needs to be initialized with the country code and name. To meet this requirement, you'll modify the `loadUser` method to also load the user's country and set it on the `user` view-model property. Modify the ./src/resources/elements/user-details.js view-model.

Listing 13.17   Handling the selection-changed event in view-model (user-details.js)

```
import {bindable, inject} from 'aurelia-framework';
import {UserApi} from '../../services/user-api';


@inject(UserApi)
export class UserDetails{

    . . .

    loadUser(name){                                          Loads the user's
        this.userApi.getUser(name).then(fetchedUser => {      country by
            this.user = fetchedUser;                         country code

            this.userApi.loadCountry(this.user.country).then(country =>{  ◁─┘
                this.selected =
                    country.code ? {"name" : country.name,
                                    "code" : country.code} :
                                   {"name" : 'Australia',
                                    "code" : 'AU'};
            });
        });
    }                                      Assigns the user's country
                                           code based on the currently
    countryChanged(evt){          ◁─┘      selected value
        this.user.country = evt.target.value;
    }

    . . .
}
```

The souped-up `user-details` page is now ready for action. Reload the project and edit a user to see it come to life.

NOTE   Although you implemented the selectize element using a custom attribute, if your goal was to create a reusable selectize component, this would be better implemented as a custom element. The benefit of using a custom element is that consumers get a more intuitive binding syntax, like `<select value.bind>`, on the element itself. The line between when to use a custom element or attribute is often blurred. Unfortunately, there's no rule of thumb, and the best approach is typically to go with what feels more intuitive to developers using the component. Sometimes the correct approach will become obvious when you reach the limitations of what a custom attribute can do. At this point, the choice to refactor to a custom element is simple.

13.4 *my-books project status*

Through the course of this chapter, you modified the user-details page to include a country picker, shown earlier in figure 13.4. This control uses a custom attribute with dynamic properties to wrap the jQuery Selectize plugin, allowing users to pick their country. You can download the completed project from GitHub at http://mng.bz/H2vV using the `git clone` command.

This chapter rounds off our exploration of Aurelia's component system. From basic components to complex custom attributes and binding behaviors, you've now got a great jump-start on the skills required for a component-driven application. In chapter 14, we'll change direction again, and you'll finally learn how to spice up your Aurelia views using animations. To use a car analogy, animations can help transform your SPA from a Volvo (functional but far from exciting) into a Ferrari (a high-performance machine that looks and feels the part). Stay tuned.

Summary

- Aurelia is a framework of strong opinions, weakly held. On the rare occasion that you disagree with its opinions, you can forge your own path using decorators.
- Aurelia has several decorators that allow you to modify conventional behaviors, for example, where a view-model's corresponding view is located to suit the needs of your project.
- Custom binding behaviors are one of Aurelia's many extensibility points, allowing you to augment a binding's behavior in any way you choose. Given this extensibility, you don't need to accept the framework you get out of the box but can mold it to suit your needs. And binding behaviors barely scratch the surface of the many extensibility points.
- Custom attributes can be made more flexible using dynamic options. With this feature in hand, you can create custom attributes that don't need to know the name of each individual property.

Animation

14

This chapter covers

- Getting started with SPA animations
- Adding CSS transition animations to your Aurelia applications

Good animations are subtle. They're the kind of thing that users appreciate, often without even realizing that they're present. Applications that use animations well feel fast, fluid, and polished. When you learn how to use Aurelia's animation framework, you'll be able to give users a high-quality experience that they'll associate with your application. The Aurelia core team have built animation hooks into key points of the framework, such as route transitions.

When it comes to animating websites, there are two main approaches: CSS transitions and JavaScript animations. Aurelia makes it easy to use either approach in your project; they both have their merits and are suited to different scenarios. In this chapter, we'll review the animation hooks provided by the framework and look at how you can use them with one of the supported Aurelia animation plugins: the `animator-css` plugin. This plugin allows you to animate pieces of your application with CSS transitions. We'll also cover the pros and cons of the JavaScript- and CSS-based animation approaches to give you a guideline for what will fit best with your project requirements.

14.1 Getting started with SPA animations

When I started frontend development, the easiest and by far the most popular method to implement animations (without the aid of a plugin like Flash) was with jQuery. jQuery makes it simple to implement the bread-and-butter animations that most applications need, such as fade-in, fade-out, slide-up, and slide-down. But in SPAs, we want to move from the imperative style of DOM manipulation to having the UI update its own state as a result of changes in the data model (which happens in Aurelia via data bindings on the view-model or route transitions handled by Aurelia's router). As such, SPA frameworks like Aurelia have different requirements and constraints for an animation library than jQuery-based pages. Because of this, SPA frameworks typically introduce an animation module that ties in neatly with the framework. This makes typical SPA animations such as route transitions easy and gives you the necessary framework hooks that can be used to animate at key points in the rendering/event lifecycle. Before we get into how you can implement animations in Aurelia, we'll look at both approaches—CSS transitions and JavaScript animations—to give you some context for when each is appropriate, and what they look like in practice. But first, let's cover some basic rules you can use to decide which parts of your SPA to animate.

14.1.1 When and what should you animate?

Have you ever run into a situation where you're using an application, but every time you try to move forward, you're forced to wait for a time-delayed animation that artificially slows down every button click or page load? When you see how easy it is to add animations to your project, it's tempting to include them everywhere, and I may have fallen into this trap once or twice myself. Instead, it's better to strategically sprinkle animations into your application only when they can make a positive impact on the UX. In general, if you're not sure whether an animation adds anything, it's better to err on the side of caution and leave it out. Here are some simple questions to ask yourself that will help you make the decision of whether to animate a user interaction:

- *Does this animation support user interaction, making it more intuitive?* An example of this is switching a button state to show a loading animation after the user has clicked it, to indicate that the request has been received and is being processed. In this case, the UX is better with the interaction in place, and it's less likely the user will resubmit the request.
- *How expensive (in performance terms) is this interaction?* Some animations are costlier than others. Adding these animations can cause the page to stutter or lag and may have the opposite effect of what you intended. Instead of adding life to your applications, these will leave your users feeling frustrated. For example, changing the `width` of an element is often more expensive than changing its `transform`. When you're considering adding an animation, it's best to first research how costly the animation is, and then test it. If it seems to create lag or spike your CPU, maybe consider an alternative or remove it altogether.

Another point is not to be afraid to remove an animation if you find that users don't enjoy it, or it generally doesn't have the expected impact. Once you've decided to animate an interaction, the next decision to make is which animation technique to use. In the next section, we'll take a quick overview of the two main animation techniques supported by Aurelia: CSS animations and JavaScript animations. Both techniques have their merits. The aim here is to arm you with the information you need to make the best choice for your project.

14.1.2   CSS animations

The first and simplest method you can use to animate sections of your web page is CSS transitions. To use CSS transitions, you declare the start and end state of an element, the change that should be applied to the element between these states, and how quickly the transition should be executed over time. For example, imagine you have a box element with a blue background that you want to transition to red on hover. You can achieve this by creating a CSS rule that includes the following three attributes:

- *Transition property*—In this case, the background color.
- *Transition duration*—In this case, how long it should take to transition to red.
- *Transition timing functions*—These control how your animation feels. In this case, you'll apply the ease function (a reasonable default transition). You can think of these timing functions like the various geometric curves you may remember from math class, where some curves start with a gentle slope and then spike quickly, some are linear, and so on. Browsers provide several out-of-the-box timing functions, such as ease-in, ease-out, and linear, to name a few. These functions give you control over your animation's timing curve.

To see the blue-to-red box-color animation in action, I've created a simple gist that you can run on GistRun: https://sean-hunter.io/css-transition-box. Take a look at figure 14.1.

Box background color transitioned from blue to red over a 0.5-second period using the ease transition function

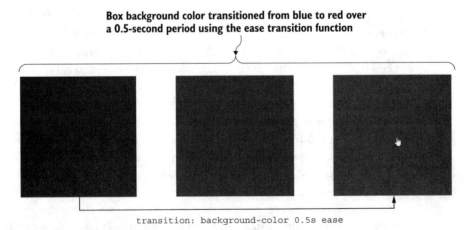

```
transition: background-color 0.5s ease
```

Figure 14.1   An example of using CSS transitions to animate a box element from blue to red

To implement this, two HTML snippets are excerpted from the gist. In the following listing, you declare a `<div>` element with a class box, which you'll then animate in the stylesheet.

Listing 14.1 CSS transition example HTML page (index.html)

```html
<!doctype html>
<html lang="en">

    <head>
        <meta charset="utf-8">
        <title>CSS Transition Example</title>
        <link rel="stylesheet" href="styles.css">
    </head>

    <body>
        <div class="box"></div>        ⊲─┐ Declares the
    </body>                                 box element

</html>
```

In listing 14.2, you define the size and initial color of the box, and then apply a transition to the element's background-color property: `background-color 0.5s ease`. This means that the background color will use the `ease` function to transition the background color during a 0.5-second period when the box moves to a different state. You then indicate that when the box is in the `:hover` state, the color should be red. With the hover state in place, the CSS transition will take care of transitioning the box from blue to red as it moves to the `:hover` state, as you saw in figure 14.1.

Listing 14.2 CSS transition example styles (styles.css)

```css
.box{
    width:200px;
    height:200px;
    background-color:blue;
    -webkit-transition: background-color 0.5s ease;
    -moz-transition: background-color 0.5s ease;     Transitions the
    -o-transition: background-color 0.5s ease;        box's background-
    transition: background-color 0.5s ease;           color property
}

.box:hover {                        Sets the color to red in
    background-color: red;    ⊲─┐  the .box:hover state
    cursor: pointer;
}
```

This example should give you a general idea of what CSS transitions are and how they can be used to animate between different element states.

> **TIP** My aim is to give you enough understanding of how this works for the coming Aurelia-specific examples, in case you haven't come across this technique so

far. As we don't have time to cover this in depth, I recommend checking out *CSS in Depth* by Keith Grant (Manning, 2018). Chapter 16 gives a great overview of the ins and outs of CSS transitions: http://mng.bz/61pQ.

Each animation approach has its advantages and disadvantages. Let's look at some things you'll want to keep in mind when deciding whether to use CSS transitions for your project.

The pros of CSS transitions are as follows:

- *No external library required*—The more external libraries that you need to pull into your project, the larger your output-application size, and the more dependencies your team members need to become familiar with. CSS transitions work out of the box in modern browsers, and, for most applications, provide all the animation functionality you'll need. You can see a complete breakdown of which browser versions support CSS animations here: http://caniuse.com/css-animation/embed/.
- *Simple declarative syntax*—You specify what you want to happen. In the blue-box animation example, you specified that the hover-state color should be red and described the transition that should be applied to the background color as the box moved into this state. The alternative to this is to use a more imperative approach, as you'll see when we come to JavaScript animations.

The cons of CSS transitions are as follows:

- *CSS transitions are not supported in older browsers.* This is only a concern for developers that need to support IE9. CSS animations came into IE in IE10, and have been there long enough that the chances of running a non-IE browser that doesn't support animations is negligible. Even in the unlikely event that the user loads your page in a browser that doesn't support animations, the browser will fail gracefully. A browser that doesn't support transitions will ignore them, and a site will move from one state to the next without animation. It's not like attempting to use an unsupported JavaScript API, which could potentially throw an error and prevent the user from moving forward in their workflow.
- *Some kinds of animations can't be achieved with CSS transitions alone.* For example, if you wanted to make the blue box bounce on hover rather than change color, you'd need to reach for a more powerful animation alternative.

In summary, you should use CSS transitions when you have small, self-contained states for UI elements (for example, :hover on a <div> element). CSS transitions are simple but powerful and, in most cases, are enough to implement the kinds of animations you need to make your Aurelia application feel fast and fluid (like fading in a view as you transition between application routes). When you need to reach beyond the limits of what CSS transitions and animations can achieve, you'll need to reach for the next tool in your animation tool belt: JavaScript animations.

14.1.3 *JavaScript animations*

With JavaScript animations, you can implement almost any kind of animation in a traditional web application. This includes all the varieties of element transformations or movement. JavaScript is also useful when you need to stop, slow down, or reverse an animation. Some examples of this include the following:

- An element that bounces when clicked
- A `<div>` that wiggles in response to an event (imagine a chat window that wiggles to alert you to the fact that you've received a new message)
- An element that swings from side to side

Anything you can do with CSS transitions can also be done using JavaScript animations. Unfortunately, at the time of writing, creating interesting animations using plain JavaScript requires quite a lot of boilerplate code. It's not as simple as calling element.wiggle to create a wiggling element. Because of this, it's more common to use one of the open source animation libraries like Velocity or GreenSock. These libraries create simple animation APIs that allow you to animate parts of your page using a less verbose and more intuitive syntax. For example, to create a shaking element using Velocity, the code would look something like this: `this.element.velocity("callout.shake")`.

As with CSS transitions, there are advantages and disadvantages to adopting this approach. Let's take a quick look at them to give you some context.

Here are some of the pros of JavaScript animations:

- You can implement almost any kind of animation you can imagine.
- Depending on which animation library you use, there's great support for older browsers, even as far back as IE8.

Here are some of the cons of JavaScript animations:

- Unless you want to implement a lot of base functionality yourself, you'll need to pull in a third-party library.
- Depending on your preference, it could also be considered a con that JavaScript animations require an imperative approach, rather than the simple declarative style available with CSS transitions.

In summary, JavaScript animations are powerful, allowing you to implement almost any animation scenario imaginable. But this comes at the cost of needing to bring in a third-party animation library and using an imperative rather than a declarative API. If you know that your application will require the more advanced animations that are only possible with JavaScript, import a library such as Velocity and use this for all your animation requirements, rather than mixing these two approaches. We won't cover the Velocity animator here, but I recommend checking out an interactive-demo page to see what's possible with this plugin: https://gooy.github.io/aurelia-animator-velocity.

14.2 *Aurelia's animation framework*

As Vildan Softic mentioned in a great article on the Aurelia blog at http://mng.bz/aOrz, the Aurelia core team started with the goal of "building animation support for Aurelia ... to enable a flexible solution that allows you to choose whatever library you like." This is a theme that repeats itself throughout the framework. Core segments of functionality, such as validation, are built in a way that enables you, as a developer, to take advantage of the vast amount of JavaScript open source libraries out there, rather than reinventing the wheel or forcing you to use a library specific to the Aurelia framework. If you already have an animation framework that you're familiar with and enjoy using, great: plug it in and get running.

If you're looking at animations specifically, the `Animator` class (part of Aurelia's templating package) provides a core set of methods. These methods are called at various points in the framework (for example, when a view is added to the DOM) to allow you to perform animations. Aurelia has two packages, `animator-css` and `animator-velocity`, that you can import into your Aurelia application to easily make use of these hooks. The `animator-css` plugin allows you to create animations using CSS transitions, whereas the `animator-velocity` plugin uses the Velocity JavaScript library instead. In the next section, we'll start by exploring Aurelia's animation API. We'll then use this API to implement CSS transitions across my-books, smoothing out some of the key state transitions such as moving between routes and adding or removing books from a user's library.

14.2.1 *The animation API*

Aurelia's templating engine uses a module called `Animator` (a part of Aurelia's templating package) to initiate animations. This module includes methods such as `enter` (called by the framework when an element is added to the DOM or placed in a DOM slot) and `leave` (called by the framework when an element is removed from the DOM). These methods each return a promise, which can be used to implement an animation asynchronously. The base implementation of these methods resolves the promise immediately and returns. By adding a plugin to the framework, such as `aurelia-css-animator`, you can override this default behavior, providing a specific animation that Aurelia should run when one of these methods is called. For example, when you add the `css-animator` plugin to your project, the `enter` method is overridden, adding functionality to add the necessary CSS classes to your element to trigger state transitions as the element is added to the DOM. Some of the common animator methods that you'll use in your Aurelia applications include `enter`, `leave`, `addClass`, `removeClass`, `animate`, and `runSequence`. We won't review each of these methods in detail here. Instead, we'll get our hands dirty implementing some of the more common animation scenarios you're likely to need in your own applications. During this implementation, I'll call out how the animator API fits into the picture to give you some context of how this works in practice.

Aurelia has several animation plugins available, but in this chapter, we'll cover the `aurelia-css-animator`, which allows you to add simple animations to your Aurelia project with minimal fuss.

14.3 CSS animations with Aurelia

The `aurelia-css-animator` plugin makes it easy to weave CSS transitions (like the one you saw in the blue-box example at the beginning of the chapter) into your Aurelia applications. You may be thinking to yourself, "That animation seemed simple; do I even need a plugin in the first place?" In fact, you're right on that count. You could take care of manually applying CSS classes to the DOM elements in your Aurelia views to trigger animations between different states. But in general, we try to avoid direct DOM manipulation in Aurelia projects in favor of letting the framework do them for us. With the assistance of the plugin, you can define the CSS required for the transitions, and the framework will take care of adding the necessary classes to your elements to trigger any associated animations. For example, when a view is added to the DOM, the animator will automatically add the `au-enter` class, and then swap this out for an `au-enter-active` class. By applying a starting state to the `au-enter` class and a transition effect to the `au-enter-active` class, hey presto—you've triggered an animation as the element is added to the DOM. This is still a bit abstract, so let's start by spicing up the book view with a fade-in transition to be triggered when a book is added or removed from a user's library.

14.3.1 Adding transitions on au-enter

The first step is to modify the book view, adding the `au-animate` attribute to the `<li>` element, as shown in listing 14.3. This step is required because Aurelia animations are opt-in. You can enable animation on an element in an Aurelia view by decorating it with the `au-animate` class or attribute. For example, animating a `<div>` would look like this: `<div class="au-animate"></div>`. You may be wondering why this class is needed. It's a simple matter of efficiency. Aurelia uses this class as a shortcut to indicate that an element should be animated to avoid the need to observe every element in the application. Enable the `<li>` book element for animation by adding the `au-animate` attribute in the view in the ./src/resources/elements/book.html file.

> **Listing 14.3   Enabling animation on the book list item (book.html)**

```
<template>
    ...

    <li class="${book.read ? 'read-book' : ''} list-group-item
    au-animate">           ◁──────┐
       ...                          Adds the au-animate
    </li>                           attribute to the book
                                    list item
</template>
```

With this in place, you need to add the necessary CSS to fade the list item when it's added to the DOM, and fade it out when it's removed. If you're working from the sample stylesheet provided in chapter 3, then you've got it easy: you've already added the necessary CSS, so don't worry about making any changes. If you're building the CSS from scratch, you'll want to add the required CSS transitions to your ./src/styles.css file, as shown in listing 14.4.

Begin by defining the state that the list item should be in when the au-enter class is applied (when the list item is initially added to the DOM). Initiate this element as entirely transparent by setting its opacity to 0. Next, Aurelia will remove the au-enter class and add the au-enter-active class, which will trigger the fadeIn animation key frame at a duration of 0.5 seconds. Animation key frames are waypoints, or key steps in an animations progress. In this animation, you've got two key frames: fadeIn, which changes the opacity on an element from 0 to 1, and fadeOut, which changes it from 1 to 0. When the list item is removed from the DOM (as a result of a user clicking the remove-book button), Aurelia will add the au-leave-activate class, triggering the fadeOut key frame over a 0.5 second duration.

> **Listing 14.4 Adding fade-in and fade-out transitions to your stylesheet (styles.css**

```
...
.books>li.au-enter {
    opacity: 0!important;          Initializes the element
}                                  to transparent as it's
                                   added to DOM

.books>li.au-enter-active {
    -webkit-animation: fadeIn 0.5s;    Triggers the fade-in
    animation: fadeIn 0.5s;            animation after the
}                                      element has been added

.books>li.au-leave-active {
    -webkit-animation: fadeOut 0.5s;   Triggers the fade-out
    animation: fadeOut 0.5s;           animation after the element
}                                      has been removed

@keyframes fadeIn {
    0%   { opacity: 0; }          Declares the
    100% { opacity: 1; }          fadeIn key frame
}

@keyframes fadeOut {
    0%   { opacity: 1; }          Declares the
    100% { opacity: 0; }          fadeOut key frame
}
```

Figure 14.2 illustrates how Aurelia triggers fade-in and fade-out animations as books are added and removed from the library by calling the animator.enter and animator.leave methods on the <li> book element. The aurelia-animator-css plugin then responds by applying the required classes to these elements to initiate the animations declared in the styles.css file.

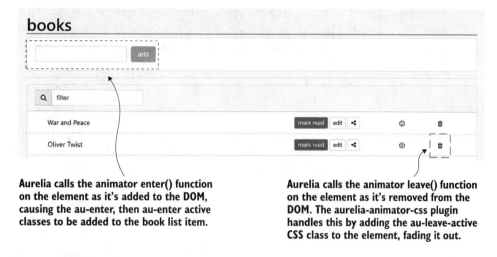

Aurelia calls the animator enter() function on the element as it's added to the DOM, causing the au-enter, then au-enter active classes to be added to the book list item.

Aurelia calls the animator leave() function on the element as it's removed from the DOM. The aurelia-animator-css plugin handles this by adding the au-leave-active CSS class to the element, fading it out.

Figure 14.2 Animations are triggered using a combination of the animator API and the CSS plugin as items are added or removed from the DOM.

If you're anything like me, at this point you'll want to see it in action. You can reload the application to see this animation at work, or you can check out a short GIF of the animation here: https://sean-hunter.io/aia-css-transition.

You've now seen how to trigger an animation when an item is added or removed from the DOM. Another common use is to trigger animations when an element is shown or hidden using the show.bind binding expression. Next, you'll add a transition to fade the index page during the show or hide transitions.

> **Transitioning between routes**
>
> To ensure that users receive a smooth and consistent experience when transitioning between the various routes in your application (some of which may have more latency than others), route navigation can be another wonderful place to weave in some more CSS transitions. The most common approach to add animations when transitioning between routes is to apply the au-animate attribute to the top-most <div> under the router-view element. For example, if each page had a section element, you could fade each page in and out by adding the au-animate attribute to this element and declaring the corresponding CSS transitions. I didn't do that in this case in order to show you how to use the aurelia-hide-add and aurelia-hide-remove transitions, and because the way we've used layout views for login and authenticated pages to conditionally include the nav-bar makes this approach awkward.

14.3.2 *Adding transitions when classes are added or removed*

You can also apply CSS transitions to elements when classes are added or removed. For example, by using the show.bind binding expression on an element, you instruct

Aurelia to apply the `aurelia-hide` class, setting the element's `display` property to none. Aurelia will apply the `aurelia-hide-add` class when the class is added, and the `aurelia-hide-remove` class when it's removed (when `show.bind` evaluates to `true`). You can then animate an element by applying transitions to the `aurelia-hide-add` and `-remove` classes. Let's look at how you can use this feature to apply a fade-in animation effect as the index page is loaded.

Because you want to selectively trigger the show and hide transitions only for certain elements, you'll need to add a class to these elements, tagging them for animation. I've arbitrarily called this class `fade-in`, but you could choose any name you want. Start by modifying the ./src/index.html file as shown in the following listing, wrapping the contents of the view inside a new `<div>` with the `fade-in` class. This `<div>` also has a `show.bind` binding expression to trigger the animation when the view has been attached to the DOM.

Listing 14.5   Adding fade-in to the `index` view (index.html)

```
<template>
    <div
        show.bind="isAttached"
        au-animate class="fade-in">
      <div class="jumbotron">
        ...
      </div>
    </div>
</template>
```

Conditionally shows `<div>` once the view has been attached

Fades the div in rather than rendering it immediately

Next, you need to modify the ./src/index.js view-model file, as shown in the following listing, to implement the `attached` callback. This will toggle the `aurelia-hide` class on the new `<div>` wrapping element. You can then add animation to this element by declaring the CSS transition to be applied as the class is added or removed.

Listing 14.6   Adding the `attached` callback to the `index` view-model (index.js)

```
import {CssAnimator} from 'aurelia-animator-css';
import {inject} from 'aurelia-framework';

@inject(CssAnimator, Element)
export class Index{

    constructor(animator, element) {
        this.animator = animator;
        this.element = element;
        this.isAttached = false;
    }

    attached(){
        this.isAttached = true;
    }
}
```

Initializes the isAttached property to false, initializing the `<div>` wrapper as hidden

Toggles the isAttached property to true, causing the `<div>` wrapper to show

As with the book list-item animation, you also need to declare the CSS states that should be applied to the <div> wrapper when the aurelia-hide class is added (by adding a transition to the aurelia-hide-add class in the stylesheet) or removed (by adding a transition to the aurelia-hide-remove class). In general, you can apply transitions as CSS classes are added or removed in Aurelia by declaring the target class name and adding the -add or -remove suffix. For example, if you had an element with a .green class, you could trigger a transition when this class was added by adding .green-add to your stylesheet. Modify the ./src/styles.css stylesheet, as shown in the following listing, to add these transitions.

Listing 14.7 Adding show and hide transitions to the stylesheet (styles.css)

```
...
.books>li.au-leave-active {
    -webkit-animation: fadeOut 0.5s;
    animation: fadeOut 0.5s;
}

.fade-in.aurelia-hide-add {
  animation: fadeOut 0.3s ease-out;
}
.fade-in.aurelia-hide-remove {
  animation: fadeIn 0.3s ease-out;
}

@keyframes fadeIn {
...
```

Adds the aurelia-hide-add CSS transition to fade out the <div> when it's hidden

Adds the aurelia-hide-remove CSS transition to fade in the <div> when it's added

If you're following along, you'll now see the index page fade in when you visit #/route or click the home link in the navigation bar, as shown in figure 14.3. You can also see this animation in action here: https://sean-hunter.io/css-transition-add-class.

Where a carpenter uses sandpaper to smooth out the rough edges of a new project, you can use simple CSS animations, like you've seen in these two examples, to

This <div> is initialized with the aurelia-hide class.
This class is then removed when the view is attached, firing the aurelia-hide-add CSS transition.
This adds a fade-in effect when the view loads.

Figure 14.3 CSS transitions are used to apply a fade-in effect to the index page as it's loaded.

smooth out any user interactions that seem jagged in your application. You can trigger these animations by applying CSS transitions when classes are added or removed from the DOM, or when classes are added or removed from an element. With these two basic techniques, you can apply subtle animations across your Aurelia projects to give them a more fluid feel overall.

With Aurelia's animation API under your belt, you've now got an understanding of each of the key APIs that you're likely to need when creating your own projects. But don't go away yet—we still have some important supporting topics to cover before you launch your first big project! When building real-world applications, we need a way of making sure that they're functioning correctly before we release them into the world. In the next chapter, you'll see how to use a combination of unit and end-to-end tests to make sure your Aurelia components are in fighting shape before you push them out into the big brave world.

Summary

- Animations, applied artfully, can give a great boost to the UX for a small amount of work.
- CSS animations are applied declaratively and are a fantastic default choice if you want to add simple animations and transitions to your Aurelia project.
- Aurelia's animator API makes it easy to add CSS animations when items are added or removed from the DOM, or when classes are added or removed from an element.
- JavaScript animations take over where CSS animations leave off and can be used to implement effects like a bouncing element or even a full animation sequence. In Aurelia, you can add JavaScript animations using the `velocity-animator` plugin.

Part 3

Aurelia in the real world

We've come a long way together on our journey to build the next big virtual bookshelf SPA. You've combined the key tools available in Aurelia's toolkit and created an application where users can log in, manage their collection of books, share them, and more. Through this development process, you've mastered technical concepts like custom elements, attributes, and value converters, and architectural concerns such as inter-component communication and the event aggregator. In part 3 of the book, it's time to battle-harden the application and push it live.

How and when you should test is always a hot topic within development teams, but today almost everyone agrees that automated testing is "kind of a good idea." In chapter 15, you'll learn how to combine unit and end-to-end tests to ensure that your SPA is defect free before you deploy it live. You'll do this by combining various testing tools including Karma, Protractor, and Jasmine, and you'll wire it all together with the Aurelia CLI.

Once you've tested your application, you need a simple, repeatable way to create a deployment package and push the appication to production. In chapter 16, you'll learn how to modify your Aurelia npm file to include a one-line command to create an optimized app package and deploy to Google's Firebase cloud service.

15

Testing

This chapter covers

- An overview of testing SPAs
- Unit testing versus end-to-end testing
- Testing services and value converters
- Testing custom elements and attributes
- End-to-end testing

Although there's still a lot of contention about the best testing techniques or tools to use, it's now almost universally agreed that some form of testing is a good idea. Having a suite of tests that proves your code works to specification enables you to iterate quickly with confidence that the features you add or change today won't adversely impact what you did yesterday. And the value of having a great test suite increases as your project grows in complexity.

With traditional client-server web development, you could generally get away with only testing the backend of the system, and maybe having a few high-level automation tests (or end-to-end tests) in place to run over the main user flows on the client side. At that point, most of the application logic was in the backend code, so by testing that part, you could have a high degree of confidence in your application's correctness. But when you change your development approach, and start building rich client-side applications with a framework like Aurelia, you quickly find that much of your application logic has shifted to the frontend. Given this shift, you'll start to see a lot of value in testing the components of your SPA project, making sure that each component continues to work as your project progresses—imagine having to manually test hundreds of components one-by-one, each time you release an updated version!

In this chapter, we'll review two of the popular SPA testing techniques: unit testing and end-to-end (E2E) testing. You'll learn why each is useful and when to apply them. You'll also learn how to use unit tests to automatically verify the correctness of common types of components. Some of the component types we'll cover include custom attributes, custom elements, value converters, and services. To round out the chapter, I'll show you how to battle-harden your Aurelia applications with a suite of unit and E2E tests, so you can spend more time creating features, and less time on manual testing.

15.1   *Testing SPAs*

As your SPA grows, so does the value you receive from having a great suite of automated tests. But this begs the question: what kinds of things should we be testing in an SPA, and what testing techniques should we use? We'll cover two main categories of tests in this chapter: unit tests and E2E tests.

Aurelia unit tests are typically written in Jasmine, using a behavior-driven development (BDD) style. BDD is a testing style that focuses on describing the overall behavior of a system in terms of business processes. For example, a BDD-style specification for your `book-list` function could read something like the following: Given a user is logged in when they visit the books page, they see their list of books. In contrast, we could state the same requirement in a traditional unit-testing style like get_books _returns_users_book_list. The BDD style is more expressive, which makes it easier for other developers on the project to read and understand.

Adopting a BDD mindset also changes your perspective, making it easier to think through each business process (or scenario) that a given feature needs to support. Writing tests in this way arguably reduces the likelihood that certain test scenarios will be neglected, leading to better overall test coverage. BDD is a large and interesting topic, but more than I can do justice to here. If you're interested in finding out more, I recommend checking out John Ferguson Smart's book *BDD In Action* (Manning, 2014). Don't be concerned if it's not crystal clear at this point though; you should get a great feel for the BDD style of testing as you follow through the examples ahead.

Within Aurelia applications, this style of tests is great for verifying the behavior components like services, value converters, custom elements, and custom attributes. The key differentiator between unit tests and E2E tests is that that the former is used to verify a component in isolation, whereas an E2E test verifies how several components work together.

Aurelia E2E tests are typically written using a combination of Protractor and Jasmine. Protractor is an E2E testing framework built on top of Google's WebDriver API. It allows you to automate one or more browsers and take your application through various test scenarios. For example, you could load the my-books application in Chrome and Firefox and verify that a user logging in with a correct username and password is correctly authenticated. This is a powerful way to ensure that all the disparate parts of your application work together correctly, and that you catch any browser inconsistencies before you release to production. We don't have time to go through a comprehensive overview of Protractor here, but if you're interested in learning more, I recommend heading over to the project's website: www.protractortest.org/#/. With this context in mind, it's time to get your hands dirty. In the next section, you'll learn how to test the key components of your project using the Aurelia CLI.

15.2 Get started testing with the Aurelia CLI

One of the most difficult things about SPA testing is getting each of the test tools to work together in the way you need them to. For example, unit tests require a combination of tools like gulp (the orchestrator), Karma (the test runner), and Jasmine (the test library) to run a suite of tests. I remember days of frustration when I first attempted to set this up by hand. It's a big learning curve and can often become a barrier to teams initiating JavaScript testing in their projects. Fortunately, the Aurelia CLI can create projects that come with the required set of test tooling for unit tests out of the box. E2E testing can also be set up with a few simple tweaks to the project's gulp build, which I've outlined in the appendix. This allows you to get up and running with your Aurelia tests much faster than you'd be able to do otherwise, and without necessarily needing to have a JavaScript test-automation wizard on your team.

When you create an Aurelia project with the `au new my-project` command, you have the option of setting up several pieces of test infrastructure as a part of the project creation. Figure 15.1 shows the initial test infrastructure created by the Aurelia CLI when you run the `au new` command.

Here are some more details on figure 15.1:

- A `test` gulp task is added to your project, which allows you to run the `au test` CLI command. This command initializes a test runner called Karma, which is responsible for executing each of the tests in your project and reporting the results. If you're interested in reading more about Karma, I recommend checking out the project website: https://karma-runner.github.io. As with the `run` command, you can run the `test` command in watch mode, which uses gulp to watch the filesystem for changes in any of your test files and automatically rerun the tests. To run the tests in watch mode, use the `au test --watch` command.
- Two Karma configuration files are added to your project: ./karma.conf.js, which contains the Karma configuration, and ./test/aurelia-karma.js, which tells Karma

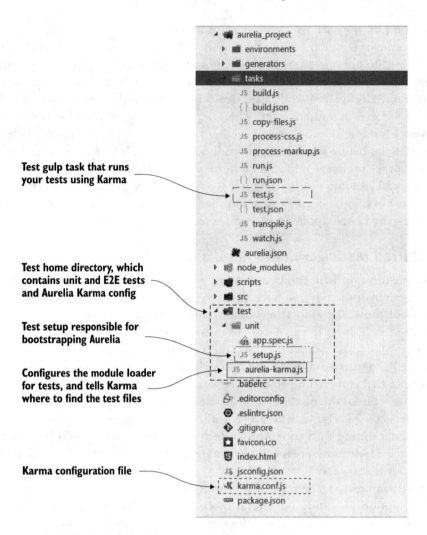

Test gulp task that runs your tests using Karma

Test home directory, which contains unit and E2E tests and Aurelia Karma config

Test setup responsible for bootstrapping Aurelia

Configures the module loader for tests, and tells Karma where to find the test files

Karma configuration file

Figure 15.1   Key files and folders added by the Aurelia CLI to give you a jump-start in testing your Aurelia projects

where to find the test source files—and in the case of a RequireJS project like yours, it configures the RequireJS module loader for the test context.

- An Aurelia test bootstrap file, ./test/setup.js, bootstraps the Aurelia framework for use in tests.

Now that you've got a basic understanding of the testing tools available via the Aurelia CLI, let's look at how you can create a basic BDD-style unit test using Jasmine, and run it using the Karma test runner via the Aurelia CLI.

15.2.1 Creating a Hello World test

Before we get into the nitty-gritty of testing Aurelia components, let's look at how you can write a basic test using Jasmine and run it using Karma via the CLI. To do this, create a new `Greeter` class that returns a greeting message. You'll then write a Jasmine test to verify that the expected message is returned. This will also give you a straightforward way to verify that the test toolchain has been configured correctly. Because you're using this class for demonstration purposes only, create it under the unit testing directory. Start by creating a new `Greeter` class at ./test/unit/greeter.js.

> **Listing 15.1   Creating the new `Greeter` test demo class (greeter.js)**

```
export class Greeter{

    get message(){                        Creates a basic Hello
        return "Hello brave world!";   ◄──┘ World message property
    }
}
```

With this class in place, you can now create a test file to verify that the expected message is returned. The Aurelia CLI has configured Karma to look for tests in any files with the `.spec.js` extension in the `test` directory. Because of this, the naming convention that you'll follow in your Aurelia tests is `{this}.spec.js`. Jasmine tests (or specs/specifications, to use the BDD term) are wrapped in a `describe` function, which is used to group a common set of tests. In this case, the `Greeter` class has only one method, but if it later implemented various kinds of greetings, you could add tests for these within the same `describe` block.

Within a `describe` block, you have one or more `it` blocks, which generally test a single unit of functionality. In this case, you have a single `it` block, verifying that the expected greeting is returned.

When you put the `describe` and `it` blocks together, you get this sentence: The `Greeter returns a greeting`. This follows the BDD style of naming specs to read like full sentences. Using this convention improves the readability of your test suite and makes it far simpler to understand what's going on at a glance, without delving into individual test implementations.

Inside an `it` block, you can add one or more expectations (analogous to test assertions if you're familiar with the corresponding unit-testing terminology). Add one expectation: that the greeter's `message` property returns the expected value. Create the greeter spec file at ./test/unit/greeter.spec.js.

> **Listing 15.2   Creating the greeter spec (greeter.spec.js)**

```
import {Greeter} from './greeter';       ◄─────────┐  Imports the
                                                    │  Greeter class
describe('The Greeter', () => {   ◄──┐
                                     │  Describes this
                                     │  set of specs
```

```
it("returns a greeting", function() {          ◄─┐  Describes what you're
                                                  │  verifying in this spec
  let greeter = new Greeter();

  expect(greeter.message).toBe('Hello brave world!');   ◄─┐  Defines the
                                                            │  message-value
});                                                         │  expectation

});
```

You now have everything you need to verify the behavior of the Greeter class. In the same way that you can run your Aurelia application in watch mode using the CLI's au run --watch command, you can run tests continually in the background using au test --watch. The wonderful thing about running tests this way is that the CLI will automatically rerun your entire suite each time you save a spec file or any of the files that make up your Aurelia project. This is useful in providing a rapid feedback loop to let you know you're on the right track. Navigate to the my-books project directory and run the au test --watch command to execute the newly created test.

This will rebuild your application bundles, so you'll see the usual tracing information that you'll be used to seeing when you run the au build or au run commands. At the end of your screen, you'll see a message like this: Executed 1 of 1 SUCCESS (0.271 secs / 0.263 secs). If you were to make the test fail, say, by changing the response message returned from the Greeter without updating the test, you'd see a test-failure message like this: Greeter returns a greeting FAILED. Expected 'Hello world!' to be 'Hello brave world!'.

Like the message indicates, the test expected to see "Hello brave world!" but instead got "Hello world!" This example is as simple as they come, but it should give you an idea of how you can create and run Jasmine tests inside an Aurelia CLI project. In the next section, we'll take this a step further as we look at how to test your first Aurelia-specific component, a value converter.

15.3 *Testing value converters*

Like many features of the Aurelia framework, value converters are simple ES2015/TypeScript classes. Fortunately for us, this makes them easy to test, because they don't have any external dependencies. Testing a value converter is a matter of importing the class from the value converter's module and creating a new instance of the class to be tested, and then executing the toView method and verifying the results. To see how this works, you'll create a test to verify that the filter value converter, created in chapter 5, filters an array of books as expected.

To simplify the spec class implementations, I created a module to specify the test data you'll need for each of the coming tests. This allows you to run the tests in isolation, without the need for your components under test to call out to the my-books REST API as they do within the application itself. This test data includes sample countries, users, and books. Create a new JavaScript file at ./test/unit-test-data.js and add the contents of the following listing.

Listing 15.3 Creating the test-data module (test-data.js)

```
export default {
    Countries: [
        {
            name: "Australia",
            code: "AU"
        },
        {
            name: "United States",
            code: "US"
        },

    ],
    Users :[
        {
            name:"Frodo",
            first_name : "Frodo",
            surname : "Baggins",
            admin : false,
            email:"frodo@bagend.shire"
        },
        {
            name:"Gandalf",
            first_name : "Gandalf",
            surname : "Olorin",
            admin : true,
            email:"gandalf@dolguldur.io"
        },
    ],
    Books :{
        Oliver :{
            title: 'Oliver Twist',
            description : 'The story is of the orphan Oliver Twist'
        },
        WarAndPeace:{
            title: 'War and Peace',
            description : ''
        }
    }
};
```

Exports country, user, and book test data

With the required test data in place, you can now create the specs for your filter value converter. In this case, you'll create only one test to verify the value converter's toView method behavior. This test should look familiar to you, as it follows a similar template to the one you saw with the greeter spec in listing 15.2.

Within the describe block, start by declaring a system under test (sut) variable. *System under test* (SUT) is a common testing term that refers to the system or object that's currently being validated by the test. For example, this could be a custom element (in the case of a custom-element test). In this case, the SUT is the filter value converter.

This spec uses another Jasmine feature you haven't encountered yet: the before-Each function, which allows you to initialize test data that's scoped to each spec. In this case, you're creating a new instance of the `FilterValueConverter` method automatically before calling the `"should filter"` spec. If you were to add more specs here, they'd each get their own instance of this class.

Within the spec itself, initialize a new array of books from the `test-data` module, and call the value converter's `toView` method, with the array of books, and the test substring of `"Ol"` (a substring containing the first two characters of the title of *Oliver Twist*) as input. Then, check that the resulting array is filtered to contain only books that have a title starting with `"Ol"`.

This basic technique of initializing the value converter as the SUT and then checking the behavior of its `toView` method is a simple but effective way to make sure your value converters are behaving as they should, without the need to perform manual UI testing.

Listing 15.4   Creating the filter value-converter spec (filter.spec.js)

```
import { FilterValueConverter }                         Imports the value
from "../../../../resources/value-converters/filter";   converter to be tested
import TestData from "./test-data";                Imports the books
                                                   test data to filter
describe("the filter value converter", () => {
  let sut;                                     System under
                                               test variable
  beforeEach(() => {
    sut = new FilterValueConverter();      Initializes a new value-converter
  });                                      instance for each spec

  it("should filter a list of books", () => {
    const books = [TestData.Books.WarAndPeace, TestData.Books.Oliver];

    const expectedResult = [TestData.Books.Oliver]

    const result = sut.toView(books, "Ol");    Executes the toView
                                               method to apply the filter

    expect(result).toEqual(expectedResult);   Checks the results
  });                                         are filtered correctly

});
```

If you've still got the `au test --watch` command running, you'll see a result similar to the following message output to your console: `Executed 2 of 2 SUCCESS (1.648 secs / 0.697 secs)`.

Exercise: Implementing the data-format value converter
Implement the data-format value converter by following this same technique.

Next, we'll see how you can use another Jasmine feature, *test spies*, to make it simple to test your Aurelia service classes.

15.4 Testing services

To simplify the remainder of your tests, I extracted some of the common utility functions from the test scenarios into a `TestHelper` class. Let's have a brief overview of these helper functions.

The `mockResponseAsync` function allows you to simulate the behavior of the `aurelia-fetch-client`'s `fetch` function. It returns a promise, wrapped in another promise, which both resolve immediately with the sample JSON body specified, rather than making a network call. For example, you could pass this function an array of users to simulate the response that you'd receive from the `getUsers` API call. This is useful to improve the speed and consistency of `HttpClient`-related tests by eliminating HTTP calls to an external service.

In the next example, we'll test components that use the Shadow DOM. The `shadow-Root` function is a straightforward way to get the `shadowRoot` node of the element with the specified query selector.

Create a new JavaScript file at ./test/unit/test-helper.js and add the contents of the following listing.

> **Listing 15.5 Creating the test helper class (test-helper.js)**

```
export class TestHelper {

  static mockResponseAsync(body) {        Simulates an HTTP
    return Promise.resolve(               fetch async call
        {
            json: () => Promise.resolve(body)
        });
  }
}
```

With the required test helper functions in place, let's create a test scenario to describe the expected behavior of the `UserAPI` service class. To keep this concise, you'll add specs to test only the following three scenarios:

- The `UserAPI` service loads a user's country.
- The `UserAPI` service loads an empty country as a fallback.
- The `UserAPI` service gets all users.

A general rule with unit tests is to only test a single unit in isolation, but because the `UserAPI` depends on Aurelia's `HttpClient` package, this presents a problem. You need a way to test the `UserAPI` methods without calling the fetch client directly, which would make an external network call.

Making these network calls from the tests presents several issues:

- The REST service may not be available under the test context.
- Some tests need to write data to the API, which would cause differences in results between test executions.
- Tests will run slower, making it less likely that developers on the team will want to run them in the first place.

Fortunately, Jade comes to the rescue again. In this case, you can use Jade's `create-SpyObj` feature, which creates a special kind of object that can be used to stand in for a dependency.

Other terms for these kinds of objects that you may be familiar with are *mock* and *test double*. The term *spy* works well, though, because these effectively allow you to spy on and record various method calls and inject your own test response in place of the response a real version of the object would return. Spy objects track all the calls you make to them, which allows you to inspect and verify them as a part of your test assertions.

For example, when you call `jasmine.createSpyObj("HttpClient", ["fetch"])`, you create a spy version of the `HttpClient` object in which the `fetch` method is replaced. Later, you'll add a fake implementation of the `fetch` method, returning a promise that immediately resolves with a set of known test data using the `returnValue` method. In this case, any time the `fetch` method is called on your spy, return the fake set of countries. When you initiate your system under test (the `UserApi` class), pass the spy object into its constructor rather than letting Aurelia's dependency-injection system inject the real version like you would in an Aurelia component. Figure 15.2 shows how to replace the real `HttpClient` implementation with a spy object while testing.

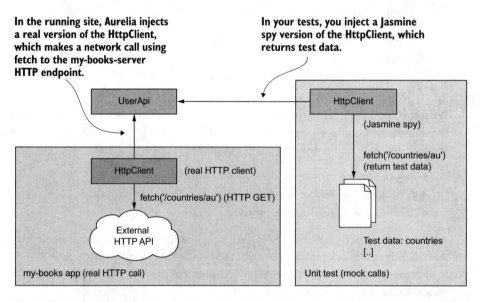

In the running site, Aurelia injects a real version of the HttpClient, which makes a network call using fetch to the my-books-server HTTP endpoint.

In your tests, you inject a Jasmine spy version of the HttpClient, which returns test data.

UserApi

HttpClient

(Jasmine spy)

fetch('/countries/au') (return test data)

HttpClient   (real HTTP client)

fetch('/countries/au') (HTTP GET)

External HTTP API

Test data: countries [..]

my-books app (real HTTP call)

Unit test (mock calls)

Figure 15.2   Spy objects can be used to avoid making calls to external dependencies when testing.

Let's take a more detailed look at the first scenario. The UserAPI service loads a user's country. In this case, you start by telling your spy to return the list of test countries imported from the test-data module. Then load a country by country code, and verify the result contains the first country in the test list. Finally, compare the recorded method calls to the spy to verify that the fetch method has been called with the expected parameter (countries?code=au).

The other two test cases follow the same technique of faking the fetch response and verifying that both the API results and the calculated REST API URL are correct. This is a useful technique for verifying that your HttpClient-dependent services are behaving correctly in isolation from an external HTTP server. Try adding a new spec at ./test/unit/user-api.spec.js.

Listing 15.6 Creating the UserApi spec (user-api.spec.js)

```
import { UserApi } from "../../../../services/user-api";
import { TestHelper } from "./test-helper";
import TestData from "./test-data";

describe("The UserApi service", () => {
  let httpClient, sut;
  let countries = TestData.Countries;
  let users = TestData.Users;

  let testUsers = beforeEach(() => {
    httpClient = jasmine.createSpyObj("HttpClient", ["fetch"]);
    sut = new UserApi(httpClient);
  });

  it("loads a user's country", done => {
    httpClient.fetch.and.returnValue(
      TestHelper.mockResponseAsync(countries)
    );
    sut
      .loadCountry("au")
      .then(result => expect(result).toEqual(countries[0]))
      .then(() =>
        expect(httpClient.fetch)
        .toHaveBeenCalledWith("countries?code=au")
      )
      .then(done);
  });

  it("loads an empty country as a fallback", done => {
    httpClient.fetch.and.returnValue(TestHelper.mockResponseAsync([]));
    sut
      .loadCountry()
      .then(result => expect(result).toEqual({ code: "", name: "" }))
      .then(() =>
        expect(httpClient.fetch)
        .toHaveBeenCalledWith("countries?code=undefined")
      )
```

Creates a spy to track calls to httpClient.fetch

Initializes the UserApi with the stubbed HttpClient

Returns a stub value whenever the fetch method is called

Checks that when loadCountry is called with a country code, you return the first matching country

Checks that the UserApi calls fetch with the expected arguments

Checks that you return an empty country when there are no matches

```
           .then(done);
     });

     it("gets all users", done => {
       httpClient.fetch
              .and.returnValue(TestHelper.mockResponseAsync(users));
       sut
         .getUsers()
         .then(result => expect(result).toEqual(users))
         .then(() => expect(httpClient.fetch).toHaveBeenCalledWith("users"))
         .then(done);
     });

  });
```

> Checks that you return all
> users by default from the
> getUsers method

If you've still got the au test --watch command running, you'll see a result similar to the following message output to your console: Executed 3 of 3 SUCCESS (1.648 secs / 0.697 secs).

Exercise: Testing UserApi methods

Implement tests to cover any of the other UserApi methods using the spy-object technique.

Next, you'll see how to use a handy Aurelia module (aurelia-testing) to test your custom element and attribute components without having to run your full project. Before starting the next section, add the aurelia-testing module to your project using the steps in the appendix.

15.5   *Testing custom elements*

Because most of an Aurelia application is composed of components, it's critical that you have a way to test them without needing to manually load the application each time. But because Aurelia's components rely on Aurelia's framework code and lifecycle (described in section 6.1), how can you emulate this in a test scenario? That's where the aurelia-testing module comes in.

The aurelia-testing module allows you to stage your Aurelia components (custom elements, attributes, and so on) inside a mini Aurelia application and make assertions about how the data binding and component lifecycle behave, as shown in figure 15.3.

To get started testing a component, you'll need to create a new spec file that imports the following dependencies:

- The StageComponent class from the aurelia-testing module. Among other things, this allows you to initialize a component using the StageComponent .withResources({full component path}) method. The withResources method returns an instance of the ComponentTester class. You can then call inView on

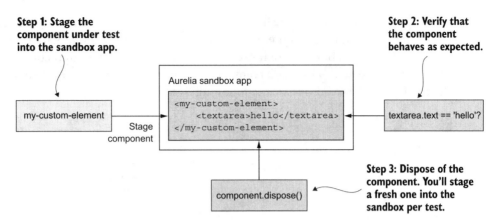

Step 1: Stage the component under test into the sandbox app.

Step 2: Verify that the component behaves as expected.

Aurelia sandbox app

```
<my-custom-element>
    <textarea>hello</textarea>
</my-custom-element>
```

my-custom-element

Stage component

textarea.text == 'hello'?

component.dispose()

Step 3: Dispose of the component. You'll stage a fresh one into the sandbox per test.

Figure 15.3 **How components are staged and tested using the** `aurelia-testing` **module**

this class, passing an inline view fragment that uses the component. For example, in a real application, your app view might use a `hello-world` component by requiring it into the view and then using it with the `<hello-world></hello-world>` custom-element syntax. Staging the component is analogous to requiring it into the view, whereas the `inView` method is like using the imported component. Using the fluent syntax, the `inView` method returns the same `ComponentTester` instance, which you can then use to data bind a sample object into the staged component. For example, if your `hello-world` component took a message, you could provide it here.

- Import the `bootstrap` class and use it to initialize a mini sandbox instance of the Aurelia application into which you'll load the component under test.
- Import `TestData` and `TestHelper`, which you created earlier.

The process required to test components is as follows. You can see these steps in action in listing 15.7:

1 Within the `beforeEach` block, stage the component using the component tester, executing any data bindings. This ensures that you get a fresh instance of the component per test.
2 Create one `it` block per test scenario. Within each scenario, you'll create an instance of the staged component using the (`component.create(bootstrap)`) Aurelia application.
3 At the end of each `it` block, call `done()` to complete the promise.
4 Dispose of the component within the `afterEach` block.

Before you put this into practice, you'll need to add a little more testing infrastructure to the `TestHelper` class that will help you interact with the DOM elements for the staged component. The last two helper functions, `clickAndWait` and `fireJQuery-EventAndWait`, are both responsible for interacting with the DOM (by clicking a button or firing a jQuery event). In each of these cases, you return a promise that contains a `setTimeout` function with a timeout value of 0. This is a test technique used to ensure that any of Aurelia's bindings that may fire because of the DOM interaction (some of which may be asynchronous) are completed before you execute the next step. Modify the test helper class as shown in the following listing.

Listing 15.7   Modifying the test helper class (test-helper.js)

```
export class TestHelper {

  ...

  static shadowRoot(querySelector) {                    ◁── Gets the shadowRoot
    return document.querySelector(querySelector).shadowRoot;    node for a given
  }                                                              query selector

  static clickAndWait(element) {        ◁─── Clicks the element and
    element.click();                          waits for the async
    return new Promise(setTimeout);          bindings to complete
  }

  static fireJQueryEventAndWait(selector, eventType) {  ◁──┐ Fires a jQuery event
    $(selector)[eventType]();                               on the given selector
                                                            and waits for the
    return new Promise(setTimeout);                         async bindings to
  }                                                         complete
}
```

Listing 15.8 tests three scenarios. You expect the `ux-text-area` component from chapter 13 to be a read-only mode initially. The first test verifies this by checking that the `text-block` element is visible. When users click the `text-block`, it should transition into edit mode, showing the `textarea` element instead.

This gives you some examples of the kinds of behavior you can verify in a custom-element-component test. Create the ./test/unit/ux-test-area.spec.js file as shown in the following listing.

Listing 15.8   Creating the `ux-text-area` spec (ux-text-area.spec.js)

```
import { StageComponent} from "aurelia-testing";
import { bootstrap } from "aurelia-bootstrapper";
import TestData from "./test-data";
import { TestHelper } from "./test-helper";

describe("UxTextArea", () => {
  let component;
  let bookDescription = TestData.Books.Oliver.description;

  beforeEach(() => {                                        Stages the ux-text-area
    component = StageComponent.withResources(      ◁──      component, registering it
      "./resources/components/ux-text-area"                 with the ComponentTester
    )
```

```
    .inView(
      `<ux-text-area
              text-content.bind="description">
      </ux-text-area>`
    )
    .boundTo({ description: bookDescription });
});
```
Aurelia HTML view markup that uses the component

Binds a test view-model to the inline view

```
function getTextAreaElement(){
  return TestHelper.shadowRoot("ux-text-area");
}
```
Helper function to get the text-area element

```
function getTextBlockElement(){
  return TestHelper.shadowRoot("ux-text-area")
                   .querySelector(".text-block");
}
```
Helper function to get the text-block element

```
function clickOkButton(){
  let okButton = TestHelper.shadowRoot("ux-text-area")
                            .querySelector("button.ok");
  return TestHelper.clickAndWait(okButton);
}
```
Helper function to click the text-area's OK button and flush any async bindings

```
function changeTextAreaValue(value){
  let componentElement = getTextAreaElement()
  let textArea = componentElement.querySelector('textarea');
  textArea.value = value;
  let event = new Event('change');

  textArea.dispatchEvent(event);
}
```
Helper function to change the text value of the text-area

Helper function to click the text-area, toggling it into edit mode

```
function editText(){
  return TestHelper.clickAndWait(getTextBlockElement());
}
```

```
it("should initialize component with a text-box", done => {
  component
    .create(bootstrap)
    .then(() => {
      let actualDescription = getTextBlockElement().innerHTML;

      expect(bookDescription).toBe(actualDescription);
      done();
    })
    .catch(e => {
      console.log(e.toString());
    });
    });
});
```
Bootstraps a sandboxed Aurelia application

Gets the text-area content

Verifies the text-area content is initially set to the bound value

Next, modify the spec to add a second test to verify that the textarea is shown on click. Because this uses Aurelia's data-binding system to show and hide various parts of the component, use the clickAndWait helper method, which will return once Aurelia's binding process is confirmed complete. Running the assertions without this helper method would lead to race conditions, and tests would be dependent on whether the binding process completed in time. Modify the ./test/unit/ux-test-area.spec.js file, as shown in the following listing, to add this test.

Listing 15.9　Adding a test to verify text-area visibility behavior (ux-text-area.spec.js)

```
...
  it("transitions to a text-area once clicked", done => {
    component
      .create(bootstrap)          ◁─┤ Bootstraps a sandboxed
      .then(() => {                   Aurelia application

        editText().then(_ => {    ◁─┤ Initializes edit mode on the text-area
                                       and waits for the async response

          let actualDescription = getTextAreaElement()   ◁   Checks that the
                                .querySelector('textarea')    text-area field is
                                .value;                       shown once you're
                                                              in edit mode
          expect(bookDescription).toBe(actualDescription);
          done();
        });

      })
      .catch(e => {
        console.log(e.toString());
      });
    });
  });
```

Logs any exceptions fired within test execution to the console

You also expect that text in this component will be saved when the user edits the value in the textarea and then clicks the OK button. The third and final test verifies this behavior. After each test, dispose of the staged component to clean up, ready for the next test. Modify the ./test/unit/ux-test-area.spec.js file as shown in the following listing to add this test.

Listing 15.10　Creating ux-text-area spec (ux-text-area.spec.js)

```
...
  it("it saves changes when ok button is clicked", done => {
    component
      .create(bootstrap)          ─┤ Initializes edit mode
      .then(() => {                  and waits for the
                                     promise to resolve
        const updatedValue = 'Updated value';

        editText().then(_ => {    ◁───────┤ Changes the value of
                                             the text-area field
          changeTextAreaValue(updatedValue);   ◁─┤ Clicks the OK button
                                                    and waits for the
          clickOkButton().then(_ => {   ◁──────────┘ promise to resolve
```

Verifies that the text-area component's text is saved →

```
let actualDescription = getTextBlockElement().innerHTML;

expect(actualDescription).toBe(updatedValue);
done();
```

← **Disposes of the component to clean up after each test**

```
      });

    });

    })
    .catch(e => {
      console.log(e.toString());
    });
  });

  afterEach(() => {
    component.dispose();
  });
});
```

If you've still got the au test --watch command running, you'll see a result similar to the following message output to your console: Executed 4 of 4 SUCCESS (1.648 secs / 0.697 secs).

> **Exercise: Testing the Cancel button**
>
> Implement tests to cover any of the test cases where the user clicks the Cancel button, and verify that the text isn't saved in this scenario.

Next, we'll look at how you can use the aurelia-testing module to verify the behavior of a custom attribute.

15.6 Testing custom attributes

You can test custom attributes in much the same way that you test custom elements. The process involves the following steps:

1. In the beforeEach block, stage the custom attribute, using the inView function of the ComponentTester with a view fragment that uses the custom attribute.
2. Add it blocks to make assertions about the behavior of the custom attribute.
3. Dispose of the custom attribute in the afterEach block.

Listing 15.11 shows how you can use the ComponentTester to verify the behavior of the tooltip custom attribute created in chapter 3. The most basic behavior to test is that when you apply the tooltip attribute to an element and hover over that element, a tooltip is displayed.

To assist in testing this behavior, you create a hoverOverElement helper function. This function returns a promise that completes when you know that any Aurelia bindings have been flushed. Start by initializing the Aurelia sandbox application with an inline view that contains a button with the `tooltip` attribute attached.

Then, use the helper function to hover over the (`hoverOverElement().then`) element, query for the tooltip element, and finally, verify that this element is present in the DOM after you've hovered over `expect(toolTip).not.toBe(null)`.

Listing 15.11   Creating the `tooltip` spec (tooltip.spec.js)

```
import { StageComponent} from "aurelia-testing";
import { bootstrap } from "aurelia-bootstrapper";
import { TestHelper } from "./test-helper";

describe("Tooltip", () => {
  let component;

  beforeEach(() => {
    component = StageComponent.withResources(          Stages the tooltip
      "./resources/attributes/tooltip"                 component, registering it
    )                                                  with the ComponentTester
      .inView(                                     Creates an inline view that
        `<button id="el"                           uses the tooltip
                tooltip="title.bind:'Remove book from list';
                placement.bind:'top'"> </button>`
      );
  });
                                                   Helper function that
  function hoverOverElement(){                      uses jQuery to hover
    let button = document.querySelector('button');  over the tooltip

    return TestHelper.fireJQueryEventAndWait("#el", 'mouseenter');
  }

  it("tooltip is shown on hover", done => {        Bootstraps a
    component                                      sandboxed Aurelia
      .create(bootstrap)                           application
      .then(() => {
                                                              Hovers over the
        hoverOverElement().then(_ => {                        inline view's
                                                              button, and
        let toolTip = document.querySelector('.tooltip');     queries for an
        expect(toolTip).not.toBe(null);                       element with the
        done();                                               .tooltip class

        });
                                              Checks that you have a
      })                                      tooltip when hovering
      .catch(e => {                           over the button
        console.log(e.toString());
      });
  });
```

```
afterEach(() => {
  component.dispose();                    ◄─┐  Disposes of the component
  });                                        │  after each test run
});
```

If you've still got the au test --watch command running, you'll see a result similar to the following message output to your console: Executed 5 of 5 SUCCESS (1.648 secs / 0.697 secs).

Exercise: Verifying bound properties

Implement a second test scenario that verifies that the tooltip attribute's bound properties such as title are used correctly.

This completes our overview of Aurelia's unit-testing functionality. You've seen how you can use a combination of Jasmine, Karma, the Aurelia CLI, and Aurelia's component-testing module to unit test your custom attributes, elements, value converters, and services in isolation.

These same techniques can also be used to test binding behaviors, computed properties, and more. We've only scratched the surface of the component-testing library's functionality. This module also allows you to manually take a component through its various component-lifecycle steps to verify the behavior at each point in the lifecycle. If you're interested in finding out more, I recommend checking out an article on the Aurelia Hub: http://mng.bz/r2tk. Next, we'll look at verifying how your application runs in the browser using Protractor.

15.7 End-to-end testing

Imagine this scenario: you receive a request from a customer to deploy the latest version of your project. You weigh the pros and cons. There have been a lot of fantastic features added in the latest release, but you haven't had a chance to check that all the existing behavior is working as it should. The risk is mitigated because you have unit tests covering each of your components and services, but you aren't 100% sure that every page in your site will work flawlessly in each of the target browsers. You must make the choice as to whether you'll manually test each page of the application in every browser. Do you even have time to do this?

At this point, you're more likely to err on the side of caution and avoid publishing the application until you can be sure that it's rock solid. But what if there was a better way? Enter E2E testing. E2E testing allows you to create tests that verify high-level scenarios (or user stories). For example, as an administrative user, when I log in to the site using a valid username and password, I can see the user-management page.

The beauty of these tests is that because they run in a real web browser, you can have a good degree of confidence that you're verifying the same behavior that your users will experience on the live site. If you have enough of these tests to cover each of the key user stories, you can be far more confident in pressing the deploy-to-live button, without feeling the need to perform a manual QA in each browser.

This all sounds promising, but how does it work in practice? In addition to the test tooling you've seen so far, you need to add another framework to the mix called Protractor. Protractor is an E2E testing framework built on top of WebDriver—an API for browser automation with the ability to drive any major web browser. Where you used Karma as the test runner for your unit tests, you'll instead use Protractor to run your E2E tests.

15.7.1   *Testing the login user stories*

To see Aurelia E2E tests in action, add a set of tests to verify the my-books login-page behavior. As with the previous tests, before beginning this section, please ensure that you've completed the required E2E test setup steps described in the appendix. Start by loading the page and verifying the following four cases, as shown in figure 15.4:

- When the login page loads, the title should be set to `'login | My-Books'`.
- When the login page loads, the header block should have the text `'my-books'`.

The first test verifies that when you load the application, you're initially directed to the login page, and that this page has the correct title.

The second test verifies that the login page has the correct header block.

The third and fourth tests verify that both failed and successful logins behave as expected.

Figure 15.4   The four test scenarios implemented to verify the login-page behavior

- When a user enters an invalid password, you should show an error message.
- When a user enters a valid username and password, they should be logged in and redirected to the /home page.

E2E tests verify your SPA behavior by automating DOM interactions (as if a user is navigating the site), and then querying the DOM at certain points to verify that it has the expected state.

For example, many SPAs will have a simple test that loads the application and verifies that the page title is set to the expected value. This is a straightforward way to ensure that nothing has gone wrong during the application bootstrap process. This test is likely to be resilient to change (it's not likely that you'll be changing how the page titles are generated that often).

But what if you wanted to check that the page displayed a specific welcome message on load? The first version of the application might have the welcome message in an <h1> tag, but in the next version perhaps this is changed to a <div>. In that case, the test would break, and you'd be forced to modify any tests that retrieved the message by querying the <h1> tag. One solution to this problem is to use the *page-object pattern*. With the page-object pattern, you create an object that represents the page you want to test (for example, WelcomePageObject). Then, each time that you need to interact with the DOM in your test suite, you add a method that implements this interaction in your page-object class. For example, to verify an application welcome message, you could add a GetMessage method to your WelcomePageObject. You'd initially implement this method to retrieve the message from the <h1> tag, but if you change the application in the next version of your application to render the welcome message in a <div> instead, it's not a problem. You'd only need to modify your page object's GetMessage method to retrieve the value from a <div>. This avoids the need to modify each test case that interacts with the welcome-message DOM element. If you're interested in reading more about the page object pattern, I recommend checking out this article by Martin Fowler: https://martinfowler.com/bliki/PageObject.html.

To test the login-page behavior, you'll need two page objects. First, you'll need an app page object, which will contain the concerns related to the application shell. This kind of page object is useful across most Aurelia applications and implements features like navigating to different routes, getting the page title, and other cross-cutting concerns. The second is the login page object, which includes functionality for entering the login-form credentials and submitting it. The login spec will use both of these page objects to implement DOM interactions in a future-proof manner, as shown in figure 15.5.

First, create the app page object. In your case, this contains only one method (get-CurrentPageTitle), which uses the browser object to get the title of the current page. Create a new folder, ./test/e2e/src, and add a new JavaScript file, ./test/e2e/src/app.po.js.

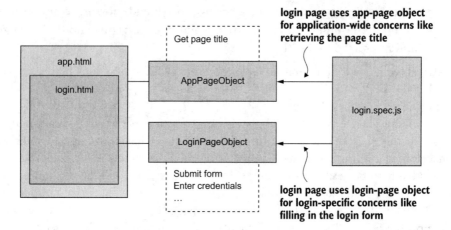

Figure 15.5   The login specification uses the app **and** login **page objects to implement the DOM interactions required to verify page behavior.**

Listing 15.12   Adding the app **page object (app.po.js)**

```
export class PageObjectApp {
    constructor() {}

    getCurrentPageTitle() {
        return browser.getTitle();          Retrieves the
    }                                        current page title
}
```

Next, create the login page object. This includes methods to enable the last three test cases related to filling in either valid or invalid credentials in the login form and submitting. You can see here a few examples of the Protractor browser API, which includes methods such as element, which takes a function that should be used to find the element in the DOM. You can retrieve an element by tagName, an Aurelia value binding, CSS selectors, and more. I recommend checking out the Protractor documentation to see a full list of the supported selectors. Create the login page object at ./test/e2e/src/login.po.js.

Listing 15.13   Adding the login **page object (login.po.js)**

```
export class PageObjectLogin {
    constructor() {}                        Gets the login-
                                            page-heading text
    getHeader() {
        return element(by.tagName("h1.brand-heading")).getText();

    }                                       Gets the username element,
                                            clears the current text, and
    setUsername(value) {                    sets it to the provided value
        return element(by.valueBind("userName"))
```

```
      .clear()
      .sendKeys(value);
  }

  setPassword(value) {                                Gets the password element,
    return element(by.valueBind("password"))          clears the current text, and
      .clear()                                         sets it to the provided value
      .sendKeys(value);
  }                                                    Clicks the login
                                                       Submit button to
  pressSubmitButton() {                                submit the form
    return element(by.css('button[type="submit"]')).click();
  }

  getLoginError() {
    return element(by.css(".card-body.login-error")).getText();
  }
}                                          Gets the login error text for
                                              invalid login credentials
```

With your page objects in place, you're now ready to write tests. These tests should look familiar. As with your unit tests, you'll also write the E2E tests using Jasmine with the BDD test style. After importing your page objects, initialize a new instance of each in the `beforeEach` block. Ask Protractor's browser object to load the browser and wait for the Aurelia page. This uses a method in the `aurelia-protractor` plugin to ensure that Aurelia's bootstrap process has completed before you run any tests.

By using your page objects to abstract away the DOM interaction code, you keep your E2E tests clean and easy to read. I won't go through a blow-by-blow account of what each of these test cases does, because the details are self-explanatory.

In case you're wondering why you call `browser.sleep` in each of the valid login tests, let me explain. You don't have a callback available to indicate when the page has refreshed after submitting the `login` button. Because of this, you can't be sure that the page will have updated to show the index page by the time the test execution reaches the `(expect(poApp.getCurrentPageTitle())..)` assertion. Adding the 200 ms of sleep gives the page enough time to transition into the next state before your assertion runs. Create the ./test/e2e/src/login.spec.js file as shown in the following listing.

Listing 15.14 Adding the `login` spec (login.spec.js)

```
import { PageObjectApp } from "./app.po.js";          Imports the
import { PageObjectLogin } from "./login.po.js";      page objects

describe("my-books", function() {
  let poLogin;
  let poApp;

  beforeEach(() => {                                  Initializes an instance
    poApp = new PageObjectApp();                      of the page objects
    poLogin = new PageObjectLogin();                  before each test run
```

Loads the browser and waits for the Aurelia bootstrap process to complete

Verifies the login page has the expected header

Submits the login form

Submits the login form

200 ms sleep to allow page transition to complete

```
    browser.loadAndWaitForAureliaPage("http://localhost:9000");
  });

  it("should load the page and display the initial page title", () => {
    expect(poApp.getCurrentPageTitle()).toBe("login | My-Books");
  });

  it("should display a header", () => {
    expect(poLogin.getHeader()).toBe("my-books");
  });

  it("it should fail to log in with invalid password", () => {
    poLogin.setUsername("Bilbo");
    poLogin.setPassword("password3");
    poLogin.pressSubmitButton();

    expect(poLogin.getLoginError()).toBe(
      "Authentication failed. Invalid user name or password."
    );
  });

  it("it should login with valid username and password", () => {
    poLogin.setUsername("Bilbo");
    poLogin.setPassword("password1");
    poLogin.pressSubmitButton();

    browser.sleep(200);
    expect(poApp.getCurrentPageTitle()).toBe("home | My-Books");
  });
});
```

Verifies the initial page title is correct (you've loaded the app correctly)

Enters invalid login credentials into the login form

Ensures the invalid login message is displayed

Enters valid login credentials into the login form

Verifies a successful transition to the homepage on a valid login

Your login scenario is ready to go, so let's test it. In the next section, I'll take you through the steps required to run your E2E tests in an Aurelia project.

15.7.2   *Running the tests*

Your E2E tests automate your application, so you'll need to have the application, along with any of its dependencies, running when you run these tests. In this case, you have the main Aurelia SPA (my-books), which you'll run on http://localhost:9000, and the my-books-server application. If you're connecting to external REST APIs in a real application, you might want to have an instance of the API running that returns mock data rather than real data and simulates write methods, like deleting or updating data. This will allow you to rerun the E2E suite at any time without worrying about whether your test data is in the correct state. Another option is to set up and tear down your test data at the start and end of the E2E test process. We won't go into the details of these testing strategies here, but if you're interested in learning more I recommend checking out Roy Osherove's *The Art of Unit Testing* (Manning, 2013).

Before you run any E2E tests, you need to start up the my-books client and server applications using the following steps:

1 In the my-books-server application, run npm run database to start MongoDB.

2 In the my-books-server application, run npm run dev to start the my-books-server node application.

3 In the my-books application directory, run au run --watch to initialize the website.

You can then execute your E2E test suite using the au e2e command.

Running the E2E tests, you should see the Chrome browser launch once for each test. Depending on how quickly the tests execute, you may even be able to watch as Protractor automatically fills out the login credentials and submits the form. After the test execution completes, you should see output like the following:

```
? au e2e
Starting 'wdUpdate'...
[14:20:00] I/update - chromedriver: file exists C:\Code\AIA\Aurelia-in-
    Action\Chapter-15-Complete\my-
    books\node_modules\protractor\node_modules\webdriver
...
Finished 'wdUpdate'
Starting 'cleanE2E'...
Finished 'cleanE2E'
Starting 'buildE2E'...
Finished 'buildE2E'
Starting 'runE2E'...
[14:20:03] I/launcher - Running 1 instances of WebDriver
[14:20:03] I/direct - Using ChromeDriver directly...
Started
...
4 specs, 0 failures
Finished in 6.189 seconds

[14:20:12] I/launcher - 0 instance(s) of WebDriver still running
[14:20:12] I/launcher - chrome #01 passed
```

When you run the au e2e command, you're effectively telling the CLI to run the Gulp e2e command you created using the steps provided in the appendix. This command executes the following steps:

1 Updates the WebDriver version.

2 Cleans the E2E-test dist directory so that you can work from a clean test build on each test execution.

3 Builds the E2E tests.

4 Launches Protractor, passing in the set of tests to execute.

TIP If Protractor doesn't launch and you don't see the gulp tasks like wpUpdate or cleanE2E logged, there's a good chance that something is missing from the test infrastructure setup. Verify that each of the setup steps in the appendix has been completed correctly and retry. If you're still having issues, try checking out the chapter-15-complete folder from GitHub, because it has all the requirements preconfigured. If the tests run but all fail, check that you have the my-books-server, MongoDB database, and my-books website running before executing the E2E test suite.

This completes our brief overview of E2E testing with Aurelia. By following the page-object pattern, you were able to abstract the DOM interaction logic, keeping it isolated from the test logic. This made for a clean and easy-to-test suite, which would be more resilient to changes in your login-related views. By adding E2E tests to cover the key user journeys throughout your application, you'll have a far better chance of avoiding breaking these journeys as you release to production. With these kinds of tests, you'll give your team a great degree of confidence in releasing your Aurelia applications to production early and often.

With your application tested (although not quite with the test coverage you'd typically be comfortable with), you're finally ready to launch. In the next chapter, we'll go through the steps required to deploy an Aurelia application to production. We'll look at configuration options, bundling optimizations, and more, and finish up by deploying the my-books application to Google's Firebase.

Summary

- By shifting to an SPA development model, you transition much of the application logic, which was previously only on the server side, into JavaScript.
- With real application logic written in JavaScript (as opposed to a jQuery widget here or there), it becomes necessary to test this logic as you would in a backend application.
- You could potentially get away with testing your applications manually to begin with, but this quickly becomes unmanageable as the number of components in your application increases.
- By combining unit and E2E testing techniques, you can ensure that your application continues to behave as expected without the burden of manual testing, saving you valuable time and allowing you to iterate and deploy quickly, even when working with larger applications.

Deploying Aurelia applications 16

This chapter covers

- Bundling an application for deployment
- Bundling and HTTP/2—things to consider
- Creating a deployment package using npm
- Deploying an Aurelia application to Firebase

In the previous chapter, you learned how to add unit and E2E tests to your application to give you the confidence needed to deploy to production early and often. But now that you're ready to go, how do you take an Aurelia application and deploy it to a live server? Fortunately, the Aurelia CLI takes care of most of the work involved in creating a production-ready application. In chapter 2, you saw that although Aurelia projects comprise many small JavaScript, HTML, and CSS files, the CLI takes these files and bundles them into two JavaScript files (a vendor bundle and an application bundle). In this chapter, you'll learn more about why the CLI bundles the way it does, and how you can alter bundles to suit the needs of your own application. You'll also learn how you can avoid the common bundling pitfalls that many SPA developers fall into by using the CLI's bundle-versioning feature. To round out the chapter, you'll prepare the my-books application for deployment and upload it to Google's Firebase.

16.1   *SPA bundling*

At this stage, the my-books application has already grown to 67 files, and that's without taking the various external dependencies into consideration. Because browsers are limited to 2–8 concurrent requests (depending on the browser), this could present some problems if you attempt to load all the files required for the application independently, as when a user first visits the site. In fact, the user would need to wait as the browser individually loaded each of these files. Suffice it to say, this UX would be suboptimal, and this is only a relatively small demo application. Imagine how much worse the effect would be loading an application with hundreds, if not thousands, of separate components.

To solve this problem, most SPAs use a process called *bundling* to combine all these individual JavaScript, CSS, and HTML files into one or more bundles. The aim with this approach is to enable the browser to load each of the application's dependencies on page load, without running into a bottleneck on the maximum concurrent requests. These bundle files can be quite large, which has an impact on the initial-page-load time. Because the files can be cached, the latency of subsequent page loads will be minimal. We have many different tools for this, including RequireJS, SystemJS, and webpack, to name a few. The Aurelia CLI bundles all applications (even in a development environment) and offers several bundling options out of the box. With the my-books application, we use the RequireJS module system, so we'll focus on this option in particular. What if you prefer a different bundler? No problem, the majority of what we'll cover in this chapter is applicable regardless of which module loader you choose.

At this point, it should be clear that bundling is a good thing, but before we move on, I'll mention a major drawback that you'll need to consider when deciding how to bundle your applications. Imagine this scenario: you bundle your application and release it to the world. Users are happy, because although the initial page load can take some time, the next time they visit the site the latency is gone, and they get a lightning-fast experience due to the browser's convenient caching capability.

About a week after release, you notice a small bug in your application that you didn't happen to catch with your E2E test suite. "No big deal," you think to yourself, "I'll make the fix and deploy an updated version." You deploy the fix and send out an email notification to let users know that the application is again running as it should. Problem solved—or is it? Half an hour after releasing the fix, you start receiving emails informing you that the bug is still there. You check the local copy, and verify that everything is working as it should be, so what's going on? Then you remember that the browser is caching the previous version of the site that you released. You can deploy the latest version as many times as you like, but users won't receive it until the cache expires. Fortunately, the Aurelia CLI provides an easy fix for this problem. By tweaking your project configuration, you can tell the CLI to automatically append a unique version number to your bundle filenames. This means that each time you make a change to any project file and deploy, the bundle filenames will change. This forces users' browsers to download the update the next time the page is refreshed. We'll cover the details of how you can enable this for your staging and production releases later in the chapter.

One caveat to the bundle-cache-drawback fix is that any time you change any file (no matter how small or insignificant), the user will be forced to download the entire application again. The default bundling strategy adopted by the CLI alleviates this to some extent. By splitting the third-party dependencies into a separate "vendor" bundle, at least you can avoid users having to redownload these each time. This alone will be fine for small- to medium-size applications, but as your application grows, you'll see benefits in splitting your application into smaller feature bundles that contain files that are likely to change at the same time. For example, in the my-books application, you could split the book-management-related files into a separate bundle, so that when these files are changed, only this submodule bundle needs to be downloaded again. We'll cover how you can split your Aurelia application into multiple submodule bundles later in the chapter.

While we're on the subject of bundling, it's important to address the topic of HTTP/2 and the impact that it has on how you should most efficiently bundle your Aurelia applications. We'll cover this next.

16.1.1 *What about HTTP/2?*

HTTP/2 is a major revision of the HTTP protocol and was introduced in 2015. The major goal of HTTP/2 is to decrease latency and improve overall page-load time by introducing several enhancements while still maintaining a high level of compatibility with HTTP/1.1. HTTP/2 is semantically the same as HTTP/1.1 and still supports the same HTTP verbs, status codes, and so on that you're familiar with. The advantage is that browsers and servers can begin to take advantage of HTTP/2 immediately, without having an impact on existing applications or infrastructure. In fact, by serving your SPA from an HTTP/2-compatible server (modern servers such as IIS on Windows Server 2016, NGINX, or a cloud service such as AWS or Firebase) and running the site in a modern browser (including Microsoft Edge, Firefox version 55 or higher, and Chrome version 49 or higher), you'll see a noticeable decrease in your application's latency with regard to client/server interactions. Several features are responsible for this latency improvement, but the major one that relates to SPAs is *multiplexing*.

Multiplexing allows you to send multiple requests over a single TCP connection in parallel. This doesn't sound that amazing until you remember that, at the time of writing, browsers support only 2–8 concurrent connections. This means that in an HTTP/1.1 world, if the initial page load for your SPA includes more files than this (as is the case when you don't bundle), you'll run into this limit quickly, and the user will be forced to wait while the browser gradually downloads each of the required files. With multiplexing, there's theoretically no limit to the maximum number of files you can download in parallel, though current browsers appear to set an upper limit of 100–256. This is a game changer in terms of how you optimize your SPA for deployment.

It's not within the scope of this book to provide a definitive guide on HTTP/2, but if you're interested in reading more, I recommend checking out an article on Google's developer site: http://mng.bz/WP1C.

At this point, you may be thinking to yourself, "Fantastic! This basically solves the problem that bundling attempts to address; let's dispense with this fiddly bundling business and serve our modules individually." Hold your horses; although many people had this reaction initially, it's now become clear that, at least for the moment, bundling still has its place. The main reason for this is that although HTTP/2 can download vastly more files in parallel than HTTP/1.1, it still has a finite limit (around 256 in Chrome or 100 in Firefox). With moderate-to-large SPAs, you can quickly overrun this limit and end up bottlenecking the application load as surely as you would with HTTP/1.1.

Hence, splitting an application into multiple smaller bundles is still generally considered a good idea, particularly for larger applications. This approach improves latency and reduces the chance that the browser will need to download the new version of a given bundle as a result of an update. As the support for HTTP/2 improves, you'll likely see benefits from continuing to split separate parts of your application into smaller bundles to take advantage of request multiplexing.

16.2 Bundling and the Aurelia CLI

In this chapter, you'll deploy a previous version of the my-books application that can be run without a dependency on the Express.js REST API. Deploying Express.js applications is out of scope here, so you won't deploy the my-books server, but if you're interested in reading more about it, I recommend checking out Evan Hahn's *Express in Action* (Manning, 2016). This will allow you to easily deploy and run the application in Firebase. Before starting this section, I recommend checking out the book's GitHub repository and changing the directory to chapter 16, using the following commands:

```
git clone https://github.com/freshcutdevelopment/Aurelia-in-Action
cd Chapter-16-Complete/my-books
npm install
```

Throughout this chapter, you'll adjust the my-books bundle configuration to enable the following deployment-related features:

- Versioning to ensure that users receive the latest version of your bundles on each release
- Splitting the book-management functionality into a separate bundle so that you can avoid reloading the entire application any time you make a change to this submodule

Before you do this, however, take a quick look at the existing bundle configuration to refresh your memory regarding what the Aurelia CLI generates. As seen in listing 16.1, the Aurelia CLI gives you two bundles out of the box. The first bundle, app-bundle.js, includes all the files that make up your Aurelia project, such as custom CSS, services, custom elements, attributes, and so on. The second bundle, vendor-bundle.js, includes third-party libraries such as the Aurelia framework itself, jQuery, and Bootstrap.

Listing 16.1   Default bundle configuration generated by the CLI (aurelia.json)

```
"bundles": [
    {
        "name": "app-bundle.js",          ◁──┐  Application bundle includes the
        "source": [                            JavaScript, CSS, and HTML files
          "[**/*.js]",                          for your application
          "**/*.{css,html}"
        ]
    },                                         Vendor bundle includes all
    {                                          third-party dependencies such
        "name": "vendor-bundle.js",   ◁──┘    as the Aurelia framework
        "prepend": [
          "node_modules/bluebird/js/browser/bluebird.core.js",
          ...
        ],
        "dependencies": [
          ...
```

The my-books index.html file includes a reference to each of these files, and they're requested when the user first visits your site, as shown in figure 16.1.

vendor-bundle.js includes Aurelia, Bootstrap, and other my-books project dependencies.

Vendor bundles can be large, and they change less frequently than app bundles, so it's convenient that they can be cached independently.

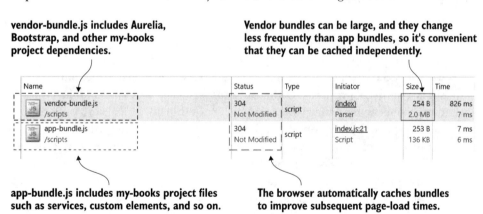

app-bundle.js includes my-books project files such as services, custom elements, and so on.

The browser automatically caches bundles to improve subsequent page-load times.

Figure 16.1   The Chrome network tab shows how the vendor and app bundles generated by the Aurelia CLI are loaded when a user visits the index.html page.

As mentioned earlier in the chapter, because of the way the project is initially configured, even if you release an updated version of the application, users won't receive it until their cache expires. In the next section, you'll solve this problem with a couple of minor tweaks to your bundle configuration to enable versioning.

16.2.1 *Aurelia environments*

Most projects I work with today need the application to run under different contexts, or *environments*. An environment can be thought of as a place you deploy and run your application. Typically, projects start their life in a development environment, which in my case is generally my local machine or a virtual machine (VM). Later, the application might move to a staging environment so that it can be reviewed and tested by users. Finally, once the application has been given the seal of approval, it moves into production—and if you can automate these environment transitions, all the better!

Depending on the application's complexity, each environment may have a separate set of dependencies. For example, you may use a local REST API in development, which transitions to a different staging endpoint URL when it moves into the next environment. It's likely that you'll also have different requirements of your application per environment. For example, in development you don't necessarily want the application to be minified because it could make debugging more challenging. In contrast, minification is essential for a production environment where the requirement is for the application to load as quickly as possible. Fortunately, Aurelia has native support for configuring sets of options per environment via the aurelia.json file. In the next section, you'll see how you can configure various bundling options per environment.

16.2.2 *Versioning bundles*

You can configure bundle versioning in the `options` section of the aurelia.json file. This section also includes settings to control whether the application should be minified (stripped of unnecessary characters to make the browser payload smaller), and whether source-map files should be used. To enable versioning, add a new `rev` (revisions enabled) property to the `options` section. You can enable bundling for all environments by setting the `rev` property value to `true`. This isn't recommended, however, because versioned bundles don't play nicely when running the `au run` command in watch mode. Instead, a preferable approach is to specify a list of environments in which versioning should be enabled by specifying the environment names separated by the ampersand (&) character. For example, a common approach is to enable it on staging and production, as shown in the following listing.

Listing 16.2   Enabling bundle versioning (aurelia.json)

```
...
"options": {
    "minify": "stage & prod",
    "sourcemaps": "dev & stage",
    "rev": "stage & prod"          ◁──  Enables bundle versioning
},                                       on staging and production
...                                      environments
```

You can run the my-books application in staging mode by passing the target environment to the CLI run command: `au run --env stage`. If you refresh the page and check the network tab, you'll see that the bundles now include a suffix generated by hashing the bundle contents. This is depicted in figure 16.2.

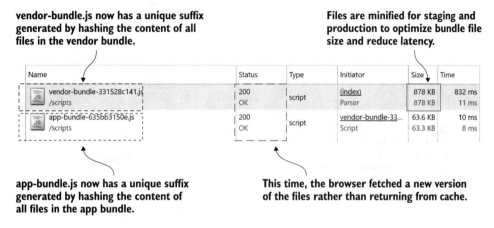

vendor-bundle.js now has a unique suffix generated by hashing the content of all files in the vendor bundle.

Files are minified for staging and production to optimize bundle file size and reduce latency.

app-bundle.js now has a unique suffix generated by hashing the content of all files in the app bundle.

This time, the browser fetched a new version of the files rather than returning from cache.

Figure 16.2   How the browser treats your application bundles once they've been versioned

Now that you've solved the problem of how to ensure that users receive timely updates to the my-books project, let's look at how you can optimize the application bundles to minimize the frequency with which each needs to be bundled.

16.2.3   *Splitting application bundles*

As mentioned earlier in the chapter, one of the drawbacks of bundling is that the user is forced to redownload the full application bundle any time a file changes. You can avoid this in your Aurelia applications by separating your files into separate feature directories, which can then be bundled separately. To see how this works, I split all the book-related functionality out into a book-feature directory, as shown in figure 16.3. Don't worry, I did the work for you on this one as a part of the \Chapter-16-Complete project on GitHub, as the purpose of this section is to demonstrate Aurelia's bundling capabilities rather than to teach you how to restructure your codebase.

To split the files from the ./books feature directory into a separate module, you need to make a few tweaks to the aurelia.json file, as shown in listing 16.3. First, you'll add a new section to the `app-bundle` configuration to exclude files under the ./books directory. This is needed to avoid duplicating the files into two separate bundles. Next, you need to add a new `books-bundle` section to bundle all JavaScript, CSS, and HTML files that you excluded from the app bundle in the previous step.

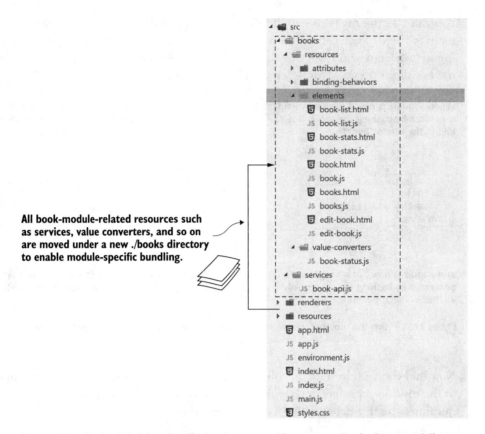

All book-module-related resources such as services, value converters, and so on are moved under a new ./books directory to enable module-specific bundling.

Figure 16.3   Book-related functionality has been moved into a new ./books feature subdirectory to enable easy submodule bundling.

Listing 16.3   Splitting the ./books feature into its own bundle (aurelia.json)

```
"bundles": [
  {
    "name": "app-bundle.js",
    "source": {
      "include" :[
        "[**/*.js]",
        "**/*.{css,html}"
      ],
      "exclude" :[
        "**/books/**/*"
      ]
    }
  },
  {
    "name": "book-bundle.js",
    "source": [
      "[**/books/**/*.js]",
      "**/books/**/*.{css,html}"
```

Modifies the app-bundle configuration to explicitly specify the include block

Excludes all files under the /books directory

Adds a new bundle configuration section for the books bundle

Includes all JavaScript, CSS, and HTML files under the /books directory in the new bundle

```
        ]
      },
      {
        "name": "vendor-bundle.js",
        "prepend": [
  ...
```

If you reload the application, you should see three bundles loaded in the browser's network tab, as shown in figure 16.4. The books bundle won't load until you visit the #/books route. This change brings two distinct advantages:

- The `app-bundle.js` file can still be cached even when files under the /books directory change.
- The `book-bundle.js` file isn't loaded until the user visits the #/books route. That doesn't improve page-load time much in this case, but in an application with several features, where users may need to use only a subset, this can provide a significant improvement.

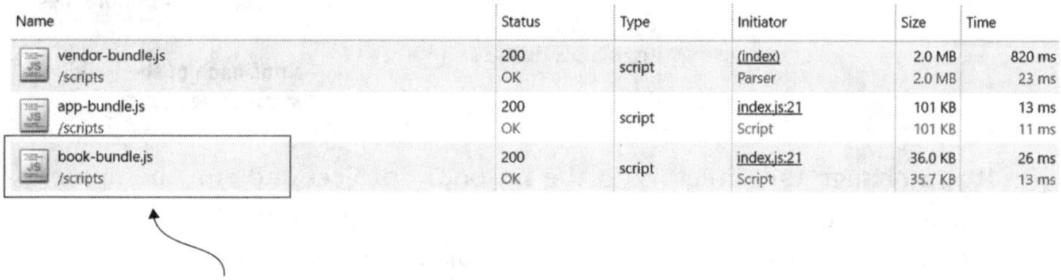

Name	Status	Type	Initiator	Size	Time
vendor-bundle.js /scripts	200 OK	script	(index) Parser	2.0 MB 2.0 MB	820 ms 23 ms
app-bundle.js /scripts	200 OK	script	index.js:21 Script	101 KB 101 KB	13 ms 11 ms
book-bundle.js /scripts	200 OK	script	index.js:21 Script	36.0 KB 35.7 KB	26 ms 13 ms

**Book feature files are now bundled into a separate bundle file.
This is loaded only when you visit the #/books route.**

Figure 16.4 Differences in my-book's network traffic once the book-management feature has been split into its own bundle.

If this technique were applied across a larger application, you could begin to make use of the multiplexing feature available in HTTP/2.

Now you understand how to bundle an Aurelia application that's ready for deployment. In the context of an Aurelia application, this means copying the bundles you've created along with other dependent files such as index.html, fonts, and images, to a web server. It's time to deploy my-books to production. Before you do so, let's review the plumbing you set up to create a deployment package. The deployment process can be done any number of ways, including shell scripts, gulp, Grunt, or any other build tool of your choice. The option you'll go with is to add a few npm script commands to your package.json file that will run a build for the production environment and copy the relevant files to a deployment directory. This deployment directory can then easily be copied to one or more production servers, using your favorite build-automation system.

As shown in listing 16.4, you first clean the deployment script and directories to clear out any previous build artifacts. You then use the Aurelia CLI to build the application in production mode to ensure that the bundles are versioned and minified. Finally, you copy the content files (such as index.html) and all bundles to the /deploy target directory.

Listing 16.4   Creating an Aurelia deployment package (package.json)

```
"scripts":{
    "clean": "rm -rf scripts/ && rm -rf deploy/ && mkdir deploy",
    "build-prod" : "au build --env prod",
    "content": "cp index.html deploy/
            && cp favicon.ico deploy/
            && cp -R fonts/ deploy/
            && cp books.json deploy/",
    "bundles": "cp -R scripts/ deploy/",
    "prepare-release" : "npm run clean
                && npm run build-prod
                && npm run content
                && npm run bundles"
},
```

Clears out any historical build artifacts

Uses the Aurelia CLI to build a production version of the app bundles

Copies all content files

Copies all bundle files

Runs each of the build steps in sequence

If you change the directory to the my-books project and run the npm run prepare-release command, the script will rebuild a production deployment package, copying it to the output directory. This should look like figure 16.5.

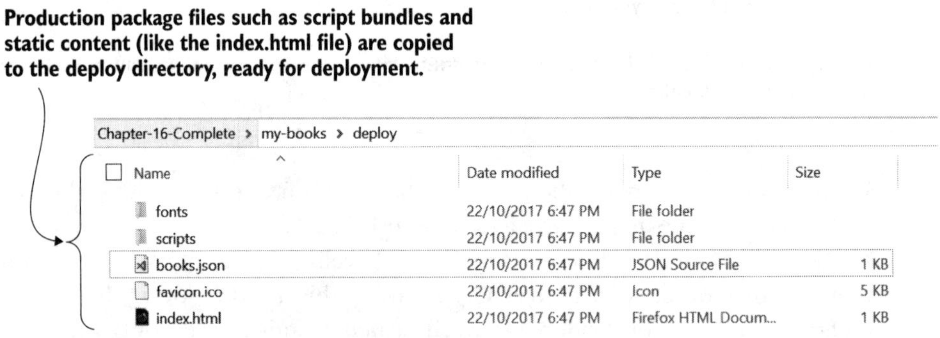

Production package files such as script bundles and static content (like the index.html file) are copied to the deploy directory, ready for deployment.

Name	Date modified	Type	Size
fonts	22/10/2017 6:47 PM	File folder	
scripts	22/10/2017 6:47 PM	File folder	
books.json	22/10/2017 6:47 PM	JSON Source File	1 KB
favicon.ico	22/10/2017 6:47 PM	Icon	5 KB
index.html	22/10/2017 6:47 PM	Firefox HTML Docum...	1 KB

Figure 16.5   The production deployment package created by the npm script

Now that you've got a deployable package, you need somewhere to deploy it! In the next section, you'll set up a new site on Google's Firebase and deploy your newly created package.

16.3　*Deploying my-books to Firebase*

In this section, you'll take the deployment package that you created using the npm script and upload it to a hosting provider. I chose Google's Firebase, which includes a collection of SaaS such as authentication, a database, and serverless functions. Although I chose Firebase for the simplicity it offers in setting up a simple hosted SPA site, you could easily follow the same process on another hosting provider such as AWS, Azure, or your own servers.

This section isn't meant to be a definitive guide to getting started with Firebase. If you're interested in learning more, I recommend heading over to the Firebase website: https://firebase.google.com/. Before you get started, you'll need to sign up for a free account, as shown in figure 16.6. This account tier has some limitations, but it comes with everything you need to get your site up and running.

Once you've created an account, log in to the Firebase console, where you can view details of your plan, create new projects, add services to existing projects, and more. Select Create New Project from the top navigation bar to create a project to host my-books, as shown in figure 16.7.

You'll then be prompted to enter your project details. Fill in the project name, ID, and hosting region, as shown in figure 16.8. The project ID determines your hosting

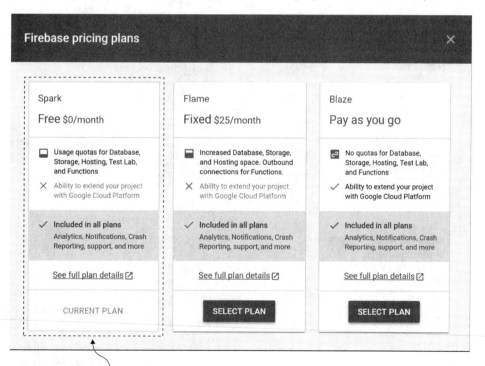

Select the free Spark tier to get started.

Figure 16.6　Pricing tiers available with Firebase. You'll select the free tier, which has everything you need to host the my-books site.

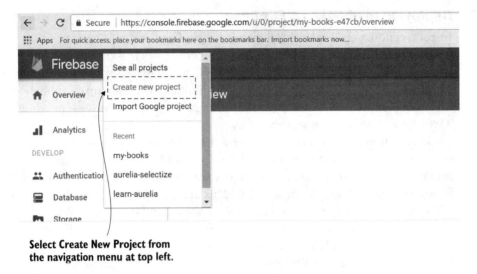

Select Create New Project from
the navigation menu at top left.

Figure 16.7   The new-project-creation option available in the Firebase console

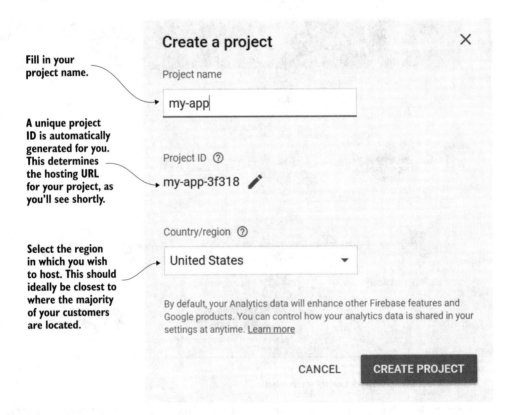

Figure 16.8   The Firebase project-creation dialog

URL, so unless you plan to associate this site with a domain name, you may want to pick something logical.

With the project in place, you're now ready to go. Switch back to the my-books project directory in your terminal and get ready for some npm action. You're going to deploy your Aurelia application to Firebase hosting, using the CLI tools. Run the commands shown in the following listing to install the Firebase CLI tools, sign in to Google, and initialize your project. When you run the `firebase login` command, a new browser will launch. You'll then need to sign in with the Google account associated with your Firebase login.

> **Listing 16.5 Installing the Firebase CLI and initializing your project**

```
npm install -g firebase-tools
```
◁─── Installs the firebase-tools node command-line application globally

```
firebase login
```
◁─── **Signs in to Google**

```
firebase init
```
◁─── **Initiates your project**

On running the `firebase init` command, the CLI will launch a wizard that will walk you through the process of creating a new hosted project. Enter "Yes" to proceed with project creation, and use the spacebar to select only the Hosting feature, as shown in figure 16.9. Firebase comes with several other serverless features, including functions and a database. These are outside the scope of this discussion, but I recommend checking out the Firebase website to learn more about these options.

Continue with the wizard, completing the remaining steps, as shown in figure 16.10.

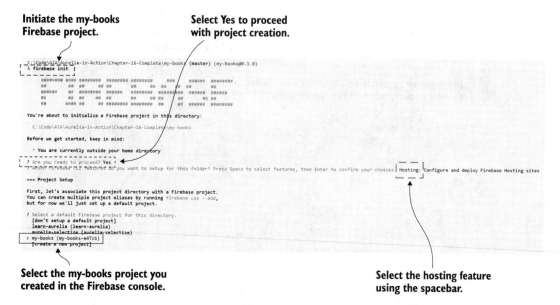

Initiate the my-books Firebase project.

Select Yes to proceed with project creation.

Select the my-books project you created in the Firebase console.

Select the hosting feature using the spacebar.

Figure 16.9 The first four steps of the Firebase project creation wizard required to initiate the my-books hosting project

Specify that the Firebase CLI should upload the contents of the deploy directory when you run the deploy command.

Enter Yes to set up the necessary Firebase-hosting configuration options to treat the site like an SPA.

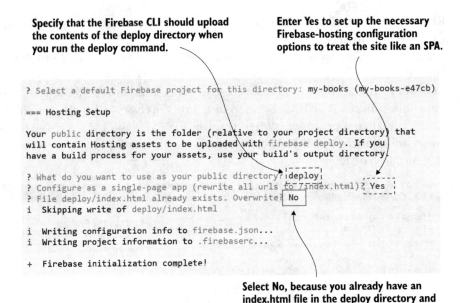

```
? Select a default Firebase project for this directory: my-books (my-books-e47cb)

=== Hosting Setup

Your public directory is the folder (relative to your project directory) that
will contain Hosting assets to be uploaded with firebase deploy. If you
have a build process for your assets, use your build's output directory.

? What do you want to use as your public directory? deploy
? Configure as a single-page app (rewrite all urls to /index.html)? Yes
? File deploy/index.html already exists. Overwrite? No
i  Skipping write of deploy/index.html

i  Writing configuration info to firebase.json...
i  Writing project information to .firebaserc...

+  Firebase initialization complete!
```

Select No, because you already have an index.html file in the deploy directory and don't need Firebase to create a new one.

Figure 16.10   The remaining steps required to initiate the my-books Firebase project, including the directory that Firebase should upload when the deploy command is run

With this project in place, you're finally ready to deploy. Run the `firebase deploy` command from within the my-books directory to upload your my-books project-deployment package to Firebase. This command will output the URL of your newly hosted application. Type the specified URL in the browser, as shown in figure 16.11. As you can see, the site's URL is taken from your Firebase project ID.

The my-books application should now be hosted at https://your-project-id.firebaseapp.com.

Figure 16.11   The my-books website hosted on Firebase

With a few simple steps, you've been able to take the my-books project-deployment package that you created using your npm script and upload it to a hosting provider. In this example, you ran the upload command manually, but this could easily be scripted as a part of your build- and deployment-automation system.

This brings us to the end of our Aurelia journey, and for you (hopefully) this is the first of many. We've come a long way, from the basic Hello World application that we started with, to the my-books site you now have running in Firebase. Congratulations on getting up to speed with the essentials needed to build the kinds of Aurelia applications that will delight your users.

I'd be thrilled to hear from you about any Aurelia projects or ideas you're working on, or discuss best practices, thoughts, or concerns on the Aurelia forum at https://discourse.aurelia.io/. Please, drop in!

Summary

- By bundling your Aurelia applications, you can achieve much better performance on a live website.
- The Aurelia CLI helps you by creating a project that bundles by default.
- Bundling introduces a new set of pitfalls regarding browser caching that you need to be aware of. By enabling versioning and splitting your bundles into feature modules, you can avoid the common issues with bundling that you may run into on a live site.
- Aurelia CLI projects include different configurations for several environments. By building your project for production or staging, you can create a deployment package optimized for a given environment.
- Once you have a production deployment package, it's a simple matter of uploading your files to your hosting provider of choice, and you're good to go.

appendix
Installation and setup

A.1 Installing Node.js

If Aurelia is a client-side framework, why do we need Node.js? Aurelia applications are prepared for the browser using the Node.js build tools such as gulp and RequireJS. Even though Aurelia applications don't require Node.js to run, we do need it to build our project into a deployable package that can be loaded and run in the browser. You can think of this like a compilation step in server-side languages like C, .NET, or Java, where you need a separate set of build tools on your development machine (such as MSBUILD on the Microsoft .NET side, or Javac on the Java side), as compared with what you need to run the deployed executable. This transformation process is summarized in figure A.1.

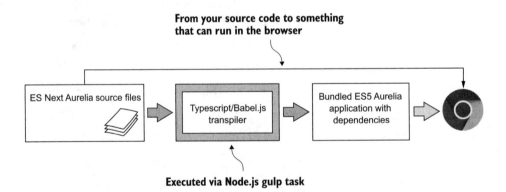

Figure A.1 Node.js is required to take the ES Next source files for your application and transform them into a package that can be run in the browser.

Download and install the current Node.js LTS from the Node.js website, https://nodejs.org/en/, using the installation package specific to your environment:

- *macOS*—You can download the Node.js installation package for macOS from the Node.js website: http://nodejs.org/#download. If you prefer the console, you can also install this with Homebrew: https://nodejs.org/en/download/package-manager/#osx.
- *Windows*—You can install Node.js on Windows by downloading and running the MSI from the Node.js website, http://nodejs.org/#download. If you prefer the console, this can be achieved using Chocolatey: https://nodejs.org/en/download/package-manager/#windows.
- *Linux*—Node.js installation on Linux is dependent on the distribution. For help in selecting the most appropriate installation method based on your Linux distribution, visit http://mng.bz/keyn.

A.2   *Installing the Aurelia CLI tool*

You can choose from the three main pathways for creating a new project with Aurelia:

- The quick-start ZIP download
- The Aurelia skeleton projects
- The Aurelia CLI (selected option)

In this book, we'll use the Aurelia CLI to create and run our project. The Aurelia CLI is a Node.js application that should be installed globally on your development machine. It allows you to do the following tasks:

- Create a new project with the development time dependencies you prefer (for example, a CSS preprocessor like SASS or plain CSS).
- Download and install npm packages into your project using npm or Yarn (a package manager developed by Facebook that improves package installation speed: https://yarnpkg.com/en/).
- Build the project, transpiling your ES Next/TypeScript source files into ES5 and bundling them for delivery to the browser.
- Host the project in a Browsersync HTTP server that autoreloads the page when changes are made to your source files.
- Unit- and integration-test your project.

After you have Node.js installed, you can install the Aurelia CLI globally using the following command:

```
npm install aurelia-cli -g
```

A.3   *Troubleshooting*

If you run into problems with the Aurelia CLI, it's likely due to one of the following causes:

- An unsupported version of Node.js (be sure you're running 6.x).
- An unsupported version of npm. To use frontend dependencies such as Bootstrap, which are installed via the Aurelia CLI, you'll need a flat directory structure for your installed packages. The flat directory structure was not supported until npm 3, so it's recommended that you update to this version before creating new projects with the Aurelia CLI. You can check which npm version you've got installed using the `npm -v` command. If it shows 3.x or greater, you're good to go. If not, then you can update to the latest version of npm using the `npm install npm -g` command.
- An outdated or broken installation of the Aurelia CLI (uninstall and reinstall the CLI using npm: `npm uninstall aurelia-cli -g`, `npm install aurelia-cli -g`).
- An outdated npm cache. If, when attempting to install the Aurelia CLI, you receive a message indicating that the `aurelia-cli` package isn't part of the npm register, try clearing the npm cache by running the `npm clear cache -g` command in your terminal. The package should then be picked up and installed correctly the next time you run `npm install aurelia-cli -g`.

A.4   *Adding Bootstrap*

In chapter 3, you style the my-books sample application with the aid of Bootstrap and Font Awesome. This section walks you through how to add Bootstrap 4 and its dependencies to an Aurelia CLI project.

> **TIP** Adding this dependency involves modifying the package.json (via the CLI), aurelia.json, app.js, and app.html files. I've created a gist to demonstrate what each of these files should look like after you've completed this setup: http://mng.bz/yk6X. If you run into any issues, I recommend cross-checking the files in your project against the files in this gist.

Installing Bootstrap 4

Begin by installing Bootstrap 4 via npm using the Aurelia CLI. Run the following command to download the node module from npm and install it in the node_modules directory. This command also takes care of modifying the aurelia.json file to ensure that the library is included in the vendor bundle:

```
au install bootstrap@4.0.0
```

> **TIP** You may be asked whether you want to install CSS resources when running the `au install` command, depending on the package being installed. In the case of a library like Bootstrap, you can select Yes to have these resources imported and configured in your aurelia.json file. Nonvisual libraries like

Lodash may have CSS libraries purely for unit-testing purposes. In these cases, it's better to select No, as you don't want these CSS files bundled with your Aurelia application.

Run the following command to include jQuery, which the Bootstrap tooltip JavaScript plugin depends on:

```
npm install jquery --save
```

In most cases, running the commands would be enough, and you'll be ready to start using the library in your project. But in some cases, the CLI is unable to automatically complete the setup. One of these cases is when something within the library that you're referencing depends on a global object. The Bootstrap 4 tooltip jQuery plugin depends on jQuery. We can still bundle these kinds of legacy dependencies into our vendor-bundle.js using a kind of hook built into the bundling pipeline. The pipeline has three main steps:

- *Prepend*—Dependencies included in this step are prepended to the start of the bundle. This is useful for dependencies that rely on an object being available globally (for example, Bootstrap).
- *Main bundle*—The main body of the bundle. Modern libraries or libraries without legacy style dependencies go here (for example, `aurelia-fetch-client`).
- *Append*—Dependencies that rely on a global object defined as a part of the main bundle go here.

Next, you'll need to reference jQuery and Bootstrap to include these in the vendor-bundle. Add the dependences shown in listing A.1 to the end of the dependencies section. The Aurelia CLI will have added Bootstrap Aurelia, so you'll need to remove that, adding these lines instead. You can cross-check this file against the gist here: http://mng.bz/9Uk7.

Listing A.1   Modified configuration to include Bootstrap library (aurelia.json)

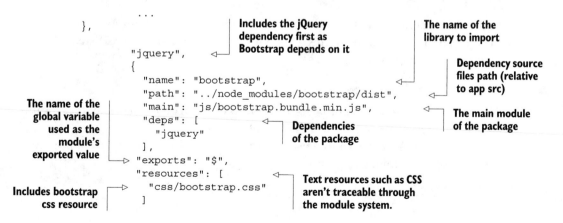

```
  },
    ...
]
```

With legacy style dependencies, such as Bootstrap, you need to give the bundling system more information as to how it should handle the items (CSS, JavaScript) that need to be included. Key points to note from listing A.1 are that you provide a specific path where the bundler should look for the Bootstrap source code (relative to your application src directory), and where the main module of that package is found (this is what you'll import when using the Bootstrap JavaScript plugins). You also indicated the value this main module should be exported as (in this case, $). This allows you to import the main module from bootstrap.min into a view-model using the import $ from bootstrap syntax. Finally, the Bootstrap library includes CSS, which, being text, isn't traceable as part of the module system; you need to list it in the resources array so that it will be injected as text into the vendor-bundle.

So far, you've completed the required steps to use the Bootstrap styles in your application by referencing the stylesheet from one of your views. To use any of the JavaScript components (such as the Tooltip) however, one more step is required. You'll need to modify the app.js view-model file to import Bootstrap.

Listing A.2 Importing Bootstrap into your app view-model (app.js)

```
import 'bootstrap';          ◁─┐  Imports bootstrap at
                               │  root view-model
export class App {
  configureRouter(config, router) {
  this.router = router;
  config.title = 'My-Books';
  config.map([
    { route: ['', 'home'], name: 'home', moduleId: 'index' },
    { route: 'books', name: 'books', moduleId: './resources/elements/books'},
  ]);
  }
}
```

In the next section, I included a set of steps required to install Font Awesome without the use of a CDN. You can skip this section if you're happy to use the CDN-based setup established in chapter 3.

A.5   Adding Font Awesome

The next dependency you'll install is the Font Awesome icon library. The steps for this are like the steps you used to install Bootstrap.

First, use the Aurelia CLI to download the font-awesome package from npm into the node_modules folder:

```
au install font-awesome
```

This automatically wires up a new dependency in the aurelia.json file, as follows.

Listing A.3   Include `font-awesome` dependency (aurelia.json)

```
{
    ...
        "dependencies": [
            ...

          {
              "name": "font-awesome",
              "path": "../node_modules/font-awesome/css",
              "main": "font-awesome.css"
          }
        ]
      }
    ]
  }
}
```

The name of the library to import

Dependency source files path (relative to app src)

The main module of the package

So far this should look familiar. You now have the font-awesome dependency installed and bundled as a part of your Aurelia project. You're almost ready to start using these dependencies, but there's one more issue to resolve first. Font Awesome consists of a CSS file and a collection of font files. The problem with what you've set up so far is that the font-awesome CSS looks for the font files relative to the font-awesome CSS file under the directory (for example, ../fonts/fontawesome-webfont.eot?v=4.7.0). To work with the Font Awesome directory structure, you need to make the font files available under ./fonts, which you can do with a new gulp task. As a refresher from chapter 1, gulp is the Node.js-based frontend build-automation tool used by the Aurelia CLI under the hood to prepare your Aurelia application to be run in the browser. Use the au generate command to generate a new gulp task that you'll use to copy the fonts from the node_modules directory to the ./fonts directory as a part of the build:

```
au generate task copy-fonts
```

Modify the newly created gulp task, aurelia_project/generators/tasks/copy-fonts.js, to what is shown in the following listing.

Listing A.4   Creating a new gulp task to copy font files (copy-fonts.js)

Takes the font files from the source location configured in aurelia.json

Imports gulp build tool

Imports the project node from aurelia.json to access paths

Creates the copyFonts function and exports it as the module entry point

Copies the font files to the target location configured in aurelia.json

```
import gulp from 'gulp';
import project from '../aurelia.json';

export default function copyFonts() {
  return gulp.src(project.paths.fontsInput)
    .pipe(gulp.dest(project.paths.fontsOutput));
}
```

You've now created a new gulp task that takes the font files from the `node_modules` directory and copies them to the ./fonts directory. The next step is to define the input and output paths that this task references in the aurelia.json file. Modify the aurelia.json file as follows.

Listing A.5   Including font input and output paths (aurelia.json)

```
...
"paths": {                           ⟵  Paths used in gulp
    ...                                  build tasks
    "fontsInput": "./node_modules/font-awesome/fonts/**/*.*",
    "fontsOutput": "./fonts"
},
...
```

Directory to copy the fonts from on build

Directory to copy the fonts to on build

Now that you've created this task, you need to include it in the build process. Do this by modifying the build.js file, as shown in the following listing, to copy the fonts after it has copied the CSS.

Listing A.6   Modifying the gulp build file to include the `copy-fonts` task (build.js)

```
import gulp from 'gulp';
...
import copyFonts from './copy-fonts';        ⟵  Imports the new
                                                 copy-fonts gulp task
export default gulp.series(
  readProjectConfiguration,
  gulp.parallel(
    transpile,
    processMarkup,
    processCSS,
    copyFiles,
    copyFonts
  ),
  writeBundles
);
...
```

Runs tasks in series (one after the other)

First reads the project configuration (paths and so on)

Runs this section in parallel, as they're independent

Includes the new copyFonts path in the pipeline

Creates the bundle files

Including the `copyFonts` task in the build pipeline ensures this task is run as part of the build when you run the `au run --watch` Aurelia CLI command.

This completes the setup of the Bootstrap and Font Awesome dependencies. Next, we'll look at how we can make use of the Bootstrap CSS dependency, combined with a custom style for my-books.

A.6   *Installing the Aurelia validation plugin*

You can install the Aurelia validation plugin using the Aurelia CLI with the following command:

```
au install aurelia-validation
```

As with the packages you've installed already, this command downloads the `aurelia-validation` plugin from npm and configures it in the aurelia.json file. Once this has been successfully installed, you'll need to wire up the plugin as part of the application-bootstrap process. As you'll recall, the main.js `ViewModel` file exports a configure function that's called by the Aurelia framework to configure environment settings as part of the application start. This method also allows you to register plugins with the application. Registering a plugin makes the resources within the application, such as exported classes, custom attributes, and binding behaviors, available for import throughout your Aurelia application. With the validation plugin installed, you now need to register it in the `configure` function, as shown in the following listing.

> **Listing A.7 Modifying `configure` to register `aurelia-validation` (main.js)**

```
import environment from './environment';

...

export function configure(aurelia) {
  aurelia.use
    .standardConfiguration()
    .feature('resources')
    .plugin('aurelia-validation');

...
}
```

Registers the aurelia-validation plugin in the configure function

With the Aurelia-validation plugin installed and registered with your Aurelia application, you can now put it to use by adding validation to the edit-book form.

A.7 Setting up my-books-server

The my-books single-page application (SPA) has a partner application, the my-books REST API. This replaces the fake backend and books.json seed file from chapter 6 onwards. This application consists of a REST API built on Node.js and Express.js, with a MongoDB database. This section walks through the steps required to get the my-books REST API up and running on your machine. The setup includes the following steps:

1. Download and install MongoDB.
2. Clone the my-books-server repository from GitHub.
3. Run the npm command to start the MongoDB server.
4. Execute the npm command to initialize the my-books-server and seed the database.

Installing MongoDB on macOS

If you're on macOS, please follow the quick-start guide on the MongoDB website: https://docs.mongodb.com/manual/tutorial/install-mongodb-on-os-x.

Installing MongoDB on Linux

You can install MongoDB on Linux by following this quick-start guide on the MongoDB website: https://docs.mongodb.com/manual/administration/install-on-linux.

Installing MongoDB on Windows

To install MongoDB on Windows, follow these steps:

1   Download the installer from the MongoDB website: http://mng.bz/xAN9.
2   Run the MSI (see figure A.2).

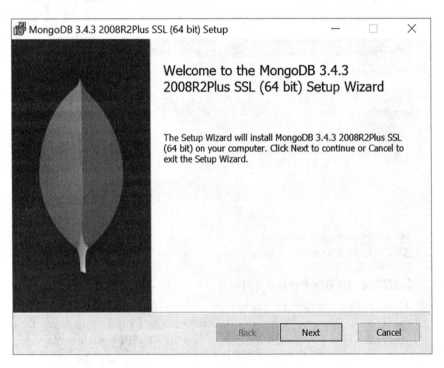

Figure A.1   Run the MongoDB MSI on your machine.

3   Add the path to the installed MongoDB binary to your system path (see figure A.3).
4   With MongoDB installed on your machine, you can run MongoDB by running the mongo command on the command prompt.

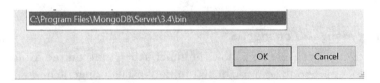

Figure A.2   Modify your system path to include the MongoDB binary.

Cloning the my-books-server repository

Clone the my-books-server repository from GitHub using the following command:

```
git clone https://github.com/freshcutdevelopment/my-books-server.git
```

Starting MongoDB server

I've created an npm command to allow you to easily launch the MongoDB server, creating the my-books MongoDB instance if it doesn't exist at the root of your my-books-server application. Before you run this command, please launch your terminal and navigate to the directory you cloned the repository into. Then run the following npm script to launch MongoDB:

```
npm run database
```

Starting the MongoDB server

The my-books-server REST API runs off a simple Express.js website. You can run this website by running the following npm script, launching the server at http://localhost:8333:

```
npm run dev
```

This script also seeds the database with the initial my-books seed data on first run. Once the site is running, you can test the various API endpoints by installing Postman (available from www.getpostman.com) and loading the Postman collection, available as part of the my-books-server GitHub repository: mng.bz/coK7.

Installing the aurelia-http-client package

The Aurelia framework comes with two HTTP clients: the `aurelia-fetch-client` package and the `aurelia-http-client` package. Installation steps for the `aurelia-fetch-client` module are included in chapter 2. You can install the `aurelia-http-client` using the following Aurelia CLI command in your terminal:

```
au install aurelia-http-client
```

After installing the package, kill your currently running Aurelia application if it's running, and rerun the au `run --watch` command to ensure that the new dependency is included in your vendor bundle (see figure A.4).

GET, PUT, POST, and DELETE endpoints are available for testing via the Postman collection.

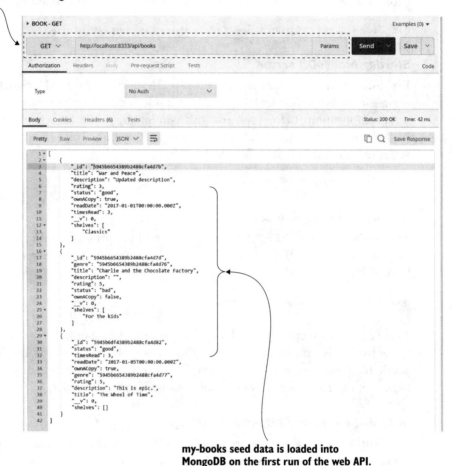

my-books seed data is loaded into MongoDB on the first run of the web API.

Figure A.1   The sample Postman collection can be used to test the my-books-server endpoints such as GET, POST, PUT, and DELETE.

Enabling my-books-server JWT authentication

In chapter 10, we secure the my-books application, connecting the my-books SPA to the JSON Web Token–based authentication system provided by the my-books-server application. To enable authentication on the my-books-server API, please perform the following steps:

1 Check out the latest my-books-server implementation from GitHub `git clone` at http://mng.bz/zu3L.

2 Reset your database so that you have a fresh instance to start the chapter with `npm run reset-database` (first ensure MongoDB is already running; see the appendix section titled "Installing MongoDB on Linux").

3 Enable authentication via the `config` file. Modify the ./my-books-server/config.js file to enable authentication: `'authEnabled'`: `true`.

4 Run the my-books REST application: `npm run dev`.

You're now ready to hit the ground running, implementing Aurelia authentication in chapter 10.

My-books-server: user credentials

Many users are prepopulated into the my-books-server MongoDB database. You can test the service under various roles by logging in with the credentials listed in table A.1.

Table A.1 The full list of user credentials used to log into the my-books-server sample application under different roles.

Username	Password
Bilbo	password1
Frodo	password2
Gandalf	password3
Gollum	password4

A.8   *My-books book-sharing-component prerequisites*

The Aurelia dialog is required to implement the book-sharing feature in chapter 12. To complete this setup, you'll first need to download the plugin from npm and install it in your Aurelia project. You'll then need to get the latest my-books stylesheet version, which contains changes specific to chapter 12 and the dialog component.

Installing aurelia-dialog

To install the `aurelia-dialog` component, follow these steps:

1 Run the following command at your terminal to download and install the `aurelia-dialog` plugin: `au install aurelia-dialog`.

2 Modify the main.js file, as shown in the following listing, to make the plugin available within the my-books application.

> **Listing A.8 Adding the `aurelia-dialog` plugin to the main module (main.js)**

```
import environment from './environment';
...

export function configure(aurelia) {
  aurelia.use
    .standardConfiguration()
    .feature('resources')
    .plugin('aurelia-validation')
```

```
    .plugin('aurelia-dialog');          ◁──┐   Adds the aurelia-dialog
                                            │   plugin to the Aurelia
    ...                                     │   startup process
}
```

Updating the my-books stylesheet

The my-books stylesheet has been updated with some required styles for the new sharing component. You'll want to download the latest version of the stylesheet CSS file from the my-books GitHub repository at http://mng.bz/6f5f, and place it in ./src/styles.css. With the dialog plugin and latest stylesheet in place, you're now ready to get started with the sample project in chapter 12.

A.9 *Installing selectize.js*

Before beginning this step, please ensure that you have the latest version of the my-books-server application. You can clone the my-books-server application using the `git clone https://github.com/freshcutdevelopment/my-books-server.git` command.

Once the my-books-server application is up to date, you'll need to download and install the `selectize.js` jQuery plugin and install configure it in your aurelia.json file:

1 Run the `npm install selectize` command from the root of the my-books Aurelia project to install the dependency.
2 Modify the aurelia.json file, as shown in the following listing, to configure Selectize to be loaded correctly via RequireJS.

> **Listing A.9 Configuring `selectize` in the aurelia.json file**

```
{
  ...
        "jquery",
        {
          "name": "bootstrap",
          "path": "../node_modules/bootstrap/dist",
          "main": "js/bootstrap.min",
          "deps": [
            "jquery"
          ],
          "exports": "$",
          "resources": [
            "css/bootstrap.css"          Adds selectize
          ]                              module reference
        },                               with a dependency
        {                          ◁──┘  on jQuery
          "name": "selectize",
          "main": "dist/js/standalone/selectize.js",
          "path": "../node_modules/selectize",
          "deps": [
            "jquery"
          ],                                         References selectize
          "resources": [                             default styles to ensure
            "dist/css/selectize.default.css"   ◁──┘  they're bundled
```

```
        ]
      },
      {
        "name": "font-awesome",
        "path": "../node_modules/font-awesome/css",
        "main": "font-awesome.css"
      },
  ...
}
```

You can now reference Selectize in a view-model using this statement: `import selectize from 'selectize'`.

A.10 *Installing aurelia-animator-css*

The `aurelia-animator-css` plugin is used in chapter 14 to enable the CSS transition animations we add to my-books.

Installing the npm package using the Aurelia CLI

The `aurelia-animator-css` plugin is an npm package and should be installed using the following steps:

1 Stop the `au run --watch` CLI command if it's already running.
2 Run the command to download and install the package: `au install aurelia-animator-css`. If you're asked whether you want to install CSS files from this package, select No.
3 The aurelia.json file will now have been modified to include the relevant configuration for this package.

Adding the plugin to the main module

Next, you need to add the plugin to your `main` module to make it available to the my-books application. Modify the main.js file, as shown in the following listing, to include the `aurelia-animator-css` plugin.

> **Listing A.10 Adding the `aurelia-animator-css` plugin to `main` (main.js)**

```
import environment from './environment';
...

export function configure(aurelia) {
  aurelia.use
    .standardConfiguration()
    .feature('resources')
    .plugin('aurelia-validation')
    .plugin('aurelia-dialog')
    .plugin('aurelia-animator-css');    ⟵  Adds the aurelia-animator-
                                            css plugin to the Aurelia
                                            startup process
...
}
```

This plugin will be available the next time you launch the application using the au run --watch command.

A.11   *Installing Aurelia testing dependencies*

The aurelia-testing plugin is used to test components such as custom attributes, custom elements, and value converters in isolation. It's an npm package, and you can install it using the following command:

- npm install aurelia-testing --save-dev

You'll also need two npm packages for E2E testing (gulp-protractor and aurelia-protractor-plugin); you can install these using the following commands:

- npm install --save-dev aurelia-protractor-plugin
- npm install --save-dev gulp-protractor

Next, you'll need to add the following Protractor configuration file to your project, which configures Protractor to use Chrome as the test browser, configures Jasmine, and registers the aurelia-protractor plugin with Protractor. Create the ./protractor.conf.js file at the root of the my-books project and add the contents of the following listing.

> **Listing A.11   Adding the Protractor configuration file (protractor.conf.js)**

```
exports.config = {
  directConnect: true,

    capabilities: {
    'browserName': 'chrome'
  },

  plugins: [{
    package: 'aurelia-protractor-plugin'
  }],

  jasmineNodeOpts: {
    showColors: true,
    defaultTimeoutInterval: 30000
  }
};
```

Following this, you'll need to modify the Aurelia project-configuration file to include the required E2E test settings, such as the location in which Protractor should look for the test files. Add a new e2eTestRunner section to the ./aurelia_project/aurelia.json file under the unitTestRunner node, as shown in the following listing.

> **Listing A.12   Adding E2E test settings to the project configuration (aurelia.json)**

```
...
"unitTestRunner": {
    ...
  },
```

```
    "e2eTestRunner": {
      "id": "protractor",
      "displayName": "Protractor",
      "source": "test/e2e/src/**/*.js",
      "dist": "test/e2e/dist/",
      "transpiler": {
        "id": "babel",
        "displayName": "Babel",
        "options": {
          "plugins": ["transform-es2015-modules-commonjs"]
        }
      }
    },
...
```

Finally, you need to create a new gulp task to execute the E2E test suite using Protractor. Add a new JavaScript file at ./aurelia_project/tasks/e2e.js and add the contents of the following listing.

Listing A.13 Adding the `e2e` gulp task (e2e.js)

```
var gulp = require("gulp");
var project = require("../aurelia.json");
var to5 = require("gulp-babel");
var plumber = require("gulp-plumber");
var webdriverUpdate = require("gulp-protractor").webdriver_update;
var webdriverStandalone = require("gulp-protractor").webdriver_standalone;
var protractor = require("gulp-protractor").protractor;
var del = require("del");
var assign = Object.assign || require("object.assign");
var sourcemaps = require("gulp-sourcemaps");
var e2eConfig = project.e2eTestRunner;

let cleanE2E = function() {
  return del(e2eConfig.dist + "*");
};

let buildE2E = function() {
  return gulp
    .src(e2eConfig.source)
    .pipe(plumber())
    .pipe(sourcemaps.init({ loadMaps: true }))
    .pipe(to5(e2eConfig.transpiler.options))
    .pipe(sourcemaps.write(".",
        { includeContent: false, sourceRoot: "/src" }))
    .pipe(gulp.dest(e2eConfig.dist));
};

let runE2E = function(cb) {
  return gulp
    .src(e2eConfig.dist + "**/*.js")
    .pipe(
      protractor({
        configFile: "protractor.conf.js",
```

```
        args: ["--baseUrl", "http://127.0.0.1:9000"]
      })
    )
    .on("end", function() {
      process.exit();
    })
    .on("error", function(e) {
      throw e;
    });
};

let e2e = gulp.series(webdriverUpdate,cleanE2E, buildE2E, runE2E);

export { e2e as default };
```

The my-books application is now E2E-testing enabled, and you're good to go. Head back to chapter 15 to get started.

index